A Nation of Descendants

FRANCESCA MORGAN

A Nation of Descendants

Politics and the Practice of Genealogy in U.S. History

The University of North Carolina Press *Chapel Hill*

Set in Arno Pro by PageMajik
Manufactured in the United States of America

The University of North Carolina Press has been a member of the
Green Press Initiative since 2003.

Library of Congress Cataloging-in-Publication Data
Names: Morgan, Francesca, author.
Title: A nation of descendants: politics and the practice of genealogy
    in U.S. history / Francesca Morgan.
Description: Chapel Hill : University of North Carolina Press, 2021. |
    Includes bibliographical references and index.
Identifiers: LCCN 2021004021 | ISBN 9781469664774 (cloth; alk. paper) |
    ISBN 9781469664781 (pbk.; alk. paper) | ISBN 9781469664798 (ebook)
Subjects: LCSH: Genealogy. | United States—Genealogy.
Classification: LCC CS47.M67 2021 | DDC 929.1072/073—dc23
    LC record available at https://lccn.loc.gov/2021004021

Cover illustration: Branching pattern © iStock.com/cienpies.

Chapter 1 was previously published in a different form as "A Noble Pursuit?: The
Embourgeoisement of Genealogy, and Genealogy's Making of the Bourgeoisie,"
in *The American Bourgeoisie: Distinction and Identity in the Nineteenth Century*, ed.
Sven Beckert and Julia B. Rosebaum (New York, N.Y.: Palgrave Macmillan, 2010),
135–52. Reproduced by permission of Palgrave Macmillan.

Portions of chapters 3, 4, and 5 were previously published in "My Furthest-Back
Person: Black Genealogy before and after *Roots*," in *"Roots" Reconsidered: Race,
Politics, and Memory*, ed. Erica Ball and Kellie Carter Jackson (Athens: University
of Georgia Press, 2017), 63–79. Used by permission of University of Georgia Press.

For my mother

Contents

Illustrations

Abbreviations in the Text

AAHGS Afro-American Historical and Genealogical Society

ASG American Society of Genealogists

BCG Board of Certification of Genealogists

DAR National Society, Daughters of the American Revolution

GSU Genealogical Society of Utah

IAG Institute of American Genealogy, Chicago

IGI International Genealogy Index

JGS Jewish Genealogical Society

LDS Latter-day Saints (Mormons)

NAACP National Association for the Advancement of Colored People

NEHGS New England Historic Genealogical Society, Boston

NGS National Genealogical Society, Washington

NYGBS New York Genealogical and Biographical Society

TJHS Thomas Jefferson Heritage Society

A Nation of Descendants

Americans' ambivalent relationship to genealogy has perplexed outsiders from nearly the beginning. In 1840, the young French nobleman Alexis de Tocqueville (1805–59) cherished the notion that democracy-minded Americans had cast aside concerns about family background. "Among democratic peoples new families emerge constantly out of nothing, while others constantly fall back into nothing," he wrote. "The thread of time is broken at every moment, and the trace of past generations fades. You easily forget those who preceded you, and you have no idea about those who will follow you. Only those closest to you are of interest."[1]

Elsewhere in *Democracy in America*'s second volume, though, Tocqueville portrayed Americans abroad as fascinated with lineage and eager to flaunt their own ties to long-ago "worthies," as contemporaries called illustrious forebears.[2] He heard sojourners from the United States crowing about their country's "admirable equality" (among white men) while insisting on exclusive company and exquisite manners abroad. He concluded that the American traveler was "secretly distressed about [equality] concerning himself." The traveler's bundle of insecurities included wishful kinship with prestigious ancestors. "You hardly meet an American who does not want to be connected a bit by his birth to the first settlers of the colonies, and, as for branches of the great families of England, America seemed to me totally covered by them." Tocqueville ascribed this practice of Americans' protesting too much to Europeans, to Americans' emphatic repudiation of "rank." "If the trace of old aristocratic distinctions were not completely erased . . . Americans would appear less simple and less tolerant in their country," he wrote, "less demanding and less ill-at-ease in ours."[3]

Just as Tocqueville presumed that individuals' manners could express broad national differences, I argue that even this particularly personal interest, namely genealogy, has been political, in the sense of reinforcing formal and informal group hierarchies. Hence this work constitutes a political history of genealogists and their practices. At first glance, the pursuit of genealogy seems so narrow as to resemble autobiography and so oriented toward specifics as to bore anyone else, except family members and people with an overlapping or similar surname.[4] But besides pursuing the question of "Who am I?" genealogists through time have also chased the inquiry of "Who are we?" The category of "us," be it a clan or an ethnic group or a nation, contains within it a "them" to serve as foil and target.[5]

My insistence that genealogy's seemingly narrow, individualistic concerns illustrate Americans' setting of "us" apart from "them," depends on a range of meanings of the adjective "political."[6] Formal meanings pertain to institutions of government. In the late nineteenth and early twentieth centuries, for example, genealogists' methods and collections buttressed U.S. state and federal laws that served white supremacy—oftentimes, the even narrower category of white Anglo-American supremacy.[7] These laws justified and reinforced African American disfranchisement; suppressed interracial marriage involving whites; encouraged the practice of eugenics, with the sterilization of incarcerated populations without their consent; dispossessed Indigenous populations; and suppressed immigration from southern and eastern Europe, and Asia, on a racially discriminatory basis.

The term "political" also contains informal meanings. In their everyday lives, Americans have used genealogy findings to enforce any number of social boundaries, particularly those interlocking hierarchies of race, class, and religion that placed white Protestants on top.[8] Illustrations of this pattern include a wave of monument building at the turn of the twentieth century. Confederate soldier statuary and white-baby wall plaques in many an American downtown and courthouse square inscribed principles that were simultaneously patriotic, racist, and hereditary, for all passersby to behold.[9] But after the 1970s, especially, the racial, ethnic, gender, religious, and class diversification of genealogists and their practices began to transcend these barriers. Civil rights activists, feminists, and others used genealogy as a tool to challenge subjugation and promote group pride among African Americans, women, American Jews, Mormons, and others who otherwise lived at the receiving end of widely shared prejudices. I do not pause during these arguments to verify descendants' claims to kinship with particular ancestors, which is outside the scope of this work and would be a research task without end. I take most of my subjects at their word because my main interest is in the political ramifications of genealogy practices for descendants, and for the genealogists they hired. Self-representations are all-important here.[10]

Genealogy's political character—and genealogy's uses for inscribing power relations—increased over time. Genealogy underwent its first growth in popularity during the Gilded Age, between the 1880s and the 1920s, when Americans became ever-more convinced that heredity explained their own and others' physical and mental characteristics, in keeping with the scientific racism that Americans at leading universities and in the most educated circles touted.[11] Genealogy's second major enlargement, in the 1970s and afterward, reified two additional sets of power relations. The first was the elevation of bio-genetic family ties, or what Donna Haraway has called "gene fetishism," over chosen forms of relatedness, such as those created by marriage or adoption.[12] Consequently, following Alex Haley's bestselling book and television mini-series *Roots* (1976–77), genealogy businesses began operating on a massive scale. Since 1999, DNA testing has reached a new level of commodification, following its enlistment for genealogy purposes. Genealogy's business history illustrates the second political dimension that recent practices have reified. Big businesses not only rewarded those with disposable income but also seques-tered information that had previously been widely accessible behind paywalls, and they threw their weight behind definitions of family that treasured procre-ation within heterosexual marriage at a time when same-sex, childless, and un-married family formations were on the rise. In sum, businesspeople set the needs of the present-day descendant as consumer above the less-commercial, and sometimes anti-commercial, goals of historical knowledge and accuracy.

Some evidence complicates my framing of genealogy's political and busi-ness histories. Even in an era of large-scale commerce, genealogists have con-sistently engaged in sharing, trading, and donating their time and information outright. These behaviors need more study. Dick Eastman, with his epony-mous online newsletter, and Cyndi Ingle of Cyndi's List (1996) have devel-oped free online clearinghouses to dispense advice and advance research on particular families, surnames, regions and other places, and ethnic groups.[13] Consider the legions of unpaid contributors to the JewishGen.org website, and the armies of Mormon faithful who, as missionaries and congregants, have entered reams of information into online databases to aid the Interna-tional Genealogical Index (IGI, 1961), FamilySearch.org (1999), and other church entities in the course of fulfilling unpaid obligations.[14] Since the 1940s, the Church of Jesus Christ of Latter-day Saints has offered content and ser-vices without charge to genealogists everywhere, scholars like myself, and others. One resource is the online, searchable FamilySearch Digital Library of genealogy writings. The church counted 13.9 million registered users (in-cluding me) of its website FamilySearch.org in late 2019.[15] Such generosity stems from the church's longstanding advocacy of increased genealogy prac-tices. Genealogists themselves have benefited not only from this plenitude but also from sharing their own findings.[16] As Gary Mokotoff, publisher of the Jewish genealogy journal *Avotaynu*, asked in 2001, "Why waste time and resources by duplicating the effort of those who came before you?"[17]

Regardless of whether genealogists share and donate information in order to conserve their own time and effort or for more altruistic reasons, these collaborative behaviors do not illustrate market capitalism's grasping, amassing, and sequestering tendencies, which is a major theme of my political and business histories of genealogy. However, genealogists' predilection for sharing and donating can harmonize with the political history of genealogy. Within the many subfields of genealogy in the United States, genealogists have shared freely and combined efforts in order to advance knowledge of particular communities. During the calendar year of 2019, the 318,000 indexing volunteers who collectively donated 10.9 million "indexing hours" to FamilySearch.org were laboring to fulfill Mormon aims, even though anyone who could get to the internet could access the volunteers' pooled information.[18] Because genealogists' predilection for sharing fosters community-building, it has reinforced the shoring up of group boundaries.

This Book's Import

I scrutinize the persistence of practices in the United States in which white Christian genealogists bundled together inherited, documented, and racial readings of Americanism. At the same time, my histories of African American, Indigenous, Jewish, and Mormon genealogists who operated before the civil rights reforms and multiculturalist convictions of the long 1960s, show the lengthy roots of each of those groups' push for respect and fairness from others, and proclamation of their distinctiveness. Understanding these two major continuities in the history of genealogy— the persistence of antidemocratic patterns in genealogy practice, and religious minorities' and people of color's longtime embrace of genealogy practices—helps us appreciate, and therefore preserve, later diversifications among genealogists. These diversifications included African American and American Jewish genealogists' waves of organizing and development of periodicals and other publications including instruction books, starting in 1977. The two groups generally worked separately from each other. Smaller-scale operations began among other ethnic and racial minorities, such as Polish Americans, Irish Americans, Hispanic/Latinx communities, and Native Americans.

My work enriches American studies overall by folding both Mormon and Native American practices into broader histories of American genealogy. United States historians have so far insufficiently incorporated Mormon histories into more general histories. Mormon genealogy practices have also been a marginal concern, until very recently, to most scholars of Mormonism and the Church of Jesus Christ of Latter-day Saints.[19] Such neglect is problematic for historians of genealogy because of the strong dependence non-Mormon genealogy practitioners from around the world have developed on the church's unparalleled collections of genealogy data and records.

A truly full history of Mormon practices requires laypeople's perspectives—obtained from unpublished writings, archival materials, and other primary sources, especially those from women—as well as prescriptions from all levels of the exclusively male priesthood and church leadership. My book's discussions of laypeople and lived experiences of piety addresses another important literature. Scholars have shown a pronounced shrinkage of Mormon women's theological and cultural status between the nineteenth century and the twentieth century's second half.[20] Consider the distance between church president Brigham Young's pronouncement in 1869—women should, he said, be "useful not only to sweep houses, wash dishes, make beds, and raise babies, but . . . they should stand behind the counter, study law or physic, or become good book-keepers and be able to do the business in any counting house, and all this to enlarge their sphere of usefulness for the benefit of society at large. In following these things they but answer the design of their creation"—and the church's proscriptions, as recently as 2003, against mothers working for pay outside the home.[21] The church and laypeople's praise for married heterosexuality and married reproduction, and combating of organized feminism, is of a piece with the church's leadership in fostering genealogy activity and, indirectly, inspiring genealogy businesses to form.[22] These interrelationships among gender conservatism, piety, and enterprise illustrates my broader principle of the seemingly personal being profoundly political, in the history of American genealogy practices.

My book is the first long history of genealogy in the United States to incorporate Indigenous people's genealogy practices. Previous historians of genealogy have placed Native American family historians outside of "European" traditions of documentation or left their practices unmentioned.[23] But the anthropologist Kim TallBear has scrutinized modern genealogists' approaches to Native American studies and modern Indigenous people's predilections for genealogy.[24] Historians, too, need to examine family history in Indian country. White Anglo-American supremacists' uses of genealogy have been a familiar story pertaining to African Americans during Jim Crow times and immigrant precincts in northern and western cities.[25] But in Indian country, the federal government used textual, racial handlings of genealogy, of European origin, to reinforce conquest. This reinforcement occurred most notoriously in the land allotment system and the promotion of assimilation that began in 1887 with the Dawes Severalty Act, which intended to break down tribal land holdings. In the 1910s, the government added blood quanta (measurements of percentages of "Indian blood") to identifications of individuals and families in order to further weaken full-blooded Indians' claims on land. In response, some Native Americans grafted text-based, patrilineal racial practices of European origin onto Indigenous practices that treasured matrilineal descent, foremothers, and oral transmission of information. My scrutiny of Native genealogy practices enhances our overall understanding of how non-Indians used genealogy to enforce colonization and of how subjugated people made their own uses of genealogy findings and methods.

A History of Genealogy Studies

Because the historical scholarship on genealogy in the United States has been thin and recent, in contrast to booming historical literatures on eugenics and genetics, historians of genealogy benefit greatly from reading across disciplinary boundaries.[26] Sociologists, anthropologists, and others in the social sciences have furnished crucial vocabularies and frameworks to genealogy studies. Numerous scholars—mainly anthropologists, sociologists, geographers, and other nonhistorians—have found (as I have) that enactments of genealogy have served descendants' present-day needs.[27] I ascribe the recentness of, and the small number of scholars involved in, tracing historical developments in genealogy, to the longstanding estrangement between historians' and genealogists' practices in the United States that began at the turn of the twentieth century with history's professionalization. Historians later repudiated any kinship with genealogy professionals, who shared historians' regard for original documents and commitment to detachment, and who were setting themselves apart from the larger, diffuse communities of genealogy hobbyists and businesspeople.[28]

But rapprochement began in the mid-1970s, when some historians realized that genealogy resources and methods could be useful, and when some genealogy professionals began applying broader-minded questions and narratives that historians favored, to genealogy itself. The grand April 1975 issue of the *New England Historical and Genealogical Register* was assembled for the bicentenary of the Battles of Lexington and Concord (1775) and boasted a cover printed in color. The contents stressed heavily footnoted history articles and book reviews by historians with doctoral degrees and university affiliations, omitting the usual fare of particular lineages within specific families that genealogist authors assembled.[29] Another pivotal development occurred in the mid-to late 1970s when historians and genealogists began characterizing the estrangement between history and genealogy as a problem.[30]

Brief histories of American genealogy began appearing in 1978, when the historian Tamara Hareven published her article on the "Search for Generational Memory." The historian Robert M. Taylor Jr. delivered a pioneering social history of family reunions as well as of genealogy activity in 1982, with his article "Summoning the Wandering Tribes."[31] Because they were pathbreaking, these brief articles could hardly avoid conflating the history of publications and institutions, such as Boston's pioneering New England Historic Genealogical Society (NEHGS, 1845), with the history of genealogy practices overall. More recent scholars have avoided that error. Their scrutiny of periods before the emergence of American institutions dedicated to genealogy in the 1840s has illustrated genealogy's persistent amorphousness.[32]

Developments since the 1990s have further thawed relations between history and genealogy. Historians' predilections for seemingly narrow topics and events, such as microhistories and local histories, have fostered deep research, using many different types of sources, on surrounding contexts. Such topics deepened dependence on source material that genealogists have also used and, sometimes, generated. Like microhistorians, genealogists use wide arrays of sources while researching narrow topics over long durations. The impressive range of records now available on Ancestry.com and FamilySearch.org has compelled historians to incorporate genealogy findings, frameworks, and motifs more than ever.[33] Not a few scholars have published histories centered around individual families, often their own.[34] These developments all served to weaken the walls between historians' and genealogists' practices that have stood for nearly a century and to encourage historians' scrutiny of genealogy and genealogists.

Within this friendly environment, in 2006, the Canadian historian Caroline-Isabelle Caron published the first book-length history of North American genealogists' practices, *Se créer des ancêtres: Un parcours généalogique Nord-Américain, XIXe-XXe siècles* (*To Create Ancestors: A North American Family Journey, 19th–20th Centuries*). Spanning two continents and three countries, including the United States, Caron's project subjected the publications, meetings, and reunions of an eminent French Protestant family, the De Forests, to textual and historical analysis. However, her book remains available only in French.[35] Apart from Donald Akenson's travelogue through Mormon genealogy processes in *Some Family* (2007), the first book-length monograph in English on genealogy's American history was François Weil's, in 2013.[36] In *Family Trees*, Weil delivered extensive primary research and crisp narratives about genealogy practices from colonial times to the present, while arguing for genealogists' search for identity, both group and individual.[37]

The old distance between genealogy and professionalized history has been shrinking since the 1980s also because of the efflorescence of public history. Historians outside university departments, such as at research libraries and museums, have published historical findings and have aspired to reach broad publics more than their colleagues in universities, countering academicians' tendency to write for each other.[38] Some genealogists have created new kinship with public historians in pursuing historical knowledge as an end in itself. The historian Susan Tucker's 2016 study of genealogists in New Orleans, past and present, articulated the sense of wonder about history that genealogy research imparts. Usually operating far outside academia and professionalized history, genealogists have built superhighways to the seemingly "foreign country" of the past.[39] Genealogy journals illustrate this commitment to wide accessibility with their occasional quick tutorials of a few pages or paragraphs, imparting basic historical knowledge that genealogists need to avoid research pratfalls. A newcomer to English colonial-era genealogy might otherwise conflate dates on the Julian calendar, used in seventeenth-century England and its colonies, with the Gregorian timekeeping used today.[40]

For their part, public historians have explicitly brought genealogists under their umbrellas in situating genealogists' practices among other forms of do-it-yourself, crowd-sourced history. Genealogy's ongoing boom seems to erode the barriers surrounding the academy and the archive, otherwise "challenging exclusive uses of the past."[41] In 2014, public history leader Jerome de Groot hailed genealogy as "fundamentally . . . *public* history insofar as it is user-generated, undertaken in public, deploying relatively democratic approaches, and interested in creating local, domestic stories and interactive experiences."[42] He intended his sanguine assessments as provocative, in order to engender further discussion. Some of his respondents, notably the Swedish scholar Carolina Johnsson Malm, have been less optimistic when they recall genealogy's past usefulness to eugenics, in both the United States and western Europe.[43]

Notwithstanding such evidence of genealogists who foster historical knowledge for its own sake and historians who welcome expansions of genealogy, no historian has yet explored a basic characteristic of genealogy practice—that it has had political uses and implications, both in government sectors and in commercial, family, and other private sectors. Nor has any study before mine linked earlier and later eras in United States history by analyzing their interplay in genealogists' practices over a long duration. The burgeoning social scientific literatures on genealogists focus mostly on the present or the recent past.[44] Among historians, François Weil chose a long time span—four centuries, ending in the present—but he weighted it toward earlier periods, with only one chapter (of six) focusing after 1900.[45] But my own work stresses later periods. The last two of my seven chapters and my epilogue range after the 1970s. I treat recent times extending to the present as well as the past, and I trace continuities as well as change in genealogists' practices. While Weil has argued that racially centered genealogy practices gave way to genealogy's democratization over the course of the twentieth century, my attention to continuities starkly illuminates persisting exclusivities.[46]

Reasons to Study Genealogy Practices in the United States in Particular

It is necessary to study genealogists in the United States because their activities furnish an array of paradoxes, groundbreaking institutions, and theories to test. Reasons to scrutinize American genealogists include paradoxes stemming from the American Revolution and geographical mobility that enrich understanding of broader themes in United States history; American genealogists' pioneering institution-building; and opportunities to explore the hypothesis that genealogy has spread more quickly in republics than in monarchies. In one major contradiction, the United States' revolutionary origins amounted to a repudiation of inherited forms of governance. The Articles of Confederation (1777), Article 6, and the U.S. Constitution (1787), Article 1, section 9, specifically prohibited governments' awarding of "titles of nobility." These bans impressed any number of European visitors; Alexis de Tocqueville was thrilled by Americans' repudiation of official, hereditary aristocracy.[47] Yet by the 1840s, the same decade in which he published the second and final volume of *Democracy in America*, the United States became the earliest Western country to see literate, middle-class populations who were not aristocrats or gentry engage in genealogy, as Weil has emphasized.[48]

We can easily explain this paradox, in which people in the world's earliest modern republic also originated mass forms of genealogy and invested in hereditary forms of identity. Having come undone from political power, after centuries in Europe in which it had inhered in monarchy and official aristocracy, genealogy in the United States became conjoined with social power in everyday settings. The nineteenth-century genealogy society, for gentlemen of leisure, favored daytime meetings on weekdays, except during July and August when members would head for mountains or the seashore.[49] Separately, but simultaneously, Mormons developed an even more expansive form of mass genealogy for religious reasons. Mormons' ministry to the dead began early in the history of the Church of Jesus Christ of Latter-day Saints (1820). By the 1840s, living people evangelized dead people, usually dead kin, by standing in for them at temple ceremonies that included baptism. These rites depended on identifying each dead person by their name, birth and death dates, and other precise information. Hence, worshippers have depended on genealogy data throughout the church's history.

Another paradox in the history of American genealogy pertains to nineteenth-century Americans' pronounced affection for genealogy while living in a time and place with a high rate of geographical mobility. Fiction's footloose archetypes range from Natty Bumppo, to the Ishmael who narrated *Moby Dick*, to Huckleberry Finn, to the hero of Horatio Alger Jr.'s *Ragged Dick*, to Jay Gatsby. Each character was in flight from his family origins, or he lived in disregard of any knowledge of such origins.[50] To Frederick Jackson Turner in 1892, accounts of moving West have embodied American history as a whole, for seeming so characteristic of the United States.[51] But those literary and real-life men on the move embodied a backlash against a countervailing urge to reconfigure one's "place." For some westbound migrants, particularly for women, the study of long-dead ancestors could furnish surrogates for family gravesites and living kindred whom they might never see again. "Even when everyone involved was in perfect health, the lack of reliable communication networks and the significant risks of travel meant that death cast its shadow over every long-term farewell" in the nineteenth century, writes the historian and physician Samuel Morris Brown.[52] Women did not directly benefit from the masculine gender privileges embedded in wandering or wield much control over family decision-making regarding whether or when to move house.[53] Those who sought to recreate old identities in new homes found that conducting genealogy activity in groups conferred on them "the thing that they lacked: namely, background. It gave them place," remarked a woman who helped found the Daughters of the American Revolution chapter in Berkeley, California, in the 1900s. She was originally from Massachusetts.[54]

Ironically, the most famous exponents of the "self-made man" in nineteenth-century America furnish additional examples of fascination with inherited origins. Benjamin Franklin (1706–90) began as a brash printer's apprentice. Toward the end of his life, he produced a canonical text about remade identity, his *Autobiography*. But he otherwise showed considerable interest in forebears. When he retired from printing in midlife to become a gentleman, he "adopted a Franklin coat of arms and began sealing his letters with it," around 1751. Seven years later, in 1758, he traveled to England to unearth more family history. His sojourn to England may be the earliest roots trip in American letters, having appeared at the beginning of his *Autobiography*.[55] Thomas Jefferson, for his part, famously remarked in an 1816 letter that "the dead have no rights . . . they are nothing," as part of a broader argument about republicanism's wiping away of monarchy. But Jefferson collected multiple works on heraldry and aristocratic descent for his extensive library at Monticello, especially after his presidency ended in 1809.[56] Ralph Waldo Emerson, known for coining the term "self-reliance" and for condemning others' genealogy fixations, nevertheless researched the same eighteenth-century clergymen among his forebears that his redoubtable "Aunt Mary" Moody Emerson had taught him to praise.[57]

In contrast to the nineteenth-century United States, societies characterized by geographical stasis often contain lively genealogy subcultures—to the point that one expert has listed stability of location of ancestral populations among the ingredients of successful research.[58] Relatively low rates of in-migration and out-migration have characterized the white population of Québec. Québec's significance in genealogy's history is due to the earliness of recordkeeping and archives formation there, including all-important notarial archives of Catholic origin. Québécois developed genealogy groups and publications starting in the 1860s, not long after such activity began flowering in the United States, and nearly simultaneously with German institution-building that Eric Ehrenreich has described.[59] Another example of booming genealogy practices within a society with relatively little internal permanent migration is the twenty-first-century United States, which has been leading the world in developing mass genealogy and DNA testing commerce and genealogy-themed entertainments.[60]

Besides the abovementioned paradoxes involving geographical mobility or the lack thereof, additional reasons to explore genealogy's history in the United States include institutions that broke new ground in world history. The Afro-American Historical and Genealogical Society, founded in Washington in 1977 with later chapters across the United States, was the earliest organized effort in any country to foster African-diaspora genealogy. Americans also brought genealogy for hire, for profit, and for entertainment up to unprecedented heights, most obviously with Alex Haley's *Roots* (1976–77) and later with Ancestry Inc. (1983). After evolving into the mighty enterprise Ancestry.com, starting in 1996, the company attracted millions of paying subscribers as well as wealthy investors. In October 2012, a private-equity firm purchased Ancestry.com, which by then had begun selling DNA testing kits for home use, for $1.6 billion.[61] Eight years later, in August of 2020, the private equity firm Blackstone acquired Ancestry.com for $4.7 billion. The company's market value had nearly tripled.[62]

History suggests that genealogy institutions have spread earlier in republics that boasted large middle classes and high literacy rates like the United States, while in monarchies, mass genealogy activity has emerged later. Genealogy's histories in Britain and France support this theory. Notwithstanding aristocratic and royal practices dating back to medieval times, and despite multiple evanescent Victorian-era periodicals, no genealogical society endured in Britain before the twentieth century. London's Society of Genealogists (1911), aimed at Britain's middling classes, developed in emulation of Boston's earlier New England Historic Genealogical Society.[63] In France—another country with venerable traditions of nobles' tracing their lineages—the anthropologist Martine Segalen has uncovered lively genealogy subcultures among postal workers and others far outside the upper classes that emerged in the 1980s.[64]

Some evidence challenges my theory. In the German Empire, for example, men from the upper bourgeoisie and the professions collaborated with aristocrats in launching a constellation of genealogy groups and periodicals, starting in the 1860s.[65] Research on Mexico, a multiracial North American republic like the United States, also counters my theory about mass genealogy's early emergence in republics because institutions there developed relatively late. Both Spaniards and Indigenous people treasured evidence of illustrious descent before Mexican independence in 1821, but not until the twentieth century's post-revolutionary decades did a dedicated genealogy society and journal survive. Mexico City's Academia Méxicana de Genealogía y Heráldica dates from 1943 and began publishing its *Boletín* in 1945.[66] Ultimately, particular features of German and Mexican history prevent Germany and Mexico from overturning my arguments about genealogy in the United States. Nineteenth-century Germany featured a relatively high literacy rate among men outside governing classes, compared with other European monarchies. The convulsive Mexican Revolution of the 1910s, which Mexicans experienced also as a civil war, helps explain the late and sketchy emergence of genealogy institutions there compared with those of the United States.[67] The theory that genealogy has flourished earliest and most widely in republics remains strong.

A Chapter Outline

My explorations of political dimensions of Americans' genealogy commitments unfold in seven chapters. In my first three chapters, I organize genealogists' practices by subject so as to recount uninterrupted histories of each major stream of activity. White Protestant populations that rebranded themselves as "Anglo-Saxon" starting in the 1840s, are the subject of chapter 1. While making some reference to antebellum times to illuminate comparisons, I show that genealogy practices expanded after the Civil War when, and because, they affirmed white Anglo-American supremacy. Reliance on textual evidence from the past, and contemporary beliefs that many social characteristics were inherited, informed genealogists' and others' racial labeling.

Mormon practices before the 1960s are the subject of chapter 2. Mormonism's commitment to evangelizing the dead, particularly dead kin, became a feature of worship starting with the church's own founder, Joseph Smith (1807–44). Nineteenth-century missions to the dead extended to all sorts of people regardless of lifetime successes—even to enemies of the religion who were dead. Subsequent Mormon activity repeatedly affirmed the principle of more genealogy for more people. Mormon practices seem to challenge my own thesis about genealogy's politics for seeming comparatively democratic and inclusive.[68] However, a closer look at commemorations in Mormon communities reveals a regard for white "firsts" and white fertility, including historical monuments to white babies, which shared much with the non-Mormon, white supremacist doings that I describe in my first chapter.

Chapter 3 recounts Indigenous practices, African American practices, and American Jewish practices from before the 1960s. The historian Charles Payne's contention about civil rights historiography, that history "is something that happens when the White Folks show up and stops when they leave," does not describe these genealogy practices, which evolved long before white Christians paid attention to them.[69] In the late nineteenth and early twentieth centuries, Indigenous people, African Americans, and American Jews discerned white Protestants' punitive, explicitly racial uses of genealogy for the attacks that they were. Ensuing protests, as genealogists expressed such protests in their work, highlighted genealogy's political dimensions. This chapter contains multiple one-way mirrors, in that practitioners often did not know about other subfields, and they sometimes characterized each other's work as hardly possible. Yet it is important to recognize that genealogy's democratization and diversification did not begin with the 1970s and *Roots* on television. Long beforehand, genealogists' methods and findings could buttress hierarchies of race, gender, religion, and class, but they could also destabilize those hierarchies.

My next four chapters move in a chronological procession rather than in a topical arrangement. After 1945, the multiple streams of genealogy practice came close enough together to play together in a fugue, in which each melody remained discernible. Trumpets sounded from Temple Square in Salt Lake City. In the 1940s, the LDS Church's Genealogical Society opened its formidable holdings of vital records there to the public, without charge. Thereafter, the church's outreach in phases included the local LDS branch library system (1962) dedicated to family history, which spread across the United States and into many other parts of the world; the International Genealogical Index (IGI), which anyone with a personal computer could purchase for home use, starting in 1984; and FamilySearch.org, starting in 1999. With these extensive resources, the church made its collections indispensable to genealogists on multiple continents.

Additional turning points occurred in the 1960s, 1970s, and 1980s when white and Christian genealogists, including Mormons, began publicizing the research of Jewish genealogists and genealogists of color. Genealogy practices within those latter groups expanded both qualitatively, as researchers began focusing outside elites to reconstruct histories of masses, and quantitatively, in a plethora of new institutions, conferences, and periodicals devoted to each specialty. The post-1945 period's inclusiveness extended across class divisions, as well as racial and religious ones, to include those Americans with foreign, unassimilated, criminal (or otherwise scandalous) ancestors as well as the poor and enslaved. Alex Haley's *Roots* embodied the diversification and expansion of genealogy practices that had been happening beforehand, including shortly beforehand—the subject of chapter 4. *Roots* also invigorated subsequent class, racial, and religious diversification among American genealogists and their research subjects, chapter 5's main concern. However, older forms of white Anglo-American and elite genealogy persisted. Diversification did not entail the disappearance of such practices. Instead, well-to-do white genealogists moved around a more crowded stage than before. In chapter 5, I discuss the praise for famous white ancestors in the 1970s and in subsequent decades.

After *Roots*, two phenomena grew that were previously unknown: the genealogy-themed entertainment, especially on television, and the large, for-profit genealogy enterprise, chiefly illustrated by Ancestry Inc. and its later incarnation, Ancestry.com.[70] Only in the 1980s and afterward did big businesses arise that were devoted to genealogy. These two phenomena, entertainment—including roots tourism, or genealogy-themed travel—and large enterprises, are the subject of chapter 6. While on-screen entertainment

DNA Story for Francesca

ancestryDNA

Ethnicity Regions

- England, Wales & Northwestern Europe   91%
- Sweden   4%
- Ireland & Scotland   3%
- Norway   2%

Additional Communities

- Northeastern States Settlers

Pie chart of author's ancestry based on author's Y-chromosome DNA testing, downloaded from Ancestry.com, 2018.

that treated genealogy was truly new in the time of *Roots*, the genealogy commerce of recent times belongs to a longer history of genealogy entrepreneurs in the United States, going back to the mid-1800s.

Published in 1998 in the science journal *Nature*, DNA test results that suggested biological relatedness between Thomas Jefferson's posterity and descendants of his house slave Sally Hemings created a media frenzy in the United States, as did subsequent quarrels and backlashes.[71] Starting around 2000, genealogy businesses large and small repackaged the DNA test as an item that consumers could purchase for home use, then send in for findings about distant ancestry. Genealogy companies represented these findings as probabilities, and in broad, seemingly transhistorical ethnic and geographic terms. Ancestry.com has illustrated my own DNA test results from a Y-chromosome test that I purchased and underwent in 2017, as a list of percentages expressed in a pie chart, starting with 91 percent from "England, Wales, & Northwestern Europe." The company sorted me and my results into an Ancestry research community labeled "Northeastern States Settlers."[72]

These DNA testing companies found market opportunities in Americans' powerful preexisting bias in favor of biogenetic kinship, seemingly more real than elected forms of relatedness, like marriage or adoption. Especially radical visionaries in the 1980s and afterward, many of them gay, lesbian, and/or genderqueer, assembled families entirely on the basis of choice, in disregard of any blood or other preexisting biological tie. During these same decades, genealogy businesses large and small found massive, untapped markets when they turned to genetic genealogy, realizing ample profits and television tie-ins. The elevation of blood over choice in the reckoning of relatedness is the theme of chapter 7, my final chapter. The profitability of genetic genealogy, and the emotionalism of genealogy-focused reality shows, made this hierarchy ever more severe.

The international spread of genealogy's diversification and commercialization, outward from the United States, needs its historians. The interest of entities around the world—including the governments of China, Ghana, Israel, and Ireland—in encouraging and even subsidizing roots travel by diasporic populations also needs historians' scrutiny.[73] For now, let us consider some otherwise disparate homegrown phenomena that have become American exports. The Latter-day Saints Church counted more members outside the United States than inside the United States, starting in 1996.[74] Our list of exports continues with the church's website FamilySearch.org. The list also cannot omit the for-profit Ancestry.com (officially independent of the church despite its Utah origins), its founders' degrees from Brigham Young University (the church's university), and its modern-day headquarters in Utah; Alex Haley's *Roots*; all those Jewish genealogical societies that developed after the first one did in New Jersey, in 1977; and the swarms of roots tourists headed for West Africa, eastern Europe, and Asia as well as to western Europe.[75] All these phenomena possess roots that connect them to those nations of descendants, genealogists for hire, and genealogy professionals contained within the United States.

Part I

Arguments about Exclusion before the 1960s

CHAPTER ONE

I Could Love Them, Too

Genealogy Practices and White Supremacy

Nearly a century after Tocqueville's sojourn to the United States in the 1830s, foreign visitors in the early twentieth century were quick to discern genealogy practices' usefulness to Americans' social pretensions and to the maintenance of power relations in the United States. In 1904, prominent German sociologist Max Weber (1864–1920) became sure that affection for aristocratic tropes was increasing rather than decreasing in America. He toured the United States for three months with his wife Marianne. The couple crossed multiple boundaries, social as well as geographical. Their destinations included Booker T. Washington's Tuskegee, Alabama, and settlement houses in Chicago and Buffalo's poor immigrant neighborhoods. The Webers also paused outside Medford, Massachusetts, to visit some of Max's maternal kin. His half cousin Laura (Fallenstein) lived there with her husband Otto von Klock and their eight children. Klock ran a typing and translation business, and he also hired himself out as a genealogist, reportedly garnering "commissions from the Astors and other established and wealthy families to conduct genealogical research."[1] Klock's ability to use both German and English aided his catering to the successful.

Max and Marianne then returned home to Heidelberg, where Max polished the draft of what became *The Protestant Ethic and the Spirit of Capitalism*, published the next year (1905). He also began to incubate theories that America was undergoing "Europeanization." Europeanization's most obvious meaning was increasing bureaucratization and the growing power of the state.[2] Another signifier of America's Europeanization "had to do with the intrusion of status-seeking norms of social honor, the 'aristocratic' pretensions of the plutocracy" in the United States, in another echo of European histories. His cousin-in-law's clients helped inspire that formulation. Weber called out some U.S. hereditary organizations, family associations, and catchphrases—"'F. F. V., or First Families of Virginia,' or the actual or alleged descendants of the 'Indian Princess' Pocahontas, of the Pilgrim fathers, or of the Knickerbockers," shorthand for ruling families of old New York. Each of these represented "almost inaccessible sects and all sorts of circles setting themselves apart."[3]

Weber's perceptions of increasing stratification in the United States, expressed in the development of hereditary organizations, articulate American genealogists' status-seeking in the late nineteenth century. White genealogists' practices became ever more explicitly racist and hereditarian. Narrowing definitions of American belonging, along the lines of inheritance, documentation, and whiteness, increased genealogy's prestige, and therefore genealogy's popularity. In part because of the dropping costs of printing and publishing, the number of published family genealogies in the United States jumped from an estimated 339 in 1868 to a total of 3,795 in 1909, or a nearly ninefold increase, as registered by the Library of Congress.[4] Family genealogies focused on only one family, one surname, or small, interrelated groups of families or surnames. Acts of documenting and publishing signified upward social mobility and high social status on the part of both ancestors who were easy to document, and descendants who were able to devote time and money to genealogy.

Affection for genealogy drove Americans to make the most of new technologies and institutions. Genealogy activity even brought some facilities into being. The creation of newspaper genealogy features and large libraries, both of which expanded access to materials on which genealogists depended, suggests a preexisting interest in genealogy even as they increased genealogy's popularity in turn. The late nineteenth century featured the development and elaboration of public libraries throughout the United States; the launching of larger research libraries such as the New York Public Library's federation (1895) and Chicago's Newberry Library (1887); and the proliferation of newspaper features, which the *Boston Transcript* pioneered. The emergence of these institutions belongs to a larger picture in which the American bourgeoisie in American cities brought all kinds of cultural institutions into being, from symphonies to opera houses to art museums to universities, with the intent of rivaling Europe's.[5] But the Newberry Library's founding figures purchased many genealogy publications for their brand-new collection, built de novo from bare ground, also because they anticipated patron requests for those materials.[6]

A newspaper that Boston's upper classes favored, the *Transcript* published readers' genealogy queries as early as the 1830s.[7] Genealogy became a regularly scheduled offering of the *Transcript* in 1876, in response to reader demand. Such features appeared weekly by 1894, and twice a week by 1901.[8] Newspaper features for genealogists typically combined information exchanges—readers' queries about particular research problems, for other readers to address—and points of advice from more experienced genealogists. The historian Katharina Hering has counted at least seventeen major newspapers that had regular genealogy features between the 1870s and 1940s, including the *Atlanta Constitution* and the *New York Mail and Express*. My own count of major newspapers with genealogy features adds at least two more, the Newport (R. I.) *Mercury*, as of 1899, and the Church of Jesus Christ of Latter-day Saints' *Deseret News* (Salt Lake City), as of 1907.[9]

Research facilities appeared in many parts of the United States during the late nineteenth and early twentieth centuries. Denver's public library expanded its genealogy offerings after it became clear that illustrious patrons, such as the wife of New Mexico's territorial governor, were traveling considerable distances to obtain the proof that they needed for their applications to the Daughters of the American Revolution (DAR) (1890) and the other new hereditary organizations of the era.[10] By the mid-1920s, other urban public libraries with collections and services for genealogists included those in Los Angeles; St. Louis, Missouri; and Chattanooga, Tennessee.[11] These examples from the West and South show the spread of genealogy-friendly institutions well outside Northeastern cities and New England diasporas in the Upper Midwest.

Genealogy practice was not racial on its face, since research could challenge a family's whiteness as much as certify it. However, the insistence on documentation embedded in Victorian genealogy practices otherwise placed these practices in Jim Crow's arsenals. State laws that imposed racial segregation, suppressed voting by people of color, and allowed the sterilization of incarcerated populations without their consent all depended on genealogical record-keeping. So did federal laws that eroded Native American tribal sovereignty and landholding and that restricted or banned immigration.[12] Private entities, such as hereditary organizations, also used genealogy to stiffen social distinctions. In all these cases, scrutiny of family histories set Americans apart from each other on the basis of race. Important to note, "European" did not yet equal "white." Gilded Age genealogy aficionados attributed racial supremacy to descendants of Protestants from northwestern Europe and Scandinavia, especially but not exclusively from the British Isles.[13] In the late nineteenth and twentieth centuries, racially delineated genealogy practices spread across boundaries of region, denomination, ethnicity, gender, and class that would otherwise have continued to divide white Protestants from each other.

Continuity and Change since Antebellum Times: Inherited Identities for Contemporary Anglo-Saxons

Late nineteenth-century genealogy practices that stressed inheritance of identity, insisted on documentation, and prized Anglo-American whiteness possessed lengthy roots. But the concept of Americanness as an inherited, racial, and documented status was contested enough before the Civil War to put genealogy aficionados on the defensive and to keep their numbers small. "The study of genealogy will never become a popular pursuit," the attorney William Whiting predicted in 1853 when serving as president of the New England Historic Genealogical Society (NEHGS), founded eight years beforehand. Whiting ascribed that organization's small numbers to widespread objections among "unreflecting minds" that "the study of genealogy is uninteresting and useless . . . that it makes no difference to us who our ancestors were, or what were their peculiarities of mental or physical constitution— that the value and respectability of every one depends upon his personal merits—that in this country, if not elsewhere, there are no hereditary rights which render a knowledge of one's ancestry either necessary or desirable." Whiting went on to dismantle each of these objections at length. But he did not challenge his own prediction that genealogy would never become popular.[14] Just months after his speech, the NEHGS closed its "rooms" for at least four months because of a shortage of funds.[15]

However, definitions of Americanness as racial and inherited had begun to spread as a result of the U.S. war on Mexico (1846–48) and mass immigration. Famine in Ireland and the failed revolution of 1848 in the German states caused mass exoduses to the United States. Population flows from Europe now included significant numbers of Catholics and Jews. The term "Anglo-Saxon" had long indicated populations and languages in antique and early medieval England that many Britons and Americans regarded as ancestral. But "Anglo-Saxon" now also indicated contemporary white Anglo-American Protestant populations, with some inclusion of descendants of Pennsylvania Germans, Dutch, and other non-British nationalities who had lived in colonial British America.[16] Starting in the 1840s and 1850s, the term "Anglo-Saxon" served to distinguish these groups from the Northeast's masses of newly arrived, desperately poor Irish Catholics, and from Mexicans and Chinese in the newly conquered West.

The American Party, nicknamed the Know Nothings, was a formidable but short-lived third party amounting to an outcry against Catholic immigration and citizenship at a time when the U.S. government had never sought to limit or otherwise regulate immigrants by group. In the mid-1850s, the American Party captured impressive numbers of local and state political offices in northern states, and repeatedly ran presidential candidates. But the worsening sectional crisis soon extinguished the Know Nothings' challenges, when northerners and southerners who bemoaned immigration could no longer tolerate belonging to the same party.[17]

Solomon Bradford Morse Jr. (born 1809) of East Boston was a forty-seven-year-old sometime accountant when his local Know Nothing "wig-wam" elected him as secretary in 1856.[18] As Morse transcribed it, the chapter's constitution bemoaned Catholics' access to government jobs, and it specified hereditary membership requirements. To gain admission to the chapter, a "brother" had to be at least third-generation American-born, with "American born parents and paternal or maternal Grand parent, or of parent or Grand parent who took an active part in the Revolutionary War in favor of this Government, and of good character." He duly performed extensive research on paternal colonial-era ancestors and on others who shared the Morse surname. He noted ominously in a "memorandum" to himself that a "family of German Jews by the name of Maas" who had arrived around 1850 and were selling clothes in Boston and New Bedford had "assumed the name of Morse."[19] He wanted to close Americanism, as his English-sounding surname of Morse represented, against those he thought lacked a birthright to it, like the Maas family. Such praise for race and documented bloodlines, bundled together, is not surprising from a man who held office in the American Party in a state where it was especially popular among voters.[20]

Talk of hereditary greatness is also not surprising when found among other Americans more affluent than Morse who were fond of heraldry. Heraldry, the study of shields and emblems, takes many forms, but throughout U.S. history and into modern times, Americans' search for relatedness to English aristocrats and luminaries, whose own claims to family arms had survived the inspections of Henry VIII's heralds in the 1500s, has dominated U.S. heraldry. Documenting kinship to such aristocrats would allow Americans, in their own minds, to claim the aristocrats' family crests as their own. Displaying such emblems on their walls, on bookplates and other smaller items of property, or in jewelry or cufflinks on their person, amounted to a public boast.[21] American interest in armigerous forebears in the British Isles was evident long before the 1800s.[22] Yet Americans openly integrated the fetishes of aristocratic descent into their cultural lives after the peace with Britain of 1815. Over time, the interest in heraldry seemed safe—no longer able to threaten republicanism. Heraldry lent a frisson of prestige precisely because of its seeming incongruity in the American Republic.[23]

Heraldry aficionados populated both halves of the nineteenth century, during earlier times as well as later times. Documenting aristocratic descent was sufficiently difficult that it constituted a formidable social barrier between those Americans who achieved documentation and those who could not. The length of documented lineages mattered more than ever after 1840, especially among northerners who complained of being swamped by newcomers who seemed unlike themselves. In 1863, the dean of British heraldry research, Sir John Bernard Burke of *Burke's Peerage*, recalled Americans' appetite for heraldry in the 1840s and 1850s. "For ten or twelve years before the civil conflict broke out, the most intelligent and zealous of my genealogical clients were on the other side of the Atlantic, all yearning to carry back their ancestry to the fatherland."[24] Burke's American clientele was so important to him that he purchased a membership in Boston's NEHGS starting in 1851.[25] Eliza Susan Quincy of Boston struggled for decades to fully document her family's relatedness to arms-bearing Quincys and de Quinceys in England. She knew perfectly well that family arms no longer commanded any "such value & meaning" in the United States, as they had before 1776. "Yet to me they are like an old coin, proving the existence of former ages, of the Crusades & the iron age of armour.-Like sea shells left on the tops of mountains they show where the tides of (human) existence have been," she wrote wistfully in 1873, at age seventy-five.[26] Documented kinship with overseas aristocrats would greatly enhance her family's already sterling reputation, in her mind.

But heraldry's lack of status in American law also lent heraldry a fluidity that freed some Americans to claim family ties to nobilities, simply in acts of purchasing representations of family arms that matched their own surnames. No U.S. law prevented Americans' appropriation of arms to which they lacked a documentable claim or the outright concoction of new coats of arms.[27] An unnamed "Yank" quoted by Frederick Law Olmsted in 1852 remarked of his family arms, apparently with a straight face, "It's the genuine thing.... I paid a great deal of money for it."[28] In contrast, Britain possessed a titled aristocracy, a College of Arms, and extensive regulation of the use of family arms. That country insisted on their patrilineal transmission, from father to son, from individual man to individual man (not from family to family).

American heraldry practices constitute the baldest illustration of how people in the same country that had scrapped European forms of hereditarian government cherished social hierarchies of class and race all the more. But praise for Anglo-Saxons, contemporary as well as ancient, also appeared in the writings of maverick thinkers. Abolitionist minister Theodore Parker and the premier transcendentalist Ralph Waldo Emerson provide examples.[29] While they did not prize aristocratic descent like heraldry aficionados did, these thinkers' prizing of Anglo-Saxon whiteness across class and geographical differences makes their racialism all the starker. While Emerson's essay on "Self-Reliance" (1841) kindled imaginations for centuries to come, his *English*

Traits (1856) has commanded less attention from posterity. He devoted that book to what he saw in England, when visiting in 1833 and again in 1847–48. His memories of stepping ashore at Liverpool made white Americans' inherited Englishness explicit: "[the] American has arrived at the old mansion-house and finds himself among uncles, aunts, and grandsires."

The inborn qualities of Englishmen, which included a talent for colonization, were an even more frequent theme for Emerson. "On the English face are combined decision and nerve with the fair complexion, blue eyes and open and florid aspects. Hence the love of truth, hence the sensibility, the fine perception and poetic construction." Elsewhere in *English Traits*, Emerson admired the rough-hewn masculinity, extending to a propensity for violence, that he noticed in living Englishmen and in ancient Anglo-Saxon royals. He carefully distinguished those qualities from the grosser propensities for violence that he attributed to men of other races and nationalities. "The fair Saxon man, with open front and honest meaning, domestic, affectionate, is not the wood out of which cannibal, or inquisitor, or assassin is made, but he is moulded for law, lawful trade, civility, marriage, the nurture of children, for colleges, churches, charities, and colonies."[30] In contrast, Emerson wrote privately, "[the] German & Irish nations, like the Negro, have a deal of guano in their destiny."[31]

During the same decades of the mid-nineteenth century, evolution's pioneers also fused race with inheritance. While the fluidity of evolution theory challenged the fixed categories of racism, which depended on belief in inherited qualities, racial science nevertheless found much nourishment in Darwinism's presumptions of competition, and notions of inherited characteristics of species.[32] Working separately, the British social scientist Herbert Spencer published on "survival of the fittest" as early as 1852, while Charles Darwin pondered human reproduction alongside other forms of animal breeding in his *Descent of Man* (1871). The British scientist Francis Galton found his initial inspiration for studying heredity in his cousin Darwin's *Origin of Species* (1859), pervaded as it was with genealogical metaphors.[33] Galton published *Hereditary Genius* first as articles in 1865 and then as a book in 1869. This work drew much notice in American genealogy periodicals.[34] He later coined and launched the field of eugenics in 1883.

Americans' regard for racial sorting and inherited greatness found a more hospitable environment after the Civil War. Genealogy practitioners who exclaimed in the 1870s that they no longer felt defensive about their interest, fused together ideas about race with convictions about heredity with new frankness. Charles B. Moore, an attorney who helped develop the New York

Genealogical and Biographical Society in 1869, aspired to evaluate human re-production along the same lines as nonhuman animal breeding. Pets and live-stock with documented bloodlines were becoming a keen preoccupation on both sides of the Atlantic.[35] "In selecting for use the best animal of a high or-der, such as a horse or a dog," Moore remarked in 1870, "it is conceded that *race* and *blood* are important; both as to intelligence and courage, i.e. men-tally, and as to size, strength, speed, and endurance, i.e. physically. Then, must not race and blood be much more important, in both departments, for *man*; the highest class of all animals?"[36]

Continuity and Change since Antebellum Times: Documented Identities

Documentation reflected social stratification so persistently, throughout the nineteenth century and in later times, that it showed more historical continu-ities than the notion of inherited status did. Genealogy practices required the accumulation of records of births (often baptisms), marriages, deaths, military service, wills and probate court documents, and other features of a long-ago person's life that fixed identity. This insistence on written evidence proved more of a social barrier in the Early Republic than it would later do. In an era when public libraries were in their infancy, when most surviving documents from earlier times existed as sole or very few handwritten copies, and when broadly accessible research libraries were nonexistent, any antebellum re-searcher needed resources—time, money, education, and connectedness to other researchers—that people who lived hand to mouth generally lacked.[37]

Large pools of Americans aspired to genealogy knowledge even when they were unable to document that knowledge. Deborah Bradford Sampson (later Gannett) (1760–1827) famously fought in disguise as a man, Robert Shurtleff, in the Revolutionary War. Raised in southeastern Massachusetts, she claimed descent from two *Mayflower* passengers of 1620, including Wil-liam Bradford, the first governor of Plymouth Colony. Her family had since fallen on hard times. Her father abandoned her mother for a common-law wife in Maine. That decision compelled her mother to go on poor relief, whereupon she sent five-year-old Deborah to live with another family as a servant. As a result, Deborah went without any formal education. In adult-hood, following the war, she did what she could to claim the Bradford name and the *Mayflower* reminder. She purchased a reprint of the first sermon preached in Plymouth Colony, and she gave her first-born child the middle name of Bradford.[38] But her case also shows that the ability to document such claims rested on some degree of affluence and leisure time on the part of the descendant and generations in between as well as the forebear.

The Flourishing of Hereditary Organizations after 1876

After the Civil War, societies devoted to genealogy per se spread beyond New England. In consultation with visitors from the NEHGS, New Yorkers formed the country's second genealogy society in 1869, the Genealogical and Biographical Society (NYGBS).[39] Philadelphia gentlemen in the Historical Society of Pennsylvania (HSP, 1824) developed such an appetite for genealogy that some split off from the HSP in 1892 to develop the Genealogical Society of Pennsylvania.[40] I will address contemporaneous developments in Mormon genealogy in a subsequent chapter. The aforementioned genealogy societies in New York and Philadelphia shared with Boston's NEHGS a membership in which professionals, merchants and other businessmen, political figures (including ex-presidents), and gentlemen of leisure predominated, along with the very occasional woman, such as the NYGBS's Elizabeth Clarkson Jay.[41]

Hereditary organizations, so-called because of their genealogy-based membership requirements, were not new as such. Recall the hereditary membership requirements for Solomon Morse Jr.'s American Party "wigwam" in 1856. But earlier examples were either small or local or—in the case of the Society of the Cincinnati (1783), made up of revolutionary officers and their eldest male posterity—they walked into a buzzsaw of objection. The Society of the Cincinnati contributed to its already controversial reputation when members converted their status, with its evocation of British aristocrats' practice of primogeniture, into a patriotic pedestal from which to express themselves on such fraught, highly political issues as ratifying the U.S. Constitution, in 1788.[42] But a new array of mass hereditary organizations emerged a century later, beginning in 1876 with San Francisco's Sons of Revolutionary Sires. Hereditary organizations went on to attract a much broader membership—numbering over one hundred thousand members, collectively, by World War I.[43]

Patriotic anniversaries command an uncanny power to stimulate commemorations and memory work among people who are already interested in the past. With the national centenary of 1876, the public appetite for nostalgia for Early America increased.[44] Shortly before the Fourth of July, a San Francisco widow suggested in a local newspaper, "Wouldn't it be a most novel but strikingly interesting idea in the programme of the procession for our city Centennial Celebration to have represented our grandparents of the

Revolution by the grandchildren now living, residents of this city?" Her own grandfather had served. In the end, eighty men marched in the San Francisco Independence Day parade, and many more sustained the Sons of Revolutionary Sires that same summer.[45] In subsequent decades, Alice Morse Earle of New York, author of numerous histories of everyday life, such as *The Sabbath in Colonial New England* (1892) and *Child Life in Colonial Days* (1899), garnered substantial advances from commercial publishers for her lengthy tomes. They ran more than three hundred pages each.[46]

In this atmosphere, the hereditary organization that mobilized itself on contemporary issues—such as the "patriotic education" of immigrants and preservation of antiquities against industry's wrecking balls—and harnessed both projects to genealogy and local history, seemed unobjectionable. The Daughters of the American Revolution (DAR, 1890), by far the largest hereditary organization, acquired many characteristics of the reform-minded women's club before the First World War and the Russian Revolution impelled the DAR's conservative elements to drive the organization to the right.[47] Hereditary organizations' efflorescence at the turn of the twentieth century contains additional significance. For substantial numbers of white southerners, white women, whites in the middle classes, and white progeny of colonial-era Dutch, Scots-Irish, German, and Huguenot (French Protestant) populations, the hereditary organization became the principal medium by which they began to conduct genealogy publicly.

White Southerners in Organized Genealogy

White, leisure-class Southerners had long practiced genealogy in the absence of dedicated institutions and publications, usually in private.[48] The "first families of Virginia" existed as a buzzword long before the First Families of Virginia formed as such in 1912. Incarcerated in Richmond during the Civil War, Union prisoner of war Reuben Bartley heard the wife of Confederate secretary of war James A. Seddon denounce his group as "'*Thieves. Murderers. Hell Monsters. Assassins.*' and," he added sardonically, "such polite epithets as the Ladies of the F.F.V.s only use to designate Union soldiers."[49] Sarah Bruce Seddon's denunciations foreshadowed the Lost Cause movement to come.[50] The mass bereavement among Southern whites from the loss of Confederate soldiers, and survivors' widespread rage over the outlawing of slavery, the withering of Southern economies, and simultaneous triumphs of Northern capitalism, all compelled white Southerners to enshrine the reputation of the bygone Confederacy. Throughout the South, immediately following the end of the war in

1865, women's and veterans' groups engaged in fundraising for mass burials and cemetery-building for Confederate soldiers, tasks for which there was no government funding. These groups also sponsored and erected monuments to soldiers and generals.[51] Edward A. Pollard's paeans to the "Lost Cause" in 1866, published in Richmond, gave the movement its name. With the return of U.S. troops to the South in 1867, in peacetime, to police state and local elections, and with the temporary disfranchisement of Confederate veterans and supporters, Reconstruction's radical phases increased white Southerners' commitment to emphasizing honorable dimensions of the Confederate struggle, and eagerness to spread that gospel. Former Confederate generals founded the influential Southern Historical Society in 1869 in Richmond.[52]

The spread of the Lost Cause movement did not compel southerners to enact genealogy publicly right away, but Lost Cause organizations took explicitly genealogical and hereditary forms later in the century. The Ladies' Memorial Associations that originated in 1865 or soon afterward were not hereditary or kin-based, strictly speaking. But Lost Cause commemoration and historical studies in subsequent decades, coupled with the insistence that race itself was heritable, invigorated genealogy activity and hereditarian sensibilities in the South. The major Lost Cause memory organizations of the 1890s (the United Daughters of the Confederacy, 1894, and the Sons of Confederate Veterans, 1896), which sponsored hundreds of monuments and pressured local schoolboards toward pro-Confederate textbook choices, both required proof of relatedness to Confederate soldiers, sailors, or supporters for admission.[53] White Southerners' public engagement with genealogy, history, hereditary organizations, and commemoration harmonized with the Democratic Party's monopolization of Southern state governments starting in the 1890s. Otherwise parsimonious governments funded state archives and history repositories for the first time in southern history. These decisions affirmed white supremacy, as did the new segregation laws, disfranchisement measures, and lynchings and pogroms that were characteristic of "Jim Crow."[54]

By extension, white Southerners at the turn of the twentieth century also showed new eagerness for the study of colonial and revolutionary eras. Northerners had long predominated among historians and schoolbook authors who wrote on Early America.[55] Two major history periodicals based in the South, the *William and Mary Quarterly* (1892) and the *Virginia Magazine of History and Biography* (1893), launched close together in time. Until the 1940s, both journals included substantial genealogy content, suggesting that their scholarly authors and readers harbored some interest in findings on

prominent families.[56] Such blending of history and genealogy also characterized the activities of white southerners in hereditary organizations. Southerners joined or helped found groups not focused on southern history per se,
such as the Colonial Dames of America (founded in New York in 1890); the
unrelated National Society of Colonial Dames of America, organized in Philadelphia the next year; the Daughters of the Revolution (DR) (1891); the
U.S. Daughters of the War of 1812 (1892); and the Sons of the American Revolution (1889). Two in the DAR's founding quintet of 1890, Eugenia Washington and Mary Desha, came from Virginia and Kentucky, respectively. Flora
Adams Darling spearheaded the founding of the DR and the U.S. Daughters
of the War of 1812 after her ouster from the DAR's leadership. Though born in
New Hampshire, she had spent her adult life in the South and was the widow
of a Confederate officer.[57] A group of Galveston women formed the hereditary Daughters of the Republic of Texas in 1891, which went on to purchase
the Alamo in San Antonio in 1905 and run it as a museum for more than a
century.[58]

White Women in Organized Genealogy

Many of the foregoing examples of southerners in genealogy and hereditary
organizations feature women, who played an increasingly central role in genealogy's history. After centuries of conducting informal recordkeeping
among their kin, white women nationwide, including southerners, inundated
the field of publicly conducted genealogy after the Civil War. Women's interest in ancestry resembled an extension of family responsibilities, and also illustrated some of the benefits of white supremacy to white women.

Families and neighborhoods had long boasted the aunt or grandmother
who stored extensive family history and local history information, with emphasis on perceived successes, in her own head. When Benjamin Franklin met
such a woman in 1758 while on his roots trip to England, he called her a "good-
natured, chatty old lady." Mrs. Eyre Whalley was married to a vicar in the small
village of Ecton, Northamptonshire.[59] So many American incarnations of
Mrs. Whalley aided genealogists' endeavors that the "chatty old lady" resembles a stock character. Male genealogists and historians considered her information to be indispensable to their research, after reaching the end of the
paper trail. Witness the checklist of John Kelly, a New Hampshire judge, in
1826 when he was not in court. "I have never spent so long a time in Exeter to
so little purpose. I examined no records-ransacked no office-made no genealogical inquiries-conversed with no old woman-and found no old Almanack.

In short I know no more about '200 years ago' when I left the town than when I entered."[60] Later in the century, women in hereditary organizations bowed before the "chatty old lady" as they ceremoniously committed her words to paper. Women in Knoxville, Tennessee, who gathered as Daughters of the Confederacy in 1898 reported their "unwritten law that every member must read [aloud] and deposit in the archives of the chapter either her personal reminiscences of 'war-times' or those of her mother and grandmother, as handed down by tradition," meaning informally, especially orally.[61] Daughters of the Confederacy insisted on the legitimacy of women's memories of the Civil War and Reconstruction.

The expansion of literacy and higher education among advantaged women brought ever more of them into text-based genealogy practices. Collectively, hereditary organizations before 1900 contained female majorities; Daughters and Dames far outnumbered Sons. Daughters also out-energized Sons, creating agenda that the men followed or did not bother to pursue. The women's calendars featured monthly meetings and earnest historical and literary study. The organizational culture of men's groups instead stressed the occasional banquet or smoker to foster present-minded networking opportunities.[62]

What accounts for women's predominance and energy in American hereditary organizations and in genealogy generally? Daughters' and Dames' historical studies appealed to a group that remained barred from most realms of professional life. Even women with college and postgraduate degrees experienced these exclusions, especially if the women married.[63] Club meetings for women often took the form of adult education, and self-education. Gender norms regarding social mobility also played a role. Women's enforced financial dependence on fathers and husbands reduced the stigma of interest in inherited relationships and other accidents of birth, while male genealogists often felt that they had to justify their interest, especially when addressing other men. In 1847, Jacob Moore of Washington eulogized a friend and fellow genealogist, as follows: "He well understood the general indifference of the public to pursuits of this nature. The direction of the living and moving crowd is onward; and he who busies himself in gathering up the memorials of the past, will be left behind,—himself and his labors too generally unrewarded and forgotten."[64] But compared to men of their race and class, women felt little need to apologize for deviating from the American archetype of the self-made man, when publicizing their ancestry, given that the archetype was out of reach for most women. Only bequests—inheritances—from their fathers, and/or financially advantageous marriages, could protect most women from poverty.[65]

Limited Class and Ethnic Diversity
within Hereditary Organizations

The white middle classes were another group more in evidence in the late nineteenth century, compared to earlier times, in publicly conducted genealogy. Middle-class inclusion, in this context, shows the heightened ability of whiteness and race to bring together people whom class differences would otherwise separate. Genealogy activity—especially successful documenting of lineages—joined manners, dress, foodways, and home furnishings in the toolboxes of Americans who wished to rise in society.[66] While genealogy pursuits projected exclusiveness when insisting on textual evidence, they became more accessible over time. With the expansion of libraries; newspaper clearinghouses; surname and place indexes; and publications in general, many of which reprinted old documents, conditions of genealogy research were not quite as arduous as they had been before the Civil War. People in less moneyed circumstances economized on other expenses or incurred debts in order to fund their interest. When Lila Dix Ball Agnew of Wahpeton, North Dakota, hired a genealogist in Boston to assemble documentation of *Mayflower* descent, the genealogist privately characterized her "little" client as "anxious for a Mayflower and thus far I have not discovered one for her; she has to be careful with her pennies and we progress slowly."[67] For someone in Agnew's position, access to this exclusive group, documented *Mayflower* descendants, amounted to a durable form of cultural capital that no amount of money could obtain if one did not already have it, and that no one could take away.

Some hereditary organizations were more accessible to white Americans with documentable forebears than others. To gain admission to the DAR, one had to prove only one line of descent, via proof of births and marriages in each generation, to a revolutionary soldier, sailor, or supporter on the Patriot side of that war.[68] The group's founding generation boasted of attracting descendants of lowly teenage drummer boys as well as high-hat officers. "Burke's peerage will have no place in this land of the free, where every man and every woman is the peer of every other man or woman, for they are sons and daughters of the highest nobility the sun ever shone upon," contended Mary Smith Lockwood in 1893, in a swipe at heraldry's fetishes.[69] This comparative inclusiveness enabled the DAR to build a large, truly national membership, when compared to other hereditary groups.

Ever-more-exclusive organizations, in which some in the upper classes walled themselves off from lower orders, were another indication of the widening range of social classes' practicing genealogy within white America. The

two Colonial Dames organizations were invitation-only. Admission commit-
tees screened the prospective member's prerevolutionary ancestors for social
and political prominence; her proof and references for her claims to relatedness; and her own clubbability and social prominence ("personal character").[70]
Later times brought the emergence of ever-smaller and more stringent hereditary organizations, such as the Baronial Order of Runnemede (1898), that aspired to trace descent to thirteenth-century nobles.[71] Notwithstanding the
stock market crash the previous year and ongoing bank failures that were roil-
ing the country, twenty-three-year-old Chauncey Devereux Stillman (b. 1907)
of New York City decided in 1930 to hire a genealogist to help him access exclusive hereditary groups in town. Having "prepared" at Groton and Harvard, and
able to supply a list of "finals clubs" to which he had belonged while in college,
he gained admission to the Society of the Cincinnati in addition to the Society
of Colonial Wars (organized in 1893), the Order of Founders and Patriots
(1896), and the Society of Mayflower Descendants in New York (1894).[72]

These predominantly white Anglo-American organizations did allow some
degree of ethnic diversity, so long as the individual was white and with documented colonial descent. The late nineteenth century showed the descendants of non-English-speaking colonists, and to a lesser extent colonial-era
Catholics and Jews, developing hereditary groups and genealogy forums as
never before. Huguenot and Dutch forebears were a longtime interest of the
NYGBS (1869). Its periodical sometimes published untranslated Dutch Re-
formed Church records. Descendants of Huguenots organized as such, starting in 1883.[73] The hereditary Holland Society came together in 1885 in New
York, and Pennsylvanians developed the much larger Pennsylvania German
Society, also hereditary, in 1891.[74] Because the Huguenot, Dutch, Scots-Irish,
and German forebears being commemorated were nearly always Protestant,
as were their descendants, mass hereditary organizations like the DAR and
the SAR remained mostly Protestant—ecumenically so, ranging from New
England and upper midwestern Congregationalists to Pennsylvania Quakers
to Southern Baptists.[75] Few groups explicitly barred Jews or Catholics, but
Americans of non-Protestant ancestry sometimes sought refuge in organizations of their own. A short-lived group called the One Hundred, descendants
of the earliest documented Jews in North America, was founded in 1889. Flee-
ing the Portuguese Inquisition in Brazil, they had arrived in 1654 in New Amsterdam in search of Dutch commitments to religious toleration, a decade
before English conquerors renamed the colony New York.[76]

Hereditary organizations and the institutions that served them, such as libraries and historical societies, expanded whiteness and Americanism to

include women, southerners, the middle classes, and descendants of non-English colonists. Individuals from all these groups served as leaders and founders of hereditary organizations. Clearly, though, hereditary groups and genealogy cultures drew ever firmer racial boundaries against people of non-European descent.

Hereditary Organizations and Race

White supremacists relied so much on genealogy findings to enforce racial distinctions that, when genealogists' results failed to clarify matters of race, consternation ensued. In earlier eras, legally speaking, up to one-quarter of nonwhite ancestry was allowable for a person to live as white or to marry someone who was white. But from the late nineteenth century onward, as late as the 1980s in Louisiana, a white person could have only one-thirty-second Black ancestry, or less. In the 1910s and 1920s, some states broadened their bans on interracial marriage while simultaneously narrowing the legal definition of "white," such as in southern states' "one-drop rule." Under Virginia's Racial Integrity Act of 1924, the merest percentage of nonwhite ancestry, whether rumored or fully documented, made an individual's marriage to a white person illegal.[77]

Consequently, numerous white, divorce-seeking plaintiffs across the country in the 1920s alleged that their spouses had fraudulently misrepresented themselves as white. The young New York socialite Leonard Rhinelander made national headlines in December 1925 when he lost his case against his estranged wife, Alice Jones Rhinelander, a mixed-race Englishwoman who had been a servant in his parents' house. Leonard's case for annulment hinged on the allegation that he had believed Alice to be fully white when they married. Though the court did not grant annulment, the wealthy Rhinelander family went about annihilating any claim Alice could make to the family's immense estate and sought to keep the couple apart permanently. Neither Leonard, who died a decade later, nor Alice, who lived into the 1980s, married again.[78]

Shortly before Leonard Rhinelander lost his suit, when the trial was still garnering much newspaper coverage, a Michigan woman panicked at her discovery. In late November 1925, Olive Harwood Lash wrote to a fellow genealogist about her great-grandfather's first wife. Living in upstate New York at the turn of the nineteenth century, Lash's great-grandfather had abandoned and then divorced her ("a nice girl–a good looking girl") shortly after she bore their third child, after he heard from her parents that she "had negro blood."

Or maybe it was Indian blood; Lash was not sure. Among the first wife's descendants, Lash discovered teachers, "scholars," and other successful people. While assuring her correspondent that she herself descended from his second wife, she nonetheless felt sullied. "I could love them, too," Lash lamented, referring to the first wife's posterity. "This is what genealogy brings ... it is the only blight on the family records of my ancestry for many centuries and I can trace far, especially on my father's side ... back thru the Saxon Princes-and many generations beyond."[79]

When Lash remarked that she "could love" her newly discovered relatives—who might or might not have bestowed the "blight on the family records" of nonwhite ancestry—she felt unable to love them. Although genealogy research could divulge family secrets, such as nonwhite forebears of families who otherwise lived as white, genealogy was nonetheless useful to the maintenance of racial distinctions simply because most unions between whites were much better documented than those occurring across racial boundaries. Lash reported that other descendants of her great-grandfather "seem to *not* have any ... records" of his first wife and her descendants, "or else withhold them."[80]

Denying strenuously that a family or person with mixed-race origins could rightfully claim to be white, hereditary organizations deliberately barred those small numbers of nonwhites who could meet their genealogy-based membership criteria. By "statute," on the initiative of members from Cincinnati, the DAR in 1894 declared an outright ban on "colored" women. More than eighty years passed before the society admitted an African American to membership, in 1977.[81] Men's organizations similarly excluded people of color, especially African Americans. Prospective members of the Sons of the American Revolution had to document their descent from a revolutionary soldier or supporter, supplying written proof of births and marriages in each generation. The Harvard-educated historian, sociologist, and civil rights pioneer W. E. B. Du Bois (1868–1963) managed to document his relatedness to the revolutionary soldier Tom Burghardt, a Massachusetts slave who had obtained his freedom with his military service. Du Bois's research satisfied the state branch of the SAR, and so the Massachusetts men voted to admit him in 1908. But the SAR's national leadership refused Du Bois because it anticipated that admitting an African American would repel white southerners from joining the Sons.[82]

Other hereditary groups used more subtle or unspoken methods of exclusion. The kinship-based United Daughters of the Confederacy (1894) hardly needed a stated ban on "colored" members, in part because there were hardly any African Americans among Confederate soldiers and sailors. The Confederate military had excluded Black soldiers until March 1865, just weeks before surrendering, and the Confederate government had withheld any promise of emancipation for slaves who served—unlike the experiences of enslaved men, such as Tom Burghardt, in previous wars.[83] The personal character requirements of most hereditary groups were an even more effective tool for barring undesirables. DAR applicants in 1894, for example, needed the endorsement of "at least one member of the National Society."[84]

Hereditary groups did not just screen against nonwhites; they marked urban spaces and other landscapes with praise for white populations' reproduction. By the 1910s, hereditary organizations were regularly funding monuments and plaques, fastened to walls or boulders, that intended to remind passers-by of the name and birthdate of the first "white" or Anglo-American baby born, or the first "white wedding," in the area. White baby commemorations were especially noticeable west of the Appalachians. Upon her seventy-fifth birthday, Harriet Godfrey of Minneapolis (born 1849) was feted by a local DAR chapter as "the first white girl of American lineage" born in the area.[85] The DAR chapter that formed in Lewiston, Idaho, in 1918 named itself for Alice Whitman (died 1839). She had been the first and only child of the Congregationalist missionaries Narcissa Prentiss Whitman and Rev. Marcus Whitman. The chapter celebrated the Connecticut-born Narcissa as the earliest white Anglo-American woman to cross most of North America, in 1836. But young Alice drowned at the age of two, whereupon warriors from the nearby Cayuse tribe slew both her parents. Nearly eighty years later, a local Daughter eulogized Alice as the "'little white Cayuse Queen.' Miners and trappers often walked many miles to get a glimpse of her baby beauty."[86] An exception in North Carolina to the midwestern and western concentration of white-baby monuments and plaques is Sallie Southall Cotton's 1890s crusade for a monument to baby Virginia Dare. Dare was the first and only child born to English colonists on Roanoke Island before the colonists' unexplained disappearance by 1588.[87]

These acts of commemoration concealed some ironies. Birth rates among native-born Americans had plunged by half during the nineteenth century, notwithstanding prohibitions on contraceptive devices and abortion that became national with the federal Comstock Act of 1873.[88] Concerns over "race suicide"—the prospect of immigrant nationalities and others out-reproducing and outnumbering white "Anglo-Saxons"—were the subject of presidential handwringing. When Theodore Roosevelt called on women and men like himself to embrace "the strenuous life," he intended that women would return to bearing large families like their grandmothers had.[89] But hereditary groups attracted affluent urban and small-town denizens with considerably smaller families than their own parents had had, or with no children at all.[90] "Race suicide" discourses nonetheless burrowed into the groups' concerns.

Hereditary organizations' publicizing of members' prestigious ancestry, in print, communicated praise for white reproduction. Such boastfulness had seemed déclassé in antebellum times, when merchant-industrialists in Boston preferred to conceal their interest from public knowledge. "You must not make it known by *name*, who gave you this information.-It is not of importance enough to any body,-and besides I should be unwilling to have it done," the merchant Peter Chardon Brooks told a historian in 1838, regarding the nine pages of detailed genealogy information he enclosed with his letter. At that time, Brooks was reputedly Boston's richest man.[91] But later generations saw no problem with publicity. Printing "yearbooks" listing descendant by name and ancestor, side by side, was a common practice in hereditary organizations. Between 1895 and 1938, the DAR published 160 thick volumes of "lineage books."[92] Hereditary groups' reputation for policing racial boundaries was such that others turned to these groups to clarify the whiteness of public figures. Democrats' rumors that Senator Warren Harding of Ohio possessed nonwhite ancestry, beset the 1920 presidential race. Republicans intended that his publicized admission to the Sons of the American Revolution and a widely distributed family tree, bundled with "pallid, full-page portraits of his mother and father," put the matter to rest. His sister Abigail belonged to the DAR. Harding won the presidency.[93]

Government Deployments of Genealogy: Impositions on Indian Country and on African Americans in the South

Genealogy proved useful not only to heredity organizations' exclusiveness but also to the state. The expansion of public genealogy activity across class, religious, regional, and gender boundaries to draw together native-born white Americans as white, overlapped in time with government policies and laws aimed at racial subjugation, with use of genealogical recordkeeping as a cudgel. Native Americans had long engaged in family history, passing down oral evidence to subsequent generations. Many reckoned their forebears through their mothers.[94]

The reminiscences of Buffalo Bird Woman/Maxi-diwiac (Hidatsa) (ca. 1839–1929) illustrate these patterns of orality and matrilineal tracing. After she reached her old age, scholars prized and recorded her memories of

Indigenous farming practices in Missouri River floodplains, before the whites came. Buffalo Bird Woman began a 1912 interview with a University of Chicago anthropologist by naming her maternal great-grandmother, Soft-white Corn, and her two daughters, Turtle and Otter. Buffalo Bird Woman then listed women in subsequent generations, to arrive at her own early life. At age six, she lost her mother to a smallpox epidemic. Two of her aunts, Red Blossom and Strikes-many-Women, along with her grandmother and great-aunt, Turtle and Otter, then raised Buffalo Bird Woman and taught her how to farm. She then began calling Red Blossom and Strikes-many-Women her "mothers."[95] Buffalo Bird Woman's family history focused on her maternal lines, she recounted it orally after likely having received it orally, and she also dispensed with the binary of immediate and extended family that mattered to whites at the time.[96] Quite simply, her aunts, great-aunt, and grandmother had become her immediate family.

Incoming Americans sought to dismantle each of these characteristics of Indigenous family reckoning, in the course of conquest. Starting in the 1880s, people in authority who intended to shrink Indian numbers and claims narrowed the already-tangled answer to the question of who was a tribal member, after centuries in which Indians had mingled with whites, Blacks, and Indians from other tribes.[97] The 1887 Dawes Severalty Act sought to break up reservations into family-size plots of land, intending that Indian families live and farm on them in the manner of white farming families. This legislation also subsidized distant boarding schools that bundled Christianization with assimilationist education of Native American children.[98] Because the U.S. government wanted Indians to live in nuclear, male-headed families, the government found it necessary to gather information on family interrelationships in order to allot the plots of land to families. Hence, in the 1890s and 1900s, government agents and some tribal members began compiling tribal allotment "rolls," lists that noted kin relationships. During Woodrow Wilson's presidency in the 1910s, which otherwise brought new degrees of racial segregation to the federal government, the administration added notations of each person's "blood quantum" (percentage of Indian ancestry), to fulfill requirements that claimants to tribal land needed to possess particular percentages of Indian "blood." A fraction now adorned each name. A fraction exceeding one-half of Indian blood placed a person's land claims in trust.[99]

While attempting the breakup of tribal identities while simultaneously trying to shrink the numbers of claimants to tribal lands, the U.S. government imposed document-based, patrilineal, and racial forms of family reckoning and, later, blood-quantum measurements, on family history practices among

Indigenous people.[100] Decades later, the Indian Reorganization Act (1934) aspired otherwise to end severalty and allotment, but the legislation linked blood quanta and other racial readings of relatedness even more emphatically with dispossession. As the federal government's first official pronouncement of just "who was an Indian," the legislation of 1934 specified at least one-half Indian blood for tribal belonging, consequently shrinking the pool of possible tribal members.[101]

The process of generating allotment rolls and later tribal membership records was not only error-ridden; it also expressed active prejudices. The lists omitted Indians who simply refused to comply with enrollment or allotment. Even when Indigenous people participated in putting together the rolls, the process often excluded those of mixed African American and Indian descent, and descendants of former slaves ("freedmen") whose masters and mistresses had been Indians. Long after the Dawes Act's repeal in 1934, these race-based and political exclusions from tribal rolls retained their ability to harm. Ancestors' inclusion on such rolls guaranteed, to descendants, access to plots of land, government employment in areas where other employers were painfully few, and other staffs of reservation life such as access to health care. The Certificate of Degree of Indian Blood remains an instrument of exclusion to this day.[102]

Governments' deployments of family reckoning and genealogy practices also subjugated African Americans. With the slave-free distinction gone, genealogy increased in importance as a sentry guarding racial boundaries in the South, where most African Americans lived before World War I, and in growing southern cities. The violent end of Reconstruction in the 1870s sank into memory, to be replaced by Jim Crow.[103] Whites developed new reminders of white supremacy befitting urban life, such as segregation of mass transit on long-distance railroads and local trolleys, mob attacks on Black neighborhoods and businesses, and exclusion or restriction of African Americans from amusement parks and cinemas.[104]

Besides southern states' bans on interracial marriage, other Jim Crow measures also depended on genealogy-focused information gathering. The disfranchisement measures in southern states after 1890, namely elevated poll taxes and non-standardized "literacy tests" that varied greatly in their difficulty, were not racial on their face. But the laws would not survive court challenges, if they made their racial purposes explicit. State governments implemented these laws to suppress African American voting, but many poor, illiterate white men also experienced disfranchisement. Some politicians found this consequence unacceptable. State-level "grandfather" clauses

(1898–1915) carved out voting rights for men who failed literacy tests, but who could otherwise meet one of the following criteria. The men needed to document either their own voting in southern elections before 1867, or document their fathers,' grandfathers,' or other kinsmen's voting in southern elections before 1867.[105]

Architects of the grandfather clauses intended to narrow the franchise in southern states on the basis of race, by linking voting rights to the times before Reconstruction's most ambitious reforms. Even though three southern states possessed Black majorities in the nineteenth century and other southern states had near-majorities of African Americans, southern voting populations had been entirely white—until 1867. The federal Reconstruction Act of that year limited the franchise in southern states to men who had been loyal to the United States during the Civil War, thus enabling Black men to vote and hold office, and temporarily suppressing the votes of ex-Confederates.[106] The grandfather laws of the 1890s and 1900s framed whiteness as an inherited and documented quality, in that familiar blend.

Government Deployments of Genealogy: Eugenics Laws and Practices

State laws that intended to suppress reproduction of supposed inferiors, also depended on genealogists' methods, assumptions, and findings. Although genealogy and eugenics differed in orientation toward past and future, eugenicists needed genealogical records. Francis Galton, who launched eugenics and was a decidedly public intellectual, reconfigured genealogical record-keeping to focus on posterity as well as forebears with the publication of his *Record of Family Faculties* (1884). He intended it for readers who, in his words, "care to forecast the mental and bodily faculties of their children and to further the science of heredity."[107] But retrospective genealogies served the purposes of eugenics, too. "[The] past record of a family is a sure indication of what its general character will be in the future," William P. W. Phillimore remarked in 1887 while citing Galton, in his advice book for American genealogists traveling in Britain.[108]

American eugenicists sought a future for the United States that featured the enhanced reproduction of human "stocks" they considered superior, and diminished reproduction by those labeled as inferior. To make their cases, eugenicists tracked social tendencies, such as crime or drunkenness, and some forms of disease, such as epilepsy, as they passed through families.[109] Charles B. Davenport of the Eugenics Record Office (founded in 1910) in

New York, along with his colleague Harry Laughlin, amassed extensive infor-mation to argue that each family was "stamped with a peculiar set of traits," depending on the "germ plasm" that distinguished the family from others. Davenport and Laughlin believed in an inherited "'determiner' for feeble-mindedness or criminality, as well as intelligence or morality."[110] They achieved their aims when at least thirty-two states, starting with Indiana in 1907, passed compulsory-sterilization legislation by the 1930s. These mea-sures sought to end reproduction by persons considered unfit, by means of surgery: vasectomies for men, and salpingectomies that severed or removed women's fallopian tubes. Across the United States, at least sixty thousand Americans—mostly incarcerated in prisons and state institutions designed for persons deemed "feebleminded" or otherwise disabled—underwent ster-ilization without their consent between 1907 and 1963. This number does not include those within private medical practices who experienced sterilization against their will.[111]

In the 1920s, eugenics expanded in popularity, as "Fitter Families" contests at state and county fairs, and a slew of eugenics publications and newly founded groups all illustrated.[112] That same decade featured an especially stark overlap between eugenics and genealogy's hereditarian premises. Stan-ford University president and biologist David Starr Jordan, and the California genealogist Sarah Louise Kimball, nourished each other's commitments. Kimball had assisted with Jordan's presentations at least since 1912, and he credited her work for inspiring the title of his 1921 *Scientific Monthly* article, "The Inbred Descendants of Charlemagne."[113] Together they published *Your Family Tree: Being a Glance at Scientific Aspects of Genealogy* (1929). Jordan possessed a household name. A public intellectual, he had combined stances for disarmament and world peace with an ardent advocacy of eugenics over the previous two decades. He was responsible for connecting the Eugenics Record Office to the woman who became its financial angel, Mary William-son Averell Harriman (1851–1932), the widow of railroad magnate E. H. Har-riman. Like other eugenicists, Jordan believed ardently in genealogy's usefulness to building the American future.[114] "The study of genealogy has received a new impulse from its bearing on Eugenics and the maintenance of racial strength," he pronounced.[115]

Kimball and Jordan sought to expand genealogy beyond its usual narrow focus on individual families and uses of historical methods, to include entire epochs and populations. Contemplating the previous millennium, when Al-fred the Great and the emperor Charlemagne had walked the earth, Jordan and Kimball sought "to deduce the fact that both of these famous worthies

are in the lineage of the great body of Englishmen and of Americans of English descent." The authors cited as evidence some unpublished genealogies
compiled by Kimball's late brother-in-law in Minneapolis. The manuscripts
"[treated] especially the Puritans and the half-mythical periods before the
Ninth Century."[116]

Jordan proclaimed his relatedness to the twelfth-century figures Isabel de
Vermandois and Henry I, King of France, through his mother, as he affirmed
the importance of heredity to explaining both the present and the future. In-
voking his expertise as a much-published scientist, Jordan considered each
"individual man" to be "the keeper and carrier of inheritable possibilities. . . .
Each man and woman so far as we know transmits to posterity not their actu-
ally developed traits but rather their inborn tendencies, the raw material, in
the development of which character may be forged." He allowed for the importance of upbringing ("euthenics") and other environmental factors, as did
other fervent eugenicists, including Galton himself. But Jordan proclaimed,
"Nurture can go no further than Nature permits. . . . Ancestry never gathers
grapes from thorns nor figs from thistles."[117]

Government Uses of Genealogy: Restricting Immigration

Genealogy practitioners and hereditary organizations also anxiously manned
the outer gates of the United States because the goals of compulsory sterilization and immigration restriction as well as apprehensions about Anglo-Saxon
"race suicide" found interconnection in the minds of men in powerful posts.[118]
After centuries of unpoliced borders, and the rapid eclipse of the Know Nothings by the late 1850s, Americans in the late nineteenth century renewed race-
based outcries against excessive numbers of foreigners.[119] In the 1870s, San
Francisco was simultaneously a seedbed of hereditary organizations, with the
Sons of Revolutionary Sires' greeting the centennial in 1876, and of mass
demonstrations for Chinese exclusion. Mining booms in the American West
had reverberated around the world. Chinese immigration to the United
States had begun on a small scale with the California Gold Rush (1848), as
had Italian immigration. Congressmen of both parties found it easy to agree
on excluding Chinese laborers, knowing that most Chinese immigrants of
the time occupied that category. The Chinese Exclusion Act of 1882 was the
first-ever federal ban on a particular ethnic group.[120]

After this legislation, unprecedented immigration ensued from other parts
of the world, in response to perpetual labor shortages in American industry.
Although "older" nationalities such as Germans and Britons continued to

arrive as they had done since colonial times, other Europeans came from places and espoused religions that seemed outlandish in Protestant-majority America. In the 1880s and afterward, masses of Poles, Italians, Greeks, Jews from eastern Europe and Russia, and other Slavic and Mediterranean nationalities joined the accustomed western European flows. Social differences that are now perceived as ethnic or religious were then portrayed as racial ones. Thomas Nast and other Republican cartoonists drew Irish Catholics as apes, implying that they were less evolved life forms.[121]

Especially in northern cities and places of industry, hereditary and genealogy organizations raised alarms at the demographic transformations of their surroundings. The bulk of the DAR's membership in the early twentieth century lived in the Northeast and the upper Midwest, places where plentiful manufacturing and construction jobs, and affordable land, attracted hordes of newcomers. The ability to assemble lengthy lineages of white colonial or revolutionary ancestry, built on birth and marriage records, enabled sorting those of native birth who descended from families that had long resided in the United States, from supposedly less American "huddled masses" and recent arrivals.[122] A Providence, Rhode Island, woman made a revealing slip of the tongue when praising the DAR's "lineage books" in 1894: "in years to come, when the country is flooded with an alien race, these careful records which we transmit to posterity will be the Doomsday Book of the United States, and show beyond dispute the purity of our nationality and the right of our sons to influence the destiny of a country which owes its existence to the patriotism of their remote ancestors." She most likely intended a comparison between the DAR's lineage books and the eleventh-century land records of England's Domesday Book; both compendia registered and announced the ownership of wealth. But "alien races" of her own time seemed to bring doomsday with them.[123]

New York City drew both praise and condemnation for being a magnet for immigration. Numerous hereditary organizations originated there, including the Sons of the Revolution (1883), the earliest mass hereditary organization in the East; the SR's offshoot, the larger Sons of the American Revolution (1889); the Society of the Colonial Dames of America (1890); the Daughters of the Revolution (1891); the first of many state-level Societies of Colonial Wars (1892); and the country's first Society of Mayflower Descendants (1894).[124] At a banquet commemorating the New York Genealogical and Biographical Society's twenty-fifth anniversary, in 1894, Edward F. De Lancey thundered that the officially non-hereditary NYGBS existed "for the purpose . . . of forming a true and firm foundation on which those who are to come after us can establish the fact that they are the descendants of the original settlers and founders of civilized life upon this continent, not of the hordes of foreigners." To applause, he contended that those descended from "original settlers and founders" are "primarily entitled to rule this country." Never mind that the NYGBS, numbering nearly five hundred, had several illustrious foreign-born members, including Andrew Carnegie, who never shed his Scottish brogue, and the Irish-born William R. Grace.[125]

Americans with genealogy inclinations feared, among other things, immigrants' Anglicization of their original names, and the supposed falsehoods that would result. No amount of documentation could offset the effects of such fluidity of identity. The DAR distributed its *Guide to the United States for the Immigrant* extensively and without charge on board ships, and in processing and detention facilities. The *Guide's* author, John Foster Carr, enjoined the reader not to change their name except when "absolutely necessary to simplify it for English pronunciation. . . . Be proud of your race, your birth and your family." The DAR bankrolled this manual's translation into eight languages by 1924, including Yiddish.[126] Name-changing practices among newer, less white immigrants and their posterity threatened genealogy's own regimens of documentation, as well as the documentation requirements on which American racial regimes depended, as grandfather laws and tribal rolls illustrated.

Resisting and suppressing immigration was not limited to hereditary organizations and white families with prestigious-sounding surnames. Immigration restriction, which depended on some part on genealogical data, also became a top priority of the state. The First World War and the Russian Revolution's aftermath made possible the racially motivated immigration restrictions of 1921 and 1924, after repeated presidential vetoes in the 1910s. These "national origins" quota systems sought to shrink immigration by reducing immigration from eastern and southern Europe in particular, and by banning Japanese altogether along with other Asian arrivals. In the first quota system, created in 1921, the quota for each European nationality was based on the number of its immigrants inside the United States, as the 1910 U.S. census documented. The 1924 system (the Johnson-Reed Act) specified the earlier census of 1890. Pegging quotas to the 1890 census curtailed further immigration from southern and eastern Europe—which lawmakers viewed as racially undesirable—because considerably smaller Mediterranean, Slavic, and Jewish populations resided in the United States in 1890, than in 1910. Consequently, populations from northwestern Europe and the British Isles received disproportionately large quotas.

The 1924 legislation also based each European nationality's quota on the numbers of residents of the United States of that origin, as the 1920 census recorded.[127] This incorporation of native-born Americans in the 1924 national-origins quotas required knowledge of their family histories. The U.S. Census Bureau hired Howard F. Barker, an expert on naming practices (onomastics), to investigate the Anglicization of immigrants' surnames in order to determine the size of the "national origins" quota for each European nationality. As Barker and the historian Marcus Hansen undertook it, this research entailed statistical analyses of surnames' appearances in censuses, rather than the endless task of tracing innumerable families and surnames across the land.[128] Distinctions between worthy and unworthy populations inhered in the Englishness, and familiarity to Anglo-Americans, of their surnames. Commissioned by the U.S. government and funded at public expense, Barker and Hansen's work and the legislation behind it reinforced American social hierarchies for more than forty years by suppressing the foreign-born presence in the United States. Ardent civil rights reformers led the repeal of the quota system in the 1960s because they detected the white Anglo-American racism and anti-Semitism behind it. The Hart-Celler Act (Immigration Reform Act) of 1965 favored family-based immigration and other criteria that had nothing, on their face, to do with race or ethnicity.[129]

Protective Coloration in Chicago

To circle back to the 1920s, immigrant Frederick Albert Virkus parlayed the intense nativist prejudices and expanding genealogy practices of the era into the largest genealogy business as yet in U.S. history, in a quest for his own camouflaging in white Anglo-America. His successes signify the intensity of Anglo-American racism among educated, affluent people at the time. Born in Germany in 1879 to Albert and Albertina Virkus, he immigrated with his family to Chicago at the age of two.[130] His education ended when he was just thirteen, when he was compelled to go to work as an "office boy."[131] His longtime employer, Albert Nelson Marquis, later became a voice for immigration restriction. Marquis was the Ohio-born founder of the *Who's Who* publication enterprises.[132] Along the way, in 1902, Virkus married a woman with an English name, Nellie Moore. By 1911, the family moved to suburban La Grange while he continued to work in the city. The Virkuses gave their three children English-sounding names: George Frederick, Lorene Elizabeth, and Robert Moore.[133]

In fostering considerable anti-German prejudice in Chicago and other American cities with large or visible German populations, the First World

War compelled Virkus to accelerate his assimilation.[134] After 1911, none of his published profiles mentioned his German birth.[135] He changed his own middle name from "Albert"—redolent to Americans of Queen Victoria's German-born, German-speaking consort, Prince Albert—to the presidential, Anglo-Saxon-sounding "Adams." By 1925, Frederick Adams Virkus left *Who's Who* to go into business for himself under his new name, as founder of the country's first-ever genealogy clearinghouse.[136] His Institute of American Genealogy (IAG) was virtually a one-man operation, but he reported soliciting more than fifteen hundred members. From an office in downtown Chicago, he published numerous reference works, lists of resources including hereditary organizations, and a periodical, *Magazine of American Genealogy*, all under his own imprint. The IAG's groundbreaking scale compelled one woman to condemn it as a "genealogy trust." She complained to Virkus in 1929 that the IAG's objective was "to control all the research work, and by so doing you will take the bread and butter out of the mouths of those of us working professionally."[137]

Virkus reached out to the major genealogy figures of the day to join the IAG so that he could list them on letterhead. He extended a hand across racial boundaries to W. E. B. Du Bois, and he disregarded some widespread religious prejudices when he solicited the prominent Mormon genealogist Susa Young Gates.[138] His contact with Du Bois contrasts with his stringent interpretations of the era's racial beliefs, which sorted European from European. His publications fetishized "The First Families of America" to the point of grouping non-English colonists, including Germans, under the heading of "Racial History," implying those races' differentness from the English.[139] He deflected attention from his own origins, not publishing on them at all, and he eschewed applying for admission to hereditary organizations even though he cultivated members and leaders of those groups otherwise. Presumably, he wished to play down his own immigrant background when among newer friends and associates. Despite or perhaps because of his own shape shifting, Virkus publicly subscribed to a powerfully hereditarian and evolutionist perspective in 1929. Genealogy benefited the descendant because "he becomes conscious of his place in the march of civilization, in the progressive evolution of mankind, and begins to realize that he is the sum total of all that for ages has gone before."[140]

As the Depression began to bite, Virkus moved on to other interests, although a *Chicago Tribune* reporter found the IAG office still operating in 1952.[141] He pursued a life of conservative activism in suburbia. Opposed to the New Deal's unprecedented level of government regulation, he lost his run for Congress as a Republican in the Democratic landslide year of 1936. Subsequently, in the 1940s, he represented his hometown of La Grange in the Illinois state legislature. The needs of small businesses, like his own IAG, were his pre-eminent concern.[142] Like other immigrants from northwestern Europe and from English-speaking parts of Canada, Virkus succeeded in concealing his foreign roots and plebeian past.[143] His activity signifies the widespread social pressures he felt to refuse ownership of his provenance and of the moniker that his parents Albert and Albertina Virkus, in search of a namesake, had originally bestowed on Frederick Albert. In the hands of the insistently rootless Frederick Adams, genealogy functioned as a vector for heredity-based prejudices.

Early Protests against Racial Forms of Genealogy

The early twentieth century's combinations of racism and hereditarian uses of genealogy occurred in cultural practices, such as Virkus's business operations, as well as in lawmaking. But from within white populations, some in the 1920s and 1930s began to challenge race-based genealogy. Following the First World War, professionalism developed in order to reform genealogy. Like historians at the time, genealogy professionals sought truths to be found in original, unpublished source material, generated close in time to the events in question. Both genealogy and history professionals also cultivated a posture of detachment from their own and others' passions, in quest of fair-mindedness.[144] Genealogy professionals protested Jim Crow's and eugenicists' selective uses of genealogy findings. The plainspoken Great War veteran and Yale graduate Donald Lines Jacobus (1887–1970), for example, encouraged other professionals to pursue research that a client would consider embarrassing, referring to the "wormy apple in a client's family tree."[145] As an eighteen-year-old in 1905, a few years before graduating from Yale College and posing for this yearbook photo, Jacobus published the first of his many genealogy articles. He became one of the earliest career genealogists.

One might not expect staid professionals to articulate the earliest white challenges to genealogy's racialization, but their commitment to candidness led them there. Here, professionals resembled the metaphorical "gray, meticulous, and patiently documentary" being who discerned the grubby reality beneath the vainglorious narrative. This was the "genealogical" method of analysis in philosophy that drew praise from Friedrich Nietzsche and, later, Michel Foucault.[146] Scrutinizing white families in eighteenth-century Connecticut in 1928, Jacobus unearthed an axe murder between siblings, with no

Donald Jacobus
yearbook photo, 1908,
Yale College.
Manuscripts and
Archives, Yale College
Archives.

legal consequences for the killer. A woman who "was with child by another man when she married" was later divorced by her husband after her subsequent infidelities came to light, at a time when wives otherwise outnumbered husbands among divorce plaintiffs.[147] Jacobus also described general "insanity." These tales of axe murders, straying wives, and mental illness came from the same colonial-era, white Anglo-American families that 1920s eugenicists considered "good."[148] Like most genealogist authors, Jacobus published much of his work privately, with limited numbers of copies, and in small-circulation journals. But he published "Haphazard Eugenics," containing the tale of the axe murder, in a widely circulating national periodical, the *North American Review*.

Did Jacobus's challenges to eugenics rob genealogy of its usefulness to white supremacy, or diminish white supremacy's dependence on genealogy? No, not at the time. His article had little immediate impact. Immigration restrictionists and eugenicists had much more powerful microphones than Jacobus's in the 1920s. They continued to blame American racial degeneration on the excessive reproduction of racial Others rather than on the behavior of people of supposedly superior races, except for criticizing their falling birth rates. Not until 1942 would the Supreme Court deem the compulsory sterilization of prisoners unconstitutional, in running afoul of the Eighth Amendment's ban on cruel and unusual punishment. People of color, and people with disabilities and mental illness, continued to experience forced sterilization long after 1945, especially while incarcerated.[149]

But genealogy professionals' work in the interwar decades, and their work's intellectual backdrop, announced the beginning of an end. Intellectuals such as the anthropologist Franz Boas were challenging the premises of scientific racism, which had depended on group characterizations of families and on inherited statuses.[150] New scientific inquiries included behaviorism, a school of psychology that assigned new importance to outward, environmental factors that shaped the individual. In psychology and psychoanalysis in general, the individual seemed ever in flux and in tension with surrounding family, particularly with parents and other immediate family members.[151] All these schools of thought implicitly dismissed ancestry as an effective explanation for successes and failures.

Genealogy's usefulness to the American state also began to recede. Eugenics institutions experienced the 1930s as a time of decline. The national-origins quota system for European immigrants, and the compulsory sterilization laws passed in more than thirty states by 1932, meant victory. The resulting decline in urgency sapped the movement of numbers and energy. The extreme, homicidal form of eugenics that became a governmental priority in Nazi Germany after 1933 also discredited American eugenics institutions even though Nazi leaders drew inspiration from state laws in the United States.[152]

In Nazi Germany, even more than in the United States, eugenics and genealogy activities walked arm in arm and proved highly useful to a government intent on separating races. Katharina Hering has documented that historians and genealogists in Nazi Germany, and earlier in Weimar Germany, reached out to forge race-based understanding with German American genealogists and historians in Pennsylvania. The Americans remained aloof.[153] Elsewhere, Nazis reconfigured longstanding German genealogy practices as a form of predation, setting apart Jews and persons of partial Jewish descent on the basis of degrees of Jewish ancestry, then dispossessing them, segregating them into ghettoes, and orchestrating racial pogroms such as Kristallnacht (the Night of Falling Glass) in 1938.[154] The next year, Nazis devised the mass killing of babies and young children (including among ethnic Germans) whom they believed to have disabilities, on the grounds that they were unfit to live and would likely pass on their conditions to future generations.[155] Nazi extremes in preying on Jews and people with disabilities, dealt a body blow to the Eugenics Record Office's reputation in the United States. After its chief financial supporter died in 1932, the ERO became increasingly dependent on outside grants. It shut its doors in 1939 after the Carnegie Institution ceased its funding.[156]

Even before the Nazis began developing their genocidal "final solution" in 1941—death camps, work camps, and massacres intended to wipe Jews from existence—the United States perceived threats from expansionist regimes in which convictions of inborn racial superiority grounded plans for world domination. After the Pearl Harbor attacks, the U.S. declaration of war on Japan compelled fascist Italy and Germany to declare war on the United States. Like never before, Americans during the Second World War confronted an enemy that sorted Europeans into superior and inferior races. Consequently, racism and anti-Semitism at home that elevated Anglo-Saxons met new challenges.[157] But erosion did not bring silencing. Racial, white supremacist forms of genealogy endured throughout the war years, and throughout the time of postwar civil rights reforms that otherwise overturned Jim Crow laws.

Conclusion

The late nineteenth century's racialization of genealogy had unified whites of otherwise varying classes, genders, regions, and religions, on the basis of race. Genealogy's usefulness to the creation of white supremacist racial hierarchies, and its deployment by governments large and small, compelled resistance from targeted groups who in turn increased their commitments to genealogy. Among those groups were African Americans, Native Americans, and two widely despised religious minorities. At different times, white Americans excluded Jews and Mormons from desirable forms of whiteness and considered each group to be racially distinct.[158] Outsiders' prejudices aside, both faiths shared many features with American genealogy at large. Both Jews and Mormons treasured descent from biblical figures, with some rejecting any distinction between spiritual and blood descent. Members of each religion voiced commitments to tracing patrilineal ancestry. The "patriarchal blessing" administered in Mormon temples is called "patriarchal" because a patriarch administers it, and also because the blessing locates the recipient in a line of paternal descent from a chosen biblical patriarch.

Yet unlike in any other major religion in the United States, including Judaism, Mormon "ordinances" (rituals enacted in temples) have long depended on genealogy activity per se. Mormons equipped one baptismal font in 2003, for example, with a "visual display unit linked to computer facilities" elsewhere, to enable worshipers to reconfirm the genealogical information on the dead person they were baptizing by proxy.[159] Such distinctiveness, and eventual leadership in fostering faith-based genealogy practices, and resulting invigoration of secular-minded practices, justifies the following chapter on Mormon genealogists.

CHAPTER TWO

Yours, for the Dead

Mormonism's Linking of Genealogy with Worship

Like no other community of genealogists in U.S. history, to date, Mormon church officials and laypeople have infused genealogical research with piety, and piety with genealogical research. Both priests and laypeople integrated family history directly into worship when they began requiring genealogy information for proxy baptism and other temple ordinances in which living people evangelized the dead. This commitment to the dead originated with the church's first generation in the 1840s. Fifty years later, with church president Wilford Woodruff's declarations in the 1890s, evangelization of the dead became explicitly genealogical, and based on blood, biological, and marital relatedness. Throughout these historical transitions, Mormons' sense of urgency, in which they compared the unapproached dead to spirits in prison, resulted in a refusal to sort worthy dead from unworthy dead. In contrast to non-Mormons' deployments of genealogy to serve social advantages pertaining to wealth, leisure time, advanced education, and connectedness to other genealogists, Mormons took a populist approach to the dead from the religion's earliest years. However, Mormon practices featured sorting tendencies—pertaining to gender and race—that shared ground with genealogy practices among other Americans. Although Mormon practices did not express more stratification than others, they were not free of stratifying behaviors pertaining to white Anglo-American supremacy and male supremacy.[1]

Egalitarian Approaches to the Dead in Early Mormon History

Mormonism began in 1820 in an upstate New York barn when a young farm boy, Joseph Smith (1807–44), reported the first of many unbidden visits from an angel. Messages quickly spread. In its early decades, the religion attracted many relatively poor and uneducated immigrants from Britain and Scandinavia.[2] Attributes of their religion scandalized contemporaries, who forced Mormons' expulsion from every U.S. community in which they settled, or that they founded, notably the river town of Nauvoo, Illinois. After state militiamen and local vigilantes assassinated Joseph Smith and his brother in 1844, and after arsonists torched the towering Nauvoo Temple, the faithful fled to the Great Salt Lake Valley in the Mexican desert, starting in the summer of 1847.[3] There, they expected, and hoped, that America would leave them alone. But after the United States conquered much of northern Mexico, Mormons found themselves on the American side of the border the very next year, 1848.[4] For the rest of the century, with much public support, including from millions of evangelical Christians, the U.S. government persecuted Mormons over religious practices that many believed threatened American civilization, including polygamy (plural wives). The Supreme Court supported the government's actions when it ruled, in 1879, that the First Amendment's guarantee of the free exercise of religion extended only to belief, not to practices, thus rejecting Mormonism's claims to religious freedom. Congress then declared polygamy a felony, in 1882.[5]

Mormonism incurred popular and governmental hostility in the nineteenth century for several other practices besides plural marriage that sharply contrasted with most Protestant and Catholic teachings. These Mormon practices included a nearly universal male priesthood in which nearly every man and teenage boy held some kind of rank and the direct revelations from God, or angels, that church presidents and other leaders frequently reported. These contacts were lengthy enough, in Joseph Smith's time, to result in the "translation" of the entire Book of Mormon from inscrutable hieroglyphics into English.[6] Living people's proxy baptisms of dead people, based on founding principles of Mormon theology, also startled non-Mormon contemporaries.[7]

Mormons were not the only nineteenth-century Americans to infuse the reconstruction of knowledge about bygone ancestors with religious purpose. In a century when Americans predicted a heaven full of departed family members and portrayed death as a moment of reunion, Christians in many walks of life articulated their interest in genealogy in biblical terms and tropes.[8] Genealogy practice itself seemed Scriptural, notwithstanding early Christians' denunciations of "endless genealogies" for distracting from God's teachings (1 Timothy 1:4). Josiah C. Pumpelly was an ardent member of the New York Genealogical and Biographical Society, with a specialization in Huguenots. He was also an instigator of early hereditary organizations, notably the Sons of the American Revolution. In 1893, when speaking to the NYGBS, he reached for the story of the prophet Ezekiel and the valley of dry bones that belonged to people long dead, that God restored to life (Ezekiel 37:1–14). "It was apparently a most unpropitious field, yet it proved to be one which it was well to cultivate," said Pumpelly. "These dry bones were found to be capable of living. There came a voice, and a shaking, and the bones came together every bone to its fellow bone; flesh and skin came upon them; breath entered into them, and they lived and stood up. That is what we are attempting. Each of us has a regard for the bones of his own family stock, and we shall soon find bone matching bone. . . . All history is but a connecting together in their proper place of the achievements of individuals."⁹ When reconstructing great men and great deeds, genealogists emulated the actions of God in the Ezekiel story. Pumpelly spoke at a time when the priorities of historians and genealogists still overlapped, regarding biographical approaches to prominent men.

Even in the midst of such representations of dry bones that had come alive, Mormon outreach to the dead stood out because living people incorporated that outreach into formal temple ceremonies. They lauded each other, predicting each other's progress through the heavens, for attempting salvation of the dead. Mormons documented and virtually baptized their dead family members and the occasional friend without regard to the dead people's own religious beliefs, moral conduct, or social status during their lifetimes. Regardless of whether the dead person agreed to baptism, while dead—an outcome that the church considered impossible to ascertain— the living person found reward in their outreach. Proxy baptisms showed a person's intent to garner more souls for the church, even when the souls belonged to already-dead people. Therefore, proxy baptism helped assure the living person's own future progress after death through multiple layers of heaven, culminating in the shining possibility of becoming a "god in embryo." Worshipers called this state "perfection" or "exaltation."¹⁰ Other criteria for salvation and exaltation included the living person's own baptism into the faith, and the living person's own marriage. Unlike the infant baptisms that many other Christians favored, the full-immersion Mormon baptisms generally occurred around age eight, or in adulthood for adults who converted.¹¹

Engagement with the dead began with Mormonism's founder. Amid a flurry of visits from the Angel Moroni in 1823, as Joseph Smith reported them, Smith heard the angel paraphrase the Bible to the effect that the prophet Elijah would "plant in the hearts of the children the promises made to the fathers, and the hearts of the children shall turn to their fathers. If it were not so, the whole earth would be utterly wasted at his coming."¹² In subsequent reports of revelations, Smith linked baptism for the dead to family relatedness even more explicitly, following an 1836 vision of his late brother Alvin in heaven. Alvin had died without being baptized into Mormonism. When Joseph wondered how Alvin's salvation had been possible, Joseph heard these words from God: "All who have died without a knowledge of the Gospel, who would have received it if they had been permitted to tarry, shall be heirs of the celestial kingdom of God; also all that shall die henceforth without a knowledge of it, who would have received it with all their hearts, shall be heirs of that kingdom.'"[13] In allowing salvation of a person who had been unable or unwilling to convert while they were alive, including those who had simply lived and died too early in time to know the church (like Alvin), Smith's declarations inaugurated the church's inclusive approaches to evangelizing the dead.

Subsequent developments in the 1840s of the major temple "ordinances" (rituals), which laypeople, including women, carried out, included the proxy baptism of dead people. Explicating the biblical verse from the Prophet Elijah again, in 1842, Smith stated, "For we without [the dead] cannot be made perfect; neither can they without us be made perfect" in that highest reach of heaven.[14] Smith's words both galvanized and described the actions of believers. Between 1841 and 1845, at least 15,722 "baptisms for the dead had been recorded" in the Mississippi River and then at the Nauvoo Temple, within a Mormon population estimated at between 26,000 and 35,000 in 1844.[15] Living people focused these virtual baptisms most often, but not exclusively, on departed family members. Joseph Smith himself limited baptism for the dead to relatives, in 1840.[16] The baptism of nonrelatives seems rare, but a few believers stood in for friends, as Lucia Allen did in 1843 for the late Sabrina Barlow, in Nauvoo. Recordkeepers listed Barlow as Allen's "friend."[17]

Contemporaries described the riverine baptisms in Nauvoo, before the Nauvoo Temple's completion. One woman wrote to her husband that in the previous week, in October 1840, "there were sometimes from eight to ten elders in the river baptizing. . . . Thus you see there is a chance for all. Is not this a glorious doctrine? Surely the Gentiles will mock, but we will rejoice to have the gospel preached to the spirits in prison and give them the privilege of coming forth in the first resurrection."[18] A visitor from New Hampshire, in 1843, voiced bemusement at the posthumous baptism of George Washington in the Mississippi. But she also noted the focus on dead family members. "Two elders stood knee-deep in the icy cold water," Charlotte Haven told her family, "and immersed one after another as fast as they could come down the bank. We soon observed that some of them went in and were plunged several times. We were told that they were baptized for the dead who had not had an opportunity of adopting the doctrines of the Latter-day Saints. So these poor mortals . . . were releasing their ancestors and relatives from purgatory!"[19] The ensuing grand Temple of Nauvoo included a massive indoor font for baptisms, the first of many in Mormonism's history. The sixteen-foot-long font was ready for use by late 1841, four years before the rest of the temple's completion in 1845.[20]

Generally opposed to discrimination among the dead, Mormons likened the dead to "spirits in prison," incarcerated in the afterlife until living people presented them with the Mormon gospel, by means of virtual baptism. Echoing the case of Alvin Smith, missionaries to the dead approached those who had died too early to convert to Mormonism, including a great-aunt of Joseph Smith's first wife, Emma Hale Smith. On that same occasion, in 1841, Emma stood in for both her parents, her sister Phoebe, and an aunt and uncle.[21] The evangelization of the dead extended also to those who had opposed family members' conversion to Mormonism. The historian Carol Cornwall Madsen describes female converts of the 1840s "whose family ties had been severed at their conversion," permanently. The women "found solace in the knowledge that they would 'stand as a savior in the midst of [their] father and mother's house,'" referring to parents and other family members who had rejected them.[22]

During these same decades of the 1840s, 1850s, and onward, traveling Mormon missionaries partook of non-Mormon genealogy cultures in New England, New York, Philadelphia, and elsewhere, while adapting those practices to their own. In 1853, Orson Pratt was living far from his wife and children in Utah, while on a mission to Washington, D.C. That year, he answered a newspaper advertisement placed by one Reverend Frederick W. Chapman "requesting information concerning the descendants of William Pratt of Massachusetts." From corresponding with Chapman, Orson Pratt obtained proof of his relatedness to the bygone William Pratt. Orson Pratt's sojourn in the East inspired him to publish a book-length family genealogy. Two decades after his Washington mission, in 1873, he claimed to have traced his family back eleven generations. Pratt adapted his genealogy activity to Mormonism when he performed an additional service for his forebears. He reported "that the families of the Pratt brothers had been baptized for about three thousand of their ancestors."[23]

The Theological Importance of Genealogy after 1894

Pratt was not the only Mormon missionary who partook of eastern genealogy activity and linked it to his own religion's obligations to the dead. Another missionary far from Utah, Benjamin Cummings, made an extended visit to the NEHGS library in Boston in 1877–78.[24] Future church president Wilford Woodruff (1807–98) also busied himself in the 1870s with the matter of proxy baptism, including of nonrelatives.[25] He experienced a powerful vision in 1877 in which dead family members, including his two-year-old daughter who had perished at home while he was overseas, were now "redeemed" and residing in heaven. That vision inspired Woodruff to arrange baptisms on behalf of one hundred literary figures and political heroes who had died too early, or too far away, for Mormon missionaries to essay their conversion during their lifetimes. The retinue included Napoleon, Edward Gibbon, Robert Burns, Goethe, Lord Byron, Lord Nelson, and John Wesley as well as every signer of the Declaration of Independence.[26]

But as church president, repeatedly citing revelations from angels or God, Woodruff later turned against such practices. He explicitly linked relatedness to preexisting family ties and ended commitments to chosen relatedness among Mormons. Woodruff and the church's turnabout against spiritual adoptions in favor of transgenerational sealings, operated as part of the broader backdrop in which he famously repudiated polygamy for the church. Reporting repeated revelations on the subject in his 1890 Manifesto, Woodruff rejected plural marriage in the face of intense pressure from the federal government, after it threatened the expropriation of Mormon temples.[27] The Woodruff presidency's institutionalization of Mormon genealogy in 1894, with the administration's creation of the Genealogical Society of Utah (GSU), further signified this renunciation of polygamy. The historian Thomas G. Alexander has argued that the church intended its new commitments to genealogy as a surrogate for plural marriage.[28] Both polygamy and genealogy conferred theological benefits in potentially advancing ever more souls toward heaven and its highest layers. Polygamy achieved this through expanding married reproduction, with some men fathering many dozens of children. After their births within wedlock—their future progress through the heavens, itself, depended on birth into earthly life—ever more children would grow up in the Mormon faith. Genealogy, when undertaken for the purpose of baptizing the dead and other temple ordinances, garnered additional souls for the church retroactively, assuming that the dead heeded the earthly efforts to convert them to Mormonism.[29] Note the explicit linking of genealogical knowledge and recordkeeping to temple ordinances, in the most sacred of spaces.

The church leadership's discouragement of polygamy and new commitment to genealogy entailed the end of spiritual adoptions common among nineteenth-century Mormons. Adults had long been declaring relatedness to higher-order priests and officials so as to "secure the salvation of their families in a worthy priesthood lineage if their own progenitors did not accept the gospel in the next life," while dead, write the historians James B. Allen, Jessie Embry, and Kahlile Mehr.[30] President Woodruff in 1894 allowed the estimated thirteen thousand preexisting adoptions to stand.[31] But he forbade any more spiritual adoptions when he declared: "let every man be adopted to his father. When a man receives the endowment, adopt him to his father; not to Wilford Woodruff, not to any other man outside the lineage of his father. This is the will of God to this people." Scholars define the endowment as a temple-administered "series of symbolic representations, special instructions, and sacred covenants that would give [worthy Church members] greater insight into their eternal origins and destinies as well as their earthly responsibilities."[32]

Woodruff intended that intergenerational sealings substitute for the spiritual adoptions. "We want the Latter-day Saints from this time to trace their genealogies as far as they can, and to be sealed to their fathers and mothers. Have children sealed to their parents, and run this chain through as far as you can get it," Woodruff enjoined.[33] Sealings are formal declarations, taking the form of temple ceremonies, that family relationships will endure through all layers of eternity.[34] Sealings now operated vertically, between generations of kin, not just between spouses or between parents and children. This premium on unending family togetherness, which included ancestors and descendants separated by centuries, required the prohibition of yet another older practice—virtual baptisms of nonrelatives. Worshipers were now no longer supposed to pursue the baptism of unrelated friends, strangers, and famous people who were dead, as Charlotte Haven had witnessed of George Washington in 1843, and as Woodruff himself had done with Napoleon and Lord Byron in the 1870s. This 1894 prohibition against the proxy baptism of nonrelatives remained in place for the next seventy years, until the 1960s.[35]

The Genealogical Society of Utah:
The Institutionalization of Mormon Genealogy

The narrow membership and insider status of the Genealogical Society of Utah (GSU) in its early years, with its umbilical relationship to the church, belies genealogy's later theological importance in Mormon history. Early GSU meetings were small enough to convene in the offices of the church historian.[36] For the next twenty years, after 1894, genealogy remained a vestigial concern for the masses of laypeople and lower-order priests. After five years of existence, the GSU counted 173 yearly and life members; the latter number remained unchanged in 1908.[37] Before the creation of its dynamic Woman's

Committee that same year of 1908, with its "lessons in genealogy" for congregants, the GSU's membership remained concentrated among men who were high up in the church and sometimes also church employees and staff.[38]

With its small beginnings, the GSU fit the overall pattern of nineteenth-century genealogical societies, including among non-Mormons. The GSU's early history fits another widespread pattern in the history of genealogy, in which genealogists built on precedent and cited the labor of others. The GSU's first president, church historian Franklin S. Richards, had sold his own personal library to the GSU, worth over five hundred dollars at the time. It would become the core of the GSU's institutional library. He continued to purchase items for the library even after he sold it. The holdings stressed the work of genealogy societies in distant eastern cities. The library included full runs of the New York Genealogical and Biographical Society's *Record* (1869), and the New England Historic and Genealogical Society's *Register*, published in Boston.[39] The earliest enduring genealogy periodical in the United States, then specializing in the documentation of white New Englanders' descent from early colonists and Revolutionaries, the *New England Historical and Genealogical Register* had begun publication in 1847. Mormons, generally, gazed at such groundbreaking genealogy publications, libraries, and societies as manifestations of God's plan. "[Thousands] of men are laboring assiduously to prepare the way, though unconsciously, for the salvation of the dead. In this the Saints recognize the hand of the Lord," concluded the church's newspaper in 1885.[40]

For the rest of the nineteenth century, relations between non-Mormon genealogists, and Mormons' connecting of genealogy to their missions to the dead, resembled a one-way mirror. Other American genealogists operated mostly in ignorance of Mormons' interest in genealogy work, within the context of deeply felt intolerance of the religion.[41] But Mormon genealogists repeatedly traveled east to see things for themselves, sometimes in pursuit of knowledge about their own forebears. Franklin S. Richards himself had visited ancestral ground in western Massachusetts in 1890.[42] GSU leaders' 1909 trip to the Library of Congress in Washington, the Newberry Library in Chicago, and additional "genealogical libraries" in Boston, New York, and Philadelphia, culminated in the GSU's launching of its *Utah Genealogical and Historical Magazine* in 1910. The travelers were current GSU secretary, librarian, and treasurer Joseph Fielding Smith Jr. (grandnephew of Joseph Smith, son of a church president of the same name, and an eventual church president himself), and former GSU secretary Joseph Christenson. The men cited the *New England Historical and Genealogical Register* directly, as inspiration for their own magazine.[43]

Gender and Race in Mormon Genealogists' Practice

Notwithstanding their widely inclusive approaches to the dead, Mormon genealogists nonetheless invested in earthly power relations that sorted living people. A stark example has to do with the gendered displacement of a prominent woman's authority, stemming from genealogy's increasing importance to the church. Before 1918, the GSU stayed small, with 108 life members and 65 annual members in 1907.[44] But in the 1900s and 1910s, among masses on the ward and stake level, there was a decided expansion of genealogy instruction and practice. The GSU after 1906, and its Woman's Committee after 1908, and elements within the Daughters of Utah Pioneers (1901), the principal Mormon hereditary organization, undertook these teachings.[45] Genealogy lessons from women, for audiences that were mostly women, belonged to a longstanding pattern in which Mormon women had performed temple ordinances for other women and tutored other women in piety generally, starting in the Nauvoo Temple.[46]

The instigator of genealogy instruction among women was Susa Young Gates (1856–1933), a club leader and women's suffragist with unusual connections to women's movements nationwide, and to non-Mormons. She helped found the Daughters of Utah Pioneers and launched one of the first magazines for girls in the United States. In addition to raising thirteen children with two husbands, Gates was a daughter of church president Brigham Young. She invested heavily in that relationship long after her famous father died in 1877.[47] While doing summertime coursework at Harvard, Gates journeyed twice to the NEHGS's library in Boston to research her father's New England lineages. These visits of 1890 and 1892 occurred years before the NEHGS admitted women to membership, in 1898.[48] She later published her research on the Young family.[49] Her peregrinations in Boston strengthened her own commitments to genealogy and helped energize her to begin teaching co-religionists, like the inspiration the later travelers from the GSU in 1909 experienced from traveling east.

Working in Salt Lake City from the GSU's library, and teaching classes there starting in 1907, Gates began formulating her *Lessons in Genealogy* and published them as a book by 1912. It was the earliest how-to book on genealogy published in the United States. The Woman's Committee of the GSU "has felt the need of printed instructions regarding the practice of genealogy," Gates explained, introducing the project. "There is practically no such book in existence; so that when the members of this Society come to the Library and wish to take up the study and practice of genealogy, there has been no way opened

Susa Young Gates,
1900. Church History
Library, Church of
Jesus Christ of
Latter-day Saints.

for them to do so, except to blunder into it as all others have done."[50] The manual's forty-five pages included basics such as "Approximating Dates," "Methods
of Recording," and "What the Country Genealogist Can Do." The sections titled "Heirship in Temple Work," "Instructions Concerning Temple Work," and
"Making Out Temple Sheets" signify that her intended audience was Mormon.
After the first edition of *Lessons* sold out, she published a second edition only a
year later.[51] Twenty years later, the professional genealogist Donald Jacobus
called *Lessons* "the best practical course in the methods of research" for novices
that he had seen. While professionals like Jacobus aimed at reforming existing
practices, including those of veteran genealogists, her instructions truly addressed beginners.[52] Gates and other clubwomen traveled throughout Utah,
holding workshops. She also ran the weekly genealogy advice and queries column in *The Deseret News*, the church's newspaper, starting in 1907.

But the ensuing masculinization of genealogy instruction, and the increasing importance of genealogy practice to Mormon worship, walked hand in hand. Joseph Fielding Smith, future church president, reported a revelation in 1918 in which he saw Jesus Christ himself ministering to the dead. This vision vested temple work for the dead with new theological importance.[53] Church authorities swiftly replaced Gates with a male colleague, Nephi Anderson, at the helm of the newspaper column. She condoned the change, as she had already been developing "lessons" in genealogy for the priesthood since at least 1915.[54] Mormon priests, past and present, inhabit a different status from pastors, priests, or ministers in other Christian faiths. Throughout Mormon history, virtually any right-thinking, right-acting male as young as twelve could become some kind of priest. An elaborate hierarchy that sorted priest from priest, extended to the topmost layers of the church. But this otherwise remarkably "universal" priesthood was closed to women and girls in Gates's time, and it remained closed a century later.[55]

In the 1920s and afterward, priesthood training for older boys and young men began to include genealogy lessons, with men as the teachers. Ultimately, a new generation of men who possessed the advanced degrees and convictions of genealogy and history professionals, and were also priesthood holders, displaced the aging Gates from the Church Historian's Office and from the work of genealogy instruction, even while they carried on her commitment to teaching novices. Only sixteen when she married her first husband, Gates had begun college but not completed it. Her successor in the Church Historian's Office, Archibald F. Bennett (1896–1965), was exactly forty years her junior and had earned a master's degree in history from the University of Utah.[56] In the late 1920s, he came close to boarding an eastbound train in pursuit of a PhD in history. Instead, he decided to stay in Utah, and to expand genealogy instruction among Mormons for the church.[57]

Gates did her best to smile through her displacement. Other scholars have pointed to her deepening conservatism on gender issues, such as women voters and birth control, as she reached her seventies in 1926.[58] When GSU president Anthon Lund complimented the toils of the Woman's Committee, she recalled demurring: "Jealousies arose and it should be the Priesthood who not only direct the affairs, control the activities, but also to them should be given the credit and praise. . . . For you remember the birds get up in the springtime and sing about the coming of the spring. They do not bring the beautiful opening of the spring." Lund responded, "Yes . . . but I notice that a great many people would over-sleep themselves if it wasn't for the birds singing in the morning."[59]

Notwithstanding such denials, her subsequent endeavors suggest that her departure had hurt, and that she perceived the end of her career as a blow to women. In the belief that "there is little or no reference to women" in existing church histories, she returned to writing a history of Mormon women with her daughter, Leah Dunford Widtsoe.[60] Additional actions illustrated her commitment to fostering women's history and genealogy simultaneously. By the time she collected historian Carl Becker's 1932 affirmation of history as people outside the academy undertook it, "Everyman His Own Historian," she had already embarked on instructing a group of people whom others considered to live outside history, in writing on their lives and times.[61]

The church enjoined men and women alike to engage in extensive remembrance in writing, especially regarding family history.[62] But in her Women's Biography class, Gates encouraged the framing of women and their daily labors as meaningful historical subjects. Held in Salt Lake City in the spring of 1932, the class attracted eighty-seven students, all of them married. Gates taught these mothers, grandmothers, and wives how to place themselves and their experiences, including "faith-promoting incidents," at the center of their narratives.[63] Her encouragement incurred skepticism from an otherwise well-disposed English professor from the church's university. He worried that her students' daily journals "will contain too much of the common place; unimportant details will clog the stream of interest."[64] She was planning to repeat the class in 1933 when she died suddenly, at age seventy-six. The Women's Biography Class expired with her. No women were among her replacements until Elizabeth L. Nichols began genealogy instruction work for the church in the 1960s.[65]

This case study of gender hierarchy as it played out in Mormon genealogy practices, shares much in common with other instances in which early twentieth-century professionalization entailed masculinization, in people and priorities. Historians illustrated this, in repudiating older informalities that allowed some degree of prominence to some women.[66] But Susa Young Gates's story has distinctively Mormon characteristics. Even though she, a daughter of a church president, was as close to the church leadership as any woman could be, her high status and her employment in the Church Historian's Office could not prevent the church hierarchy's rejection of her status as a leader in the teaching of genealogy methods. The more the church leadership cared about spreading engagement in genealogy throughout the wards (local congregations of between seventy and one hundred families) and stakes (gatherings of wards), the more the church designated genealogy instruction as men's work.

Distinctively Mormon patterns of race and genealogy reckoning are less obvious because they shared even more with contemporaneous practices in the rest of the United States, than patterns of gender and genealogy did. White Christians' incorporation of nineteenth-century notions of race, including Anglo-Saxonism, into their readings of holy texts, fired their enthusiasm for genealogy. Nineteenth-and early-twentieth-century Mormons illustrated this broader pattern. Both groups, American Protestants overall, and Mormons, imported an amalgam of Anglo-Saxon racial reckoning, British Israelism, and sometimes American Israelitism into their biblical interpretations. Both Mormons, and American Protestants generally, understood the Hebrew Bible's heavily genealogical accounts literally, when they posited their own descent from the various twelve tribes of Israel. In these American representations, these biblical forebears originated in ancient England and elsewhere in northwestern Europe. Dark-skinned people, especially those of sub-Saharan African descent and appearance, seemed to have inherited God's curse on Cain and on Cain's posterity. The sociologist Armand Mauss and others found residues of these racial readings of Christianity among white Mormons in recent times.[67] Mauss also found that leading figures in the GSU, including Archibald Bennett, who was Susa Young Gates's successor at the Church Historian's Office, and Joseph Fielding Smith Jr. deeply invested in racial, literal readings of holy texts while in their GSU capacities. Gates herself bundled lessons on race with lessons on genealogy, in her *Surname and Racial History* (1918). Her table of contents included these chapter titles:

- Seth and Shem
- Disobedient Races Descended from Shem
- Ham, his Descendants and Tribes
- Japheth, his Descendants and Tribes
- Racial Beginnings in Europe
- Where the Races and Tribes Settled in Europe
- English History, 55 B.C. to 1066 A.D.[68]

The white-pioneer trope in Mormon culture, most evident in Pioneer Day pageantry, also amounted to celebrating white reproduction. Bennett remained fully aware of Gates's earlier innovations in teaching genealogy and history, and he went on to expand them considerably among Mormons. When she died, he reached for the metaphor of the white, westbound pioneer when he eulogized her as an "intellectual" version of Daniel Boone, "with restless urge and intrepid courage blazing trails out into the trackless and unexplored wilderness of thought, that others might follow and build securely along the paths she marked out for them."[69] Mormons channeled particular energy into honoring histories surrounding the white pioneer, enacting grand reenactments every July 24. Pioneer Day marked the anniversary of when the first migrants, in flight from persecution, arrived in the Great Salt Valley.[70] Just weeks after the first newcomers came, on July 24, 1847, the small community by the lake greeted its first baby. Named for church president Brigham Young, Young Elizabeth Steele (later Stapley) was born on August 9.[71]

Later in the nineteenth century, Mormons celebrated both hereditary organizations and white reproduction, as when they developed their own hereditary organization in response to religion-based exclusions from other such groups. From the 1850s until Woodruff's presidency in the 1890s, church leaders had repeatedly enjoined the faithful to engage in plural marriage, reporting multiple revelations from God or angels on the subject. Plural wives had been the order of the day. Susa Young Gates was one of fifty-four children that church president Brigham Young had fathered, with nineteen different wives. His marriages to eight additional women were childless.[72] Coming of age as federal law redefined polygamy as a felony, Gates never lived in a plural marriage, but she did criticize the hostility to polygamous descent that operated against all Mormons.[73] She helped develop the Daughters of Utah Pioneers in 1901 because contemporary hereditary organizations, notably the DAR, turned down applicants with polygamous forebears, even when those same applicants could document revolutionary descent.[74] From Gates's perspective, the DAR's ban denied to Mormon women a set of privileges to which their racial status, and their families' generations of residence in the West, should have entitled them.

For most of her own long life in isolated desert towns in Utah, Stapley (died 1938), who had begun as the white baby of 1847, found honor as a living monument. That status does not mean that she personally believed in white supremacy; Paiute neighbors repeatedly sought her out for her midwifery skills. But during those same decades of the late nineteenth and early twentieth centuries, organizers of parades and local newspapers feted Stapley for being a "first."[75] The festivities surrounding her were, in some ways, distinctively Mormon. The white pioneer symbol bore a particular poignancy for a group of people whom other Americans had forced into exile, and for descendants of that group. But these same features of Mormon history—the veneration of white babies, other white "firsts," and of white-pioneer descent—articulate praise for racial propagation generally. Such praise was also a familiar sound in non-Mormon cultures around the United States that explicitly linked genealogy to racism.

Conclusion

From the church's earliest decades onward, Mormon priests and worshippers refused to judge and sort the dead according to contemporary standards of success and morality. Instead, worshippers viewed all dead as incarcerated, until rituals that living people undertook among themselves, freed the dead and allowed them to proceed through the multiple layers of heaven. These inclusive discourses about the dead show a world of differences between Mormon approaches to genealogy, and other Americans' filtering of their family trees at the time. Inclusive Mormon approaches to the dead were so different from those of non-Mormon contemporaries, that they foreshadowed future revolutions in genealogy practices among non-Mormons, namely, their embrace of warts-and-all approaches to their ancestry starting in the 1970s. By then, no ancestor seemed too poor or too foreign or too shameful to embrace as one's own.

But in the meantime, the Mormon engagement with the dead belonged to broader American histories of genealogy and male supremacy, and of genealogy and white supremacy. The church's genealogy instruction work, as church staff like Bennett undertook it, contained a bundle of commitments to male supremacy, and operated against an American backdrop in which non-Mormon genealogists, too, trafficked in the names and statuses of men. From the 1910s onward, persisting into later eras, the church anxiously sought to expand male audiences for genealogy among the faithful, starting when the church designated genealogy research and instruction as a priesthood responsibility. Reaching more men signified genealogy's escalating importance to Mormon worship. Even though other white Americans represented nineteenth-century Mormons as not white, or less than white, and subjected them to racial hostility, Mormon genealogists' practices, hereditary organizations, and interpretations of holy books nonetheless praised Anglo-American whiteness.

While white supremacist dimensions and male-supremacist dimensions of Mormon genealogy practices were not, in themselves, all that different from those of non-Mormon contemporaries who were white, these practices' coexistence with inclusive approaches to the dead set Mormon practices apart. This blend of exclusiveness and inclusiveness, and concern over the dead's incarceration in the meantime, compelled the church in the twentieth century to foster interest in genealogy among ever-broader audiences in the United States. Salt Lake City Temple official Harry Russell instigated the collection effort that became the Temple Index Bureau. This ocean of index cards listed dead people's genealogical information and the temple ordinances that living people had undertaken on their behalf. The bureau's purpose was to avoid duplication of labor at temples, where officials (like Russell himself) wished to avoid having congregants perform the same ordinance multiple times on the same dead person. Russell, who had converted to Mormonism in adulthood, regularly signed his letters "Yours, for the Dead."[76] In the meantime, in many other parts of the United States, genealogists pursued inclusive approaches to their ancestors, for purposes other than dead people's spiritual welfare. Genealogists' results often buttressed white supremacy, but genealogical research also articulated protests in favor of civil rights, racial fairness, and an end to discrimination and abuse.

CHAPTER THREE

Hereditary Greatness

Early Genealogical Efforts among Native Americans,
African Americans, and American Jews

Like many other periodicals of its time, the National Association for the Advancement of Colored People's *The Crisis: A Record of the Darker Races* (launched in 1910) invited readers to send in baby pictures for a "virtual" spectacle. Such displays were a tradition at American fairs. The displays subjected babies, small children, young women, and sometimes whole families to similar assessments of size, growth, and conformity to beauty and health conventions, as were used to judge livestock.[1] But in *The Crisis* editor W. E. B. Du Bois's hands, the long-distance baby contest, conducted through the mail between 1914 and 1918, also refuted a number of principles of white supremacy in keeping with *The Crisis*'s status as a premier organ for civil rights, with an otherwise progressive-minded, multiracial readership. Rather than choosing a few contest winners, Du Bois reprinted a total of eighty-nine photographs in the October 1914 children's issue, that he had culled from more than five hundred submissions. Displaying a crowd seemed more powerful than showing a few who stood above it. He identified the children only by their state of residence. In subsequent contests, he adorned the pages of photographs with short biblical verses or lines of poetry, continuing to withhold the children's names.

The photographs showed round-cheeked cherubs and schoolchildren who were painstakingly dressed in white or light-colored clothing, carefully groomed, and generally Black or mixed-race. The older children's toys, bicycles, and schoolbooks positioned them far from child labor, which was still widespread in factories, mines, and agriculture in the 1910s.[2] These seemingly innocuous representations, that nonwhite babies, toddlers, and children could be clean, prosperous-looking, and well cared for, contested a bundle of racial stereotypes. Published during the same decades in which white-baby monuments were erected across the country, *The Crisis*'s photographic exhibits of young children affirmed African American reproductive health at a time when Black physicians felt compelled to address the social-Darwinist assertion that African Americans' high rates of fatal illnesses and infant mortality demonstrated their inferiority to whites and forecasted a vanishing race. "The

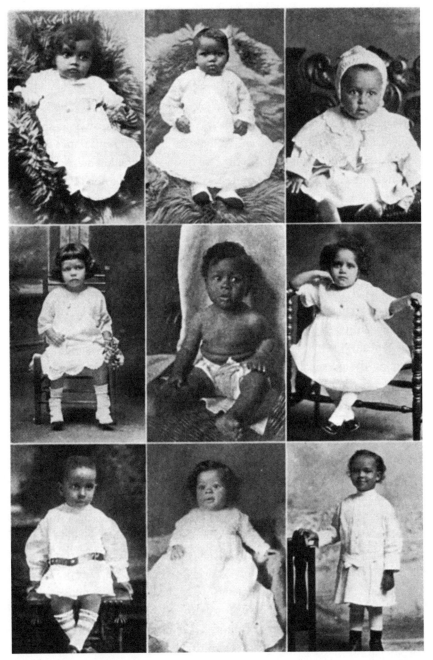

Readers' baby and toddler pictures from "Shadows of Light," *The Crisis: A Record of the Darker Races* 12 (October 1916): 294.

Negro, like other races is susceptible to what the environment dictates, and is amenable to the pernicious and insidious ravages of diseases in a similar proportion and in a most exact ratio, just as other races of men," protested Dr. Monroe A. Majors from Chicago in 1906.[3] When Du Bois himself disparaged the "fiction of the physical degeneracy of Negroes" in 1914, he recognized the presumptions of white supremacy that lay behind whites' exclamations about African Americans' premature deaths.[4] Wordlessly, the procession of impeccably dressed, round-cheeked children also affirmed the endurance of Black and brown people's family ties in the face of wars of attrition on such bonds.[5] Loving hands had bathed the youngsters, laundered and ironed their clothes, arranged their hair, and photographed them in a pleasing light. Loving attitudes had garnered the children's cooperation. Babies and toddlers sat peaceably before the camera.

Native Americans, African Americans, and American Jews were three different, disfranchised groups whom Anglo-American Protestant whites considered to be racially distinct from themselves. But members of these three groups, working separately, undertook substantial genealogy activity in the early to mid-twentieth century, long before the 1960s' civil rights reforms. This genealogy activity bore substantial political freight while simultaneously affirming the personal. To argue that nonwhite people and non-Christians were worthwhile subjects of biography, autobiography, and family history amounted to a stand against Jim Crow because such assertions drew choruses of denial. In 1914, U.S. senator James K. Vardaman of Mississippi argued that "the negro" had never built monuments "to . . . perpetuate in the memory of posterity the virtues of his ancestors" and therefore had never "created for himself any civilization."[6] Precisely because genealogy practices lent themselves to political uses by private entities such as hereditary groups, and by governments intent on racial subjugation, genealogy practices also amounted to potent arguments for racial equality, fairness, and progress.

As compared to the violence that U.S. state and federal governments inflicted on African Americans and Native Americans, and European states' subjugation and segregation of Jewish populations, anti-Semitism in the United States took more nebulous forms. Such prejudices against American Jews were most noticeable in workplaces, on college applications with explicitly genealogical requirements intended to detect Jewish ancestry (that particular surnames supposedly indicated), and in real-estate transactions.[7] While numerous scholars have affirmed the rewards that American Jewry gained by claiming whiteness and gradually rising to middle-class status, those same Jews nonetheless confronted Christians' racist, explicitly hereditarian efforts to curtail Jewish immigration and to exclude successful Jews from universities, resorts, and other perquisites of American bourgeois life.[8]

My histories of Jewish, Native American, and African American genealogists contain some ironies. Some affirmed the belief that their or others' lineages demonstrated hereditary greatness, a principle that white Christian genealogists also held at the time, who cited eugenics pioneer Francis Galton's 1869 book directly: *Hereditary Genius*. Genealogy practices also exposed class and education hierarchies that distinguished elites—the Black "talented tenth," acculturated Native Americans in the East, and successful Jews whose forebears had lived in America for many generations—from less privileged masses among their respective peoples.[9] Still, early twentieth-century white Anglo-American supremacy was so intense as to drive people together, transcending distinctions of class, color, region, denomination, language, ethnicity, and (among Indigenous people) tribe, band, and clan that would otherwise have thrust them apart. While working within their own groups and separately from each other, Native Americans, African Americans, and American Jews shared legacies of genocide: European invasions of the Americas followed by numerous epidemics and wars, mass trafficking of enslaved Africans across the Atlantic and within the United States, and the Holocaust in Europe. Attempted eradications of populations, channeled through memories that descendants' communities carefully maintained, added poignancy to the genealogist's work of listing, naming, and recounting reproduction.

Indigenous People's Family Reckonings

The people in the following examples represented particularly advantaged layers within Native American populations. These examples also reconfirm genealogy's political dimensions pertaining to colonization. The genealogists in question operated in protest of the continuing dispossession of Indigenous people and of white supremacist attempts to monopolize history and popular memory of the American past. In 1878, Zerviah Gould Mitchell (1807–98) of North Abington, Massachusetts, published information on her own maternal lines that she had obtained informally, largely by firsthand or secondhand word of mouth, from foremothers. Through her mother, she claimed descent from the seventeenth-century sachem Massasoit and from his second son, Metacomet (King Philip), of King Philip's War infamy in the 1670s as well as from Metacomet's sister-in-law, Weetamoo (their descendants intermarried). Weetamoo was the bejeweled "severe and proud dame" that the Puritan captive Mary Rowlandson beheld in 1676.[10] Two centuries later, comporting herself quite like a "severe and proud dame," the seventy-one-year-old Mitchell waged a decades-long dispute with the state of Massachusetts over its agent's theft of $1,500 worth of lumber from her land. The land had been in her family since the seventeenth century, when Massachusetts Bay Colony had awarded it to another of her forebears, Benjamin Tuspaquin, for fighting against Metacomet's forces and alongside the English in King Philip's War.[11] Mitchell and her collaborator publicized her descent from Massasoit, Metacomet/King Philip, Weetamoo, and Tuspaquin in a gesture of protest, in the guise of the book *Indian History, Biography, and Genealogy* (1878).

Mitchell engaged a white, published historian—retired general Ebenezer Weaver Peirce (1822–1902)—to be both amanuensis and microphone. The fifty-four-year-old Peirce framed his "Indian history" of King Philip's War around Mitchell's topics, while she obtained commitments from 494 subscribers—including officials at the New England Historic Genealogical Society, the abolitionist Wendell Phillips, and the poet Henry Wadsworth Longfellow—to purchase the book.[12] A mother of eleven children, with only six of them still alive in 1878, the widowed Mitchell studded her lineage with other facts that she considered important. Those included her own and some of her adult daughters' educations and the Indian names borne by three of them. Mitchell also proudly included illustrations of two of her daughters posing in knee-length Indian dress.[13]

Mitchell's work looked forward as well as backwards in time. Her unmarried, self-supporting daughters, with their advanced educations, personified the era's independent "New Woman." Mitchell had herself benefited from academy-level schooling, and she had taught private school in Boston. But she simultaneously followed Indigenous traditions of matrilineal reckoning. She credited her maternal grandmother Lydia Tuspaquin Wamsley, a talented horsewoman and herbal healer with a "retentive memory," according to Mitchell, for the information on their shared descent from Massasoit. But I suspect that Mitchell obtained the information from her own mother, Phebe Wamsley Gould, unless Lydia had written things down. Mitchell was only five years old when Lydia drowned in 1812. She had been gathering herbs on a steep shore when she fell into a deep lake.[14]

For all their praising of contemporary women's agency, Mitchell and Peirce's 1878 collaboration on *Indian History, Biography, and Genealogy* also illustrated many of the era's other social barriers. The well-connected Mitchell and her forebears came from an advantaged layer of Indigenous life in New England. Mitchell and Pierce published their work privately, in her

Massachusetts hometown, with the help of hundreds of subscribers. Even with Mitchell having to wage her own protracted struggle against dispossession, she and Peirce lived far removed from ongoing conflagrations farther west. Following mining booms in the sacred lands of Dakota Territory's Black Hills, the U.S. government abrogated recent treaties and waged wars of dispossession against Indigenous populations in the Great Plains and western mountains to force them onto reservations. Such extremes as government bounties for the mass slaughter of bison, with which the state intended to starve out Native resisters, drew outcries from white reformers in eastern cities, like those who had signed on as Mitchell's subscribers. Mass assimilation and Christianization for Native populations in the West resembled a humane alternative, at the time.[15]

Mitchell and Pierce's publication also illustrates gender and class stratification. Mitchell's name does not appear on the book's title page or spine. I suspect that she stepped behind Peirce because his past publications in local history, his educational attainments, and his status as a white man—and as a one-armed veteran—would enhance the book's authority and draw attention to her protests and litigation.[16] But in nearly any population, people with published or otherwise widely recognized royal ancestry embody a small elite. Even non-Indians noticed Mitchell's bloodlines. Her storied maternal progenitors caught the attention of the leading American aficionado of royal ancestry, Charles Henry Browning of Philadelphia, presumably when *Indian History, Biography, and Genealogy* fell into his hands. Five years after her and Peirce's book appeared, Mitchell's name and her descent from Massasoit found inclusion in the first edition of Browning's *Americans of Royal Descent* (1883).[17]

Like Mitchell, some Native dissenters in later times voiced Victorian-era genealogy's underlying premise of hereditarian greatness, thus displaying the power of that paradigm. In 1930, two women in Chicago, the opera performer and entrepreneur Tsianina Blackstone (Cherokee-Creek and formerly Tsianina Redfeather), and Anna Fitzgerald (Chippewa), an attorney's wife, gave the name "First Daughters of America" to their pioneering group. This was the first-ever women's club for American Indians. Formed at a time of escalating pan-Indian consciousness, the group's priority was to educate others in Native American history and about ongoing protests.[18] The "First Daughters" moniker constituted a powerful retort to the Daughters of the American Revolution and like-minded hereditary groups, in that the First Daughters boasted family ties to earlier generations in America than any Colonial Dame could claim. Though not requiring genealogical documentation for membership, the First Daughters limited admission to "women of Indian Blood or Indian and white blood"—implicitly drawing a line against Indians who also possessed African ancestry, as ongoing land allotments and tribal governments had already done or would later do.[19] Indigenous exclusions of Black and multiracial populations with Black ancestry persisted into the next century.

Slavery's Challenges for Genealogists

The following sections of this chapter will address African American history, starting in the time of nineteenth-century slavery. Freedom suits and bids for manumission, as historians have explored them, have revealed some enslaved people's ability to reckon their ancestry over multiple generations. In areas that the long-distance domestic slave trade affected less, such as in South Carolina's specialized rice economy, such knowledge of family history was occasionally possible. A photograph that the historian Tera Hunter has published shows five generations of an enslaved family in coastal Beaufort.[20] As a rule, though, the race-based chattel slavery that reigned in Early America and the United States operated to divorce enslaved people from their own personal information and knowledge of forebears as well as from living relatives. An estimated one in three enslaved families experienced being torn apart by the nineteenth-century domestic slave trade, but enslaved people experienced the absence of kin and family information even when no one forced them to move over long distances.[21] New state laws that criminalized slaves' education, in the 1820s and 1830s, were another feature of enslavement that suppressed recordkeeping. As a result, an estimated ninety to 95 percent of slaves remained illiterate in the 1860s.[22] Most also experienced a distinct lack of control over their working hours, especially when laboring by moonlight in the booming cotton-and sugarcane-producing areas of the Deep South.[23] Antebellum U.S. censuses listed the numbers of slaves per household, sorted by gender and age, while withholding their names.[24] Such omissions did not make future genealogists' and descendants' tasks any easier.

But the feature of slavery that most robbed slaves' descendants of genealogical knowledge departed from deep-seated English, British, and American patrilineal traditions. Starting with a 1660 Virginia statute, in the earliest surviving English colony in North America, and continuing until slavery was outlawed in 1865, slaves inherited their slave status from their mothers—a sharp exception in a society in which most people inherited surnames and property from fathers. Any child born to an enslaved woman shared her enslaved status; therefore, any birth added to her owner's assets. As a result of these laws requiring the matrilineal descent of slavery, and other laws designating slavery as a lifelong and hereditary status, owners reaped financial rewards from en-slaved women's reproduction.[25] Combined with colonial and nineteenth-cen-tury laws that banned interracial marriage, the matrilineal descent of slave status also enabled white fathers to forego any responsibility for children they sired with enslaved women, contrary to what a free woman's premarital child-bearing would legally require of her baby's father.[26]

Exploitation of enslaved women worsened after Congress outlawed Amer-icans' participation in the overseas slave trade in 1808. The enslaved popula-tion increased fourfold between the American Revolution and the Civil War, mostly through natural increase in which births exceeded deaths. As a result, stories of sexual predation are common in histories of enslavement. "What tangled skeins are the genealogies of slavery!" reflected the former slave Har-riet Jacobs in 1861, in her memoir *Incidents in the Life of a Slave Girl*. Here, Ja-cobs was recalling her daughter Louisa's christening in North Carolina thirty years earlier. Jacobs chose for her baby's middle name "the surname of my father, who had himself no legal right to it; for my grandfather on the paternal side was a white gentleman."[27] Sexual exploitation's rewards for slavers cre-ated painful contrasts to the married rectitude that Victorian genealogists and historians, including Jacobs, prized in forebears and among themselves.

Documenting marriages and births was difficult enough for those white researchers whose ancestors had been unchurched, not especially prominent, geographically mobile, or in common-law (private) marriages, in which cou-ples cohabited, declared themselves married, and appeared married in the eyes of friends and neighbors. But common-law marriages went without church solemnification. As early as the 1730s, Parliament sought to outlaw them by requiring the public posting of impending marriages and formal li-censing. Common-law marriages' informality might otherwise enable big-amy. But such marriages persisted well into the nineteenth century among whites, especially in frontier areas and the South.[28] Common-law marriages have often eluded genealogists' efforts to document them as they do not ap-pear in church records, and throughout Early American history, religious au-thorities were the only ones to systematically record births or dates of baptism, marriages, and deaths. The city of Philadelphia was the earliest sec-ular entity to begin keeping vital records, in 1807.[29]

Marriages between enslaved people appeared inconsistently in records, depending on whether an individual slaveowner or overseer decided to log such marriages. Throughout the history of American slavery, enslaved people married each other. Masters' and mistresses' behaviors ranged from allowing slaves to choose their spouses and marry for love, and bankrolling wedding festivities, to choosing spouses for enslaved people and forcing their pairings. Especially after 1800, slaveowners' efforts to convert slaves to Christianity entailed their encouragement of marriage generally. However, enslaved people's marriages lacked any legal or licensed status that would prevent the forced separation of married couples that was characteristic of slave trading. Because enslaved people resembled chattel in the law, the law had about as much regard for their marriages as it did for marriages between farming tools. Enslaved people's marriages endured at slaveowners' pleasure.[30]

For enslaved people's kin and descendants, the documentation requirements of American genealogy research were exceedingly difficult to meet. That research demanded literacy on the part of forebear and descendant as well as substantial control over one's time. Frederick Douglass pointed at these realities when he stated flatly in 1855 that "genealogical trees do not flourish among slaves."[31] His pronouncement applies even to exceptional cases. James Madison Hemings (1805–77), an Ohio carpenter, could perform the unusual feat among former slaves of tracing his ancestry back three generations. Sixty-eight years old in 1873, Madison Hemings told a friendly white newspaperman that his old master, Thomas Jefferson, had fathered him and his siblings during his decades as a widower. Madison—along with his mother, Sally Hemings, and his siblings—had been mixed-race house slaves who worked in close proximity to Jefferson. Following his death in 1826, his will quietly emancipated Sally and those of her children who had remained at Monticello—his plantation in Charlottesville, Virginia—or otherwise allowed them to leave. But after Sally died nine years later in Charlottesville, her children, including Madison and his younger brother Eston, departed for neighboring Ohio.[32] The brothers had been free for decades when slavery finally became unconstitutional in 1865.

House slaves like the Hemingses, and other enslaved people who lived in close contact with whites, endured a great likelihood of experiencing sexual pressures from them. Every generation (save Madison's own) of his maternal lineage showed relationships between enslaved women and white men that produced children. His great-grandparents included an unnamed "fullblooded African" woman and an English sea captain. Their daughter, Madison's grandmother Elizabeth Hemings, became the "concubine" (said Madison) of her master, John Wales, and the mother of Sally.[33] Three of Sally's biological grandparents had been white. She lived before the invention of photography, but white strangers exclaimed at the pulchritude of Sally and other Hemings women at a time when the word "fair," meaning light-complected, was synonymous with beauty.[34]

The Hemingses' case was unusual because some of their white kin in the Wales family publicly acknowledged their relatedness to Hemingses. Sally was the widely recognized half-sister of Jefferson's wife, Martha Wales Jefferson (1748–82); Martha and Sally had had the same biological father. But the Hemings family's exceptionality also proves many rules about slavery. One rule required silence on the subject of white paternity. Strangers and friends in Ohio remarked on Eston's reddish hair, talent for the violin, and other resemblances to Jefferson. "[Five] white residents of Chilicothe" recognized Eston's features in a statue of Jefferson that they saw while on a visit to Washington.[35] But Madison never revealed the sources of his information. Very likely, he had obtained it from conversations with his mother or other maternal relatives because he made assertions about Jefferson's fatherhood that most whites, including the otherwise loquacious Jefferson, considered unspeakable.[36] Other aspects of the Hemingses' family history illustrate slavery's tendency to rend families. At least two of Madison's siblings, Beverly and Harriet, went on to live as white after escaping Monticello permanently. Madison corresponded with them after moving to Ohio, but he never saw them again.[37] American slavery and racial divides wrought havoc on the family togetherness on which later genealogy researchers depended.

African Americans' Genealogy Practices after 1865

Many recently enslaved people strove mightily to find their relatives after slavery was outlawed in 1865. A yearning for reunion caused many a Southern road to fill with freedpeople.[38] In later times, African Americans and mixed-race people recognized that many whites bundled racial hostility with organized genealogy. But many did not internalize their exclusion from public genealogy activity. Former slaves, free Blacks, and their descendants displayed some interest in being able to name, and track, their forebears, including when surviving textual evidence would not enable them to document their findings.[39] Researchers turned to shared morphological (phenotypical) resemblances, orally transmitted lore, and other non-textual forms of evidence to build their knowledge.

This use of non-written evidence is not unique to African Americans. White genealogists did the same, using lore to bridge gaps or vacuums in written records and then, in turn, reconfirming the information in other records. While the nineteenth-century historian Leopold von Ranke, who did much to frame historians' professional practices, famously insisted that original, written documents were all, genealogists could hardly afford to eschew evidence obtained from lore. Researching narrower topics (family lines and/ or surnames) over longer periods of time than historians usually favored, required the use of broader arrays of source material.[40] Trustees of the Newberry Library in Chicago in 1904, for example, deliberately undercounted the annual number of books and pamphlets that Genealogy Department patrons requested for retrieval because they "often use a great number of volumes for a single reference. In such cases but 10 percent of them is recorded." The number of items that genealogy patrons requested during that single year exceeded 54,600.[41] Because genealogists needed to rely on more varieties of source material, including informal and non-written forms, NEHGS founding figures from the 1840s such as Lemuel Shattuck, and authors of instruction manuals all condoned the limited use of oral evidence ("tradition") obtained from interviewing family members and neighbors ever since. Typically, authors stipulated that genealogists reconfirm the veracity of the information they obtained from "tradition" in other, textual sources.[42]

Despite these overlaps in practice with white genealogists, such as the limited use of non-textual evidence, most African Americans' alienation from the means of producing identity documents during slavery, and the difficulties in documentation that descendants faced, resulted from specifically racial forms of subjugation. Jim Crow stalked Black researchers even in the library. Public libraries in the South either excluded Blacks altogether or relegated them to inferior, segregated facilities.[43] Twentieth-century published indexes of surnames and places gathered from genealogy periodicals, family genealogies, and other genealogy publications often omitted African American and other nonwhite families' surnames. Genealogists depended on these indexes for streamlining their research.[44]

Consequently, in the absence or dearth of documentation, some African Americans studied overlaps in outward appearance as an indicator of relatedness. The mixed-race writer and educator Caroline Bond Day (1889–1948), born in Alabama, was a graduate student in anthropology at Harvard in the 1920s when she contacted numerous families, many already known to her, for her thesis titled "Negro-white families in the United States," which she published in 1932.[45] Focused on physical anthropology—her advisor, Earnest A. Hooton, helped develop the field in the United States—Day showed a keen interest in her subjects' and their ancestors' external racial appearances. She included her own and her husband's families in the study.[46]

Day situated her scholarship within the ongoing scholarly challenges to scientific racism in the 1920s and 1930s, that such anthropologists as Melville Herskovits and Franz Boas were mounting. "You have doubtless seen the article in 'Opportunity' concerning the work of Prof. Herskovitz [*sic*]," Day wrote to a Chicago woman in 1927. "Well, this is more or less the same kind of work, except that I believe I have secured a more highly selected group of people than the average white worker would get in touch with."[47] She intended to vindicate the successes of dark-skinned African Americans to demonstrate that even "Negroes . . . of unmixed blood" succeeded in their careers, sent their children to college, ushered their children into professional careers, and enjoyed seaside vacations and second homes.[48] Instances of upward social mobility among dark-skinned people with African features constituted an especially powerful refutation of white supremacy, from her perspective.

While other social scientists of the era draped their human research subjects and their locations in pseudonyms, such as in Robert and Helen Lynd's *Middletown* (1929), Day made no attempt to conceal the identities of her research subjects.[49] When she politely asked to see family photographs and collect other data that included real names, likenesses, and incomes; evaluations of skin color and racial quanta (fractions indicating percentages of white or nonwhite blood); and measurements of facial features, some of her subjects balked against their public display. A longtime friend, sixty-nine-year-old Mama Penney from Mississippi, was not amused by Day's questionnaires about ancestry, color, facial features, and attainments. "[Oh], Carrie dear, raking out those horrid ancestral skeletons is so painful I tried to bury them a long time ago," Penney objected. She added that for her mother, whose own father was reputedly white, "the past was a closed book."[50] Day aspired to research five hundred families, but, in the end, only 346 families appeared in her book.[51] However, those who embraced the political dimensions of Day's project, including W. E. B. Du Bois, consented without hesitation to having their names and family photographs published.[52] Such people knew full well that displays of their faces and lineages, combined with evidence of successes, affirmed contemporary struggles against white supremacy. "What a pleasure it is to know that our people are accomplishing great things!" exclaimed an educator from Georgia. "They have it in their blood from centuries back-so why shouldn't they?"[53] Like many educated people of his era, Ernest C. Tate of the Sparta Agricultural and Industrial Institute took the principle of inheritance of success through the "blood"—hereditary greatness—for granted.

Even with such resourcefulness as Day's, accounts of African American genealogists' practices otherwise stressed the scarcity of information. In 1928, John Wheeler of Atlanta determinedly held on to cherished mementoes, as he gently resisted Day's information-gathering for her project. His wife Margaret complained about misplaced family photographs, amid her own plans to aid the study. But she later recovered a snapshot from one of John's pockets. He had had it "a long time. Says he hasn't anything of his childrens to carry around," she told Day.[54] Still other African Americans turned to imagination, to fill the emptiness left by the voids in their knowledge of forebears. Poetry enabled Langston Hughes (1902–67) and others to reach out to pasts that history had otherwise denied them. Hughes's grasp extended across oceans, and he rejected distinctions between earthly and spiritual ancestors in "The Negro Speaks of Rivers." He composed the poem at age eighteen and published it in *The Crisis* the next year, 1921. He dedicated the poem to ardent historian and genealogist Du Bois.[55] "I've known rivers," remarked Hughes's character.

> I've known rivers ancient as the world and older than the flow of human
>   blood in human veins.
>
> My soul has grown deep like the rivers,
>
> I bathed in the Euphrates when dawns were young.
> I built my hut near the Congo and it lulled me to sleep.
> I looked upon the Nile and raised the pyramids above it.
> I heard the singing of the Mississippi when Abe Lincoln went down to
>   New Orleans, and I've seen its muddy bosom turn all golden in the
>   sunset.
>
> I've known rivers:
> Ancient, dusky rivers.
>
> My soul has grown deep like the rivers.

Hughes biographer Arnold Rampersad has analyzed this poem as an expression of father-loss and parricide. "The Negro Speaks of Rivers" also reaches for forebears, in explicitly linking ancient pasts with the present. Hughes's theme of inheritance through multiple generations made this poem a favorite of African American genealogists' later meetings and family reunions.[56]

Genealogy Practices among Descendants of Free Blacks

There are some exceptions to the rule of particular difficulties of African American genealogy, stemming from enslavement and later racial discrimination, but even these exceptions reinforce that rule. In contrast to slaves' posterity, people who descended from free Blacks had some success in proving colonial and revolutionary descent using textual evidence. The novelist and journalist Pauline Hopkins (1859–1930), a lifelong New Englander, was born in Maine to a Virginia freedman and his wife. Among Hopkins's maternal forebears were some prominent Black abolitionists in Boston, including Susan Paul. Hopkins, who had presumably obtained this knowledge from her mother, wore these lineages proudly. Naming contemporary hereditary organizations, she proclaimed herself a Black "daughter of the Revolution" at Boston's Faneuil Hall, upon the 1905 centennial of William Lloyd Garrison's birth.[57] Hopkins was apparently unable to document her more remote ancestors in her own lifetime, but her recent biographer, Lois Elizabeth Brown, has reconstructed Hopkins's descent from Nero Caesar Paul. This enslaved man from New Hampshire won his freedom in the 1760s after fighting in the French and Indian War.[58]

Another New Englander, namely W. E. B. Du Bois, could also document his descent from free Blacks. During the same years that he published *The Souls of Black Folk* (1903), performed extensive social-science research on the lives of contemporary Blacks, and spearheaded civil rights meetings, Du Bois publicized his own and others' revolutionary descent. Following his rejection from the Sons of the American Revolution in 1908, he encouraged the Boston reformer Floride Ruffin Ridley's cofounding of the first major hereditary organization for African Americans, the Society of Descendants of New England Negroes (1930). Du Bois served as the group's honorary president and promoted the group in *The Crisis*.[59] Both Hopkins, the "daughter of the Revolution," and Du Bois shared some of the hereditary organizations' attitudes toward proud ancestry. It meant a great deal to document descent from past greatness and also to refute white attempts to monopolize the pleasure of basking in ancestors' reflected glory. Du Bois, Hopkins, and like-minded people also sought to educate their audiences on the multiracial nature of colonial life and American struggles for independence. They operated in distinct contrast to the bleached histories—in which all the actors were white—that white hereditary groups and most published historians presented at the time.

But Hopkins, Du Bois, and others who could document their free Black ancestry back to colonial and revolutionary times also illustrated Black communities' internal stratification. Du Bois's own theory of the "talented tenth," from *The Souls of Black Folk*, matters here.[60] While Hopkins and Du Bois descended from African Americans who had lived free, those descended from slaves often could not locate their ancestors in the range of textual sources— church records, land and other government records, probate records, military records, censuses—on which genealogists relied. Arduous working conditions, laws forbidding education, permanent family separations, and destitution combined to prevent most enslaved people from appearing in or generating historical records. Consequently, and unintentionally, they left their posterity grasping even for small figments of information. For example, Lizzie Warrenton Wells, an enslaved cook, grew up in a family of ten in Virginia. But when she was still a child, at age eleven, her master sold her and a sister away to Mississippi. Following emancipation in 1865, Wells moved to Memphis with her husband, and she began to read and write. She told her children that her own "father was half Indian, his father being a full blood. She often wrote back to somewhere in Virginia, trying to get track of her people, but she was never successful," her daughter, the journalist Ida B. Wells, recalled from Chicago.[61]

Black genealogy practices, like white genealogy practices, reveal that the demands of genealogy research on one's time, finances, social networks, and education limited genealogy activity to a privileged stratum, to the point of signifying genealogy's prestige to others. But anyone who was nonwhite, including wealthy and highly educated people, endured the slings and arrows of discrimination and violence. Anna Julia Cooper's maxim of 1892—that "when and where I enter, in the quiet, undisputed dignity of my womanhood, without violence and without suing or special patronage, then and there the whole *Negro race enters with me*"—found much confirmation in daily life.[62] Upward social mobility invited particular hostility. Lynch mobs and race rioters, as in the self-identified "white-supremacist" pogrom in Wilmington, North Carolina, during the 1898 election season, targeted Black newspaper editors and others in the Black middle class.[63] Black genealogists' practices seemed especially threatening to white supremacy when genealogists located lifelong New Englanders, famous white people like Thomas Jefferson, and other attributes that whites valued in the ancestry of African Americans. Unearthing nonwhite progenitors of white families destabilized whiteness's walls all the more.

American Jews' Genealogy Practices as a Push against Prejudice

Before the 1960s, Jewish genealogists and their labors went largely unrecognized by professionals and businesspeople in American genealogy, who were generally non-Jewish.[64] Although non-Jews and some Jews overlooked such endeavors, Jewish genealogists' activities in America possessed a lengthy history. Nineteenth-century Americans, including Jews, blurred distinctions among genealogy, biography, and history. Both the New England "town histories" of the antebellum years and the early volumes of southern history periodicals, such as the *William and Mary Quarterly* (1892), held that genealogy findings were a necessary dimension of historical knowledge.[65] In its own earliest issues, the periodical of the American Jewish Historical Society (1892) interspersed genealogy content with history articles, as did the more international, multidisciplinary *Jewish Quarterly Review* (London, 1888).[66]

The earliest book-length Jewish family genealogy appeared in the United States in 1917. Rabbi Malcolm Stern's later dictum for genealogists, that "the prominent are easy to find, the obscure more difficult," certainly holds true in this example.[67] The New York financier August Belmont, son of the other famous financier August Belmont, expended over $17,000 in contemporary dollars on an ambitious account of his paternal forebears.[68] An acquaintance first suggested the project in 1897.[69] The younger Belmont commissioned this opus from Richard J. H. Gottheil of Columbia University, a scholar of the ancient Mideast whose extensive publications included Sephardic lineages.[70] Over the centuries, following the Spanish and Portuguese Inquisitions that began around 1492, the Belmont clan and many other Jews had fled the Iberian Peninsula for Holland and Germany. The project called for an author conversant in many languages and accustomed to difficult research conditions in Europe. Belmont turned to the polyglot, well-traveled Gottheil because he sought to have the Belmonts traced all during their peregrinations before his father's 1837 arrival in the United States.[71] The learned Gottheil showed little interest in more ordinary Jews. He gazed down his nose upon diamond dealers he encountered outside Amsterdam who possessed the Belmont/Brandon name but were "much wanting in the dignity and the position that characterized their ancestors."[72] Like most family genealogies, *The Belmont-Belmonte Family: A Record of Four Hundred Years* was published privately, in the end.

Later Jewish genealogy practitioners in the United States critiqued the American racism that operated against Jews. Anti-Semitism worsened across the western world after World War I, with haters in the United States framing Jews as an inferior race, as haters did elsewhere.[73] The "national origins" immigration quotas of 1921–65 provide an especially glaring example. There was no discrete quota for Jews, but these quotas' suppression of southern and eastern European immigration targeted "the demographic Jewish heartland" in Russia, the Ukraine, and Poland.[74] Distinctions between longtime Americans and newer immigrants, which were all-important for some Jews, had little meaning for American universities in the 1920s that imposed admissions quotas intended to limit Jewish numbers on campus, and for homeowners whose restrictive covenants banned both Jewish and Black purchasers. As happened to the Black middle classes, Jewish upward mobility and assimilation invited particular bigotry.[75] Americans who treasured Anglo-American whiteness continued to sort European from European as the twentieth century went on. The historian Leonard Dinnerstein posits that anti-Semitic rhetoric from politicians and celebrities worsened during the Depression and World War II, with the war years representing "antisemitism at high tide" in the United States. But the historian Kirsten Fermaglich extends this periodization after 1945. Ensuing pressures and discrimination resulted in 1960s civil rights activism on behalf of Jews as well as people of color. The Civil Rights Act of 1964 penalized religious discrimination as well as race discrimination.[76]

Some Jews responded to increasing anti-Semitism by changing their names in an attempt to modulate their Jewishness when dealing with outsiders—and also, as Fermaglich has suggested, to ease their entry into the middle classes.[77] The wealthy mercantile Cabot tribe was so lofty that in an old Boston rhyme, the "Lowells speak only to Cabots, and the Cabots speak only to God."[78] In 1923, in the same year that Congress passed a stringent new federal copyright law, members of that same gilded clan angrily sued Harry and Myrtle Cabot (formerly Kabatchnick) of Philadelphia for name infringement. Hereditary organizations, genealogy societies, and the Historical Society of Pennsylvania all sided with the Boston Cabots in the suit. Stability of names given at birth, especially of men's names, was all-important to historians, genealogists, and, of course, to all those who detested foreigners, foreignness, and acts of supposed imposture that would result from such fluidity of naming. Recall Solomon Bradford Morse Jr.'s hostility in the 1850s toward the Maas family of Jews that had reportedly rebranded itself Morse. But despite their own prominence and their many allies, the Cabot plaintiffs of 1923 lost their case. Defendants Harry and Myrtle Cabot were entitled to their current name as far as the court was concerned.[79]

Jewish resistance to anti-Semitic pronouncements from American politicians and others took another form besides name changing: publicizing Early American Jewish history. Throughout the 1920s, a New York couple, Dr. Walter Max Kraus and his wife Marian (née Nathan), amassed extensive documents and information about colonial and revolutionary-era Jews. Both husband and wife came from families who had lived in the United States for the past century, like the Belmonts. Drawing on colonial-era lineages, Walter in particular undertook to "prove that half the people in the *Social Register* here in America had Jewish blood in their veins," a friend wrote in retrospect. Later, in 1934, the divorced Walter founded a hereditary organization, Society of Americans of Jewish Descent. He named its equally evanescent periodical,

The St. Charles, for the vessel that had borne the first Jews to North American soil, in 1654.[80] Both entities lasted only a year or two and were probably casualties of the Great Depression.

Locating and naming long-ago Jews whose near descendants included elite Protestants with Anglo surnames, as the Krauses were doing, challenged contemporary racial prejudices that elevated white Anglo-American Protestants over others. Asserting the longevity of the Jewish presence in America, going back to mid-seventeenth-century Sephardim in New Amsterdam, challenged hereditary organizations' positioning of Americanism's arbiters as a closed circle containing those who were white, documented, Christian descendants of Christian colonists. Walter Max Kraus's attempts to develop a hereditary organization for descendants of Early American Jews constituted a retort to the mainline, mostly Protestant hereditary organizations of the time that had long fetishized "firsts" in history, and, in some cases, aspired to Magna Carta and early medieval English descent even though documentation was scarcely possible.

Jews' interest in America's earliest Jewry became even more ardent after the Second World War. Genocide rendered the U.S. Jewish community the world's largest, in its numbers, in any one country. Before the war, that status had belonged to Poland. But 90 percent of the three million Jews there perished in the Holocaust.[81] Those Americans who created the American Jewish Archives in 1948, at Cincinnati's Hebrew Union College, spoke in assimilationist terms. The emergence of a new, hybrid Jewish man in America would usher in a bright future for world Jewry. Rhetorically turning his back on the ashes of Europe, the historian Jacob Rader Marcus intended the repository he cofounded on the Ohio River "to collect the records of this great Jewish center [America], not after it has perished, but while it is still young, virile, and growing."[82] The three hundredth anniversary, in 1954, of the first Jewish arrivals in North America seemed all-important.[83]

Dr. Walter Max Kraus died in 1944. After remarrying, Marian Nathan Kraus Sandor donated the voluminous files accumulated during her first marriage to the American Jewish Archives as soon as it opened.[84] That act launched the career of American Jewish genealogy's leading figure, Rabbi Malcolm H. Stern (1915–94). A Reform Jew, he was simultaneously known for supporting African Americans' civil rights struggles in Norfolk, Virginia, where his congregation was.[85] From Cincinnati, Marcus good-naturedly told Stern to "do something" with the Kraus/Sandor files. They became the empirical core of Stern's *Americans of Jewish Descent* (1960), and they informed his subsequent historical publications on Early America.[86] The small Jewish communities of the colonial and revolutionary periods grounded twentieth-century Jews' efforts to assert their right to a lasting home in the United States.

Conclusion

Genealogists among Indigenous people, African Americans, and American Jews all operated long before the rest of America, including some other African Americans and American Jews, realized that members of those groups could and did trace their ancestry. Such activity not only predated *Roots* (1976–77) but prepared the ground for *Roots'* unanticipated success. Transformations in Jewish genealogy practices in the 1960s—namely the turns toward Holocaust consciousness, eastern European histories, and "history from the bottom up" that prized workers and tradesmen alongside rabbis and successful businessmen—illustrated forms of genealogy's diversification that reverberated far outside Jewish communities. Inclusive forms of genealogy after 1945 inspired activities among Americans of other nationalities, too. Overall, genealogists who practiced less traditional forms of genealogy pushed away at racial, class, and religious distinctions in the United States in the first half of the twentieth century, as well as the second.

Part II

Arguments about Inclusion

Spectacle and Commerce

CHAPTER FOUR

There Has Not Been Such a Book

Precedents for Alex Haley's Roots after 1945

Roots found unanticipated success in 1976–77 because multitudes of genealogists and others had long prepared the cultural soil in which Alex Haley dug for information.[1] He contended that the scarcely possible was in fact possible, that an African American could document his descent through generations of enslaved people, back to a named African forebear who had lived two centuries beforehand. But he and others mischaracterized *Roots* as unprecedented. "In America, I think, there has not been such a book," he told his agent in early 1965. "'Rooting' a Negro family, all the way back, telling the chronicle, through us, of how the Negro is part and parcel of the American saga."[2] On the contrary, Haley's own research processes for *Roots* illustrated expansions in genealogy activity that had either already occurred or were ongoing. *Roots* ended up flourishing in ground that others had already primed.

After 1945, two factors in particular increased genealogy's popularity: cheaper and faster travel to libraries, resulting from the beginnings of commercial air travel and interstate highway systems, and continually dropping costs of publication. Americans' decisions to allocate resources toward making records available, and traveling for genealogy purposes, mattered even more. Demand for genealogy materials caused libraries, historical societies, and publishers to increase their genealogy offerings. More of those things further stimulated demand for, and travel to, genealogy materials. What contemporaries called decolonization in the 1950s and 1960s also helped, inadvertently, to ready the ground for *Roots*. The two world wars had ground down the grand British, French, Belgian, Dutch, and German Empires to the point that independence struggles in their respective Asian, African, and oceanic colonies began succeeding. A bevy of newly independent countries now festooned world maps, not least Haley's own maps in his mind.

Closer to home, widespread upward social mobility in the United States and increasing diversity on campus created new interest in the histories of working-class and poor people, women of all kinds, and ethnic, racial, and religious minorities. Commitments to social history, or "history from the bottom up," had originated among French historians, but the field found a hospitable environment in the United States at a time of extensive civil rights reform and widely affordable higher education. An appetite for social history was evident off campus as well as on campus, particularly among Jewish genealogists who ranged outside rabbinates to track descent from more ordinary villagers and tradespeople in eastern Europe, from where the majority of American Jews' forebears had come. Social history also possessed an umbilical relationship to reform movements and revolutions, chief among them the struggles for African American civil rights. Civil rights reform, Black nationalism, and calls for Black power all expanded African American genealogy practices, including Haley's own practices. The 1970s' ethnic revivals among Irish Americans, Italian Americans, Polish Americans, and other ethnic minorities illustrated the "third generation" truism that the grandchildren of immigrants, the third generation in America, collectively remembered what their fathers and grandfathers preferred to forget.[3] Ethnic revivalists repudiated assimilation to Anglo-American Protestant ways in their roots travel, genealogy practices, and historical research.[4]

An even more important factor in preparing the ground for *Roots* was its author's own advance publicity and fame. Haley already bore a household name because of his unanticipated bestseller, *The Autobiography of Malcolm X* (1965), and his frequent articles and interviews in *Playboy* and *Reader's Digest*. His writer's block, difficulties finishing the *Roots* manuscript, and financial need engendered arduous lecture tours in the early 1970s. His preexisting popularity as a journalist and historian helps explain why large audiences came to hear a talk on a work in progress. His oratorical prowess made him a compelling pitchman for his project and an unexpectedly congenial one for whites who might have been expecting more confrontational approaches.[5] Haley's activities before 1976 contributed to *Roots'* successes in the end. In 1972, he announced his descent from Kunta Kinte in the *New York Times*— four years before publishing the book.[6] His audiences' receptiveness indicates preexisting interest in Haley's aspirations to reconstruct his descent from an enslaved man who had known Africa, and from generations in between.

Histories of Technology, Travel, and Information

Innovations in technology, travel, and information, combined with Americans' deliberate channeling of time and other resources into genealogy, all helped account for *Roots'* later popularity. Librarians who have surveyed the three decades following World War II, between 1945 and 1975, have posited an "'information explosion,' *i.e.*, the almost unbelievable increase in the publishing of new, revised, and old information."[7] But Americans in this same era also introduced some new restrictions on obtaining the kind of family and demographic information that genealogists prized. World War II, as experienced at home in the United States, temporarily increased the number of unwed mothers, as most contraceptive devices and abortions remained illegal and scarce until the turn of the 1970s. Secret, closed adoptions involving strangers and paid agencies increased in wartime, and they continued long after the war. People involved in these adoptions placed documents out of reach that would divulge birthdates and other family information, a staple of genealogy research.[8] The outcry against government surveillance and lists of enemies of the president during the Vietnam War era prompted other restrictions on the obtaining of information about citizens. The 1970s saw new "privacy" laws, such as the Family Educational and Right to Privacy Act (FERPA) of 1974, which universities now commonly employ. Such "privacy" laws also had the effect of constraining genealogists' access to personal and vital records on which there had been no restrictions before.[9]

The new plenitude was otherwise overwhelming. It included printed historical documents, surname and place indexes, and family genealogies. Documents came into public view in the 1960s and 1970s that pertained to early decades of the twentieth century, a period of great interest to white ethnic minorities and Jews. For example, the 1900 U.S. Census was opened in its entirety for public viewing in 1978, an especially poignant event given the loss of 99 percent of the 1890 Census to a 1921 fire in the U.S. Commerce Building in Washington.[10] And, starting around 1975, passenger lists for nineteenth-century sailing ships and steamers that bore immigrants, and naturalization records for that same period, were now translated, printed, and published.[11]

With long-distance travel cheaper and faster than ever, and ever more publications of historical documents of interest to genealogists, genealogy patrons flocked to large repositories such as the National Archives in Washington after 1945.[12] These postwar decades also saw legions of travelers visit the Genealogical Society of Utah (GSU) library (later the Family History Library) in Salt Lake City, that the church oversaw and staffed with missionaries. Utah's genealogy tourism after 1945 reversed the old pattern in which Mormon leaders and missionaries traveled east to research genealogy and scrutinize genealogy facilities, as had occurred in 1877, 1890, and 1909.[13] Before 1944, only GSU members could view the organization's formidable collections without charge. Consequently, the only library in the United States devoted solely to genealogy materials and serving genealogists was the New

England Historic Genealogical Society's library in Boston. But following the GSU's opening of its collections to nonmembers in 1944—its fiftieth anniversary—non-Mormons breached the mountain curtain in large numbers to find unparalleled collections of historical documents as well as Temple Index Bureau card files, containing genealogical information, that missionaries and others were committing to microfilm.[14] The GSU's new accessibility belongs to a broader pattern in which, in the 1940s, the church absorbed the previously freestanding GSU, including its Temple Index Bureau. The church redesignated them its Genealogical Department.[15]

Four years after Joseph Fielding Smith's famous 1918 vision of Jesus Christ himself engaged in evangelizing the dead, the GSU had developed its bureau. The index's purpose was to prevent further duplication of labor at already-swamped temples, the only places where the faithful could undertake virtual baptism, intergenerational sealings, and other ordinances.[16] Travelers from far away—including Gilbert Doane, who came in 1930 "to consult the genealogist of the Sherwood family about a problem in my ancestry"—gaped at what they saw: "over five million names in a huge card file, which serves as an index to thousands of sheets of family records. It is part of the belief of the members of this church that the family is a unit in the future paradise," he informed his readers in 1937.[17]

Information on these cards served as the nucleus of the mammoth Mormon databases of post-1945 times. Gradually, the church and the GSU transferred the information onto an even more accessible format, which enabled multitudinous copies and facilitated preservation. Early in the 1930s, colleagues in the church's History Office passed around a *Popular Mechanics* article "describing a newly developed camera for taking microfilm pictures." Microfilming facilitated the duplication and preservation of any written text. Church workers adopted microfilming technology early and par excellence. Not only did microfilming pack a lot of data onto a small object that could fit into a pocket, but it was "non-inflammable [sic] and durable as the best rag paper," explained Archibald Bennett, from the church's History Office.[18] The Second World War's dire threats to European repositories lent new urgency and speed to the church's projects, launched officially in 1938.[19] Time and time again, missionaries armed with photography equipment compelled archives to consent to their microfilming of documents, with the delivery of duplicate rolls to the archives, free of charge.[20] These massive operations in the wartime and postwar decades resulted in millions of microfilm rolls of genealogical data, with the negatives and master copies stored in the bombproof and fireproof Granite Mountain Vault (1963), hewn out of one side of Little Cottonwood Canyon in Utah.[21] In 1954, Roberta S. Wakefield of Washington's National Genealogical Society spent a rapturous fortnight in Salt Lake City. "One need stay weeks to half-way explore even those references most interesting and helpful to his own problems. Then there are the MICROFILMS! They are there by the thousand and the machines to read them! If only you had the time!" All seventy-nine film readers were in use during her visit.[22]

Because of the intertwined booms in microfilming and recordkeeping, access to Mormon resources became de rigueur for career genealogists and hereditary organizations in the 1950s and afterward, regardless of whether they themselves were Mormon. In 1953, when she otherwise reported being "broke," Winifred Holman, a professional genealogist outside Boston, purchased a lifetime membership in the GSU. In turn, the church hired her to "straighten out" the New England colonial-era ancestry of nineteenth-century church leader Franklin D. Richards.[23] Later in the 1950s, the Society of American Archivists was among those professional organizations that held its annual meeting in Salt Lake City, having solicited an article from Bennett for its professional journal. The archivists came in awe of Mormon recordkeeping.[24] Post-1945 hereditary organizations renounced old prejudices against applicants with polygamous ancestry, in part because the church's herculean collection efforts directly benefited the organizations' own numbers by facilitating the genealogical research necessary for applications. By 1949, enough Utahans had amassed the documentation that would admit them to the General Society of Mayflower Descendants to form Utah's first Mayflower Descendants chapter.[25]

The church itself intended to invigorate genealogy practices among Mormons as well as non-Mormons and visitors to Utah with its lifting of the old prohibition of temple work done on nonrelatives—friends and strangers—in 1961. After church president Wilford Woodruff first forbade the practice in 1894, well-connected laypeople used back channels to minister to departed friends. In friendly contact with the president of the LDS Temple in Manti, Utah, in 1920, Susa Young Gates arranged to have three fellow feminists—May Wright Sewall, Anna Howard Shaw, and Rachel Foster Avery—baptized by proxy. While claiming Avery as a distant relative, she referred to all three as her late "friends."[26] Church officials otherwise discouraged congregants from "extracting names, regardless of family relationship," as occurred in Mesa, Arizona, in 1936. "Name extraction" from historical records entailed the amassing of birthdates, death dates, marriage dates, and other genealogical information that was necessary for temple ordinances.[27] When the church did begin allowing name extraction and temple ordinances to be done on nonrelatives in 1961, the church imposed some limits on the practice. The deceased had to have been born at least 110 years prior to anyone essaying their baptism. When closely related survivors gave explicit permission for temple work, the departed needed to have been born at least ninety-five years before.[28] Generally, however, the dramatic enlargement of the pool of allowable dead people after 1961 created ever more ways for living people to pursue their own salvation.

The church freely and widely disseminated the genealogy information that it garnered from temple workers and distant missionaries, and that came pouring in once the church began allowing "name extraction" and temple work on nonrelatives. In 1962, the church began developing a nationwide and, later, international web of local libraries dedicated to genealogy and family history research. Without leaving their vicinity, a researcher could borrow and read rolls of microfilm from Utah by means of their local LDS repository, without charge. More than twenty such libraries were in place by the summer of 1965, only three years later. By 2012, more than 3,400 such family history centers existed worldwide.[29]

Paradoxically, given all these tales of traveling genealogists, improvements in travel and communication after 1945 bolstered local history and genealogy by enabling many others to remain on their home ground.[30] Major repositories of all kinds, besides the network of LDS family-history libraries, catered to patrons who wanted or needed to remain close to home while undertaking research. By the mid-1960s, the U.S. National Archives developed a "unified mail service operation," whereby U.S. residents could order "a standard search to be made for their ancestors from among pension, military service records, Federal census schedules, and immigration passenger lists." In 1970, there were 102,000 such mail requests and a considerable backlog, especially in the Military Service Section.[31] Later in the 1970s, the ability to obtain information over long distances "on an urge" were such that a Crockett, Texas, woman complained about the inferior level of service from the Daughters of the American Revolution's own library in Washington, where call numbers were not yet in use. "It seems shamefully regrettable that I cannot enjoy any benefits of our Library . . . without going there in person," she wrote to the *Daughters of the American Revolution Magazine*. "Every other library in our country makes its services available for stipulated considerations. Oftentimes the answer is given to one direct question for only a [self-addressed stamped envelope]" with which the sender assumed the cost of postage.[32]

Jewish Genealogy Practices in the 1960s and 1970s:
The Shtetl That Memory Built

Affection for social history, on and off campus, expanded genealogy practice in the long 1960s and also helped prepare the ground for the success of *Roots*. Historians asserted that knowledge of working people, poor people, women, recent immigrants, enslaved people, free people of color, and all manner of other populations that professional historians and many cultural institutions had previously neglected, was not only possible but necessary for a full under- standing of the past.[33] Jewish genealogy practices illustrate the new commit- ments to social history especially well. Rabbinical research continued to have its adherents, but there was considerable new appetite for tracking more ordi- nary Jews through history. Following the 1954 tercentenary celebrations of the earliest Jews' arrival in North America, Jewish genealogists shifted their interests toward eastern European populations, in part because so many Americans descended from them. Two hundred thousand descendants of mid-nineteenth-century Jews from German states and elsewhere in central Europe, and smaller numbers of descendants of colonial-era and revolutionary- era Sephardic populations (such as the poet Emma Lazarus), had already been present in the United States when larger numbers began flowing from eastern Europe. Two and a half million Jews from eastern Europe immigrated to the United States between 1870 and 1924, with a low rate of return com- pared to other immigrant groups.[34]

As hostility toward unassimilated foreigners began to wane among Amer- icans in the 1950s, interest in the history of bygone eastern European Jewish populations increased in the United States. Ironically, although racial hatred inspired both the rise of Nazi Germany and the 1920s "national origins" quo- tas, both events, especially as viewed in retrospect, did much to quell anti-Semitism and anti-Catholic prejudices and the racial prejudices that had sorted European from European.[35] World War II poster artists praised America's multitudinous nationalities in representing them as lists of di- verse surnames—including characteristically Jewish surnames like Co- hen—to foster patriotic pride and highlight the differences between the United States and Nazi Germany.[36] By then, low percentages of new immi- grants in the population heightened Americans' impression that earlier im- migrants, including Jews from eastern Europe and their near descendants, had assimilated. For more than four decades, between 1921 and 1965, the na- tional-origins quotas suppressed immigration from Europe and Asia. Con- sequently, the percentage of foreign-born in the U.S. population hovered at a low 4.7 percent in 1970, in contrast to 14.7 percent in 1910 and 13 percent in 2010.[37] Before the 1970s, "immigration history" indicated studies of ethnic diversity among western Europeans in the British colonies, the revolutionary era, and the Early Republic—Marcus Hansen's specialty.[38] But in the 1960s and 1970s, also a time of immigration reform, immigration history pertaining to later decades (between the 1880s and the 1920s), and to Mediterranean, Jewish, and Slavic nationalities, began developing as a scholarly field and as a topic of interest for public historians, local historians, and genealogists.[39]

Heightened Holocaust consciousness among Americans, spreading beyond survivors and their kin, also explains the eagerness to reconstruct eastern European Jewish history. Before 1961, the Nazis' genocide lacked its own name in English as a discrete event. Only after the publicity surrounding the Eichmann trial in Israel did the genocide acquire its shorthand of "the Holocaust."[40] Americans' civil rights activism on behalf of Jews as well as people of color, and Holocaust remembrances, explicitly linked racism and anti-Semitism to mass killing in the 1950s and 1960s.[41] Increasing Zionism (support for Israel as an explicitly Jewish homeland) and Holocaust consciousness intertwined, in the minds of many Americans. So many Holocaust survivors moved to Israel after 1948 that the leading Jewish genealogist Sallyann Amdur Sack told other Americans, in retrospect, that "as a result of the Holocaust, and the return to Zion, Israel has become the source of our roots in a virtual sense."[42] With threats to the small country in the wars of 1967 and 1973 that invasions from neighboring Arab nations posed, the earlier, vanished world of eastern European Jewry now seemed all the more precious because survivors were now experiencing new perils.[43]

In the 1960s, significant cultural happenings simultaneously represented a culmination of what had come before while stimulating subsequent events, in a foreshadowing of *Roots'* later expansions of historical consciousness. To modern historians, a "shtetl" (Yiddish for "town") indicates the pre-World War II Jewish neighborhood or community within the otherwise multi-ethnic eastern European country town. Nazi Germany eradicated most shtetls when it invaded Poland (1939) and the Soviet Union (1941) and massacred Jewish populations there. But Yiddish-language literature and theater among these same early-twentieth-century eastern European populations, and retrospective portrayals such as the Broadway musical *Fiddler on the Roof* (1964), portrayed the shtetl to resemble, instead, a small, poor village where everyone was Jewish and knew each other.[44] In postwar America, Jews and others ardently preserved this homogeneous version of the shtetl. This all-Jewish village in eastern Europe and Russia was memory's shtetl, a place in the past that later generations cherished.

Jerry Bock, Sheldon Harnick, and Jerome Robbins based their musical *Fiddler on the Roof* on Shalom-Aleichem's earlier Yiddish-language fiction. The show did not portray genealogy doings per se. But when it premiered on Broadway in 1964 and on movie screens in 1971, as an immediate critical and financial success, *Fiddler* set memory's shtetl, the new appetite for recalling eastern European Jewish life, and the social history of workers to music, rhyme, and dance. The milkman and antihero, Tevye, and his wife, Golde, with their marriageable daughters; the butcher Lazar Wolf; and everyone else in the small, all-Jewish village of Anatevka, Russia, in 1905 were working people. The plot of *Fiddler* was ethnically specific enough to teach non-Jews about Jewish history basics, as did the song "Sabbath Prayer" and denouements involving pogroms and eventual exile from Anatevka. Lazar Wolf appeared with his suitcase packed for Chicago, in the final scene. But *Fiddler* was universal enough to appeal far outside its ethnic and religious context, with its stories of youthful rebellion over marriage choices, parental bewilderment, and adult children's farewells. With frequent revivals and easy adaptability to school and amateur stages, *Fiddler on the Roof* created considerable awareness of the history of eastern European Jews, so many of whom had died in the Holocaust, in addition to signifying preexisting interest in that history. Alisa Solomon has described Jerome Robbins's own roots travel in 1959 while visiting Poland, as he searched in vain for the site of his father's ancestral shtetl, years before directing and choreographing *Fiddler*.[45]

Because the reconstruction of eastern European Jewish history was a leading priority of American Jews' genealogy and other public-history efforts, there is reason to believe that *Fiddler on the Roof* stimulated those efforts in the United States. In a mutually reinforcing process, eagerness on the part of library patrons and booksellers compelled the publishing of ever more records pertaining to early twentieth-century immigration. These publications and purchases in turn attracted ever more patrons and customers. Young Arthur Kurzweil, newly graduated from Hofstra University in 1970, had often journeyed in his mind to his father's native shtetl in Poland. "Every time I sat and had daydreams about the little town, I felt warm and at home," he wrote, despite never having been to Poland. Note that he defined his father's shtetl as a little town, not as a neighborhood or quarter. During his initial visit to the New York Public Library's Jewish Division, he was amazed at the diversity among other patrons. "There were young Chasidic men leaning over rare rabbinic texts, and middle-aged Reform rabbis preparing for a future sermon.

There were college women writing term papers on history, and scholars writing books on obscure subjects." Some were reading Yiddish, "a language barely known to me . . . and others were strict observers of the Law, a way of life which I have never known."[46]

He was also taken aback to discover that others shared his interest in history and family history. Gradually, he located a 1963 memorial book (yizkor) of the extinguished Jewish community of Dobromil, that survivors in the United States had published. He glimpsed his great-grandfather, a tinsmith named Avraham Abusch, in a group photograph of a trade organization. The discovery "changed my life" because the image "said one thing to me . . . 'You have a past and a history, and you can discover it if you want.'"[47] Less than a decade after stepping into the NYPL, Kurzweil became a coeditor of *Toledot*, America's earliest Jewish genealogy periodical (1977–85), with Steven W. Siegel and contributing editor Rabbi Malcolm Stern. The name *Toledot* is Hebrew for "descendants." Kurzweil later published an advice book aimed at more devout Jews, *From Generation to Generation: How to Trace Your Jewish Genealogy and Personal History* (1980), that resulted in multiple editions.[48]

Before the 1970s, beginners in genealogy expressed frustrations at the exclusivity built into existing American genealogy advice, which generally addressed white Anglo-Americans in search of documented colonial and revolutionary descent. Around 1963, for example, twenty-one-year-old Dan Rottenberg of Philadelphia embarked on "tracing my family tree." Describing his ancestry as "exclusively Jewish," he found little help in instruction books. "All the references to church and parish registers, to Revolutionary War pension records, and to European coats of arms were worthless to someone whose ancestors (a) never belonged to a church or parish, (b) arrived in America long after the Revolution, and (c) knew nothing about coats of arms—except to run for their lives when they saw one coming."[49] His joke about heraldry illustrated the shortage of genealogy instruction that was relevant to Jews. He went on to publish the earliest how-to manual on Jewish genealogy for Americans, *Finding Our Fathers* (1977). Like Kurzweil, Rottenberg managed to publish his book with a commercial publisher. He also cofounded, with Neil Rosenstein and four other men, the country's first Jewish Genealogical Society that same year.[50]

This New Jersey-based group was the earliest Jewish genealogical society in world history—after the Holocaust. There had been earlier, organized activity among Jewish genealogists in Weimar Germany, before the Nazi takeover of 1933. The Berlin ophthalmologist Arthur Czellitzer was extending longstanding German genealogy practices to other Jews when he founded the Gesellschaft für Jüdische Familienforschung (Society for Jewish Family Research) in 1924. Its accompanying German-language periodical endured until 1938.[51] The gesellschaft boasted more than three hundred members in 1926 and persisted for much of the 1930s before Nazism and war extinguished it. Czellitzer's wife and children managed to escape to America, bearing new English names, but the doctor lost his life in the Sobibor death camp.[52] One gesellschaft member, the historian Hanns G. Reissner, survived to publish an account of this enterprise in 1977. Another member, the architect Siegfried Ascher, struggled to develop a Jewish Genealogical Research Society of Palestine in 1940 after he fled to Jerusalem.[53] That society does not appear to have lasted.

More Seemingly Impossible Family Histories: Black Genealogy and Civil Rights Reform

Many American Jews overlooked Jewish genealogy endeavors. "Do Jews have genealogies?'" one man asked a high school friend turned genealogist, around 1980.[54] Other Jews rejected the enterprise altogether, condemning Jewish genealogy for fostering self-centeredness, or stigmatizing genealogy on the grounds of its uses in Nazi Germany to track and attack Jews as a race.[55] Similarly, some African Americans consigned family history to the realm of impossibility. In despair over the numerous, race-specific obstacles that separated so many African Americans from autobiographical facts, some turned their back on the whole enterprise of reinforcing self-worth or group pride through ancestor tracking. Malcolm Little and others in the Nation of Islam substituted "X" for the surnames of their birth, scorning those surnames as slave names and spurning the broken histories behind them.[56]

But ongoing decolonization abroad, civil rights reform at home, and Black history's expansion all invigorated African American genealogists' efforts. While the independence of African countries from European empires kindled the imaginations of African diasporas around the world, an older American tradition found new fuel. African American genealogy activity retained its strong, historic affinity with civil rights struggles. The Association for the Study of Negro Life and History's *Negro History Bulletin* published genealogy content on Black and mixed-race families as a protest against Jim Crow segregation in the 1940s and 1950s. In 1943, editor and historian Carter G. Woodson wrote on "Negro Women Eligible to be Daughters of the American Revolution" in response to the DAR's notorious exclusion of the Black opera singer Marian Anderson from its auditorium's stage in Washington in 1939.[57]

Black genealogy's connection to civil rights advocacy was especially visible on the local level. The Pittsburgh area, where numerous African Americans from the South had found manufacturing jobs, proved to be fertile ground. Pittsburgh was home to the proud Black newspaper the *Pittsburgh Courier* and Joel Augustus Rogers's column, "Your History," which ran from the 1920s to the 1960s. The Jamaican-born Rogers (1880–1966) often described the nonwhite ancestry of white public figures and publicized interracial liaisons in history, in order to impeach segregation. His most famous, self-published oeuvre was *Sex and Race: A History of White, Indian, and Negro Miscegenation* (1942). Another work that did not otherwise find a publisher was his *Five Negro Presidents* (1965).[58] Also in Pittsburgh, the first-ever group devoted to Black genealogy, spearheaded by Florence Ball-Jones and the Western Pennsylvania Research and Historical Society, organized in 1965. Ball-Jones's effort apparently died out soon afterward.[59] But in 1970, a Pittsburgh-area family decided on a yearly reunion, nicknamed itself the "Cousins," and soon drew in hundreds of kin from around the country to the point of becoming a popular annual event for decades.[60]

Such flurries of activity among African Americans before *Roots* occurred not only because of the new ease of obtaining information or getting to it but also because the content of the information now included people like themselves. Civil rights confrontations and reforms, including the desegregation of higher education, injected new energy into the field of Black history and, by extension, Black genealogy. Activists such as the Reverend Wyatt Tee Walker, who had long worked alongside the Reverend Martin Luther King Jr., understood the importance of usable pasts for Black communities when he began assembling materials for a history library in 1965.[61] Patrons now approached library catalogs and counters with the conviction that it might be possible, after all, to document their own forebears, even if the paucity of writings entailed reading against sources that whites had generated. Interviewed in 1965, the New York Public Library's Timothy Field Beard reported that the past two years had witnessed a dramatic increase in African American patrons' making their way past the marble lions that guarded the Fifth Avenue doors. "All ethnic groups are using our materials more than ever before," he told an interviewer. "Take the Italian people, descendants of early 1900s immigrants; now they are conspicuously here, seeking their roots. Before them it was the Irish. It's a regular pattern that we see; the Negroes really are just starting."[62]

One important civil rights text of the time period was a family history. The jurist, poet, and minister Pauli Murray (1910–85) is best known for forging new trails in African American civil rights and in women's struggles against what she called "Jane Crow." She also anticipated movements in defense of lesbians and gays and challenges to gender normativity. Murray had been born Anna Pauline but she took the more androgynous name Pauli, and she kept it for the rest of her life. In her youth, she explored living as a man, sometimes wearing men's suits, at a time when both homosexuality and cross-dressing indicated mental disease when otherwise not treated as crimes.[63] Eschewing marriage and motherhood, she quietly maintained a decades-long partnership with an Englishwoman, Irene (Renee) Barlow, until Barlow's death in 1973. Settling into a female gender identity by the time she reached midlife, Murray labored on *Proud Shoes*.[64]

Murray's schoolteacher aunt, Pauline Fitzgerald Dame, legally adopted her when she was still a child, after her parents died. She grew up around Pauline's two surviving sisters, Sallie Fitzgerald Small and Marie Fitzgerald Jeffers, as well as her Fitzgerald grandparents, Robert and Cornelia Smith Fitzgerald.[65] These were all maternal kin. When still in her teens, Murray began transcribing, at length, the recollections of the "race aunts" who had raised her. Her Aunt Pauline wrote down her own memories of family.[66] The white poet Stephen Vincent Benét applauded the young Murray's plans for a book based on her aunts' reminiscences. He marveled in 1939 that "nobody as far as I know has really tried to sit down and do a 'Buddenbrooks' or a 'Forsyte Saga' . . . from the negro [*sic*] point of view."[67]

Murray's stay in Washington's segregated Freedmen's Hospital in 1951 illustrates not only her own genealogy inclinations but multiple other ardent family historians within the Black bourgeoisie. Washington's African American life included eminent high schools, universities, and exclusive social clubs.[68] While hospitalized, Murray recognized another patient, Ethel Just, as Ohio State University's "first Negro woman graduate" and a longtime English teacher. Murray told her aunts that Just was "one of Washington's 400, I think, and the elderly friends who come to see her belong to the old established families of tradition."[69] One visitor was seventy-four-year-old May Belcher, who soon became friendly with Murray. Like Murray's grandfather, Robert Fitzgerald, Belcher's father and paternal grandfather had fought in the Civil War as Black Union soldiers. Murray and Belcher "had a wonderful time together building family history," Murray told her aunts. "She seemed so pleased to see and talk with me, and I showed her all the family album (Mil's book)," indicating her sister Mildred, "with the five Fitzgerald sisters, and all the relatives. She said that she was so stimulated by our chat and that she believed she would try to document her family history for her younger nieces and nephews as a result of our conversations."

Like Caroline Bond Day and her research subjects, and African American genealogists generally, Murray based some of her family reckonings on shared morphology—outward appearance—as well as on oral and written recollections that she had obtained from her aunts. During that same hospital stay, she reconnected with her seldom seen cousin Sam Fitzgerald, aged sixty-seven, when she "saw him standing at the Hospital Canteen counter when I went down to get some cigarettes. I looked at that old Fitzgerald jaw and something rang a bell. I said, 'Your last name wouldn't be Fitzgerald, would it?' He said, 'Yes.' I said, 'It wouldn't be Sam, would it?' He said 'Yes.'" He later aided Murray in drawing up a Fitzgerald family tree. "So it is a small world," Murray told her aunts, "and if we check back far enough, we will discover that the whole human race is related."[70]

The next year, 1952, a stinging job rejection from Cornell University increased her commitment to researching the book. She departed for archives and interviews in Pennsylvania, Delaware, North Carolina, and Virginia, in order to reconfirm the information she had gathered about the Fitzgeralds and her grandmother's family, the Smiths. "I was curious to know how far a Negro family in America can push into the jungles of its mysterious origins," she ruminated in 1954, in notes to herself.[71] She found additional material on enslaved and free forebears going back to the eighteenth century, to solidify her case for the family's deep American roots and patriotism. Amid the loss of her now-elderly aunts, as they died one after another, she published her findings.

Murray's *Proud Shoes* (1956) proved to be a major precedent for Alex Haley's *Roots* (1976). Both stories reconstructed lineages from the time of slavery. Both stories originated with information that the authors had obtained orally, at first, from older female relatives from the maternal side of their families. Both authors assembled multiracial family trees—in Murray's case, Black, white, and probable Cherokee—that included white forefathers. In *Proud Shoes*, Murray recounted that her grandmother, Cornelia Smith Fitzgerald (1844–1924), was born a North Carolina house slave and that Cornelia's master, the white attorney James Sidney Smith, was her own biological father. When Sidney had forced himself on a house slave named Harriet, Cornelia was the result. Neither Sidney nor his sister, Mary Ruffin Smith, ever married or reported other children. After Mary survived Sidney, she bequeathed some of the family land to his only child. But Cornelia and her husband later incurred Ku Klux Klan attacks on their land ownership and theft of their property during Reconstruction.[72] Cornelia maintained contact with her Aunt Mary long afterward, and she took her children, including her daughter Pauline (born

Pauli Murray posing with a copy
of *Proud Shoes*, 1956. Schlesinger
Library, Radcliffe Institute,
Harvard University.

1870), to visit her. Writing in 1944, Pauline retained this childhood memory of encountering her white forebears: "I would wander into the parlor look at the Smiths and their ancestors in huge picture frames on the walls. Wherever I would turn their solemn eyes would follow me so that I would turn and run out again."[73] But Aunt Mary left much of the rest of the family land to the University of North Carolina at Chapel Hill, which then excluded Blacks. In a subsequent bitter twist, that university rejected Aunt Mary's great-grand-niece Pauli Murray's graduate school application in 1938, on racial grounds.[74]

In 1956, *Proud Shoes* found publication with a commercial press, and it received warm reviews in northern newspapers.[75] "The contrast between the two lines which meet in the marriage of her grandparents is beautifully done," the African American writer Roi Ottley remarked, in the *Chicago Tribune*.[76] Yet Murray's efforts did not give rise to additional publications and institutions in African American family history. Most African American genealogists considered the field to have emerged after *Roots,* two decades later. Murray's depiction of grandmother Cornelia's deeply felt cultural and religious identification with her white Episcopalian forebears, who had also been her and her mother's captors, helps explain why later Black-genealogy canons omitted *Proud Shoes.*[77] Out of print by the early 1970s, it was overlooked to the point that Alex Haley understood *Roots* to be unprecedented.[78]

Differences in each author's approaches and intended audiences also explain the neglect of *Proud Shoes* until recent times. Haley wrote as a storyteller, a journalist, and a popularizer. Murray wrote as a scholar and a poet, with literary aspirations. Her previous publications ranged from poetry to law articles, a world away from Haley's mass commercial appeal. Murray admitted to having shared the passionate work habits of genealogists while researching *Proud Shoes:* "[my] own exhilaration over successfully tracking down clues to the past sometimes bordered on a mild sort of lunacy, a common affliction of genealogical buffs." But she did not publicly identify as a genealogist, unlike Haley, who folded his own genealogy research and genealogy-driven emotions into the plot of *Roots,* especially the book, and into the publicity surrounding *Roots.* His book, and the articles that predated it, appeared at a time when genealogy was reaching new heights in popularity, much more so than in the 1950s.[79] Additional reasons for the oblivion surrounding *Proud Shoes* in the 1960s and 1970s include Haley's own timing. Already celebrated as Malcolm X's bestselling biographer, he published *Roots* following calls for Black power and Black-is-beautiful pride.[80] The determined African and African American parents and grandparents of *Roots* illustrated that ethos. That same mentality made more assimilationist personages—like the light-skinned, devoutly Christian Cornelia Smith Fitzgerald—seem like painfully obsequious relics.

But the twin impact of *Roots* in 1976–77, and Murray's simultaneous fame in 1977 as one of the first women to be ordained an Episcopal priest, brought *Proud Shoes* back into print. In the final years of her life, Murray rallied her far-flung siblings to help maintain neglected family gravesites in North Carolina.[81] Having counted three races in her own family tree, she strove to foster mixed-race people's pride in their plural identities—long before it became possible for Americans to identify themselves as belonging to more than one race on U.S. census forms, in 2000.[82] In a 1975 group letter to her siblings, Murray envisioned their reunion in Washington as "an imaginative stunt tied into the Bicentennial, a possible publicity feature to show 'White America' that 'Mixie America' can be both proud of its ethnic origins and feel related to American tradition."[83]

Civil Rights Consciousness among White Genealogists

Awareness of racism among some white genealogists in the 1950s and 1960s, especially in liberal precincts, explains their interest in histories and genealogies of African Americans. A discussion among professional genealogists in the 1950s concerned a subject that would still create consternation sixty years later. The presence of Blacks, mixed-race persons, or Indians in the otherwise white family tree seemed to impeach descendants' claims to whiteness.[84] Because interracial marriage (especially involving whites) was widely outlawed in Early America, genealogists were often unable to trace interrelationships between white and nonwhite individuals.[85] Such connections often went undocumented and, for professionals generally, research seemed hardly possible in the absence of documents. Instead, Donald Lines Jacobus and his client Edgar Francis Waterman (b. 1875), himself an assiduous genealogist, reframed their Waterman family genealogy as a surname history.

Starting in 1939, Jacobus and Waterman published information on Watermans in the United States generally, including those they could not trace to white colonial-era Watermans in Massachusetts and Connecticut.[86] This approach allowed research on recent immigrants, non-Christians, and even non-whites. In the third and final volume (1954) of *The Waterman Family*, Jacobus and Waterman published lineages of German-and Russian-born Wassermans and Watermans. These were Jewish (and, in one case, German Evangelical) people and included Wassermans who had changed their surname to the more English-sounding "Waterman."[87] Jacobus and Waterman then briefly listed fragmentary lineages of Watermans of "African and Amerindian Descent." They informed the reader that Black and Indian Watermans had both descended from New England slaves held by "more prosperous" white Watermans. The Indians had been enslaved following King Philip's War in 1675–76. The authors also noted cryptically, without further comment or citation, that the "Negro Watermans . . . are believed to be of mixed Negro and White descent."[88] Jacobus and Waterman published this third volume in a landmark year for civil rights (1954), when the Supreme Court aspired to desegregate public education in *Brown v. Board of Education*. Jacobus turned sixty-seven that year, and Waterman was nearly eighty years old. Unusually for older whites in the 1950s, the authors acknowledged the multiple races and ethnicities, and the histories of enslavement and immigration, contained in one English-sounding American surname. The authors went one further in respecting the name-changing decision from Wasserman to Waterman. Such respect was unusual among genealogists, since fluidity in naming greatly complicated their labors.

The expansion of African American history as a scholarly field, studied keenly even in predominantly white universities, compelled additional white genealogists to start working with genealogists of color and on nonwhite history projects.[89] Jean Stephenson, for example, was born in Texas around 1892, in a place and time decidedly in Jim Crow's grasp.[90] After moving to Washington in her twenties and earning a doctorate in law, she became a major figure in professionalized genealogy, particularly in the DAR's internal reforms of its admissions procedures toward more rigorous documentation and improved historical accuracy.[91] The summer of 1965 found Stephenson in the National Archives, giving encouragement to a bewildered Alex Haley as he embarked on researching the project that would later become *Roots*. She also connected him to Ball-Jones in Pittsburgh. Without naming Stephenson publicly, he later made numerous references to the well-dressed white woman from the DAR who had aided him in the archive.[92]

White genealogists' discussions of Black genealogy, and media interest in the topic, increased in years to come. "The black people of our country have become actively and proudly interested in their history. . . . Family history should be an integral part of this new interest," remarked a white archivist from the National Archives in 1971. He chided Washington's National Genealogical Society (NGS) for its lack of interest in "offering membership to minority peoples" at such a late date, despite its location in a city that was nearly three-quarters Black (71.1 percent) in 1970.[93] In the same year of 1971, the first instructional articles on "Black Genealogy" appeared in professional genealogy journals, in which authors remarked on the field's particular difficulties of documentation.[94] During the next spring, the *Wall Street Journal* began to take notice of African American genealogy. Reporter Peggy J. Murrell interviewed numerous Black studies and Black history experts of the time, within and outside university walls.[95]

Warts-and-All Approaches to Ancestry in the 1970s

Americans' growing affection for warts-and-all genealogy research in the 1960s and afterward—in rejection of the filtering practices characteristic of earlier times—also prepared the ground for *Roots*. Historically expansive Mormon attitudes toward the dead anticipated the inclusive forms of genealogy that other Americans now embraced. "You are not looking for kings and heroes, but just to identify your own ancestors. As they must accept their descendants, so we must accept them," stated Elizabeth L. Nichols in 1972 in a Mormon instruction manual.[96] A man from the church's Genealogical Society (formerly the GSU), interviewed anonymously in the early 1980s, elucidated this perspective from the standpoint of World War II and the Cold War, in an increasingly militarized America. "It used to be that we wouldn't do [temple] work for suicides or murderers, but then we thought, what about guys who went to war and shed innocent blood? They had to obey the law of the land.... So now we just ... provide the vicarious ordinances for everybody, and leave it to the Lord to decide if there will be forgiveness."[97] In the United States at large, no matter how humble, poor, enslaved, or foreign forebears had been, they deserved recognition from the descendant because relations between ancestor and descendant felt indelible.[98] Few forebears seemed unworthy of naming and describing publicly.

Praise for forebears even included scandalous ones. An Indiana man, for example, lovingly subtitled his family genealogy *Grandpas, In-laws, and Outlaws* (1976).[99] People who located proverbial horse thieves among their forebears no longer cloaked those horse thieves in shame and silence but joked about them as people would do with any other embarrassing relative whom they planned to retain as kin. Harold Felty of the Illinois State Genealogical Society remarked to a *Newsweek* reporter in 1976, "It's a bit of a status symbol to have a verified horse thief in the family."[100] The next year, a Jewish genealogist from Bothell, Washington, defended her enduring interest in rabbinical genealogy on the grounds that this supposedly elitist pursuit derived its main purpose from studying all Jewry. She, too, invoked horse thief heritage. "If the royal and rabbinic lines are the only ones written and recorded that carry one back past the Middle Ages, then naturally we hope to connect with some of those because it means we have DISCOVERED SOME ANCESTORS. If there were compiled genealogies of horse thieves spanning those centuries, we would search those too, looking for our people," wrote Judith Allison Walters.[101]

There were many reasons for embracing characteristics in a forebear that in earlier times seemed unworthy of ownership or public airing. The reasons include the previously mentioned rise of "history from the bottom up," especially as Americans outside the academy experienced that transition. A second reason for the emergence of "warts and all" genealogy research in the United States has to do with the flurry of literary activity, cultural productions, and scholarship known as the "ethnic revival." The ethnic revival included roots travel, as memoirists and other authors directly connected histories of diasporic populations in the United States to histories of the old country. Examples are the scholar Richard Gambino's *Blood of My Blood: The Problem of the Italian Americans* (1974) and the journalist Michael J. Arlen's

Passage to Ararat (1975), "a subjective account of a journey back to his Arme-nian forebears."[102] A third reason is Americans' predilection for the public discussion of the self. More than ever, knowledge of ancestry brought within reach the self-knowledge that seemed basic to the descendant's psychological well-being, especially when the descendant publicly announced it.[103] I will explore in subsequent chapters the intensifying genetic consciousness and commercial activity that heightened these emotional benefits for the descen-dant, of knowing more about their forebears, as well as the reverse, mutually reinforcing phenomenon in which genealogy's emotional benefits became a major selling point for businesspeople.

Another characteristic to treasure in one's ancestor was foreignness. As lo-cating progenitors in the old country became ever-more feasible, that knowl-edge became ever-more desirable to Americans. In one sense, roots travel to western Europe after 1945 did not represent much historical change. Ameri-cans had been making pilgrimages to their ancestral Britain since colonial times. Recall that Benjamin Franklin opened his autobiography with his own family-history sojourn to England in 1758, with his son and a few slaves ac-companying him.[104] Recall Ralph Waldo Emerson's sense of shared ethnicity when traveling to England. Remember the American genealogy fetishists that Alexis de Tocqueville or his friends encountered in France sometime before 1840. But the beginnings of commercial air travel in the late 1940s brought decided increases in international genealogy tourism, as did airline deregulation in 1978. In 1960, the third edition of Gilbert Doane's advice book, *Searching for Your Ancestors*, added a chapter titled "Getting Ready to Cross the Atlantic." It was retitled "Bridging the Seas" in the two subsequent editions of 1974 and 1980, to include sojourns beyond western Europe.[105] American roots travelers to Europe included Alex Haley in 1966, in search of information on his Irish forebears.[106] Diasporic genealogy tourism started ap-pearing on government agendas in destination countries. By 1977, the Irish government's Genealogical Office was "scheduled to expand owing to soar-ing world-wide requests," amounting to ten thousand callers and "several thousand letters" annually.[107]

The aspiration to research ancestors overseas now spread among Ameri-cans who did not descend from Britons. American Jews gazed across the Cold War's iron curtain at ancestral ground in Eastern Bloc countries and the Soviet Union. By the 1980s, a few stubborn souls reached such countries to try to reconstruct information on forebears, as Daniel Rottenberg did in eastern Czechoslovakia in 1975.[108] And African Americans contemplated newly drawn West African nations. In 1960, only three years after Ghanaian independence (1957), Pauli Murray was already encountering "Negro visitors from the United States" in Ghana who had the "romantic notion of 'coming back to Mother Africa to see my people.'"[109] Haley famously made two sojourns to Gambia in March and May 1967, as he sought more proof about Kunta Kinte, who had been kidnapped into overseas slavery two centuries beforehand.[110] Having been a British colony, Gambia gained independence in 1965, just two years before Haley's trips.[111]

The idea of American interest in African roots did not, of course, originate with Haley. His endeavors followed more than a century of American Black nationalists' rhetorical outreach to other Black populations around the world, especially to Africans, as well as Garveyite Black nationalists' attempts in the 1920s to develop businesses in Liberia. The antihero of Haley's first book, *The Autobiography of Malcolm X* (1965), most clearly articulated Black nationalism's re-invigoration, and fostering of kinship among Blacks internationally, in the 1960s. For sound reasons, journalists have called for both Malcolm X and his widow Betty Shabazz, a longtime friend of Haley, to receive more credit for inspiring Haley's later African odysseys than they have.[112] Haley did not mention personally going to Africa until after Malcolm died in February 1965. Six months earlier, upon completing the *Autobiography of Malcolm X*, Haley garnered an advance and a book contract from Doubleday for his second project, which he planned as a family history centered largely on Tennessee. Although Haley mentioned a "Mandingo" man, name unknown, among his distant forebears, in January 1965 when writing to his agent, he did not speak of actively researching this man until the summer and fall of 1965.[113] "[By] now," he wrote in October, referring to his second project, "deep into the book's writing, I know that to make it full-circle I will go to Africa's one-time slave coast and return here, symbolically, by ship."[114] Ultimately, in contrast to Murray's *Proud Shoes*, Haley in *Roots* broke new ground in aspiring to track his slave ancestry back across the Atlantic. His innovation in this area lay in explicitly connecting international travel to African American genealogy practices.

Conclusion

Alex Haley's own strenuous publicizing of his descent from Kunta Kinte fell on ears that had long been poised to hear his messages. Starting in 1972, Haley announced his revelations in speeches and in media dispatches around the country. One venue was the National Archives' two-day conference in 1973 on "Federal Archives as Sources for Research on Afro-Americans."[115] The next summer, *U.S. News and World Report* proclaimed, in tune with the ongoing ethnic revival, the American Indian Movement's fame on television, and the flourishing of Black history, "Increasing numbers of blacks, Indians, and children and grandchildren of immigrants—no longer content to submerge themselves in the 'melting pot' of American society—are flocking to libraries to learn more about their own family heritage."[116] Well before the *Roots* telecast, in other words, a widely read national news magazine informed readers that nearly everyone was performing genealogy. Months later, in December 1974, ABC-TV made an unprecedented move. "No network ever had bought the advance rights to an unpublished book," marveled a reporter.[117] Haley submitted his completed book manuscript to Doubleday in late 1975, months after he began meeting with screenwriters and producers about the television show during the previous spring. This timing explains why the *Roots* television series appeared only four months after his book.[118] To commit such resources to an unfinished work carries considerable risk. But media executives embraced these risks when they signed Haley's contract in 1974 because Haley's talks and articles—and his previous successful work on Malcolm X—convinced them of the project's future popularity.

Since the mid-1960s, Haley had sought, on multiple continents, proof of his descent from Kunta Kinte and his enslaved American descendants. Haley's genealogical and historical research occurred on ground that others had long been preparing. External factors matter, to this racial, religious, and ethnic diversification among genealogists—including Haley—that occurred before *Roots*. These developments include information's proliferation in libraries; the spread of "history from the bottom up," on and off campus; dropping costs and increasing speed and convenience of travel; and the Church of Jesus Christ of Latter-day Saints' commitments, as an institution, to the amassing and dissemination of genealogical data without cost to the user because of the church's persistent linking of genealogy with worship. External developments after 1945 also include civil rights reforms and Black nationalism's revival; decolonization in Africa, Asia, the Pacific, and the Caribbean; and intertwined Holocaust consciousness and support for Israel among American Jews in the 1960s and afterwards. But closer examination of these developments reveals masses of genealogists, historians, librarians, scholars, and others making deliberate decisions. These Americans maximized these outside developments' potential advancement of their knowledge. Genealogists enabled and prolonged some of these developments, notably travel and long-distance research that some performed without going far from home and that compelled others, including Haley, to board airplanes. The next chapter traces *Roots'* afterlives and ensuing continuities as well as transformations in genealogists' practices.

CHAPTER FIVE

Diversification and Discontentment
Roots (1976–1977) and Its Afterlives

Roots accelerated transformations within genealogy practice and American society at large. But in the long run, *Roots* also signified the persistence of genealogy practices that reinforced social norms pertaining to race, class, religion, gender, and documentation. A series of events in a single year, 1977, including the broadcasting of the *Roots* show that January, illustrates the diversification among genealogists and their practices that *Roots* accelerated. Published at the end of September 1976, *Roots* topped the *New York Times* bestseller list for over five months, starting in November. It sold over 1.5 million hardcover copies within eighteen months and more than 4 million paperback copies by 1994.[1] The television series *Roots* aired four months after the book's publication. Catching media executives by surprise, an American audience of unprecedented size, 130 million people, watched the last of the eight consecutive nightly episodes on the ABC network on January 30, 1977.[2] Two days later, on Tuesday, February 1, a photographer captured a jubilant autograph seeker with her copy of *Roots*, as she stood with Alex Haley. The line behind her at the Broadway department store at the new Fox Hills Mall in Culver City, California, measured a mile and a half long.

Roots immediately expanded genealogy activity among Americans of all sorts. Major repositories such as the National Archives saw the numbers of patrons, and patrons' phone calls, jump dramatically and remain much higher than previous levels. On one Saturday shortly after the *Roots* show aired, patrons waited in line for four hours for genealogy services at the National Archives in Washington. Over the next two years, the Archives measured a 70 percent increase in genealogy research requests.[3] In Salt Lake City, the Latter-day Saints church facilities served twice as many patrons in the first half of 1977 as during the bicentennial summer of 1976.[4] Smaller repositories also experienced a surge in interest in genealogy. Phebe R. Jacobsen, an African American librarian and archivist at the Maryland Hall of Records, a state repository, had aided Alex Haley's research on slaves in 1968. Still at her post when *Roots* appeared, she published an account of genealogy patron increases and transformed workplace procedures titled "The World Turned Upside Down."[5]

Alex Haley with autograph seekers with their copies of *Roots*,
Culver City, California, February 1, 1977. The line was a mile
and a half long. Bettman via Getty Images.

Four months after the *Roots* television broadcast, in May 1977, the archivist James Dent (Jimmy) Walker, the five women, and the one other man who founded the Afro-American Historical and Genealogical Society (AAHGS) in Washington likely had *Roots* on their minds. The AAHGS's formation made the United States the first country to sport a society dedicated to Black-diaspora genealogy.[6] The AAHGS's second meeting, in October, attracted more than seventy people. It matters even more to history because its large turnout validated the founding meeting and boded well for the organization's endurance.[7] The founders sought to book Alex Haley for the group's first banquet, planned for early 1979, because "you brought so many of us together under your inspiration and leadership."[8] Institutions dedicated to African American genealogy continued to form, such as the AAHGS's periodical, which launched in 1980. By 1993, the AAHGS claimed chapters in twenty-two cities and towns around the country, including one in Chicago (1989). The aftermath of *Roots* also witnessed the birth of freestanding local organizations and periodicals that were independent of the AAGHS but shared its focus on Black genealogy, such as the Afro-American Historical and Genealogical Society of Chicago (1979).[9]

In addition to the airing of *Roots* and the formation of the AAHGS, the year 1977 saw publication of the first full-length instruction book on African American genealogy, *Black Genealogy*, by Charles L. Blockson (assisted by Ron Fry). Most genealogy instruction books were previously published in limited runs, often privately or in other nonprofit arrangements such as with university presses. Exceptions that had interested commercial publishers, namely Gilbert Doane's first edition of *Searching for Your Ancestors* (1937), featured one-size-fits-most approaches that fit white Anglo-American Protestants the best. But in the flush of excitement in the publishing business over *Roots'* unanticipated success, Blockson convinced a commercial publisher, Prentice-Hall, to publish *Black Genealogy*. The later months of 1977 witnessed yet another turning point in the history of race and genealogy in the United States. Making headlines in October, the Daughters of the American Revolution at last admitted an African American after eight decades of maintaining a stated ban on "colored" members. The new member, Karen Batchelor Farmer, was a twenty-six-year-old, college-educated housewife and mother from Detroit.[10]

The year 1977 saw similar, unprecedented institution-building in American Jewish genealogy, including the first-ever U.S. society dedicated to it and advice publications that reached broader audiences. Early in 1977, a few men in New York founded the genealogy periodical *Toledot*. They included Arthur Kurzweil, who simultaneously oversaw a recurring newspaper feature, "Finding Jewish Roots," for *New York Jewish Week*.[11] That October, the six men who met in the New Jersey suburbs to organize the first Jewish Genealogical Society (JGS) cited *Roots* as an inspiration.[12] The author Dan Rottenberg was among them. Within that same year, he published his genealogy instruction book for Jews, *Finding Our Fathers*, with the trade publisher Random House. The Jewish Genealogical Society of 1977 inspired numerous additional Jewish Genealogical Societies to form in American cities and towns—forty groups by 1992. The city of Las Vegas boasted two.[13] Along with the ubiquitous Rabbi Malcolm Stern, Gary Mokotoff of the journal *Avotaynu*, successor in 1985 to *Toledot*, found it necessary to develop a federated Association of Jewish Genealogical Societies (1987). Putting together meetings had become increasingly complex because so many local groups had formed.[14] Organizations and meetings devoted to Jewish genealogy emerged elsewhere in the world, such as in Israel, Britain, and Australia.

Roots' Afterlives: Post-1977 Transformations in Genealogy Practice

The diversification during the year 1977 continued in the years and decades following *Roots*. Much anecdotal evidence suggests that reading or watching *Roots* inspired genealogy activity and family reunions in subsequent years among people who were not African American as well as among people who were. For example, Stanley H. Balducci of Mechanicsville, Virginia, composed a fan letter to Alex Haley in which he credited both the book and the series for "inspiring me . . . to research my own ancestry," which he labeled as "Virginia and Maryland ancestry on my mother's side, and Italian ancestry on my father's side." Balducci's efforts "did fill a certain void in my life: to search for one's identity and meaning in today's world."[15] A majority of genealogy patrons (58.6 percent of a sample of more than four thousand) at Chicago's Newberry Library in 1981 reported having begun their research in, or since, 1977. The survey's authors attributed this finding more to *Roots*, in which genealogy research was itself a theme, than to the recent bicentennial celebrations in 1976.[16]

Publications and local groups emerged among other ethnic and religious minorities in the mid-and late 1970s, and these too were unprecedented. Irish Catholics and Polish Americans created new genealogy institutions such as Chicago's Irish Ancestry Workshop (1975). "Like to Sleuth?" quipped founder Bea Brennan McGuire, whose workshop's acronym (CIA) matched the Central Intelligence Agency's; as was common among genealogists, McGuire compared genealogy research to detective work.[17] Irish Americans also published primary documents of interest to genealogists and demographers, such as nineteenth-century "Missing Friends" ads that had first appeared in the Irish American newspaper the *Boston Pilot*. The New England Historic Genealogical Society reprinted these ads en masse to aid the reconstruction of Irish Catholic lineages, starting in the 1980s.[18] The Polish Genealogical Society's founding and proliferation occurred soon after the *Roots* broadcast, with the group's launch in Chicago in August 1978. The next year, the group reported membership in thirty-four states, including Connecticut and Houston, Texas, by 1984.[19] During these same years, genealogy advice aimed at additional ethnic and racial minorities began appearing. Jessie Carney Smith's guide to *Ethnic Genealogy* (1983) resulted from a 1979 symposium on the subject at Fisk University in Nashville, aimed at Native American, Asian American, and Hispanic populations as well as at African Americans.[20]

Within a broader context in which Americans paid increasing attention to Native American history, Indigenous genealogists turned out new advice literature and other publications in the years following *Roots*. Widely read histories appeared in the 1960s and 1970s, such as Dee Brown's *Bury My Heart at Wounded Knee* (1970) and Vine Deloria Jr.'s *Custer Died for Your Sins* (1969), that expanded awareness of atrocities that Native Americans had experienced among non-Indians. The American Indian Movement's protests in 1973 and afterward were widely televised. Even more significantly for historians and genealogists, the National Archives in Washington hosted a grand "Conference on Research in the History of Indian-White Relations" in June 1972. Presenters spoke on Indigenous family history, among other topics.[21] With research on Indigenous people gaining more attention and resources, the Stanford English professor N. Scott Momaday (Kiowa) had just published his memoir *The Names* (1976), in which he achieved "his realization of himself in his family's history," when *Roots* appeared. When a white reporter interviewed him, Momaday briefly sketched Native American genealogy practices, affirming the importance of oral histories obtained from women: "It is a matter of going to the old people who remember things. . . . You learn of things through family tradition. Generally speaking, the Indian has a very good sense of the oral tradition. The older folk understand they are the repositories of these stories and feel an obligation to pass them on."[22]

But Native Americans, and Hispanics and Latinx people, did not engage in institution-building to the same extent as African Americans and American Jews, in part because of the unusually segmented nature of Indigenous and Hispanic genealogy studies. Compilers of resources for Native Americans sometimes did not know about each other's endeavors, as theirs was an especially decentralized field. Larry Sullivan Watson (1941–2016), editor of the *Journal of American Indian Family Research* (1980–93), quoted an unnamed "well informed person" to the effect that "no one can be an expert in Indian genealogical research.'"[23] He explained, "It is very difficult for a single individual to be familiar with the records that are available for an individual tribe, let alone all the different tribes that are recognized as tribal entities as well as those who have now lost their identity or have not been recognized by the federal government or a state."[24] Watson's Oklahoma-based periodical, which focused most on the "Five Civilized Tribes" and on Oklahoma history, did not appear in contemporary bibliographies on Native genealogy.[25] In Washington State, Cecilia Svinth Carpenter (Niqually) published her pioneering 1984 instruction book *How to Research American Indian Blood Lines* as a typescript with a spiral binding. A revised edition appeared three years later. Watson did know about Carpenter's book, at least its later edition.[26]

The years following *Roots* witnessed unprecedented institution-building among Hispanic and Latinx genealogists, as happened among other American genealogists who focused on non-European ancestry. By 1979, local organizations in Texas, including the Tejano Genealogical Society of Austin (1977), were coming together in the statewide Annual Hispanic Genealogical and Historical Conference.[27] But Hispanic and Latinx genealogy, as a field, remained diffuse, divided by populations' provenance and by color politics.

The "Hispanic" or Latinx designation encompassed those Americans of Mexican, Spanish-speaking Caribbean, and other Latin American descent. The term referred alike to recent immigrants and also to those whose forebears were present in Texas, Puerto Rico, New Mexico, Alta California, and elsewhere before the U.S. conquest of those areas in the nineteenth century. The terms "Hispanic" and Latinx referred to users of a variety of languages: Spanish, English, and Indigenous languages from Mexico, from historically Spanish islands in the Caribbean, and from Central and South America. "Hispanic" and "Latinx" also encompassed a range of colors and racial identities, ranging from European to Indian to Black to mixed-race, that Anglos did not fail to notice.[28] Writing in 1902, a California woman wished to recruit white women descended from Spaniards into the DAR, to commemorate Spain's assistance to American independence in the eighteenth century.[29]

For much of the twentieth century, those Latinx authors who wrote in English presumed interest in European, Christian forebears. The Catholic priest Angélico Chávez's compendium *Origins of New Mexico Families* (1954), reprinted in 1992, is the earliest example I found of an English-language genealogy publication by a Latinx author.[30] New Mexico generally constitutes an outlier, in Latin American history. Indigenous and Spanish-Mexican cultures persisted there long after U.S. takeover in 1848, and Spanish-Mexican families intermarried with Anglo newcomers more than they did in other places.[31] Chávez's endeavor of 1954 did not inspire subsequent works on Hispanic or Latinx genealogy in the United States. His surroundings help explain why, as documenting Spanish-Mexican forebears may have been more difficult outside New Mexico.

Illustrating the earliness of Spanish colonization of North America, Chávez (1910–96) began his list of Spanish surnames in 1598—nine years before Englishmen founded Jamestown, England's first surviving North American colony, and twenty-two years before the *Mayflower* sailed. As a Catholic priest, Chávez had clear religious reasons for fervently praising the Spanish conquest and Christianization of North America. But the families he profiled also prized Spanish descent and ethnicity per se. In a 1954 statement that appeared unchanged in the 1992 reprint, he assured the reader of the "general preponderance of Spanish blood" among New Mexico's early colonizers. "Some initial Aztec admixture, which has to be mentioned here for having already appeared in print, was admitted by individuals in some cases, but often as not was cast as a false aspersion on a par with immorality or a lack of culture."[32] In the 1940s and 1950s, when Chávez undertook his research, rumors of mestizo or partial Indian ancestry resembled a slur against a family's reputation. Spanishness embodied a racial characteristic as well as a religious one. As late as 1984, one Anglo genealogist's how-to instructions for tracing "Hispanic" descent in the United States specified travel to Spain, and he focused nearly exclusively on archives in Spain. Without saying so, he presumed that his audience would be interested mostly in tracing European ancestry.[33] Interest in mestizo (white-Indian) ancestry, or Indigenous ancestry, or African ancestry, had not yet permeated the field of Latinx and Hispanic genealogy in the United States in the 1970s and 1980s—at least not in its formal institutions or English-language publications.

Genealogy Professionals and Controversies Surrounding *Roots*

In the years surrounding *Roots*, some genealogists, historians, archivists, and librarians from underrepresented communities shared professionalism's ethos. The Black librarian Roland C. Barksdale-Hall, for example, objected to the author Nora Louis Hicks's reliance on lightly sourced oral histories. A retired Black schoolteacher in the New York area, Hicks published multiple family genealogies, beginning with *Slave Girl Reba and Her Descendants in America* in 1974. She drew on interviews with her kin to assert that her forebear Reba, who had been of mixed "African" and French descent, had been captured in Madagascar and brought enslaved to South Carolina in 1828 at age thirteen. Writing in retrospect, Barksdale-Hall commended Hicks for "compassionately [addressing] miscegenation, race relations, family solidarity, and their fruits" during slavery in 1974, before *Roots* further popularized discussion of those subjects. But to reconstitute Hicks's research on Reba, he complained, one would personally have to meet with Hicks. "It should not be like this. I cannot overly emphasize the point: our research should be repeatable and our publications should contain footnotes and/or a list of sources of materials and documentation," Barksdale-Hall told readers of the AAHGS's journal.[34] He shared professionalized genealogy's commitment to scholarly transparency, with research that others could inspect and follow through the author's use of full citations. He and others also sought firmly documented truths derived from original documents, preferably textual.

Accepting oral evidence to some degree, however, was necessary for genealogy's diversification. African Americans, in particular, used non-textual evidence to research forebears who had gone without educations, leisure time, and the likelihood of generating writings, or being mentioned in records, such as censuses or probate records, that future generations might access. In 1972, the historian and genealogist Elizabeth Clark-Lewis interviewed a great-aunt and great-uncle about their shared family history. Five years later, she published carefully documented archival findings that reconfirmed her oral-history findings on enslaved forebears dating back to 1820s Virginia. One of the first African Americans and one of the few oral historians to publish in the National Genealogical Society's *Quarterly*, she credited her relatives' "testimony" for leading her to the documents.[35] Clark-Lewis was a cofounder of the AAHGS in 1977, and she served as a longtime vice president of that group. Like some other genealogy professionals, notably Rabbi Malcolm Stern, Clark-Lewis went on to publish as a historian. In 1994, she published *Living In, Living Out*, a pioneering history of Black women who worked as domestic servants.[36]

Like African Americans, some Native Americans adapted professionalism while adopting it. Indigenous people had long been interspersing document-based, patrilineal, and racialized methods that white Americans had imposed on their communities with Indigenous practices of orally recounted family histories, often traced through mothers. After Larry Sullivan Watson launched the *Journal of American Indian Family Research* in Lawton, Oklahoma, in 1980, he continuously stressed the importance of written evidence and the use of original documents, arguing strenuously for the feasibility and necessity of such studies of Native Americans. His frequent instructions ("Arrow Tips") in research methods in textual sources, especially in archival repositories, reveal familiarity with historians' research methods and librarianship as taught in academia.[37] "The most important principle to remember in researching an Indian family line is to proceed as if one were working with an Anglo-Saxon or European problem until one can no longer find the individual(s) in the usual records. When the person no longer appears in the census, marriage records, land records, etc., of the area they resided in, then the researcher must start to consult the records of the Indian tribes of the area," Watson advised his readers in 1981.[38] His journal also reprinted myriad documents, including tribal rolls that listed names with blood-quantum fractions next to them. Like Watson's efforts to foster wise uses of textual sources, Cecelia Svinth Carpenter's *How to Research American Indian Blood Lines* also exemplified professionalized genealogy because the need for instruction to reform existing practices was a basic tenet of professionalism.[39]

The scandals surrounding *Roots* that cropped up shortly after the show suggest an especially discomfiting moment for professionals of color. Doubleday steadfastly marketed the book *Roots* as nonfiction in the 1970s and continued to do so forty years later. But uncertainty about the accuracy and even the factuality of Haley's claims dogged the text's promises. Shortly after *Roots*' publication, some scholars took Haley at his word—that he had successfully documented his descent through generations of enslaved people, back to the stolen Kunta Kinte. In a 1978 article, likely drafted some months beforehand, the historian Tamara Hareven argued that *Roots'* power resided in its factual revelations. Without that "final linkage to Africa, [Haley's story of the search itself] would not have electrified the public," she wrote.[40] But others, including genealogy professionals, reviewed *Roots* as a novel.[41] While characterizing *Roots* as fictional resembles an attack on the text, these skeptics shared some ground with the author himself. Repeatedly, Haley defended blending fact with imaginative reconstructions, portraying "faction," the blending of fact and fiction, as a positive good. He described his writing of *Roots* to the *New York Times* as follows: "The beginning is a re-creation, using novelistic techniques, but as it moves forward more is known and it is more factually based."[42]

Compounding the confusion over *Roots'* status as nonfiction, historians, journalists, genealogy professionals, and others publicized the text's inaccuracies, beginning with the historian Willie Lee Rose's critique in the *New York Review of Books* in November 1976.[43] In Haley's narrative, young Kunta Kinte had come of age in the 1700s surrounded by his tight-knit, multigenerational family. In an indelible image, later echoed in Disney's *The Lion King* (1994), proud father Omoro lifted his infant son to the starry African sky. The family lived in the secluded, peaceful village of Juffure, located in what is now Gambia. However, drawing on the work of historians such as Philip Curtin, Willie Lee Rose and, later, the *London Times* revealed eighteenth-century Juffure to have been a busy, slave-trading entrepot with some white residents.[44]

Haley recounted that Kunta Kinte was then kidnapped and sold, transported to Maryland in 1767 on the slave ship *Lord Ligonier*, renamed Toby Waller, and enslaved in Virginia for the rest of his life.[45] But by 1981, the historian Gary B. Mills and the genealogist Elizabeth Shown Mills located the enslaved man Toby Waller in multiple documents that predated 1767, some as early as 1763, meaning that Waller was present in North America years before the *Lord Ligonier* arrived.[46] The Africa specialist Donald Wright publicized earlier findings by the Gambian scholar Bakari Sidibe (1973) that Haley's Gambian informant of 1967 had not been the "griot" Haley had supposed him to be. His answers to Haley's questions had been massaged for the occasion.[47] Other revelations included unattributed copying of others' work. For example, the Black writer Margaret Walker (later Alexander) had published the novel *Jubilee* in 1966, an early rejoinder to Margaret Mitchell's nostalgia for plantation life in her bestselling novel *Gone with the Wind* (1936). Opposition to plantation nostalgia was also a major theme of *Roots*.

Walker and two others, working separately, brought suit against Haley in the spring of 1977 for copyright infringement and plagiarism. Haley settled one of these suits, that the anthropologist and writer Harold Courlander brought, for $650,000, but Walker's own suit failed.[48]

For some, *Roots'* broader truths as a story about the Middle Passage, and about slavery's violations of family ties, transcended these flaws. African Americans outside academia stood by *Roots* because attacks on Haley's texts felt like attacks on the race. Haley had himself marketed his heavily autobiographical project as an autobiography of African Americans generally. In 1973, he portrayed his endeavor not as "the story of a family" but "the saga, of us as a people." To him, Blacks all shared the same "common generic background; . . . every single one of us without exception ancestrally goes back to some one of those villages, belonged to some one of those tribes, was captured in some way, was put on some one of those slave ships, across the same ocean into some succession of plantations up to the Civil War, the emancipation, and ever since then a struggle for freedom."[49] Shortly after the book's publication, the educator Nancy L. Arnez returned the favor when she remarked that *Roots* "helped destroy the chilling ignorance of who we are as a people" and had "given our proud heritage back to us."[50]

However, African Americans in subsequent decades were not unanimous in defending *Roots*. Instead, they divided among themselves over whether the fictional dimensions of *Roots* impeached its veracity. Divisions grew over time. While relations between Alex Haley and Black genealogy professionals were friendly during *Roots'* immediate aftermath, the scandals surrounding *Roots* directly challenged professionalized genealogy's premises: that knowable truths existed in original documents and that inaccuracy was a worst-case scenario.[51] Professionals of color risked particular attacks for standing by *Roots* in the 1980s and 1990s, as gulfs in understanding widened between academia and the public when it came to history, and as popular history became more entertainment-focused.[52] Haley's own work belonged to that bigger picture of polarization. His television dramas such as *Palmerstown, U.S.A.* (1980) and its sequel, *Palmerstown* (1981), grafted tales of interracial friendship and love affairs onto segregated 1930s Tennessee. A *New York Times* critic sniffed of *Palmerstown*, "the producers are now aiming to establish a niche somewhere between 'Little House on the Prairie' and 'The Waltons,'" two other highly sentimentalized, nostalgic entertainments of the era.[53] Consequently, perhaps, the professional genealogists, librarians, archivists, historians, and other scholars who published in the AAHGS's journal eschewed discussion of *Roots* even when Haley died in 1992, and as *Roots'* anniversaries rolled by. The 1973 conference at the National Archives on "Federal Archives as Sources for Research on Afro-Americans" (at which Haley spoke) loomed much larger for the *Journal of the Afro-American Historical and Genealogical Society* (JAAHGS), when recounting the history of Black genealogy, than did *Roots* and Haley's speeches and articles beforehand.[54] However, *Roots* remained a touchstone for AAHGS branches. Haley himself referred to *Roots* as a "saga," but compilers of a finding aid to papers that Chicago's AAHGS chapter maintained in the 1990s, remembered *Roots* onscreen as a "documentary."[55] To some in the United States, *Roots* resembled nonfiction.

Continuities in Genealogy Practices after *Roots*, Regarding Race and Gender

Scholars have presumed that the democratization of genealogy practices, and the undeniable diversification of genealogists that *Roots* accelerated, chased off older, racial, eugenics-inflected traditions in genealogy.[56] Instead, some genealogists in the 1970s, 1980s, and beyond continued to presume that Americanness was inborn and inherited, to stress the history of white people, and to insist on the exclusive use of textual sources—a practice that in itself reinforced race and class-based exclusions. Famous white ancestors deserved particular praise.[57] The years 1976 and 1977 saw an invigoration, not a decline, of research on long-ago white Anglo-American forebears. Why would the celebrations of historical anniversaries—including the three hundred and fiftieth anniversary of the *Mayflower's* arrival, in 1970, and the hoopla-ridden American bicentennial celebrations, in 1976—*not* foster more interest in descent from eminent white forebears from Early America and revolutionary times?[58] The quest for roots was ubiquitous. Besides *Roots*, another book with history themes that was adapted for television in 1976–77—Jack Shepherd's *The Adams Chronicles: Four Generations of Greatness* (1975)—simultaneously promoted interest in genealogy and in one of the nation's elite, founding families.[59]

The largest hereditary organizations, devoted to fostering awareness of colonial and revolutionary history, never stopped growing even after *Roots*. Apart from a blip in 1974–75 when it raised its dues, the almost entirely white National Society, Daughters of the American Revolution, grew nonstop after 1945, and it experienced record-breaking growth in the years following the U.S. Bicentennial.[60] *Roots* went unmentioned and unadvertised in the DAR's magazine during the same months that saw saturation coverage of Haley and *Roots* elsewhere in the press. But by the end of 1976, the DAR allowed use of its library in Washington for a planned retrospective television special on the making of *Roots*. Haley and his assistant George Sims, who was also African American, were filmed doing research there. "This is an example of the intention of the DAR to cooperate as much as possible with the news media," the DAR's president told members. The organization had retained a public-relations firm.[61] While the DAR admitted its first African American member that year of 1977, admission of a second African American did not occur until the mid-1980s, after much scuffling in court. A third Black woman gained admission in 1993, sixteen years after *Roots*.[62]

Race, color, and class politics, as they played out in genealogy practices, did not just show the persistence of white supremacy. Social hierarchies operated among Americans of color and religious minorities as well as against them. African Americans had long been sorting themselves not only by class, education, and color but also by free, literate antecedents versus enslaved ancestors.[63] African Americans continued to do so after *Roots*. The particular difficulties of researching enslaved people were such that David H. Streets published *Slave Genealogy* by 1986, an instruction book specifically for slaves' descendants and anyone else researching the subject.[64] A decade later, Chicagoans founded the International Society of Sons and Daughters of Slave Ancestry (1997), a dedicated hereditary organization. Its purposes included fostering community among those experiencing the particular difficulties of tracking lineages among enslaved people and educating others on the subject.[65]

When African Americans did find records of their forebears in the years surrounding *Roots*, too often, lineal ancestors included white male predators. But there are some exceptions to the pattern of the absent white biological father. For example, the revolutionary soldier in the ancestry of Karen Batchelor Farmer, the first known African American in the DAR, was William Hood, an Irishman who had served in a Pennsylvania militia. Her relatedness to Hood occurred not through his male descendants but through a white woman. Jennie Daisy Hood had married Prince Albert Weaver, who was Black, in Cleveland in 1889, two years after Ohio ended its ban on interracial marriage. The Weavers became Farmer's great-grandparents.[66] But in 1965, Haley reminded readers of the *Tuesday Magazine*, aimed at African Americans in Chicago, that they could "expect to encounter at least one white male ancestor. Almost always, the elders' oral histories include exactly who was this white parent—the owner of the plantation, his sons, an overseer or whoever."[67] *Roots*' storyline included numerous enslaved women who endured sexual coercion from white men. Haley himself made numerous attempts and trips to research his own white ancestry, before and after *Roots*.

Another instance in which new-spirited genealogists and old-fashioned ones enforced social hierarchies among themselves, pertained to gender. History's early twentieth-century professionalization had featured the displacement of women's authority and was profoundly linked to masculinity and had included historians' repudiation of fellowship with genealogists. Later generations of historians, librarians, and other professionals—including some genealogists—continued to represent genealogists as unmanly.[68] A male genealogist in 1972 blamed libraries' refusal at the time to permit interlibrary loans of genealogy materials, and other examples of what he saw as "discrimination" against genealogists, on the presence of a certain kind of woman among them. "The average genealogist of the '70s would like to be spared the image of the little old lady who idolizes her ancestors just as much as the librarians would like to eradicate the image of the bifocaled, bunned, spinster librarian," he complained.[69] He wished for his own field to undergo a more complete masculinization and professionalization, than it had.

As this next example shows, Jews were hardly the only Americans to subject the stereotypical genealogist's excessive attention to detail, emotionally freighted filiopietism, and apparent amateurism to gendered insult. But in one instance, a Jewish historian, the socialist thinker Irving Howe, disparaged genealogists in powerfully gendered terms, to critique social transformations among Jews that he found disturbing. Leftist intellectuals in 1970s America despairingly ascribed the era's tribalism and particularism to the withering of 1960s radicalism. Simultaneously, Howe was bemoaning American Jewish populations' becoming ever more middle-class and suburban.[70] He had previously dismissed other popular entertainments with historical themes. While admitting to nostalgia for the immigrant Jewish past he himself had known, Howe had disparaged *Fiddler on the Roof* shortly after its appearance in 1964, in the pages of the American Jewish Committee's magazine *Commentary*.[71]

In a 1977 commencement address at Queens College, just months after *Roots* attracted its television audiences of unanticipated size, Howe publicly reduced Jewish genealogists' practices to the wishful thinking of "middle-class Jewish ladies." The use of the word "ladies" captured, from his perspective, the superficiality inherent in the era's genealogy boom and predilection for entertainment. The male editors of *Toledot* took offense at Howe's metaphorical "ladies," saying, "We detect, in his choice of the word 'ladies,' a snide air which we resent."[72] But Howe's small-minded "middle-class Jewish ladies" were not just a metaphor to him; he was summarizing conversations with actual people. Howe recalled in his commencement speech that he "suggested to them, not very graciously, that if they were serious they would first try to learn their people's history and then they might see that it hardly mattered whether they came from the Goldbergs of eastern Poland or the Goldbergs of the western Ukraine."[73]

Howe's remarks followed genealogists' criticisms of his book. He had recently published the transformative social-history work *World of Our Fathers* (1976) about Jewish life in eastern Europe, Jews' subsequent immigration, and their working-class life in the early twentieth-century United States. Howe and the editors of *Toledot* considered each other's interests overly narrow. Howe's detractors thought his book excessively reduced European Jewish history to denizens of the shtetl, the country town, and neglected urban Jewry.[74] But with his remark about middle-class ladies and Goldbergs, Howe showed that gendered archetypes could be useful to someone committed to other kinds of social sorting, including historians' continuously setting their approaches apart from those of genealogists.

Bitter Continuities for Indigenous Genealogists following *Roots*

The expanded audiences for family histories of some oppressed groups, as *Roots*' popularity showed, coincided with depressing reminders of continuity for others. Native Americans had ridden a rollercoaster of U.S. government progress and punishments, such as those reforms in the New Deal's Indian Reorganization Act (1934), interspersed with government hostility, such as the 1950s plans for tribes' "termination," when the government refused to share authority with tribal governments over tribal populations. The 1950s also featured numerous instances of government-ordered family separations, with high rates of white families adopting Indigenous children whose parents and kin were still living.[75] Subsequent red-power uprisings compelled the government to turn once again toward acknowledging tribal sovereignty by broadening its acknowledgment process.[76] Starting in 1978, tribes that the government had not previously recognized as tribes, such as during treaty negotiations, hired genealogists to aid them in applying for federal acknowledgment—now the principal means of obtaining federal benefits and compensation. Genealogists Ruellen (Rudi) Ottery (b. 1927) and Eva Butler of Connecticut found employment with the Brotherton tribe, in its quest for compensation for New York lands promised in a treaty of 1838.[77] Yet the documentation necessary for federal acknowledgment processes depended on documented descent of tribal belonging. And information on tribal members of old, including their names, usually derived from bias-and error-ridden instances of information collecting—namely, the old allotment rolls that government and tribal officials had compiled following the Dawes Severalty Act (1887).[78]

Ironically, such rolls proved useful to some Indigenous genealogists and historians. As the anthropologist Kim TallBear has written, "Where the federal policy project of the nineteenth century was to *de*tribalize, what has happened in effect is a *re*articulated tribalization of Native Americans in blood fractions and through bloodlines" in recent times.[79] For example, George Morrison Bell (b. 1901), a retired superintendent of buildings and grounds in the Claremore, Oklahoma, schools, included tribal roll numbers and blood quanta for all possible kin in his family genealogy of 1972, including those of his wife, himself, and their children. He listed himself as one-quarter Cherokee and his wife and fellow researcher, Dana Iva Bluejacket Bell (b. 1904), as nine-thirty-seconds Cherokee and also of Shawnee descent.[80] Note that the Bell family reported having a large percentage of white ancestry: three quarters, in George's case. To have modern-day tribal identity depend on the old allotment processes illustrated racial hierarchies that continued to operate among Indigenous people, especially against Native people who also possessed African descent and African Americans who descended from slaves that tribespeople had owned. These convictions have had real consequences, namely racial exclusion from tribal membership.[81]

Genealogy's Own Methods as Illustrating Continuities after *Roots*

The history of American genealogists after 1977 contains many other examples of continuities in which genealogists and others who served them reinforced race, gender, and class hierarchies. But internal features of genealogists' practices reinforced social exclusiveness even more effectively. Genealogists' favoring of textual source material reinforced all the social advantages built into historical figures' ability to leave writings behind when they died or to warrant mentions in others' records. And genealogists' and others' prizing of blood ties (shared biological substance) and marriages as proof of relatedness did even more to reflect social exclusivities elsewhere in American life. Births, marriages, and deaths among the poor, the enslaved, free people of color, Indigenous people, religious minorities, those who did not use English, and recent newcomers to America often eluded documentation.

For genealogy professionals, historical texts lay closer to truth for having been written, even if they sometimes contained false or misleading information. Archives containing written evidence, by and large, did not seem to contain outright biases or exclusions in the eyes of genealogists, to the extent that archives could for historians. The historian Glenda Gilmore remarked in 1996, "The made-up quality of white southern accounts in archives had to be my starting point" when writing *Gender and Jim Crow*. She found especially valuable records pertaining to African American women's clubs in a closet at Livingstone College, a historically Black college in Salisbury, North Carolina. Other records seemed untouched since their placement in a century-old bookcase, far from the hushed, gilded special-collections sanctums at historically white universities and state historical societies.[82] In contrast to historians who cultivated skepticism of textual sources, given all the prejudices built into records' preservation or loss, genealogy professionals maintained their trust in printed source material. They continued to view non-textual evidence with suspicion, especially when researchers gathered such evidence in retrospect.[83] Affirmations like Elizabeth Clark-Lewis's, defending limited retrospective uses of oral evidence, remained rare in genealogy periodicals—including in the *Journal of the Afro-American Historical and Genealogical Society*, with its high percentages of Black authors.

Following *Roots*, as before *Roots*, genealogists of all sorts continued struggling with the reality that the socially advantaged people of history were better documented than the disadvantaged. It was difficult to find the names of poor transients in source material, especially in the land and probate records that genealogists considered indispensable. "[Records] related to the descent of real estate form the backbone of all genealogy," baldly stated the American Society of Genealogists' 1960 volume, which its authors and editors intended as a last word on professionalism.[84] As Daniel Rottenberg had noted, non-Christian forebears did not appear in church registers of marriages and baptisms that otherwise served as valuable sources because of vacuums elsewhere in colonial life. Spanish and French colonies in North America boasted comprehensive notarial records amassed under the Catholic Church's leadership, but in Spanish, French, and English colonies alike, government-funded collection and maintenance of vital records was absent.[85]

As a result of all these internal features of genealogy practices that reinforced social exclusions, after 1977 as well as beforehand, writings from genealogy societies, professional genealogists, and hereditary organizations alike retained a preoccupation with forebears who had been propertied white colonists in British North America, or Britons, or nobility—groups that were especially well-documented. In 1965, visitors to the New England Historic Genealogical Society's library in Boston, as a group, seemed most interested in aristocratic provenance: "Among those questions most frequently asked . . . are those pertaining to heraldry and the right to a coat-of-arms, perhaps one used by a grandfather, or some other relative."[86] Apart from heraldry, interest continued in researching white English speakers more generally. In the 1980s, librarians widely agreed that *Roots* had transformed the demographic makeup and priorities of genealogist patrons as well as swelling their numbers. Yet the Newberry Library survey of four thousand such patrons from 1981 nonetheless suggested relatively little interest in "programs on ethnic, racial, or religious groups." This sample showed much more interest in traditional program topics, such as particular source materials like probate records, or specific geographical areas like New England.[87]

Leading periodicals published relatively few items on Black and Jewish forms of genealogy or pertaining to other ethnic minorities and people of color. Such periodicals as the *New England Historical and Genealogical Register* were located in, and most focused on, historically homogeneous areas. The *Register* and professional genealogy's redoubt, *The American Genealogist* (originating in Connecticut and later headquartered in Iowa), both favored early New England. It had been a less diverse region, with fewer Catholics, Jews, and non-English speakers than in colonial New York and Pennsylvania, and fewer enslaved people than the southern colonies had. The *Genealogical Helper* of Logan, Utah, aimed at do-it-yourselfers, boasted a paid circulation of 29,414 by 1977, which swamped the *New England Historical and Genealogical Register*'s 4,194 in 1975.[88] Circulating information on white, Protestant populations all over the United States, with the occasional disquisition on Italian or central European research, the *Genealogical Helper* operated from a mostly white, Mormon context and assumed a mostly western European-descended readership.[89]

The forebears of African Americans remained distinctively difficult to document. As previously noted, federal censuses did not list enslaved people as named individuals. The *Journal of the Afro-American Historical and Genealogical Society* stressed assessments of particular bodies of evidence, such as Confederate tax assessments or mortuary records—for their usefulness to Black genealogists. Such source studies vastly outnumbered studies of particular lineages.[90] The reverse was true in white-dominated genealogy journals of the same period, whose featured articles were often tissues of surnames arranged in numbered generations.[91] White Anglo-Americans who had set the tone for genealogy practices in the United States could often trace paternal lines back into early colonial history, and sometimes further back into sixteenth-century England. But among African Americans, it was unusual to be able to document one's ancestry back to the 1790s, the time of the first federal census.[92] The archivist Jimmy Walker, a principal founder of the AAHGS in 1977, could only map his ancestry back to the 1850s. African Americans dubbed the 1870 federal census, the first one undertaken after slavery was outlawed, "the brick wall" because of the relative difficulty of documenting earlier forebears.[93]

Overseas roots travel was decidedly less affordable to African Americans than to others, and therefore infrequent. A financial angel, *Reader's Digest* co-owner Lila Bell Wallace, had underwritten Alex Haley's sojourns to Ireland, London, and Gambia in the 1960s at considerable expense.[94] Those who lacked friendly philanthropists in their lives had less access to travel. The AAHGS's journal, launched in 1980, did not publish an account of overseas tourism until 1986, when Alice Suggs of Washington traveled to Ireland to research her white ancestry.[95] The next year featured the journal's first account of roots travel to Africa. Gwendolyn Hackley Austin of Maryland claimed an enslaved woman brought from Guinea around 1793 as her own great-great-great-great grandmother. She journeyed to Senegal in an unsuccessful effort to discern the original name of this "African Lady." But by the time Austin returned home, she was able to identify the tribe and the location in Senegal where her own otherwise mysterious family custom, "slipping up behind someone on his birthday and greasing his nose," prevailed.[96]

Roots Itself as a Reason for Continuities in Genealogy's History

Roots itself and its reception provide additional examples of persisting racial and other hierarchies in Americans' social and private lives. Haley wrote searing, melodramatically presented tales of wrongs committed against slaves and free Blacks.[97] He defied genealogists' expectations, including his own initial doubts, when he seemed able to document his descent from Kunta Kinte in Africa.[98] Haley's vivid life stories of enslaved people, such as Kunta Kinte's daughter Kizzy and her entrepreneurial son Chicken George, helps explain why many who were not African American, or in the United States, found inspiration in *Roots*' characters for their own toils and freedom struggles, from Ireland in the time of the Troubles, to Taiwan, to apartheid-bound South Africa.[99] *Roots* did break new ground in the United States in invigorating less traditional genealogy practices and in educating others who had not known about such practices. Only 10 percent of the 130 million Americans who viewed the final episode, on January 30, 1977, identified as Black, a lower proportion than African Americans' 12 percent share of the U.S. population at the time. The slight underrepresentation of African Americans among *Roots* viewers may result from Blacks' lower rates of access to televisions and to the leisure time that would allow them to watch the lengthy show over eight consecutive nights. But the percentage also illustrates the show's appeal to those who were not Black.[100]

Roots otherwise lent itself to remarkable degrees of appropriation by those who were not Black because Haley, and many in his audience, explicitly linked genealogy findings to individual self-esteem.[101] He promoted an anodyne, easily adaptable understanding of genealogy's importance to the descendant's emotional well-being. In May 1977, only months after *Roots* appeared on television, he asserted in *Reader's Digest* that "in all of us, there is a hunger, bone-marrow deep, to know our heritage—to know who we are and where we have come from. Without this enriching knowledge, there is a hollow yearning. No matter what our entertainments in life, there is still a vacuum, and emptiness, and the most disquieting loneliness."[102] Haley packed five emotions into those three sentences. The library-sciences scholar Russell E. Bidlack echoed his point a few years later: "Not only did Alex Haley inspire thousands of Americans to seek their roots, he also provided dramatic proof of the importance of those roots to the individual psyche."[103] *Roots'* messages about emotional well-being foreshadowed the consumer market for large-scale genealogy commerce that emerged in the 1980s and afterward because those messages, like genealogy commerce generally, catered to the emotional needs of the descendant.[104]

Haley's stated animus against Black militancy also appealed to non-Black audiences and helps explain whites' appropriation of *Roots*, notwithstanding its Black principal characters and heroes. Haley, who identified as conservative within the spectrum of African American politics, was an avowed Republican in the 1960s, with other Republicans in the family. His businessman brother, George, won election as a Republican state senator in Kansas in 1964.[105] The decidedly unsympathetic 1959 CBS documentary on Malcolm X titled *The Hate That Hate Produced* had inspired Alex to interview Malcolm and to begin work on *The Autobiography of Malcolm X*. Haley voiced similar distaste for separatist Black nationalism when explaining his second project to his agent in 1963 as "portraying the pastoral simplicity and the root Christian culture of the 1930s Southern Negro—who migrated to the ghettos where he has fermented into today's black racism that has given us Malcolm X."[106] Initially suggested by a white *Reader's Digest* editor, this project's title was, at first, "Before This Anger."[107] After retitling the project "Roots" in 1972 and refocusing it on Kunta Kinte, Haley carefully absolved contemporary whites of blame by ending his tales well before the present.

The book and show went on to inspire genealogy practices in directions that Haley probably did not intend. The usefulness of *Roots* to Confederate genealogy was ironic given Haley's explicitness about plantation slavery's brutalities and about post-slavery violence against Blacks. White southern and neo-Confederate forms of genealogy had been stirring to new life long before *Roots* aired. The Sons of Confederate Veterans (SCV) and its kindred organization, the United Daughters of the Confederacy, had politicized Confederate descent since their origins in the 1890s, joining retrospective toasting of the Confederacy to contemporary forms of racial subjugation. But the Supreme Court's *Brown* decision in 1954, and other signs of federal support for civil rights in the 1950s and 1960s, infused the Confederate (Southern Cross) flag with new meanings. The stark, horizontally positioned "X" on the red background bundled together white southerners' massive resistance to the federal government's "Second Reconstruction" and civil rights agitation, continued adherence to Jim Crow, and pride in Confederate heritage. Numerous southern states redesigned their flags after 1954 to evoke the Southern Cross, if their flags lacked the design already.[108] Against this backdrop, the Sons of Confederate Veterans organization within Alabama grew from three chapters in the early 1970s to "about fifty" chapters in the early 1990s. John Napier III, a retired Air Force colonel and SCV organizer there, credited *Roots* for his organization's growth. He recalled, "A lot of the attempts of southern whites to find their roots came when Alex Haley made 'Roots' a national preoccupation. There are people in these old country towns who 10 years ago couldn't have told you who their grandfather was, and now they'll bore you to excruciating tears about the Civil War and genealogy."[109]

Only two months before *Roots* aired on television, while the book *Roots* topped bestseller lists, the first television airing of the *Gone with the Wind* film (1939) also illustrates the continuities in genealogy reckonings after *Roots*. Before November 1976, Americans could access this popular Oscar winner only in theater revivals. *Gone with the Wind* skillfully carried forward cinematic tropes about slavery and Reconstruction that *Birth of a Nation* (1915) had first popularized, without the latter's polarizing visions of uniformed Klansmen's sharing heaven with a haloed Jesus. Antebellum Georgia in *Gone with the Wind* was a tranquil, harmonious world that later was lost. Plantation nostalgia came complete with wisecracking mammies and other enslaved sidekicks who stood by Scarlett O'Hara, a fresh-mouthed 1920s flapper in the corsets of a Victorian plantation belle. Reconstruction was a misbegotten time. Black politicians in comically loud suits and shoes traipsed through the backdrop of Scarlett's new life of independence and tragedies.[110]

A record-breaking 65 percent of American TV audiences tuned in to *Gone with the Wind*. Only *Roots'* final episode two months later, which attracted a never-before-seen 75 percent of the viewing public, exceeded *Gone with the Wind's* turnout.[111] Americans' residual affection in the 1970s for *Gone with the Wind* accompanied the surge in whites' triumphalist genealogy activity at the time of the bicentennial and of *Roots*, and not just among southerners. A retired librarian in Michigan stated anonymously in the mid-1980s that, in retrospect, "*Roots* was somebody else's family history, not necessarily yours." This librarian and other whites whom a sociologist interviewed "made it very clear that the Bicentennial was far more important to them personally and for their organizations" than was *Roots*.[112] Historians and others who study the 1970s, in retrospect, have avoided such distinctions. Instead, they have experienced some difficulty in disentangling the two events from each other when considering the events' cultural impacts.[113]

When Diversification Became Collision

Genealogy's diversification after *Roots* created additional unintended consequences. An institution's commitment to diversity belied a lack of understanding of some of its patrons. In phenomena not related to *Roots*, the late 1970s and early 1980s saw intensifying Holocaust awareness in the United States, from gatherings of survivors to presidential proclamations to TV miniseries.[114] Counting and naming the dead seemed newly important in a Jewish context concerned about falling numbers in the United States due to intermarriages with people of other faiths and increasing levels of nonaffiliation among the young.[115] In a mutually reinforcing process, expanding Holocaust consciousness invigorated Jewish genealogy practices, and Jewish genealogy practices heightened Holocaust consciousness among Americans. Holocaust consciousness was especially evident among grown children and grandchildren of survivors and of Holocaust dead. These descendants often showed a greater zeal for family history than did previous generations, whose pressures to assimilate were less known to the young.

David Einseidler of Los Angeles had lost his father, a rabbi, to the genocide in Poland. He joked in 1987, in the journal *Avotaynu*, that his keen interest in genealogy might be weakening his marriage. He likened his predilection to "a love affair. Some days my wife has to remind me that it is after midnight. Nu, who cares about sleep? She says she would be better off if I had a live mistress.

But it wouldn't work. Where would I find a mistress who could do rabbinic genealogy?" his favorite subject. David Einseidler then displayed a lineage that he had tracked through his father and his father's mother. He listed streams of rabbis going back to the tenth century, while admitting that his documentation was incomplete. That same year, 1987, he presented these findings, rendered in elaborate calligraphy, as a ceremonial gift to his thirteen-year-old granddaughter at her bat mitzvah ceremony, which marked her coming of age in the faith.[116]

The YIVO Institute for Jewish Research, a multilingual archive in New York City, embodied Holocaust survivorship as much as any American institution could. The YIVO Institute had originated as the Yidisher Visnshaftlekher Institut (Yiddish Scientific Institute) among learned Jews in Vilna, then in Poland, in 1925. The archive narrowly escaped destruction in the Second World War. Jewish archives brigades spirited away irreplaceable materials to safety in America.[117] Fifty years later, "[people] seeking roots ... are by far the largest category of reader" at YIVO, noted one librarian in 1996. Following her retirement, another librarian discovered an empathy with genealogy patrons that she had not expected to feel. Dina Abramowicz "might once have preferred to dedicate herself only to academic projects," said Arthur Kurzweil, the genealogy impresario who interviewed her—in a statement that presumed genealogy's estrangement from scholarly endeavors. But now Abramowicz called genealogy "a natural interest" and "the requirement of an intelligent mind, of a conscious mind. . . . At certain periods of your life, you start to want to find out what happened to your parents," she remarked. "How many times have I heard, 'Unfortunately the parents didn't tell us anything; unfortunately the parents spoke a different language and didn't want us to learn this language, and we don't know anything about them.' I think it is the survival instinct of a people trying to find out who they are," referring to American Jewry generally. "They feel a gap in their consciousness."[118]

Holocaust consciousness also expanded non-Jews' awareness of Jewish history, including in places and cultures far distant from major Jewish populations. The Church of Jesus Christ of Latter-day Saints consistently sought to foster more genealogy among more people. In 1969 and again in 1980, the church hosted World Conferences on Records. The 1969 gathering in Salt Lake City, with an estimated seven thousand in attendance, constituted the largest genealogy-themed meeting to date in the United States. Among the WCR's hundreds of presentations, which stressed European and Early American content, there was an item on Jewish genealogy. The Israeli archivist Daniel J. Cohen spoke on "The Gathering of Jewish Records to Israel."

The conference also drew new attention to Indigenous practices. The archivist C. George Younkin presented on the "Historical and Genealogical Records of the Five Civilized Tribes and Other Indian Records."[119] *The American Genealogist* editor George McCracken remarked to his readers, "We would have thought that genealogy was impossible for Amerindians but we presided at a paper on that very subject!"[120] Younkin's paper from 1969 later became one of the first publications in modern times on Native American genealogy.

In June 1978, some eighteen months after *Roots* aired on television, the Latter-day Saints church president Spencer W. Kimball reported a revelation that effectively allowed Black men into the Mormon priesthood. Also, no longer would the church exclude African American women and men from engaging in temple work. The ban on Black priests, dating from the 1850s, had been especially conspicuous in a church in which "the entire male membership . . . [was] a membership of priests" otherwise. Small numbers of men from other nonwhite populations—from Samoa, Kiribati, Japan, and the Navajo tribe—had earlier gained access to the priesthood.[121] To devout Mormons, this turnabout of 1978 constituted a directive from an often-inscrutable God. The earthly context of Kimball's announcement also matters. African Americans who were Mormon, and those in Utah, had protested the discrimination at least since the 1950s.[122] Mormonism was rapidly expanding around the world, including into such countries as Brazil that had substantial African-descended populations. Lifting the ban would presumably facilitate the efforts of missionaries overseas. The 1980 World Conference on Records featured Alex Haley as a speaker. This was not the first time he had spoken under church auspices; he had appeared at Brigham Young University in 1972, and he had visited Utah again in 1977.[123]

Reflecting the new racial and religious diversity among genealogists, a motley crowd journeyed to the genealogy resources in Salt Lake City in the years following *Roots*. When a missionary at the church's Genealogical Library greeted "a man and his daughter" one day, she lost her composure after finding out that the visitors were from Israel. She had just seen microfilmed lists of names of "Jews who perished during WW II." "Suddenly I started to cry and couldn't continue the presentation, so I took them to the elevators (fortunately we were alone) and told them of the above experience. So many of the pictures we see of these poor people in concentration camps make them look more like pieces of wood than human beings. I had been suddenly filled with the realization that many of them were loving fathers and daughters just as these two were."[124]

But the history of Holocaust consciousness within Mormon facilities would soon prove ironic. The church's post-1961 encouragements, within limits, of proxy baptism done on behalf of unrelated friends and strangers created an enthusiasm that compelled some congregants to flout the church's rules. These people stood in for Jews who had perished only a half century earlier in the Holocaust, instead of choosing among those dead who had been born at least one hundred and ten years before. *Avotaynu* publisher Gary Mokotoff first became aware of these virtual baptisms in 1993, when he spotted the name of the famous Amsterdam diarist Anne Frank in the church's International Genealogical Index (IGI). Frank had perished at age sixteen in the Bergen-Belsen concentration camp in the early months of 1945. Her account of her family's years of doomed concealment, interspersed with comments about her own coming of age, in her diary posthumously found their way to American stages, film, and schoolchildren's readings lists.[125] Akin to a bibliography, the IGI guided the reader through the vast array of microfilmed and microfiched data obtained from around the world and from Mormon families' own records. The information was not only genealogical but also included temple ordinances, notably baptisms, performed on behalf of dead people.[126] The virtual baptism of persons killed fifty years beforehand—only forty-eight years, in Frank's case—violated the church's rules.

In 1994, Mokotoff pronounced the proxy baptism that Frank had undergone "particularly repugnant to Jews. It reminds us of the centuries of persecution against Jews where our ancestors were given a choice; be baptized or suffer death."[127] Virtual baptisms served as hurtful reminders of other instances of forcible conversion to Christianity in Jewish history. In imperial Russia, young Jewish boys conscripted into the Tsar's army had experienced pressure to convert to Orthodox Christianity, the state religion, with conversion being a stated government goal and entailing full-body baptism. Stories of coerced baptisms reverberated within Russian Jewish diasporas' collective memories, including in the United States.[128] In the 1990s, neither American Jews nor American Mormons, by and large, believed that dead people could communicate with the living, to agree or not agree to religious conversion. The virtual baptisms felt nonconsensual to living Jews.

At the time that Mokotoff discovered Anne Frank's listing in the IGI, Jewish genealogists, like others who were not Mormon, had otherwise been finding treasure in Utah. Three times between 1986 and 1994, *Avotaynu* organized research seminars in Salt Lake City for Jewish genealogists and others in Jewish studies. In 1993, Sallyann Amdur Sack, the editor of *Avotaynu*, was eager to see better facilities in Israel for genealogy tourists, having held research seminars there for years. "Although I live physically in the United States, there is no doubt that Israel is my home emotionally," she reflected from Maryland.[129] For the time being, she considered Salt Lake City the premier destination for people in her field. Records in Salt Lake City concerning Jews surpassed those of New York City, with its plethora of Jewish-history repositories, and those in Washington, D.C., with the U.S. National Archives and the new U.S. Holocaust Memorial Museum. Church facilities and services in Salt Lake City also ran ahead of Jerusalem's own libraries and museums in Sack's estimation in 1993.[130]

But the 1994 Jewish genealogy research seminar in Utah was advertised in the same issue of *Avotaynu* in which Mokotoff broke his story, which would recur for decades to come: "Mormons Baptize Holocaust Victims."[131] Long after the church formally repudiated the practice in 1995, Mormon laypeople went on quietly baptizing Jews who had perished in the Holocaust.[132] Indignation grew. While *Avotaynu*'s leadership continued to sponsor annual research tours to Salt Lake City after 1994, subsequent advice books for Jewish genealogists, as in 2004, omitted mention of the Utah research facilities and stressed the repositories on the East Coast and in Israel.[133] By 2012, after nearly fifty years of "name extraction" from old records and too many violations of name extraction's limits, the church resumed its old ban on baptizing nonrelatives, including "celebrities and Jewish Holocaust victims."[134] In the end, genealogy practices among Mormons and Jews in the United States broadly illustrate the persistence of group politics as they played out through the seemingly personal endeavor of genealogy. A swiftly growing religion with a strong conversion ethic that reached far into the afterworld, uncomfortably shared American space and sometimes collided with other faiths and other histories.

Conclusion

The controversies that Mormon genealogy practices created, when interacting with genealogists of other faiths in the 1980s and 1990s, illustrated the social and political tensions that *Roots* had heightened in genealogy practice more broadly. The diversification among genealogists that *Roots* both signified and fueled did not displace older traditions among white Anglo-American Protestant, or Mormon, genealogists. With all the new publications and societies devoted to Jewish, African American, Indigenous, and Latinx genealogy following *Roots*, genealogists who specialized in white Anglo-American Protestants, *Mayflower* passengers, and British colonial and revolutionary America found a more crowded stage.

My next chapter will treat *Roots* as an engine of innovations in the business world. Haley's texts created considerable possibilities for others' appropriations of them. He combined an emphasis on emotion with a determination to reach broad, white audiences. The book, and show's unexpected, record-breaking popularity, convinced entrepreneurs and investors that market demand was sufficient for a constellation of large genealogy enterprises and genealogy-focused mass entertainments. Never before the 1980s and 1990s had genealogy been so profitable or so explicitly linked to present-day emotional gratification.

CHAPTER SIX

Genealogy for Hire and for Profit

Although genealogists began hiring out their services in the mid-1800s, Alex Haley's *Roots*—especially on television—transformed the genealogy industry by exposing mass-market demand. That turning point followed more than a century during which evanescent, usually one-person or family businesses characterized for-profit genealogy. Genealogy businesses big and small, earlier and later, projected a come-as-you-are ethos toward customers and clients, and catered to the descendant's needs in the present. Haley brought these practices to new heights by repeatedly stressing that genealogical revelations aided the individual's well-being. Recall his statement in *Reader's Digest* in 1977: "in all of us, there is a hunger, bone-marrow deep, to know our heritage—to know who we are and where we have come from. Without this enriching knowledge, there is a hollow yearning."[1]

History's broader picture of Americans' fascination with the self and with psychological health in particular, helps explain *Roots'* thundering reception in the 1970s and the subsequent growth of genealogy businesses and entertainments.[2] Suzanne Hilton wrote in her semi-humorous guide to genealogy in 1976, "You will be surprised, often delighted, with each new discovery, and never bored. How could you be? It's all about *you!*"[3] In his "Me Decade" essay of 1976, which he published in *New York* magazine just weeks before the book *Roots* appeared, the acerbic satirist Tom Wolfe described the era's "new alchemical dream" as "changing one's personality—remaking, remodeling, elevating, and polishing one's very *self* . . . and observing, studying, and doting on it. (Me!) This had always been an aristocratic luxury, confined throughout most of history to the life of the courts, since only the very wealthiest classes had the free time and the surplus income to dwell upon this sweetest and vainest of pastimes." Positing the "Me" pastime's recent spread to the American middle classes, Wolfe described that pastime's harmony with the era's religious turmoil, revolutions in heterosexual activity and marriage (including politicians' "wife-shucking"), women's liberation, and consumer capitalism.[4]

Marketers and advertisers embraced tropes of individual gratification, self-fulfillment, and the self-polishing that Wolfe described to sell products and services. Enough of the public bought such products and promises for this self-oriented trope to bear fruit because it kept repeating.[5] Messages of self-fulfillment carried such cultural weight that self-fulfillment's absence fueled jeremiads. For Betty Friedan in her *Feminine Mystique* (1963), the suburban housewife's frustrated potential as an individual human being was a major theme.[6] These broader cultural discourses of self-fulfillment explain the confluence of the record-breaking audiences for *Roots* and the apotheosis of commercialized genealogy and genealogy-focused entertainments afterwards.

But commercialism in genealogy had its critics and dissenters. Genealogy professionals were foremost among them. For much of the twentieth century, including in the *Roots* era, professionals tried mightily to reform the field of genealogy in pushing other genealogists toward reliance on original source material rather than on secondhand information. Professionals also prized historical accuracy, including at the cost of present-day contentment, and emotional detachment from source materials' revelations. Such reforms did not succeed; hobbyists and the businesses that served them continued to dominate the field numerically and to characterize the field to others. But scrutinizing professionals' anticommercial backlashes can enhance our understanding of commercialism's influences.

Professionals illustrate the history of genealogy's embedded power relations because they introduced new hierarchies based on expertise and social connectedness. But genealogy businesses and the mentalities behind them represented an even more emphatic degree of exclusivity in their hoarding and monetization of family history information. The posthumous auctioning of Alex Haley's estate in 1992 is a case in point. He died beset by debt in part because his purchases in the years since *Roots* had included ten homes.[7] His brother George arranged to auction off Alex's assets to pay off creditors, amid other family members' objections. Gregory Reed, a Detroit attorney, outbid public university libraries, museums, and archives that possessed considerably fewer resources than he did to purchase treasures that would otherwise enhance understanding of Haley and Malcolm X.[8] Reed sequestered valuable items, such as a draft of *The Autobiography of Malcolm X* (1965) with Malcolm's annotations, privately for decades. Such materials came within the reach of libraries and archives only after Reed filed for bankruptcy in the summer of 2018, twenty-six years later.[9]

Another theme of this chapter is the rise of genealogy-themed entertainment, on screen and in the form of tourism. The earliest genealogical television show dates from 1954, when a TV station in Provo, Utah, aired Brigham Young University's twenty episodes of *What's Your Name?* Topics included President Dwight Eisenhower's lineage, "Mayflower Descendants," "Scandinavian Forefathers," and "Pocahontas and Her Posterity."[10] But *What's Your*

Name? did not inspire other shows, nor did it air nationally, in the 1950s. Genealogy as a mass spectacle originated with *Roots* in 1977. Tourism evolved as another form of entertainment as well as a seedbed of business opportunities. An important dimension of *Roots* and its advance publicity was Haley's popularization of genealogy-focused travel beyond western Europe and Britain, when he went to Gambia to research his descent from Kunta Kinte. Subsequent onscreen entertainments fueled roots tourism while simultaneously depending on such tourism for their plotlines. Starting in the early 2000s, viewers of reality-television shows vicariously followed celebrities and non-actors to destinations where their ancestors had walked.[11] Entertainment and commercialism alike reached new, unprecedented heights in the years following *Roots*, with *Roots* itself as a contributing factor. These heights followed many generations of entrepreneurialism in American genealogy.

The Long History of Genealogists for Hire

Genealogists for hire who were American found a market well before the Civil War. The appetite within the antebellum bourgeoisie for heraldry and other forms of prestigious British descent resulted in a tidy living for Horatio Gates Somerby (1805–72), a Massachusetts-born lawyer living in England. In the 1850s, numerous families who had prospered from New England's industrialization hired Somerby, who conducted his business by mail.[12] The efflorescence of hereditary organizations after 1876 created a much broader market for genealogy services. Collectively, these groups attracted over one hundred thousand Americans by World War I and over two hundred thousand by the 1970s.[13] The groups' very existence increased the prestige attached to genealogy practice. "More digging for ancestors has probably resulted from the desire to belong to this organization than has come about through any other impetus," Gilbert Doane wrote of the DAR in 1937.[14] The resulting demand for genealogists' expertise enabled paid jobs in genealogy for the first time. In 1899, for example, a married woman in Brooklyn, Annie Arnoux Haxtun (Mrs. Milton), was serving as "editress of the genealogical department of the *New York Mail and Express*."[15]

Genealogists' advertising during the early decades of hereditary organizations makes clear that those organizations generally served the needs of their present, before or unless they adopted values of professionalized genealogy (from inception, in the case of the General Society of Mayflower Descendants, and in the 1950s, in the DAR's case).[16] In the first volume of the DAR's magazine, in 1892, George Washington Ball of Washington, D.C., advertised his services for a five-dollar initial charge "to make investigation for parties desiring to become members of any of the Revolutionary Societies."[17] Fourteen years later, Edward A. Claypool's list showed the further proliferation of hereditary organizations. This Chicago entrepreneur offered Claypool's Ancestral Chart Blanks for $1.25 each, and he advertised "perfecting ancestral lines for membership in the Society of Mayflower Descendants, Colonial Dames of America, Society of Colonial Wars, Holland Society, Daughters of Holland Dames, Order of the Founders and Patriots of America, Sons of the Revolution, Sons of the American Revolution, Daughters of the Revolution, Daughters of the American Revolution, etc."[18]

Starting in the early 1890s, hereditary organizations published ascendant lineages that began with the living descendant and moved backwards in time, in another indicator of serving contemporaries' needs.[19] These lineages illustrated a self-centered form of genealogy from descendants' perspectives, as these lineages put the descendant and client first, in contrast to the customary descendant lineages that moved forward in time from the ancestor in the past, and that implicitly prioritized historical knowledge.[20] Earlier genealogists, from John Farmer in his *Genealogical Register of the First Settlers of New-England* (1829) to Charles Henry Browning's seven editions of *Americans of Royal Descent* (1883–1911), all tracked lineages forward in time and (in Browning's case) ended with living descendants.

Concentrating in and around major cities, the one-and two-person operations of genealogy commerce were small indeed. Not even the hungriest entrepreneur in the early twentieth century could put much hope in genealogy as a moneymaker. Frank Allaben (1867–1927) of New York proffered advice along with his company's family-history blanks when he published *Concerning Genealogies: Being Suggestions of Value for All Interested in Family History* in 1904. The Oberlin College graduate devoted many of the book's seventy-one pages to peddling his company's wares and services, including searches in New York City's many repositories for ten dollars per surname. By 1909, he founded his own business devoted to genealogy. As with many other such businesses, Allaben's began as an eponymous publishing company; he later renamed it the National Historical Society. He also performed research for individual clients, as did his colleague and eventual partner Mabel Washburn (1874–1950). A New Yorker who stayed single, she took over the business and published another instruction book, *How to Trace and Record Your Own Ancestry* (1932), after Allaben died.[21] Like Allaben, Washburn bundled advice with advertisements for services and products, but with a twist. In a chapter titled "If You Consult a Professional Genealogist," she peddled her own reputation—reprinting, at length, flattering newspaper coverage in the *Brooklyn Eagle* of her services and her satisfied customers.[22]

An even more ambitious commercial firm was Frederick Adams Virkus's Institute for American Genealogy (1925) in Chicago. Like Allaben, Virkus developed his own eponymous publishing company for genealogy materials, sold family-history blanks, and offered searching services to clients. Unlike anyone before him, he created a genealogists' clearinghouse to streamline the exchanging of information and contacts. He built a network of over one thousand subscribers.[23] Like Browning, Allaben, and Washburn, Virkus trafficked in prestigious origins for prominent Anglo-American families of his time and cultivated relationships with Daughters, Dames, and Sons. Although he eschewed talk of William the Conqueror of the eleventh century or other early medieval progenitors, Virkus, like other businesspeople of the time, assumed that many white Americans of northern European descent were related to sixteenth-century aristocrats overseas, on the basis of surnames in the Americans' ancestry that matched those in the aristocrats' families.[24] The persisting American affection for heraldry, and its determinedly unregulated nature in a country that outlawed governments' awarding of titles of nobility, lent itself to commercialization and salespeople's promises.

Businesspeople hoarded information regarding prestigious ancestry as they hoarded other forms of capital. A dispute involving Henry FitzGilbert Waters (1833–1913), an older-generation genealogist who pushed back against such behaviors, illustrates the tensions that genealogy's monetization created. The Boston attorney John Tyler Hassam, head of the NEHGS's Committee on English Research in the 1880s, predicted great media excitement in the United States—amounting to a formidable fundraising tool for the New England Historic Genealogical Society—if its representative in England, the American-born Waters, managed to document the ancestry of John Harvard (1607–38). The Puritan cleric in England had bequeathed his library and crucial funds to the infant college (1636) in Massachusetts Bay Colony that Puritans later, posthumously, named for him.[25] Nineteenth-century Americans, including Hassam and Waters, considered John Harvard to be Harvard College's outright founder. In 1884, Hassam prodded Waters to give all his time in England to "the Harvard problem": "now is the time when the information is especially valuable. . . . If we could announce it at the commencement dinner that the mystery was solved, the news would spread from one end of the country to the other."[26]

The following April, Hassam congratulated Waters on his findings but asked him to keep them "a profound secret from every one."[27] Waters apparently did not because one James Rendle scooped the Harvard discovery. The Boston press caught wind of the matter by August, repeating Rendle's gossip. Hassam sputtered at Waters's indiscretion in having bared his "bosom" to someone who turned out to be a friend of Rendle.[28] Waters unrepentantly defended his "frankness" with his "brother antiquaries." In his "enthusiasm" over his John Harvard findings, he had made "the workers," meaning fellow researchers at the British Library, "warm friends of me and the work."[29] In the end, Waters's loose talk did not harm his standing. Already a Harvard College alumnus (1855), he garnered an honorary master's degree at the 1885 Harvard commencement dinner for his findings on John Harvard.[30] The fifty-two-year-old's penchant for sharing information with peers seemed old-fashioned in recalling the hosts of "brother antiquaries" and town historians who had divulged and traded information in antebellum New England.[31] But Waters's stance was simultaneously forward-looking. His implicit critique of capitalist tendencies to hoard information foreshadowed professional genealogists' later critiques of commercialism.

In the meantime, publicity was among the intangibles that genealogy businesspeople monetized. In 1929, Frederick Adams Virkus in Chicago likened media attention to dessert. "Bread and butter has been the diet of too many genealogists and one thing we should like to do in that direction is to vary that diet by adding some cake and pie to it. The cake and pie will be added by the interest and consequent activity in genealogy, engendered by [Virkus's *Magazine of American Genealogy*], where the subject had not heretofore been thought of," he charged.[32] In addition to "interest" and media attention, the descendant's contentment resembled a form of wealth. The New York entrepreneur Mabel Washburn understood in the depression year of 1932 that family history could provide an emotional lift: "It gives one just a little more courage to face life when it is hard, and makes one carry the head a little higher, to remember a specific person back in the family somewhere who has stood out in history for bravery in the face of danger, and achievement."[33]

Professionalization as an Anticommercial Backlash, 1930s Onward

Genealogy's runaway commercialization during the Great Depression provoked such vehement objections that it culminated in genealogists' development of their new professionalized sector. Professionals forged a collective identity by 1940 and, thereafter, they pushed back against the descendant-centered and ahistorical priorities of businesspeople. Instruction manuals were an important specialty of professionals because they assumed that gene-alogists should not—and could not effectively—be self-taught. Neither of the two major genealogy journals of the time noticed or reviewed Henry Reed Stiles's *Hand-Book of Practical Suggestions* (1899), perhaps the earliest published example of advice in which a professional intended to elevate ge-nealogy. Stiles, a New York physician, wanted his fellow genealogists to fol-low scientific methods in which original research shaped conclusions and could be replicated. In 1930, Donald Jacobus published his own trenchant how-to, *Genealogy as Pastime and Profession*, privately in New Haven with a run of only one hundred copies.[34] But seven short years later, in 1937, the Ne-braska librarian Gilbert Harry Doane (1897–1980) managed to publish his own instruction book, *Searching for Your Ancestors: The Why and How of Ge-nealogy*, with a commercial press (McGraw-Hill). He persuaded trade and university presses to publish the four subsequent editions of his advice book, ending in 1980. Doane congenially addressed the do-it-yourself genealogist, but his guidelines on heraldry followed the stringent reforms that profession-als advocated. The only rightful American claimants to coats of arms were male individuals (not families) who could document paternal descent from arms holders, also individual men, who had in turn obtained authorization in writing from the College of Arms in Britain.[35]

Genealogy's expansion as a hobby during the Great Depression explains Doane's success in bringing genealogy instruction to large audiences. "Here's a job you can't lose," remarked *American Magazine* in 1933, of hobbies gener-ally.[36] Having published its genealogy query exchanges and advice twice a week since the 1890s, the *Boston Transcript* began in 1930 to publish them four times a week and in every issue starting in 1936.[37] Genealogy had been a costly and time-consuming endeavor in the nineteenth century. Now, cursory re-search was possible for as little as the cost of a newspaper or magazine sub-scription, or trolley or subway or bus fare to libraries. Walking was even cheaper. NEHGS librarian Josephine Rayne reported from downtown Bos-ton, "The use of the Library reading rooms by members and visitors during the year 1933 was the greatest in the history of the Society" and "made heavy demands upon the staff."[38]

The New Deal programs of Franklin D. Roosevelt's presidency also indi-rectly expanded genealogy practices. The creation of the Social Security sys-tem in 1935 resulted in new requirements to document one's birth and parentage in order to obtain unemployment and old-age insurance and other benefits. The Works Progress Administration's job-creation programs engen-dered a flurry of local-history publications in 1935 and afterward, including travel guides and the transcription and printing of old documents from Salem, Massachusetts, to New Orleans.[39] The flowering of local history in the 1930s fueled interest in family history; genealogy and local history had long walked arm in arm. The 1934 completion of the U.S. National Archives was another important turning point in the history of American genealogy. Hereditary organizations, historians, and genealogists, including professionals, benefited from the new, streamlined availability of government and military records to the public. All three communities had been lobbying for a publicly funded national archive for decades beforehand.[40]

Genealogy's new popularity in the 1930s resulted in an ever-expanding market for businesspeople, including outright grifters. For-profit genealogy ran to such fraudulent excesses as the shadowy Media Research Bureau, which peddled "'reports' on various 'families,'" typically "abstracted from a number of published works on usually unrelated people of a common surname," as a skeptic put it. The bureau sold these reports "through small-space periodical or newspaper advertising, and by direct mail solicitation of all persons of the same surname in the telephone directory." The bureau kept prices "low enough" (below five dollars) to avoid legal action, it hoped. In response to the bureau's actions and other, similar examples, indignant genealogists who were already attending the 1940 American Historical Association meeting in New York conceived the American Society of Genealogists (ASG), a small, invitation-only group that intended to "elevate the profession." The group limited its membership to fifty illustrious, much-published fellows, and it solicited new members only after fellows died or left the group.[41]

One of the ASG's first actions was to sue the Media Research Bureau for mail fraud. The group won that battle, but the overall war remained frustrating for professionals. With other business concerns taking the bureau's place, finding marks across the country, professionals turned to developing a slew of new institutions to foster more professionalism.[42] The years after 1945 brought the first national and international seminars of genealogists, developed to advance education and expertise in genealogy.[43] A string of workshops called the National Institute of Genealogical Research met repeatedly at American University in Washington in the 1950s and beyond. A similar set of workshops convened at Samford University in Alabama.[44] The year 1964 saw the formation of the Board for Certification of Genealogists (BCG), by which professionals developed credentials and licensing for the profession. Passing the BCG's rigorous examinations entitled the already-published genealogist to place a "C. G." (Certified Genealogist) after their name when publishing, or when publicizing their services.[45]

Some Mormon genealogists and others in western regions also embraced professionalism. The Church of Jesus Christ of Latter-day Saints' Genealogical Society (formerly the GSU) and the Utah Genealogical Association, founded in 1971 and independent of the church, developed similar credentialing and accreditation systems for Mormon and Utah-area genealogists, to the eastern examples I described above.[46] Another important figure in Mormon professionalism was Noel Stevenson, a former district attorney in Southern California who published rigorous how-to manuals starting in the 1950s.[47] In that same decade, the church-run Brigham Young University began offering the United States' first college-level courses on genealogy. Faculty and university administrators shared professionalism's tenet that genealogists needed educating and that they benefited from studying with experts within the field.[48]

The most important components of professionalism's critique of commercialism were professionals' insistence on nonprofit operations and fostering of historical knowledge and perspectives. Before the twentieth century, genealogists and historians had been accustomed to enjoining the public at large to buy their books, as Alice Morse Earle had in the 1890s, or to rounding up friends and eminent strangers to purchase subscriptions, as John Farmer in 1829, Lemuel Shattuck in 1841, and Zerviah Gould Mitchell in 1878 had each done to fund their respective tomes on genealogy. But professional genealogists in the 1920s, 1930s, and afterward favored the noncommercial advancement of knowledge, much like historians did when they began coalescing in universities, colleges, government agencies, historical societies, and in other nonprofit venues during that same timeframe.[49] Professionals did not reject all forms of accumulation, as many of them supported themselves by soliciting clients. But professionals did not incorporate their activities as publishing companies or other businesses, nor did they hawk products or services, in the style of Allaben, Washburn, and Virkus. Readers of *The American Genealogist* knew all about Donald Jacobus's resolutely anti-commercial operations in Connecticut. Though he periodically hired himself out to clients, his journal accepted no paid advertising. He reported doing all the typing himself, eschewing clerical assistance. Remaining single all his life, he never owned a car, and he lived with his mother and muse, Ida Wilmot Lines Jacobus, who mentored, proofread, and indexed his work until she died in 1952. Though Donald had grown up in a city (New Haven) and lived there until his thirties, the Jacobuses intermittently lived on a farm and raised their own chickens and vegetables, presumably to reduce cash purchases.[50]

Besides repudiating profit-seeking, professionals like Jacobus also insisted on pursuing unvarnished historical truths to be discerned from original documents, regardless of what consternation such findings might create in living people.[51] This emphasis on studying the past for its own sake amounted to another stance against commercialism because present-day emotional contentment was so noticeable among businesspeople's priorities. Heraldry in the United States was a field notorious for shaky evidence and high emotional stakes. Flushed with hope, entrepreneurs and hobbyists maintained that surname matches between American and European aristocratic families indicated relatedness. Duplicate surnames convinced Charles Henry Browning of Philadelphia, compiler of the seven editions of *Americans of Royal Descent*, that he could bridge numerous lineages of important people, including himself, back to William the Conqueror.[52] Charlemagne, Edward III, and other early medieval monarchs, in addition to Magna Carta "sureties," also appear in his books as progenitors of Americans. But as early as 1860, learned genealogists had called out this fiction, that matching surnames in themselves indicated relatedness.[53] A century later, Americans far and wide were still repeating this untruth, and professionals repeatedly challenged it. Writing in 1965, Gilbert Harry Doane rejected most royal pedigrees of Americans as "little more than sentimental patchwork in which a few pieces of real silk have been featherstitched to others of cheap shoddy by the thread of imagination."[54]

Through the decades, professionals called out falsehoods that commercial genealogists had committed or spread. In 1976, George McCracken, the Iowa classics professor who succeeded Jacobus in editing *The American Genealogist*, and the career genealogist Milton Rubincam built a hall of shame for deceased colleagues who had been notorious, among professionals, for outright concoctions. McCracken and Rubincam included Horatio Gates Somerby, Frederick Adams Virkus, and Charles Henry Browning on their list. Likening it to the Roman Catholic Church's bygone index expurgatorius, "a list of works which it compiled to warn the faithful not to read them under penalty of punishment, those on our list are so unreliable that nothing they say should be accepted without clear and unmistakable verification," McCracken explained.[55] Conversely, professionals within Washington's National Genealogical Society (NGS) developed the National Genealogy Hall of Fame in 1981 to honor meritorious career genealogists for their publications and for their reinforcement of professionalism's ethos. Henry FitzGilbert Waters, that early critic of commercialism, posthumously received a berth.[56]

Notwithstanding such rewards, professionals ultimately failed to arrest the commercialization of genealogy. Professionals and hobbyists (and the entrepreneurs whom hobbyists patronized) resembled "Two Nations," remarked one despairing professional in 1984. "P. T. Barnum missed his calling when he neglected to become a genealogist."[57] Self-taught, unaffiliated, and commercialized practices continued to dominate American genealogy practice at large, both numerically and culturally. Of the more than four thousand people surveyed who used the Newberry Library's collections in Chicago in 1981 for genealogical purposes, 93 percent had never presented "a program on genealogy; 87.2 percent had never published on genealogy; and 47.6 percent did not belong to any genealogical society."[58] Each of these would increase the possibility of professional scrutiny of a genealogist's research.

Entrepreneurialism in Genealogy after 1945

The Everton family's operations in Logan, Utah, illustrate genealogy professionals' frustrations in chasing off commercialism, and business principles in genealogy, especially well. Over four generations, the Evertons outstripped Virkus's enterprise in Chicago to develop the largest American genealogy business to date. The Evertons' most important innovation was their forum for the everyday, self-taught genealogist—their periodical called the *Genealogical Helper* (1947–2009). Its cofounder, Walter M. Everton (1876–1950), had been running a family hardware business and servicing typewriters in Logan when, around 1935, he began publishing a Saturday genealogy column in a local newspaper. Seven years later, in 1942, he published a family genealogy.[59] Eleven years later, he and his wife, Pearl, privately published their advice book, *The How Book for Genealogists* (1946). Interest was such that in 1947—which Walter and Pearl knew to be the centenary of the *New England Historical and Genealogical Register*'s first issue—they launched the *Genealogical Helper*.[60] Its paid circulation outstripped that of any other genealogy periodical by 1967. The *Genealogical Helper* reported a paid circulation of 12,500 that year; by comparison, the *Register* reported a paid circulation of 3,413 in September 1969.[61] After only twenty years of operations, the Evertons published the third edition of their *Handy Book for Genealogists*, a reference work that had already sold 49,000 copies, in 1965, and they published the third edition of their *How Book for Genealogists* in 1967.[62] After Walter died, his and Pearl's posterity—their son George B. Everton Sr., daughter-in-law Ellen Nielsen Everton, grandson George B. Everton Jr., and granddaughter-in-law, Louise M. Everton—continued to operate Everton Publishing and the *Genealogical Helper*, as did Walter and Pearl's great-grandson, Alma Lee Everton.[63]

Like entrepreneurs farther east, the Evertons operated their periodical and eponymous publishing company as a business. George B. Everton Sr.

announced in 1965 that subscription costs would rise because other costs were also going up.[64] And, like other entrepreneurs, the Evertons sold blank forms, advice books, and (in their case) reference works from their publishing company. But the family went one better. By the end of the 1970s, the range of products sold at discount in the *Genealogical Helper* extended to a $199 home photocopier and electric typewriters. The Evertons also offered a discounted carpet sweeper. With a chuckle, they intended it to "create more free time for tracing your ancestors."[65] The family's estrangement from the values of professionalism was such that, in 1975, the historian Samuel P. Hays used the *Genealogical Helper* to illustrate how genealogists and professional historians had been working in "separate worlds."[66]

The Everton dynasty's operations shared much in common with genealogy commerce generally. The family explicitly addressed and serviced the do-it-yourselfer, as the *Genealogical Helper*'s masthead slogan (of 1947–75) made plain: "Published Especially for Those Who Wish to Do Their Own Genealogical Research." The *Genealogical Helper*'s extensive clearinghouses, directories, and published advice intended to ease ongoing projects, rather than presuming that research's corruption or ineptitude as professionals were doing, when they pushed reform. The Evertons' operations possessed some distinctively Mormon characteristics, though. As Mormon genealogists had long been doing, the Evertons ignored normative distinctions between ancestors that were "worthy" and those that were obscure, or those that were moral or immoral. All the dead seemed to need attention. The *Genealogical Helper*'s post-1975 masthead slogan, "Dedicated to Helping More People Find More Genealogy," communicated the longstanding Mormon belief that the more people—Mormon or not—engaged in genealogy, the closer everyone drew to fulfilling God's plan.[67]

The *Genealogical Helper*'s aloofness toward heraldry and heraldry reform also illustrates Mormon entrepreneurs' lack of interest in many earthly distinctions among ancestors. Americans' desire to map descent from nobles and royals overseas was a major preoccupation of genealogy businesspeople and hereditary organizations, generally. Commercialism's detractors—professionals who were located mainly on the nation's coasts and in large cities—found many faults with existing heraldry activity. Therefore, heraldry and heraldry reform were familiar subjects to readers of the *New England Historical and Genealogical Register*, the *New York Genealogical and Biographical Record*, and in multiple professional redoubts: *The American Genealogist* (1922), based in Connecticut for decades, and the *National Genealogical Society Quarterly* (1912), based in Washington. The latter regularly featured content on heraldry and on roots travel to England.[68] The Jewish genealogy journal *Avotaynu* (1985), which also issued from the East Coast, at one point published coats of arms to accompany discussions of Americans' descent from eminent medieval-era rabbis and thinkers.[69]

Some of the genealogists who paid the Evertons for inclusion in their directories included heraldry as a specialty. But the *Genealogical Helper*'s feature articles eschewed the subject altogether, and the *Helper*'s precursor in Utah, the church-run *Utah Genealogical and Historical Magazine* (1910–40), also avoided discussion of heraldry, apart from a few items in its first decade.[70] Writing from Maryland, the British librarian P. William Filby complimented Mormon patrons in 1987 for banishing royal and aristocratic fetishes from American genealogy practice at large. Over the past thirty years, "genealogists no longer believe or try to prove royal and titled descent, perhaps because of the thousands of LDS members who research scientifically, wishing only to find their forebears no matter what their background might be."[71] Filby overstated his first point, about genealogy practices at large, as the historian Forrest D. Pass has found a persisting market for purveyors of "royal and titled descent" among Americans, extending into modern times.[72] But Filby did accurately represent many Mormon researchers' apathy toward heraldry.

One reason for this apathy is that authors of Mormon instruction texts cared as much, if not more, about descent from figures in the Bible and the Book of Mormon, such as Abraham and Seth, as about relatedness to royals and aristocrats.[73] Convictions of relatedness to biblical personages was integral to Mormon worship. Among the lessons in genealogy that priesthood training offered in 1930–31 was on "The Birthright Tribe" in the Bible, a reference to the biblical tribes of Israel.[74] A patriarchal blessing that church patriarchs conferred upon Archibald Bennett in 1921, as his daughters transcribed it, placed him in the "lineage of Ephraim."[75] Especially before the 1970s, Mormon believers understood biblical descent literally, including racially. But others in the 1970s and afterward began separating these two matters, interpreting biblical descent as depending on the descendant's embrace of the Christian gospel, and challenging blood-and heredity-focused readings of the subject.[76]

Genealogy's Profitability Following *Roots*

Genealogy in the United States entered a new era of lucre after the *Roots* book and telecast of 1976–77. In both texts, and not just because of the marketing of "Roots Maiden" tee shirts and other merchandise, Alex Haley imparted many of the values of commercialized genealogy.[77] Starting in 1977 and continuing long afterward, journalists repeatedly characterized genealogy as one of America's most popular hobbies, with only stamp collecting, gardening, and, later, online pornography as rivals.[78] A historians' survey of over 1,400 randomly selected Americans in 1994—many of them located using telephone books—found that over one-third of this largely unfiltered group reported having "investigated the history of their family in the previous year" and that nearly two-thirds had attended family reunions.[79] This example, from shortly before the internet came into common use, suggests the wide reach of genealogy commerce and entertainments and of the emotional sustenance they provided.

The large-scale enterprises devoted to family history research of the late twentieth century were a world away from earlier times' small offices. Recent Brigham Young University (BYU) graduates founded Ancestry Publishing Inc. in 1983 in Utah. Its slick, photograph-laden, full-color *Ancestry* magazine challenged the Evertons' plainer paper periodical. Ancestry also published some landmark advice books in the 1980s and 1990s, including Paul Andrew Andereck and Richard A. Pence's *Computer Genealogy* (1985).[80] The 1980s otherwise marked the fruition of nonprofit activity, with genealogists making the most of personal computers (available starting in 1981) to broaden research communities over long distances. Genealogists shared and traded information using networked computers and online bulletin boards. The "nets. root" newsgroup originated in 1983, and the ROOTS-L mailing list launched in 1987, both named in tribute to Haley's *Roots*.[81] Other important actors of the decade included the church's genealogy complexes in Salt Lake City, which began offering the International Genealogy Index (IGI) for sale to the public in 1984. The church had been maintaining the IGI internally as a computer database since 1961. It packaged the IGI—first on floppy disks, then on compact disks (1988)—for anyone with access to a computer.[82]

Nonprofit activities among American Jews in the 1980s, which vastly popularized genealogy among them, also need discussion. Susan E. King founded JewishGen.org in Houston in 1987. Its first incarnation was as a computer bulletin board. King attributed her effort to two inspirations. The year before, she had found information on little-known relatives on her father's side. They had been buried in nearby Galveston at a time when America's Jewish population was more geographically dispersed, across the Midwest and South, than after 1945 when it concentrated in northern cities and on the coasts.[83] In 1986, King was also in the process of unearthing the names of her mother's birth parents. "Although I never had the opportunity to share this information with my mother," who was comatose then and soon to die, "the desire to learn more about who I am, who she was, and why I am still who I am still holds."[84] Like many genealogy impresarios, King directly linked information on long-dead kin to one's own emotional well-being.

The gathering of research communities across long distances in unprecedented numbers, as happened with users of JewishGen.org through the 1980s and 1990s, eventually drew attention from entrepreneurs and investors due to their seemingly limitless growth possibilities. With the internet coming into broad accessibility in the mid-1990s, and with much commerce coming online, two major events in genealogy's popularization occurred. Ancestry Inc. launched its own website, Ancestry.com, in 1996, which paying subscribers helped fund. The nonprofit Church of Jesus Christ of Latter-day Saints' own genealogy website, FamilySearch.org, went online in 1999. The church availed its site's users without charging them. In decades to come, the church shifted from shipping microfilm rolls to its local family-history libraries to furnishing digitized records online. In 2017, the church ended its microfilming of items for FamilySearch.[85] Again, the church furnished these resources without charge. Yet another service that the church freely shared, in the 2010s, was the "digital file format" that genealogists have used when storing information, called GEDCOM (Genealogical Data Communications).[86] What enabled such generosity, in furnishing extensive genealogy services and records for free? In 2010, the non-Mormon genealogist Buzzy Jackson pointed to the church's requirement that members tithe ten percent of their income, as an important factor.[87]

Writing separately, the sociologist Christine Scodari and the cultural-studies scholar Julia Creet have recently portrayed the official separateness between the church's nonprofit FamilySearch operations and the for-profit business Ancestry.com, as a mutually beneficial and harmonious relationship. Scodari has related that "LDS representatives" from the church in the 2010s "[suggested] that Ancestry.com's continued success is in their interest."[88] In part through subscription fees, Ancestry.com generated enough profits for investors to bet successfully, twice, on its future expansion. The private-equity firm Permira purchased the company for $1.6 billion in October 2012. With its primacy in the direct-to-consumer DNA testing business and forays into health reporting, the company's business never stopped growing.[89] Unlike the church, Ancestry.com currently charges most of its users between $19.99 to $49.99 per month, or at least $99 per six months.[90] In 2020, Ancestry.com reported more than three million subscribers worldwide. The company also generated $1 billion in revenue. Amid the COVID-19 pandemic's blows to world economies in 2020, Ancestry's successes continued because of its array of products and services to use online and in the home. In August of 2020, in the midst of the pandemic, the private-equity firm the Blackstone Group bought the company for $4.7 billion, nearly triple the amount of its purchase price in 2012.[91] (I will discuss direct-to-consumer DNA testing, the company's fastest-growing sector, in the next chapter.)

Among genealogists, as elsewhere in American life, the internet's increased speed and efficiency in delivering information required a considerable financial outlay from content providers. Businesses and nonprofit operations expected customers to fund it through increased fees, if businesses and nonprofit operations did not absorb the cost some other way, such as through fundraising. A variety of factors sorted users into haves and have-nots, in the proverbial "digital divide."[92] Genealogy sites' paywalls and an array of other costs have excluded the poor, the less educated, the older, the rural, and non-English speakers from the latest and most comprehensive information and the speediest research methods. In 2003, when the nonprofit New England Historic Genealogical Society inaugurated its website NewEnglandAncestors.org (now AmericanAncestors.org), impressive user statistics accompanied the organization's yearly budget, which showed nearly half a million dollars spent annually on "content development for the Society's website" alone.[93]

The commercialization of historical research and genealogical research in the internet era (after 1995) reinforced preexisting power relations among Americans especially forcefully. Business interests and businesspeople had long preferred to keep source material and knowledge out of public sight, including scholars' sight, by declaring information to be proprietary or otherwise privately held.[94] Modern corporations went one better. In her 2016 documentary on "data mining," and again in her 2019 book *The Genealogical Sublime,* Julia Creet has argued that Ancestry.com and other companies' users and subscribers have lost control over information they have submitted, in order for companies to copyright and possibly to sell access to that information.[95] Katharina Hering and Creet have each reported on the federal government's handing over of official records, such as U.S. censuses, to Ancestry.com. Digitized versions of these records became commodities in themselves, able to be bought and sold. When companies paid to have these records digitized, the records became searchable, preserved from fire or other destruction, infinitely replicable, and accessible to users who did not have to leave their homes to engage in research. However, access to government records' digital copies was now in the hands of a for-profit company with paying subscribers. Users and subscribers risked having that access disappear if the company ever folded or decided for some other reason to withhold access.[96]

Political Dimensions of Mass Genealogy Commerce

How has genealogy commerce comported with the history of genealogy practices' usefulness to maintaining or challenging power relations? Businesspeople maintained power relations with their insistence on paywalls and also through their insistence on family, gender, and marriage normativity. Each of those three topics resembled a political and cultural battleground in the 1980s, 1990s, and afterward. Affirmations of married heterosexuality in American culture and politics did more than coincide with the genealogy-business boom. Each occasionally struggled on the other's behalf.[97] The Republican Party's fusion of libertarianism and the religious right proved a winning political combination, starting in 1980. Conservatives worried that the family, which they defined as two married people of opposite sexes and with children, was eroding. In 1992, Los Angeles erupted in deadly riots after a suburban jury acquitted white police officers whom a passerby had videotaped beating an unarmed Black man. Speaking a few weeks later to the Commonwealth Club of California, U.S. vice president Dan Quayle rooted inner-city poverty and crime in the female-headed family. The Indiana Republican famously castigated the televised representation of single motherhood on the comedy *Murphy Brown*, in which the lead character had a baby "alone" without punishment or condemnation. Although Murphy Brown was white, Quayle went on to position poor African Americans as a moral foil for behavior he wished to encourage. "It's time to talk again about family, hard work, integrity and personal responsibility," he said. "We cannot be embarrassed out of our belief that two parents, married to each other, are better in most cases for children than one. That honest work is better than hand-outs—or crime."[98] A few years later, a Republican-majority Congress passed the Defense of Marriage Act of 1996, banning same-sex marriage nationally.[99]

Indeed, as conservatives charged, heterosexual childbearing and marriage were slowly coming unmoored from each other. The draconian federal legislation that newly limited marriage rights to monogamous heterosexual couples failed to reverse this trend. Marriage rates had begun declining in the 1960s and continued declining, while divorce rates simultaneously climbed. Changes in divorce law now allowed "irreconcilable differences" as grounds for marital breakup. Plaintiffs no longer had to prove in court that their spouses had harmed them to end their marriages. Divorce rates peaked with couples who married during the 1970s and early 1980s, with 35 percent of them breaking up before their fifteenth wedding anniversaries.[100] The pace of divorce slowed afterwards only because Americans were contracting fewer marriages, and these were likelier to endure.[101] Consequently, the turn of the century featured increased numbers of single and childless adults, ever-decreasing birth rates among the native-born, and rising percentages of babies born to unwed couples and single people. Starting in 1971 and continuing throughout the next half century, native-born women in the United States gave birth at a rate lower than the replacement rate of 2,100 births per one thousand women. Immigration, instead, caused the U.S. population to grow.[102] From 5 percent of American babies in 1962, the rate of births out of wedlock shot up to 18 percent by 1980 and 41 percent by the recession year of 2009.[103] Statistically speaking, marriage and marriage before parenthood seemed less necessary than ever to heterosexuals, at the same time that the federal government newly restricted marriage rights to them.

Those legions of unmarried parents at the turn of the twenty-first century included same-sex couples and gay and lesbian individuals who had gone to some lengths to bear and raise children. Accidental or unplanned pregnancy was highly unlikely in such cases. These adults' bonds with each other, and with their children, otherwise lacked any legal standing before the 2000s.[104] The federal government gave no legal quarter to same-sex relationships, let alone marriages, before 2015, but Vermont passed the nation's first civil union law in 2000 in an effort to work around the federal Defense of Marriage Act. Thirty-six more states followed suit in the next fifteen years.[105] Courts' and state legislatures' upholding of same-sex marriage rights—following activists' decades of pushing—broke the heterosexual monopoly on representations of "family." The Supreme Court's legalization of same-sex marriage nationwide in *Obergefell v. Hodges* (2015) overturned the Defense of Marriage Act.[106]

In theory, the proliferation of same-sex couples, marriages, and families with children; unmarried heterosexual couples or single people with children; or the uses of assisted reproductive technologies, such as in-vitro fertilization and surrogacy, that became common after 1978, need not hamper genealogists' practices.[107] All that would need to change to enable family reckoning that deviates from married, monogamous, heterosexual reproduction, is the method of recordkeeping and notation of lineages. One genealogist explored such possibilities in a 1995 article titled "Numbering Your Genealogy—Special Cases: Surname Changes, Step Relationships, and Adoptions."[108] But others rejected such remedies.

The Church of Jesus Christ of Latter-day Saints had long told married couples to bring as many souls as possible into earthly existence, so that everyone, including the husband and wife themselves, could begin progressing through the heavens after they died. Men and women alike had to marry during their lifetimes to enable this process.[109] Utah, with the highest percentage of Mormons of any American state, has also featured some of the country's highest marriage rates and birthrates.[110] These prescriptions for adults to be married, to produce children while married, and to limit sexual activity and childbearing to marriage operated in harmony with other obligations to perform proxy baptisms, intergenerational sealings, and other ordinances in which descendants went about evangelizing dead forebears. These obligations also defined marriage as an emphatically heterosexual institution, with reproduction at its core.[111] Members of the same church plunged into state-level struggles against same-sex marriage rights, most notably in California in 2008. Afterward, the church quietly acknowledged some damage to its mission work and reputation when it condemned other forms of discrimination on the basis of sexual orientation and gender identity, pertaining to housing and employment, in the state of Utah and in Salt Lake City. In other words, the church supported expanded rights for lesbian, gay, bisexual, transgender, and genderqueer people in these two areas. But even following the Supreme Court's *Obergefell* decision that affirmed the constitutionality of same-sex marriage, the church insisted, in public statements, on its all-important theological principle of married, heterosexual reproduction.[112]

Like Latter-day Saints church authorities' opposition to same-sex marriage, business interests' filtering of genealogy data also expressed opposition to nonnormative family formations. Businesses usually cast the widest nets possible, to attract potential customers. Businesses often hesitate to draw attention to divisions among customers, or worsen those divisions, because doing so may diminish sales.[113] But genealogy businesses in the 1990s, 2000s, and 2010s treated nonnormative family formations as unworthy of attention. The unofficial interconnectedness of nonprofit and for-profit sectors, as in the case of Ancestry.com and the Church of Jesus Christ of Latter-day Saints, helps explain the affirmations of married heterosexuality and rigidly patriarchal naming practices. The church has marketed its "standard double" system of family recordkeeping, extending to software packages' blank forms, to the world. In so doing, the church has imposed cultural uniformity on past and present by presuming that each child has, or had, two married parents of opposite sexes, with the wife taking her husband's surname and the family possessing only one surname. But the historian Donald Akenson has located in European history multiple instances in which otherwise heterosexual, monogamous marriage practices did not follow the "standard double" model of naming. He pointed to the scarcity of surnames among Swedes before 1900, for example. This software's forms and blanks also prevent notation of the matrilineal tracing of names and identities that has long prevailed among Indigenous people in the Americas, Africa, and elsewhere outside the Western world. Writing in the mid-2000s, before the *Obergefell* decision, Akenson observed correctly that same-sex marriages and childbearing also did "not fit into the Mormon computer program and, effectively, evidence of their existence is elided in the LDS data base."[114]

In 2017, a decade later, the New York librarian Robert Sink pointed to other holes in the vast array of online services that otherwise covered American genealogy practices like a blanket. He was seeking information that both genealogy businesses, and sometimes living kin and descendants, wished to conceal about the past, in their desire to serve present-day needs. Sink's topic was female librarians in New York who lived quietly as couples in the 1940s and 1950s. Not only did he bump into paywalls when researching the women's personal and family information online but he also realized that certain kinds of information were absent altogether. Ancestry.com's otherwise remarkably comprehensive searching process did not incorporate the police records, divorce records, or other items containing material that might embarrass living people even though they might otherwise shed light on his and others' histories.[115] Sink's experiences suggest that for genealogy businesses, what did not draw sufficient numbers of eyeballs, or otherwise generate favorable publicity, seemed unfit for airing.

Commercial genealogy activity, especially as it has operated online, did not take all by storm despite impressive numbers and growth. Corners of genealogy practice remained impervious to new technologies and levels of access to information. Some who could afford computers and internet access at home eschewed new technologies or used them sparingly when performing genealogy work. These genealogists have maintained allegiances to paper notebooks, paper documents, face-to-face conversations with family members and strangers, gravestone inscriptions, and other off-line research methods.[116]

Widespread, common names can be difficult to research online. More fundamentally, professionals and other Americans have voiced apprehension about the unreliability of online information. Internet genealogy has relied greatly on secondhand sources as well as on present-minded research.

Therefore, the internet has served as an immense vector by which past and present errors have spread and have endured permanently. Information published on FamilySearch.org has often originated from Mormon families' self-reported "temple sheets." Such findings, and crowd-sourced findings such as the "Family Tree of Humanity" (2012) that the leadership of the church sought to assemble at FamilySearch.org, have been unverified findings.[117] No one has systematically filtered this information for errors or supported it with citations or links to original documents. "[Although] the church collects records and compiles databases, it does not try to control how the tens of millions of people use these records and resources; nor does it attempt to check submissions for accuracy," the historian Amy L. Harris has written.[118] Although some submitters have included citations to original records, the church has not required them to, and so the information base is unevenly supported.

Professionals in genealogy have long urged other genealogists to avoid using already-published material on a family name, and they have emulated the legal profession more than the historical profession in their rejection of most secondhand knowledge as hearsay. Only information from original documents or family lore that originated close in time to the ancestor in question, and that genealogists could reconfirm in other sources, could approach the status of historical fact.[119] Recent instruction manuals, such as Tony Burroughs's *Black Roots* (2001), have paired professionals' ethos with modern skepticism about internet genealogy. Burroughs, cofounder of the Afro-American Historical and Genealogical Society of Chicago in 1979, encouraged neophytes to begin with conversations with family members, then to go through all the phases and varieties of research in face-to-face interviews or correspondence with older kin. Then it was time to turn to tangible primary documents on paper and in stone, obtainable from archives, libraries, and cemeteries. He left spare and very specific use of the internet for the very last.[120]

Some Americans continued to report an appetite for tangible forms of evidence for positive reasons, not just because of apprehensions. Americans' persistent roots tourism in the internet era has been prima facie evidence of their enduring eagerness for face-to-face encounters, and for gravestone inscriptions, homes and real estate, documents, and other corporeal artifacts that ancestors left behind. One anthropologist has remarked of genealogy tourism in eastern Europe after the Cold War ended, in the early 1990s, "humans remain sensual beings, and they are ill at ease with information that can only be perceived as a representation of itself."[121] Such travels are also part of the post-1977 landscape of genealogy-themed entertainment.

Television and Tourism

Especially in the book *Roots*, Alex Haley's own research process proved nearly as much of a "saga" as the characters and incidents he found while tracing the previous seven generations of his maternal ancestry. In *Roots* on television, and in the follow-up TV special of 1978 called *Roots: One Year Later*, as well as in the sequel of *Roots: The Next Generations* (1979), Haley served up the earliest presentations of genealogy revelations as onscreen drama. After *Roots*—and not before—genealogy practices featured in television plotlines, including in some unexpected places.[122] The "little old lady in tennis shoes" trope that has dominated outsiders' stereotypes about genealogists meant that genealogy was not an obvious inspiration for children's entertainment.[123] Yet in a *SpongeBob SquarePants* cartoon, "Pest of the West," which first aired on the Nickelodeon cable channel in 2008, the young title character found emotional fulfillment in researching ancestors after a wise friend ushered him to the town library. Consulting a town history enabled SpongeBob to name his forebear, and to benefit from knowing that in bygone days, SpongeBuck had "saved the town." Shaped like a kitchen sponge, the yellow, rectangular SpongeBob contentedly wiped vast amounts of seabird guano off a statue that turned out to be the likeness of the long-ago SpongeBuck, now with a polished reputation. The episode's writers gently spoofed Americans' emotional investments in genealogy while simultaneously taking them to heart.[124] In addition to such fictional entertainments, reality shows played an important role in genealogy's popularization and commercialization—a phenomenon I cover in the next chapter.

Genealogy tourism has a much older and longer history than onscreen entertainments. But following the end of the Cold War, more destinations became accessible.[125] After 1991, heritage tourists—many of them Jewish—swarmed eastern Europe to such an extent that "[no] visitor to [Poland] can look through a camera viewfinder and be assured that another American or Israeli will not suddenly appear to mar the 'pristine' view," remarked the anthropologist Jack Kugelmass.[126] Roots tourism to West Africa also boomed. Many African Americans affirmed the truth of Haley's text for reasons having to do with racial indignities past and present. "I don't care what people say about how he wrote the book. He touched thousands and millions," remarked the Chicago entrepreneur Amy Hilliard-Jones in 1994. When *Roots* first aired in 1977, she had been one of only twenty-eight Blacks in her Harvard Business School class of 746.[127] "Black students watched it instead of studying. We cried and laughed with each other. It was a watershed—we started having family reunions. My father came from a family of 13 brothers and sisters. It was a logistical challenge—we got on computers—the oldest spoke and then the youngest," she told Anne Romaine, a white journalist and antiracist activist who was planning a biography of Alex Haley before her untimely death in 1995.[128] In retrospect, Hilliard-Jones and her husband Earl Jones pronounced *Roots* "[the] start of Afro-centric conversion" for Americans, meaning that it fostered ever-deeper interest among African Americans in their African origins and in Africa generally.[129] The show's utopian, scrubbed representations of sub-Saharan Africans in its early episodes were unusual, even extraordinary, within 1970s network television. Sub-Saharan Africans were absent altogether from the animated show *Tarzan: Lord of the Jungle* (1976–78), which I personally recall from Saturday morning cartoons. This 1970s incarnation of Tarzan did not resemble a Black African, although his brown skin and dark hair did set him apart from the pallid Tarzan of earlier times.[130]

In the 1990s, the Joneses oversaw McDonald's contests that funded "Homeland Tours" to Senegal and Gambia. The first one, in 1994, included surviving members of Haley's family, including his first wife and two of his adult children. Ninety-six contest winners, seven of them white and eighty-nine of them Black, accompanied them.[131] Upon arriving in Juffure, Gambia, the reputed home village of Kunta Kinte, the Americans received copies of *Roots* and Alex Haley tee shirts from their hosts. Children greeted them with cries of "toubob," meaning white person or European; "fortunately," reported the anthropologist Paulla Ebron, who accompanied the tour, "there was no translation or else there would have been consternation in the group," which was mostly African American.[132] Later in the 1990s, Ghanaian TV continuously rebroadcast *Roots*. Ghana alone attracted ten thousand American visitors per year.[133]

Conclusion

Genetic genealogy commerce, focused on selling DNA tests for home use, has been all-important to the major developments described in this chapter. Large, profitable genealogy businesses arose in the 1980s and afterwards, along with nonprofits that vastly expanded genealogy activity, from JewishGen.org to FamilySearch.org. Genealogy-themed spectacles appeared after *Roots*, as did expansions of roots tourism beyond western Europe. In the next and final chapter, I will describe increasingly hereditarian assumptions about family relations and the consequent commercial expansion of genealogy-driven DNA testing after 1998. Reality shows' broadcasted "reveals" began appearing in the United States after 2003. In these junctures, nonactors and celebrities were filmed while receiving their DNA test results or confronting documents containing previously unknown information. The televised "reveal" belongs to an important theme in the history of genealogy as done for profit: businesspeople's and entertainers' trafficking in emotions.

Among feminists and sexual minorities, family-building proceeded on the basis of affinity, sometimes to the exclusion of blood ties, during the same decades that genealogy's array of businesses and entertainments boomed. But among other Americans, including the millions who availed themselves of genealogy-focused DNA testing, widespread confidence in genetics to explain identity combined with stubborn, older convictions that blood relatedness was more real, and believable, than relatedness based on choice. Many early twenty-first-century Americans favored especially irremovable ways of setting people apart from each other.

CHAPTER SEVEN

Chosen Kin versus Genetic Fetishism

The Traffic in Genealogy-Driven DNA Testing since 1998

Starting in 1999, nearly fifty years after scientists' discovery of DNA's structure in 1953, genealogy businesses began to offer DNA test kits for consumers' use in the home.[1] Consumers would then send their samples to laboratories for genetic analysis and reporting. The goal of successful tracing of ancestry sets genealogy-driven DNA testing apart from DNA testing done for medical or law enforcement purposes, and also from DNA testing that aspires to demonstrate or refute biological relatedness among living relatives, such as paternity testing.[2] Genealogy-directed DNA testing, also known as genetic genealogy, instead focuses on groups who lived long beforehand. Genetic genealogy companies monitor overlaps in DNA characteristics between clients and sample populations who supposedly share genetic overlaps with historical populations. Some companies also report on shared DNA characteristics between clients and other users.

DNA testing for genealogy purposes increased in profitability throughout the 2000s, when a plethora of large and small businesses formed, and in the 2010s, when big genealogy businesses began developing their own genetic sectors. And as with 23andMe (2006), new companies formed whose original and main purpose was genetic genealogy.[3] These businesses reinforced the hierarchy that elevated genetic relatedness over kinship based on choice. Granted, Americans had privileged biological relatedness over nonbiological relatedness long before genealogy-focused DNA testing appeared. With such exceptions as Mormon culture in the nineteenth century, when adoption commanded theological importance, Americans had long considered blood relations to be more "real," for seeming more fixed than chosen relations, such as those created by marriage or adoption. Until recently, even scholars labeled elected relations "fictive kin," stressing the acts of imagination that went into chosen forms of kinship.[4] The vast profits and bottomless promises that advertising and reality-show entertainments made further elevated genetic forms of kinship in American culture.

Within the genetic genealogy industry, enterprises big and small followed old traditions among genealogy businesspeople of deploying the descendant's or client's emotional contentment as a marketing tool and of mining the past to serve the descendant or client's present-day emotional needs. But Americans' reasons for purchasing DNA test kits for genealogy purposes were social as well as psychological. Such testing commanded particular appeal for those who experienced difficulty in documenting their ancestries. DNA test results have taken their place among other non-textual forms of evidence that genealogists have long used to research family history, including oral evidence and morphological scrutiny of outward appearances. Recall that Pauli Murray reconnected with her cousin Sam Fitzgerald in 1951 after spotting his "old Fitzgerald jaw." Jews with forebears in eastern Europe found that shifting boundaries placed the same town in multiple countries within a villager's lifetime.[5] But because DNA results measure probability rather than aiming at historical accuracy, scholars rightfully argue that such results are qualitatively different from those obtained from written evidence.[6]

Critiques of the cultural importance of blood descent in recent times, and of genetic relatedness's considerable profitability, illustrate well that very importance and profitability. Learned people have published numerous objections to genealogy culture, undue fixations on the past, and essentialist views of group identity and the individual self. To scientist Richard Dawkins, for example, genealogy practices obscure humans' descent from, and considerable genetic overlap with, nonhuman animals.[7] Witness social scientists' jeremiads against the fetishization of heritage and consequent cultural propensities to look backward, such as the geographer David Lowenthal's *The Heritage Crusade* (1996). Others have expressed concern about a revival of eugenic thinking in the wake of the first Human Genome Project's completion in 2003 and because of consumers' enthusiasm for genetic testing.[8]

From other vantage points, feminist and gay, lesbian, and genderqueer genealogists have also mounted keen critiques of broader cultural biases towards treasuring biological relatedness. In explicitly rejecting patrilineal and reproduction-centered forms of family reckoning, these critiques amount to an overturning of existing practices and assumptions. Merely to unearth a woman forebear's birth name and birthdate demanded a level of commitment that often amounted to feminism, among genealogists. Surviving historical records otherwise emphasized the deeds and names of men, as soldiers, landowners, businessmen, clergy, and heads of household. Some genealogists went one further in valuing foremothers' deeds, including careers of those who had stayed single, within a field that otherwise valued women most who bore children while married. Gays, lesbians, and self-identified queer populations, and scholars who studied them, rejected the valuing of biological and genetic inheritance even more soundly. Building families and declaring relatedness solely on the basis of choice, as Kath Weston found in her anthropological study *Families We Choose* (1991), or on the basis of "fellow-feeling," as Donna Haraway called it in 1997, amounted to a revolution against commercialized genealogy and blood-based normativity in family reckoning.

Gender-Based Sorting and Feminist Practices among Genealogists

Paternal and patrilineal descent has defined American family culture and law for a number of economic, cultural, and religious reasons. (Enslaved status, inherited through mothers, is a notable exception, along with many Native American tribes' tracing of names and social status through mothers.) The Bible's own prizing of patrilineal descent has been particularly influential in U.S. history. Recall the parthenogenetic father-and-son lists of the Book of Genesis, in which accounts of begetting omitted any mention of women.[9] In U.S. history, alternative forms of family—ranging from female-headed households to single parents to same-sex couples and parents to modern "found families" that base themselves entirely on choice—have drawn condemnation as well as outright suppression. Kath Weston researched family formations in gay neighborhoods in San Francisco in the mid-1980s, as deaths from AIDS were mounting among people in their prime of life. Weston noted that the *San Francisco Chronicle* "insisted on a policy of refusing to list gay lovers as survivors" in obituaries, "citing complaints from relatives who could lay claim to genealogical or adoptive ties to the deceased." Weston's equation of "genealogical" with biological relatedness is commonplace but misleading, since the equation excludes affinity-based relatedness from genealogists' scrutiny.[10] Consequently, members of "found" or "chosen" families that have formed online, as well as in person, have proudly and accurately branded such family-building as queer. Truly, these kinspeople were operating in defiance of widely shared norms in disregarding any preexisting biological overlap in the course of family formation.[11]

Comprehending feminist and queer critiques of patrilineal and patriarchal family reckoning, and of reproduction-centered genealogy, requires first a longer history of gender politics among American genealogists. Women in many historical periods have been held responsible, and held other women responsible, for what the anthropologist Micaela di Leonardo has called "kin work," genealogy included. For Leonardo, kin work extended to other forms of emotional labor, such as the sending of greeting cards, visiting, and creating elaborate holiday celebrations.[12] Genealogy has long been an important part of women's gendered responsibilities and ascribed as female, even though men have dominated professional journals, entertainments, and business sectors, particularly in leadership positions. Recent surveys of rank-and-file genealogists have found large female majorities. Pamela J. Drake's sample of 4,109 Californians in 2001 was 72.2 percent female. More than three quarters of the sociologist Jackie Hogan's smaller sample from 2019 were women. Hogan pointed to other samples of genealogy professionals that were also three-quarters female.[13]

Americans in the twentieth century derided the "chatty old lady," the voluble, elderly, amateur informant who had seemed so helpful to antiquaries and gentleman historians in earlier times. Women with new access to archives and libraries, higher education, and white-collar careers and professions viewed the "chatty old lady" as a threat to their own legitimacy. Men, too, considered her a threat to genealogy's overall reputation. Granted, the pattern of gendered displacement of women apparent from history's professionalization was less evident among genealogists.[14] Although the year 1952 found Winifred Lovering Holman of Boston glumly counting the small numbers of other "ladies" invited to become fellows of the fifty-member ASG, professionals' ranks included meaningful numbers of women.[15] For every gendered insult from those who bemoaned the continuing predominance of amateurs among genealogists, a male professional addressed his illustrious female colleague as if she were his illustrious female colleague. An example is professionals' bereavement when Lucy Mary Kellogg of Michigan died suddenly in 1973. A fellow of the ASG, she was the longtime editor of the Society of Mayflower Descendants' stringent Five Generation Project. Its authors, moving forward in time, sought to document the first five generations of descendants of *Mayflower* passengers. When the project's first volume appeared in 1975, which Kellogg had edited before she died, *The American Genealogist* editor George McCracken praised her and the other compilers for having proceeded with "laudable caution, accepting nothing from previous writers on these families which cannot be documented by reference to the primary documents. They have also rigidly excluded all romantic notions, all praise of the heroism of the Pilgrims. What we have is the bare bones of information supplied by the extant records and the most logical conclusions that can be derived from them."[16] This was high praise indeed, from a professional. Accordingly, professionals of all genders represented their prescriptions as antidotes to the Victorian sentimentalism and moralistic approaches—too often culminating in wishful thinking—that they ascribed to mothers, aunts, and grandmothers. Ineptitude took the shape of a "dotty," often elderly, woman. Following *Roots*, in 1984, a woman professional derided "The Gospel of Aunt Lizzie," shorthand for a family's undue faith in lore that it obtained from oral conversations with elderly kin. "There is no such thing as the Gospel According to Aunt Lizzie," she and her husband, a history professor, complained. Haley "developed such an attachment to his old aunt's story that he could accept no documentary evidence that deviated from it."[17]

But the "chatty old lady" trope gained new respectability in the 1970s and afterwards among genealogists who embraced oral history methods, or who otherwise highly valued ethnic, religious, and class diversity in genealogists' and historians' practices. Alex Haley's lectures and articles preceding *Roots* included an item in the *Oral History Review*'s inaugural volume, in 1973, as oral history in itself was a major concern for him.[18] His research's initial basis was conversations with his maternal grandmother, Cynthia Murray Palmer (1871–1949), which he reconstructed from memories of his Tennessee childhood. Haley recalled in 1974 that she had "pumped that saga into me as if it were plasma, until I knew by rote the story of the African, and the subsequent generational wending of our family through cotton and tobacco plantations into the Civil War and then freedom."[19] He also drew on his memories of conversations among Cynthia's sisters—Liz Murray, who taught school in Oklahoma (and whose name inspired the later talk of "Aunt Lizzie"), and Matilda "Till" Merriwether—as well as "Cousin" Georgia Anderson of Kansas City, who was Cynthia's daughter and Alex's aunt. They had all died by the 1970s, including Cousin Georgia in 1964. Alex eulogized this quartet, especially grandmother Cynthia, as "*griots* in their own ways" in the final pages of *Roots* in 1976.[20] Appearing in a bestseller, the "chatty old lady" had now reached celebrity status. Six years later, in 1982, Rabbi Shmuel Gorr of Jerusalem counseled American Jewish genealogists "that 'there is a germ of truth' in every family *bubba meisha* [grandmother's tale]."[21] Rabbi Gorr, too, joined in rehabilitating the "chatty old lady's" reputation.

In claiming descent from Kunta Kinte through his mother's forebears, Alex Haley embarked on an especially difficult form of genealogy. Not only did women practitioners of genealogy, the "chatty old lady" included, experience gendered condescension, but the experience of researching female ancestors and maternal lines educated researchers of all genders about gender politics in American history. In a patrilineal culture in which people obtained their surnames and property through their fathers, maternal lineages followed circuitous paths that often ended in frustration for genealogists. The historian Laurel Thatcher Ulrich has compared antebellum women to the furniture and other portable household items that they brought into their marriages. Even women's names resembled movable chattel when girls moved into adulthood and marriage, compared to the fixed names of boys and men.[22] Genealogists consequently experienced difficulty in tracing fore-mothers' whereabouts, birthplaces and birthdates, or deaths. Even maternal ancestors who were male could be hard to research.[23]

One way to manage the silences surrounding women in many historical records was to call attention to especially illustrious foremothers, including those with theological heft. In pushing back against American genealogy's patrilineal and paternal biases, the New York law professor Helene Enid Schwartz published a disappointed review of Rottenberg's *Finding Our Fathers* (1977), the first guide to Jewish genealogy for Americans. She wished that Rottenberg "could have found a more appropriate title for his book. As the popular button points out, 'We are also the children of Sarah, Rebecca, Rachel and Leah.'" She listed these biblical matriarchs in response to Rottenberg's opening statement that "many Jews can indeed trace their lineage back to Adam."[24]

Other genealogists highlighted more recent forebears. Unlike more radical feminist thinkers, Pauli Murray treasured her blood relatives, but her family memoir *Proud Shoes* (1956) nonetheless illustrates feminist forms of genealogy practices. She explored her maternal lines and told stories of foremothers as well as forefathers. She expressed pride in having come of age in a house full of women, at a time when such pride was hardly fashionable. In a 1968 interview, the fifty-six-year-old was well aware that the Black unmarried mother was being blamed for social pathologies of all kinds, most notably in the government's recent Moynihan Report of 1965 that ascribed inner-city crime and misery to the female-headed family.[25] In response to her interviewer's question about her experiences as an orphan, she represented herself as having been "a loved child. All of the older people loved me. . . . I was a member of a family that had a tradition. So even though there was not the immediate mother and father image, there was the sense of belonging to something. This is why I sometimes ponder the whole question of the ghetto child in the fatherless home, and I'm not at all sure that it's just a mere absence of a father. It might well be the absence of a tradition; the absence of a feeling of belonging."[26] Murray unknowingly created a contrast to *Roots'* later affirmations of male-headed families and multiple Black fathers through the generations, from Kunta Kinte to the emancipated blacksmith Tom Murray.

Within feminism's great awakening in the 1960s and 1970s, some genealogists redoubled their efforts to confer visibility on foremothers whose very names patrilineal customs had buried. Christine Knox Wood of Lubbock, Texas, probably did not identify as a feminist, since she published her family genealogy, *Those Reeves Girls: A Study of the Descendants of Five Sisters* (1973), while veiled in her husband's name. Only a discerning reader could locate the fifty-year-old Mrs. James Moses Wood Jr.'s own maiden name, birthdate, and parentage, deep inside her book. Wood nonetheless scaled gender hierarchies in striving to trace foremothers and their children, including married daughters, over multiple generations. The five sisters in question lived in North Carolina and Alabama in the early nineteenth century, with their children numbering as many as twenty per sister. A reviewer marveled that the Reeves sisters' parents "have no known descendants bearing their surname, and . . . their posterity all bear different family names."[27]

Other practitioners pushed back against hierarchies by steering away from the praise for married fertility that normative genealogy practices expressed. In American, western European, and other patrilineal contexts, childless couples and single people had long been represented as withered stumps within family trees. Generations of daughters with no sons born, or sons who survived long enough to reproduce within marriage, represented ground where family identities, as fathers' and husbands' surnames expressed them, went to die.[28] Feminist-minded genealogists directed attention to familial feats instead. For example, Amy Sunners published a family genealogy as a homemade video on YouTube in 2010, using stills from family photographs. She honored a great-great aunt and a great-aunt on her father's side. Bertha Sunners, a Russian-born midwife who cared for New York tenement dwellers, was arrested in 1919 for aiding an abortion. Her daughter Elizabeth Sunners became a fully credentialed physician in 1930, and she served with the Coast Guard in World War II and with Margaret Sanger's birth-control organizations. Genealogists who were more old-fashioned would have ignored Elizabeth for remaining single and never bearing children of her own. Those two facts about her life were beside the point for her grandniece. Speaking in her video, Amy made the link between researching foremothers' careers and encounters with the law, and a descendant's feminist commitments, especially explicit. "Elizabeth and her mother paved the way for the second wave of the women's rights movement. . . . The freedom and equality that I enjoy in 2010 is in part due to the fearlessness of the women who came before me."[29]

Kinship and Family Formations Based on Choice

Radicals and more utopian thinkers went further in challenging patrilineal tradition and praise for reproduction, by assembling families on the basis of affinity. Audre Lorde's memoir *Zami: A New Spelling of My Name* (1982) is a case in point. A major African American feminist and lesbian poet, with family roots in the Caribbean country of Grenada, the footloose Lorde (1934–92) met lovers and friends easily when moving to new places and going among strangers in the 1950s and 1960s. For women, particularly for lesbians and other women who were their own heads of household, she appropriated American literary traditions of wandering, thereby challenging histories in which wandering expressed masculine gender privilege. Examples from the time of her adulthood include Jack Kerouac's *On the Road* (1954) and the 1969 film *Easy Rider*. But Lorde's peregrinations did not entail severing herself from her origins. Instead, she felt lovingly bound to foremothers. She recounted her family background as a female-only kinship stream, extending to the spiritual kinship she experienced with female spirit-beings. After leaving her mother's house in New York at age seventeen, she met other women out in America whose "shapes join Linda," her mother, "and Gran'Ma Liz and Gran'Aunt Anni in my dreaming, where they dance with swords in their hands, stately forceful steps, to mark the time when they were all warriors."[30] The scholar Cheryl A. Wall wrote of *Zami* that Lorde's "impetus is to break free of the constraints of the Western patriarchal construct that defines family as the vertical transfer of a blood line."[31]

Lorde, and Pauli Murray before her, belonged to sexual minorities. They put aside married reproduction with men at a time when even rumored homosexuality exacted high costs in workplaces and smacked of disease as well as of crime.[32] Murray and Lorde's orientation toward other women informed their regard for foremothers and, in Lorde's case, for like-minded women who were not originally related to her. Even more emphatic examples of family relationships built solely from affinity, come from the creation of gay and lesbian "sexual politics, sexual communities" in American cities, starting in the 1970s. In these neighborhoods, people thrived who were committed to living openly as gay or lesbian. They opened businesses such as bars and bookstores and specialized in parades, protests, and other forms of community organizing.[33] In San Francisco in the 1980s, unmarried, often childless gay men and lesbians assembled with other adults, often in search of surrogates for their families of origin from whom they felt estranged. These newfound families did not always contain the nucleus of a couple. Platonic friends and sometimes ex-partners also belonged to the webs, which stretched across many rooftops.[34] These families matter to the history of genealogy because their members ignored ties created by reproduction and, by implication, genetics even more completely than Lorde had. The feminist theorist Donna Haraway eschewed biological relatedness, too, when she stated in 1997, "I am sick to death of bonding through kinship and 'the family,' and I long for models of solidarity and human unity and difference rooted in friendship, work, partially shared purpose, intractable collective pain, inescapable mortality, and persistent hope."[35] In such critiques, the nuclear family privatized love and time spent together that should instead breach the bonds of *Homo sapiens* to embrace the earth at large at a time of climate emergency, Haraway remarked in 2018.[36]

Genealogical Bewilderment before 1998: Affirmations of Genetic and Blood-Based Kinship

Such affirmations of queer family reckoning were scattered, compared to the more widespread regard for blood and genetic forms of kinship among laypeople (nonscientists) in the 1970s and afterwards. Long before the advent of commercial at-home DNA testing, a particular signifier of Americans' regard for hereditary ties was the outcry from adults who, in their infancy or early childhood, had been adopted by strangers working through adoption agencies. Adoptions in earlier times had often occurred informally and openly within extended families. For example, Revolutionary War veteran Joseph Plumb Martin (1760–1850) nonchalantly recounted his own grandparents' adoption of him at age seven. He lived with them until he went to war and reached adulthood.[37] But closed, secretive adoptions became customary between World War II and the 1960s, a time when births out of wedlock were climbing; abortion and contraceptive devices remained outlawed, including for married couples until 1965; and "illegitimate" births were the stuff of shame. Adoptions usually occurred between strangers, with hired adoption agencies acting as mediators. Adults expected babies never to know their birth parentage, or to need or desire to know it, so adults sequestered from view or destroyed outright adoptees' birth certificates and other information about their origins.[38] Feeling robbed of birth information, adult adoptees understood the benefits of genetic family reckonings especially keenly because they experienced constant reminders of their absence, especially after genealogy businesses and entertainments began to boom.[39]

In 1965, a critic of these secretive adoptions labeled the subsequent unhappiness of adult adoptees "genealogical bewilderment." The diagnosis spread, especially after the jeremiad *The Adoption Triangle* (1978) popularized the term. Importantly, "genealogical" here was synonymous with "biological."[40] Secret, closed adoptions and the concealment or destruction of birth documentation seemed ever more wrong, once the ability to document genetic origins seemed essential to bodily health as well as to emotional wellness. A New Jersey woman who was active in the Adoptees' Liberty Movement Association (ALMA) (founded in 1971) remarked in a genealogy periodical that when a child grows, he "wishes to know what other people can take for granted, who he is, and who his parents were," but "he alone of United States citizens is refused his original birth certificate." Note her reference to "who he is." Knowledge of one's birth family seemed synonymous with psychological well-being.[41] This author also viewed access to one's own birth documentation as a bedrock right.

Consequently, Alex Haley's *Roots* simultaneously undercut racial and class exclusivity in genealogy practices while, to many adoptees, reinforcing exclusion. African Americans had long endured being unable to name their "furthest back person" for reasons pertaining to enslavement and racial discrimination. But a descendant of slaves now seemed able to document his lineage back to African shores. *Roots'* treasuring of blood relatedness was apparent to one white genealogist in 1980. The book and television show "more than any other single work stimulated the man in the street to inquire about the genetic, cultural, and other forces that contributed to making him the person that he is."[42] *Roots'* hereditarian premises were also apparent to Cynthia A. Ortega, who wrote a letter to the *New York Times* immediately following the 1977 broadcast. She reported having labored in vain against the sealing of her own adoption record. "Mr. Haley's book and the television show have dramatized a need that I think most people have: to identify with someone who can give them a sense of continuity and of belonging. Those of us who were adopted and who would like to know who our real parents were are being told that we will just have to ignore this need." From her perspective, Haley had been free to go into the National Archives and trail his "Aunt Liz."[43]

Genealogy professionals and hereditary organizations' officials in the 1970s and 1980s undoubtedly compounded adoptees' consternation when they, too, portrayed genealogy activity as nearly synonymous with genetics. A frequent contributor to genealogy journals, the geneticist Thomas H. Roderick defined genealogy in 1971 as "the attempts to determine through historical and biological evidence the true genetic relationships of members of a family."[44] In 1984, DAR president Sarah King enjoined members' participation in a genetic study conducted by Vanderbilt University's Department of Endocrinology, in which the subjects were asked to complete "medical-genealogical charts." King explained the decision to the membership as follows: "We are the products of those who have gone before and we hope to put our genealogy to work for the protection of future generations." She presented the decision to take part in genetic studies directed at medical research as having been "a goal of [her] administration."[45]

Marital ties seem an exception to this pattern of privileging blood and genetic relationships. It was common for genealogists to research their spouses' forebears, to whom they presumably had few or no biological ties.[46] Family reckoning need not necessarily reject elected kin. But even though matrimony fit within, and even defined, normative definitions of family, most instructional literature in the 1970s and 1980s excluded family ties based on choice from definitions of relatedness. An individual could not rightfully claim descent from their adoptive family or stepfamily even when they felt chosen by the parents who had raised them, or when their own birth information remained out of reach. In 1978, the DAR's leadership stated its refusal to admit women who claimed revolutionary descent through adoptive parents or stepparents. Chief registrar Elizabeth Cox White remarked, "Our love and sympathy go out to the parents of these 'chosen' children, but the fact remains that these children are not from your blood line. We are a lineal Society and to be eligible for membership you must have a direct blood line back to your Revolutionary ancestor through legal marriages."[47] To conceal proof of a child's adoption when compiling genealogies, fretted Milton Rubincam, a dean of professional genealogy, in 1980, meant that "future generations would be completely misled and would be tracing their lines to people with whom they would have no genetic connection."[48]

Mormon authors mounted some challenges to genetic definitions of genealogy. Exclusivity based on indelible, biological forms of relatedness did not suit a belief system that stressed more genealogy for more people. Nineteenth-century Mormons' engagement in spiritual adoptions before the 1890s foreshadowed later acceptance of affinity as family glue. Rubincam wrote in repudiation of what he called "dishonest" statements—against truth—in Virginia H. Rollins's 1975 instruction text pertaining to Mormon temple work. "Adopted children are recorded as if they were born of the parents," wrote Rollins, in statements that Rubincam indignantly reproduced in his review. "No indication of adoption need be made unless you wish. . . . Because of the legal nature of adoption and, often, the absence of information of any other parentage, any adopted person is tracing his 'real' ancestry when he traces his adoptive parents' lines."[49] During the same decades, the Logan, Utah-based *Genealogical Helper* regularly published advertisements from the Adoptees' Liberty Movement Association. A few executives lived this principle, too. George B. Everton Jr., president and publisher, and his wife Louise M. Everton, vice president and book review editor, were the third generation of Evertons to operate the business and the periodical. In 1983, Louise told readers that she and her husband had adopted at least four children.[50] However, church authorities also praised married reproduction to such an extent that, in later times, Ancestry.com moved easily into marketing DNA tests for genealogy purposes. In their very nature, these tests fetishized biological relatedness, including to living strangers and to long-dead people whom the client could never know personally. These purely genetic connections, which excluded any real-time affinity (in the case of long-dead populations), were worlds away from the like-minded spirit beings that Audre Lorde greeted as her kin.

Genetic consciousness intensified at the turn of the twenty-first century, particularly among nonscientists and in popular culture. Writing in 2000, the historian Evelyn Fox Keller found considerably more confidence in genes' explanatory power in the media and among laypeople than among professional scientists, who were then distancing themselves from the concept of the gene as overly simplistic. "Perhaps it is time we invent some new words," remarked Keller, regarding scientists' impatience.[51] Subsequent research on epigenetics, a field that researches environmental alterations of genes, has fulfilled her scenario. From scientists' perspectives, publicized instances of genetic "chimeras" and other rare instances in which biological relatives share no DNA similarities, have demolished simplistic scenarios of vertical, linear genetic inheritance. Human genetic inheritances do not amount to symmetrical fractions, with precise quarters from each grandparent, so much as asymmetrical "chunks." A child often shares much more genetic material with one parent or grandparent than with another.[52] Yet the certainty that linear representations of one's biological antecedents were necessary for bodily and mental health increased among laypeople and nonscientists.[53]

Like other modern memoirists, the law professor Patricia Williams began her 1991 account, *The Alchemy of Race and Rights*, long before her own birth. Her maternal great-great-grandmother had grown up enslaved in Tennessee. At the age of eleven, the girl was sold to an attorney, who impregnated her the next year. Many generations later, Williams's own mother told Williams that her legal prowess was in her blood—inherited from their white forebear, the slave master. Williams simultaneously embraced her mother's account and felt troubled by it. "Reclaiming that from which one has been disinherited is a good thing," she reflected wryly. In other words, it should be a good thing. "Self-possession in the full sense of that expression is the companion of self-knowledge. Yet claiming for myself a heritage the weft of whose genesis is my own disinheritance is a profoundly troubling paradox."[54] While Williams choked on the presence of a slaveowner and sexual predator in her family tree, her mother was far from unusual in voicing an emphatic genetic determinism among Americans, long before the turning points of 1998–99.

Affirmations of Genetic and Blood Kinship after 1998: The Rise of Genetic Genealogy Commerce

Genetic knowledge of oneself undeniably carried new benefits for medical knowledge, as understandings of genetically caused conditions broadened.[55] Laypeople's valuing of genetic relatedness also created the market conditions for personal DNA tests focused on ancestry to emerge as a commodity. I have seen no marketing of DNA testing for genealogical purposes before *Nature's* 1998 article, "Jefferson Fathered Slave's Last Child," which presented DNA test results from Thomas Jefferson and Sally Hemings's male descendants.[56] The Jefferson/Hemings study drew wide public notice by pulling together several potent and controversial themes, including founding fathers as slaveowners, interracial sex, and sex outside of marriage. During these same months in late 1998 and early 1999, President Bill Clinton's infidelities and his impeachment and trial for perjury attracted their own blanket media coverage in the United States. Each of these two major news stories about presidents' extramarital sex with younger women fueled interest in the other story.

Historians had long rejected the allegations—that had originated with a mudslinging political enemy—that the widowed Jefferson (1743–1826) had fathered six, possibly seven, children with his house slave Hemings (1773–1835). Political acrimony was intense in their lifetimes. Jefferson's first inaugural speech in 1801 included famous affirmations of free speech in politics and a peace offering to his opponents. Naming the dominant factions of the day, his own faction first, Jefferson declared that "we are all Republicans, we are all Federalists."[57] But the Federalist pamphleteer James Callender remained unimpressed, and he later expressed his disgust with the president by repeatedly taunting him about his mistress. A Scotsman removed to Philadelphia, Callender had previously expressed distaste for the casual breaching of racial boundaries between enslaved people and white masters that he noticed when visiting Virginia. Screeds against "dusky Sally" from Callender and others who begrudged or disliked Jefferson, combined with Jefferson's own stated distaste for Black people—and his descendants' strenuous efforts to name other possible fathers of Sally Hemings's children—exiled the allegations about Hemings-Jefferson relatedness from academia for generations.[58]

But by 1997, the law professor Annette Gordon-Reed had reexamined a vast if circumstantial body of textual evidence, to argue that Jefferson had indeed fathered Hemings's children. She incorporated Lucia Stanton's observation that Jefferson, and no other male that his grandchildren and others had named later on, had been present at his plantation, Monticello, when each of the Hemings children was likely conceived.[59] Gordon-Reed also renewed the scrutiny of items that earlier historians had dismissed, particularly Madison Hemings's newspaper interview from 1873. She pointed to preferential treatment that Jefferson, his overseers, and his posthumous estate gave to Sally Hemings and her children. Jefferson and overseers allowed those Hemingses who left Monticello to continue on their way, while aggressively pursuing other enslaved people in flight from Monticello as fugitives.[60] In his will, Jefferson manumitted Sally, in a private act of emancipation. After he died in July 1826, his estate either manumitted each of the Hemings children still at Monticello or permitted them to leave quietly. But the estate auctioned off at least 130 other enslaved people six months later, in January 1827, in order to pay Jefferson's mountainous debts.[61] This action likely inflicted trauma on a massive scale, as it severed the slaves' ties to family, friends, and accustomed homes.[62]

Centuries later, the media attention that Gordon-Reed's 1997 book, *Thomas Jefferson and Sally Hemings: An American Controversy* attracted, drew the interest of scientists and other scholars, including the historian and Jefferson biographer Joseph Ellis. They were eager to apply DNA testing technology to the question of Jefferson's fathering of the Hemings children. The scholars sought male descendants for a Y-chromosome-based examination of genetic overlaps among Jefferson, Hemings, and Woodson kinsmen. Descendants of another Monticello slave, Thomas Woodson, had long maintained that Jefferson had fathered him, too. Since the only surviving children of Jefferson and his wife Martha (died 1782) were daughters, and because only males carry the Y chromosome, the scientists had to settle for male descendants of Jefferson's uncle, Field Jefferson. The scientists tested male posterity of Eston Hemings, not that of his older brother Madison, because only Eston had a continuous male line. Test results showed a very high probability of biological relatedness. Field Jefferson's and Eston Hemings's descendants shared a rare haplotype. But the testing revealed no such overlap between Jefferson and Woodson descendants.[63]

Did the extraordinary thinker who wrote the Declaration of Independence and conceived the First Amendment engage in the commonplace, but largely unspoken, extramarital sex that slavery incentivized? Evidence pointing to an affirmative answer, from DNA test results as well as documents, was mounting. Combined with whites' residual distaste for interracial sex and an ongoing wave of interest in histories of American founding fathers, the evidence drew a considerable outcry.[64] Shortly after the *Nature* article appeared, the organization that ran Monticello as a historic site that attracted half a million visitors annually to Charlottesville, the Thomas Jefferson Memorial Foundation, ceremoniously affirmed the truth of Jefferson's fathering of the Hemings children in a series of resolutions published in January 2000.[65] So did the president of the United States. When President George W. Bush's administration celebrated the anniversary of Jefferson's birthday at the White House on April 12, 2001, it invited Hemings descendants as well as those descended from Jefferson's white children. Gesturing at the multiracial gathering, the president thanked "all the descendants of Thomas Jefferson who are here. . . . No wonder America sees itself in Thomas Jefferson."[66]

But an angry backlash had already begun among scholars, historians, genealogists, and others who founded the Thomas Jefferson Heritage Society (TJHS) in Charlottesville in April 2000. In a report issued on the same day as the White House ceremony, in an effort to divert media attention away from Washington, the TJHS contended that the DNA test results had proved only that some Jefferson man had fathered Eston Hemings and that more than two dozen other Jefferson kinsmen were alive at the probable time of Eston's conception.[67] In 2002, those TJHS members and others who controlled access to the Jefferson family burial ground in Charlottesville ritually voted, seventy-four to six, to continue banning burials of Hemings descendants there. The group simultaneously voted down another proposal to set aside land for the burial of descendants of all enslaved people at Monticello, not just Hemings descendants. These votes occurred despite, and perhaps because of, the bundle of evidence from newly assembled historical records and new evidence from the DNA study that suggested the Hemingses' relatedness to the Jefferson family.[68] The old Civil War and Jim Crow-era insistence on segregating nonwhite from white, even in death, persisted into the newborn century.[69] Decades later, historians and other scholars continued to pile into this struggle to deny Hemingses' relatedness to Thomas Jefferson.[70]

In the meantime, the publicity surrounding those *Nature* articles of 1997–98 that included findings on the Jewish priestly order called the Cohens as well as on Jeffersons, Hemings, and Woodsons, created a fertile environment for businesses to begin proffering direct-to-consumer DNA testing pertaining to long-ago ancestry.[71] In 1999, Family Tree DNA, "the first genetic genealogy company" of many, was launched in Houston.[72] Smaller companies included the Black-owned business African Ancestry, which entrepreneurs

Rick A. Kittles (also a scientist at the University of Arizona) and Gina M. Paige created in 2003.[73] In the mid-and late 2000s, Kim TallBear counted six different DNA testing companies that courted Native American consumers and tribal membership officials.[74] The field vastly expanded after 2007, when the price of genetic testing began to drop.[75] For her 2016 book, the sociologist Alondra Nelson counted thirty-eight companies that proffered "genetic-genealogy-testing services."[76] Three years later, the sociologist Jackie Hogan found "eleven leading companies" in the field to study.[77] A January 2020 study counted seventy-four companies, in all, in the direct-to-consumer genetic ancestry testing business, and twenty-six million DNA tests sold across the world in the previous two decades.[78] Over time, these companies offered three main categories of DNA testing. Y-chromosome testing, which Jefferson, Woodson, and Hemings descendants undertook for the *Nature* article, focused only on males and only on the paternal side, and usually cost the least. Mitochondrial testing revealed maternal ancestry only. Autosomal testing—the most expensive and specialized option—tracked both males and females in one's ancestry and maternal and paternal sides of the family. In the early 2010s, autosomal testing was available only under the trade name AncestryDNA.[79]

The proliferation of DNA testing for genealogy purposes signified, and also fostered, an even more solid confidence in the importance of biological relatedness to family reckonings than did previous genetic findings. The Australian journalist Christine Kenneally described the alerts that clients of major DNA testing and analysis companies could purchase as of 2012–13. These clients received an email when some other customer possessed "one or more largeish segments of DNA that look exactly the same."[80] Pondering a great-great grandfather who died long before she was born, and who was impossible for her to know personally, Kenneally reported feeling a new closeness to him. Authorities in Britain had shipped the fifteen-year-old boy to Australia after accusing him of stealing a handkerchief. Not only had Kenneally, his descendant, "spoken to people who have spoken to people who once spoke to him," but her emotional investment in genetics also informed her feelings: "he is here with me, and not just in my thoughts. This isn't a metaphor but a fact, as real as the Himalayas. There is information within me that came from him." "The ancestors are us and are in us," members of the Forest/de Forest family remarked to a scholar, having commissioned DNA research.[81]

For genealogists of all kinds, personal DNA analyses can illuminate corners of the past that omissions or untruths in surviving print documents and archives, or destruction of those materials, have darkened. Therefore, DNA test results have joined other forms of non-textual evidence, including family lore obtained orally, in researchers' toolboxes.[82] DNA testing has special poignancy for African American, Jewish, and other practitioners who otherwise have particular difficulty tracing their ancestry using documents.[83] However, DNA test results suggest one's genetic ancestry in vague and sometimes historically misleading terms. Results show overlaps between customers' DNA samples and databases of samples taken from present-day populations. But companies usually withhold details about these populations.[84] Moreover, DNA test results have assigned a permanence and significance to ethnic and geographical labels that neither history nor genetic science support. There have not always been English or Irish or Yoruba.[85] Results can indicate a client's genetic similarity to people who are living or dead but at the same time lack the dates, localities, affinities, and decision making—and above all, the names—that are characteristic of family history.

Genetic Genealogy as Entertainment Spectacle

Genetic genealogy became an entertainment staple of reality television in the 2000s, paralleling its emergence as a lucrative industry and in keeping with the overall proliferation of genealogy-themed entertainments, including tourism, after 1977. Maury Povich's talk shows that featured paternity DNA testing as a recurring theme were an important antecedent from the 1990s that persisted into the next decade. The nonactors who appeared as guests on Povich's shows foreshadowed reality shows' casting of nonactors or actors playing themselves.[86] In 2003, the BBC documentary *Motherland: A Genetic Journey* became the earliest genetic-genealogy entertainment. Multiple Britons of African-Caribbean descent beheld their Y-chromosome DNA test results, which often revealed white male forebears, while on camera.[87] The history of genealogy-themed reality-based television continued with *Who Do You Think You Are?* in 2004, a commercial show about celebrity bloodlines in which celebrities played themselves; and Henry Louis Gates Jr.'s programs on PBS—*African American Lives* in 2006 and 2008—which focused on the stories and lineages of real people.[88] *Who Do You Think You Are?* and *Motherland* originated in Britain, not the United States. But entertainments from outside the United States have shaped American history nonetheless, since the two shows succeeded to the satisfaction of executives and others who monitored U.S. ratings. The American adaptation of *Who Do You Think You Are?* with U.S. celebrities, launched in 2010. The era's largest genealogy business, Ancestry.com, sponsored the show, with "the company's products . . . quite conspicuously integrated into each episode." In 2010–12, when the show was on network television, subscriptions to Ancestry.com's websites grew by more than 40 percent.[89] NBC canceled the show in 2012, but it found new life by 2015 on the TLC cable channel.[90]

An individual's decision to publicize their purchased DNA results on television illustrates some basic features of genealogy commerce, past and present: the act of consumption, the quest for media attention, and the infusion of genealogy quests with emotion. In the juncture on reality shows called the "reveal," the camera records and broadcasts the descendant's surprise, distress, or joy at revelations from their DNA results or from documents. The "reveal" bears some resemblance to pornography for the voyeurism it inspires in the viewer, to witness the expression of strong feelings that some would prefer to experience off-camera. I personally was glad to be alone in my house when I opened the email from Ancestry.com that contained results of my own genealogical DNA test.

Other objections to television's "reveal" suggest a more serious theft of group sovereignty from Native American tribes and individuals. Regarding the Lumbee, Indigenous people in the Carolinas, the historian Malinda Maynor Lowery has described a combination of ancestry as tribespeople recognized it, residence in particular places, and behaviors in keeping with Lumbee culture, such as use of the Lumbee language, as the major bases of Lumbee belonging. Many Lumbee agreed on these criteria.[91] The writer Louise Erdrich, whose mother was Chippewa/Ojibwe, refused in 2010 to have her DNA analyzed in order to have her "reveal" broadcasted on Henry Louis Gates Jr.'s *Faces of America* show. Family members had told her, "It's not yours to give, Louise."[92] She and Chippewa tribal elders instead "[understood] her DNA to be communal property."[93] But for Americans who were not Indigenous, consumerism, genetics, and individualism became ever more yoked together. Indigenous leaders' outcry in 2018 at Senator Elizabeth Warren's publicizing of her own DNA test results, which suggested partial Native American descent, constituted an even more vivid illustration of the following principle. Entertainers and consumers, including Warren and other public figures, effectively usurped tribes' decision-making regarding who belonged and on what basis, in favor of criteria that were purely genetic and that commercialism had engendered.[94]

Conclusion

As feminists from Pauli Murray to Audre Lorde to Donna Haraway have shown, the act of dissenting from the late twentieth century's preoccupation with biogenetic relatedness, now with so much money at stake, amounted to an affirmation of queerness and defiance of normativity. As the century turned, genealogy moved ever closer to commercialized genetics. Americans rooted social identities and individual identities in the ever more distant past and made them ever more indelible. DNA test results themselves cannot deliver names, but the vast numbers of people who have purchased DNA tests, and who have watched others react to their results while on camera, have nonetheless communicated eagerness for fixed identities obtained from knowledge of lineages. Communities of genealogists and others who have especially valued genealogy-focused DNA test results, might not otherwise find family information in historical records. Both ancestor and descendant faced barriers to family knowledge resulting from slavery, poverty, language barriers, and/or belonging to a despised religious, racial, or ethnic minority.

Delores (Dee) Woodtor (1945–2002) of Evanston, Illinois, oversaw the Newberry Library's efforts to expand its holdings in African American history and genealogy in the 1980s, to increase diversity among its patrons and improve relations with African American genealogists. She later published a manual for them, *Finding a Place Called Home* (1999). Her files include reflections on practicing genealogy and engaging in roots travel as a Black person. Around 1991, she drafted a letter advising a colleague who ran a genealogical society to tell members to expect a "few obstacles" on research trips to the South. "Many people hire local researchers, so I don't suppose it is a surprise to see Black genealogists when they show up. . . . No one can deny you public access to a court house once you arrive."[95] Such objections to genealogists' diversity as Woodtor expected her colleague to encounter, illustrate that diversity's detractors continually experienced diversification as a threat.

There's No Market for Being Told We're All Related
Genealogy's Politics, Revisited

The historian Kirsten Fermaglich has found that in New York City, following the 9/11 terrorist attacks of 2001, those who petitioned courts for name changes often sought to shore up current and past identities, in contrast to earlier generations of New Yorkers who had pursued name changing in order to break with past identities and to pursue a better future as part of the middle class. Twenty-first-century Arab and Muslim immigrants approached courts to change their names in order to achieve uniformity of names in records. Eliminating inconsistencies and errors in the copying of names, from document to document, had become all-important.[1] In principle, "no fly lists" required accurate recording of names that allowed verbatim reconfirmation in other documents. Coincidence alone does not explain why lucrative genealogy businesses, genealogy-themed reality television, and the traffic in genealogy-driven DNA testing ballooned during the same decades as the federal REAL ID legislation (2005) that aspired to lock in names and other post-9/11 forms of government "identity policing" that the political scientist Magdalena Krajewska has described.[2] All these practices harnessed people to whom they had been before, up until the present day. DNA testing results went further, in shackling one's identity to one's forebears.

This chaining of present-day personhood to past personhood that the pursuit of genetic revelations expresses emphatically illustrates genealogy's political dimensions, past and present. Genealogists' articulations of struggles for inclusion—as well as exclusion—have continued into today. Genealogists of all genders have represented foremothers' full lives, beyond marriage and reproduction, in family genealogies, and they have striven to impart the voices and stories of women whose very names would otherwise remain unknown. Genealogists of color, and those from religious minorities, have gathered what they could—textual evidence, interviews of their kin, and morphological reckonings—to help reconstruct their ancestry. In writing as an African American descended from enslaved people, Alex Haley proved a transformative figure in genealogy's inclusiveness as well as in business and entertainment histories. His book and onscreen entertainments not only articulated many of previous generations' genealogy longings. Haley's infusion

of genealogical quests with the frankly expressed emotions on which genealogy businesspeople had long depended heavily influenced the later development of large-scale genealogy enterprises and the boom in consumerist
genetic commerce.

Elsewhere in the United States, in the nineteenth century, Mormons' spiritual engagement with the dead helped set their religion apart as a despised
oddity. But since the 1940s, Mormons' own escalating predilection for genealogy and their direct use of genealogical research findings in worship in order to enhance outreach to the dead have proven crucial to the Church of
Jesus Christ of Latter-day Saints' prosperity and missionary efforts. The
church's facilities, software, microfilmed treasures, and databases have all
compelled tourists to flow into Utah and uncountable others to visit church
libraries while online. Operating separately from the church, but working
alongside it, Mormon businesspeople and those from Mormon backgrounds
repeatedly developed the largest genealogy businesses to date—starting in
1947 with the Everton family's publishing company and continuing in the
1980s with Ancestry Inc. That company begat Ancestry.com in 1996, and it
became the largest genealogy business to date (2021). DNA testing has
proven an especially lucrative sector. To the extent that genealogy-driven
DNA testing has been useful to Americans for whom reliance on documentation has been difficult or impossible, genetic genealogy has advanced racial,
ethnic, religious, class, and other kinds of diversification among genealogists.
But queer definitions of family that stress affinity and choice, such as Audre
Lorde's in *Zami*, have enhanced genealogy's diversification even more. Lorde
and other builders of "found" families have opened genealogy to ever more
fluid readings of descent and relatedness.

But even more starkly than genealogy's older incarnations, genetic genealogy illustrates genealogy's persistent capacity to create and maintain social
hierarchies and power relations.[3] An especially obvious set of exclusions, in
recent times, has stemmed from genealogy's unprecedented commercialization. Genealogy businesses elevated findings that pleased their customers
and attracted new ones. Often these obligations entailed reinforcement of
heteronormativity and married reproduction. Genealogists who research
women and/or maternal lines in the United States continued to have to
struggle against an emphatically patrilineal historical record as well as
present-day recordkeeping practices that prize the male-headed and male-
named family. Families huddled under the roof of a husband's surname remain predominant in software packages and in other services and products
for modern genealogists.[4]

Genealogy has also persistently served as a tool for white supremacists, eugenicists, and nativists (those hostile to immigration), and this pattern has become even more evident with the rise of genealogy-driven DNA testing. Scholars hoped in the 1990s and 2000s that innovations in genetics, including direct-to-consumer DNA testing, would weaken the meanings of racial and ethnic differences because genetic scientists make nonsense of such differences: "99.9% of the human genetic code is identical in every person," wrote the authors of a study of laypeople's understanding of DNA test results.[5] Scrutiny of human genomes, the first completed in 2003, also served to weaken distinctions between humans and other animals; humans and mice share impressive percentages of genetic material.[6] Genetic descent began with the human species: long before documentation or rumors of relatedness could be possible or detectable for later generations, long enough ago to find a countless number of ancestors for everyone living today. But genealogy based on records reaches back a millennium, at most, but usually a handful of centuries.[7] The lineages that genealogists document, like other characteristics that people use to sort each other into groups, comprise a tiny percentage of one's genetic endowment.

But now that ancestry-driven DNA testing has acquired vernacular, less scientific uses among businesspeople and customers and governments around the world, interpretations of test results have clearly reinscribed racial, ethnic, and national differences.[8] The sociologist Wendy D. Roth and colleagues found that "The methodology of ancestry testing itself may ... reify races as essential genetic realities by suggesting," falsely, "that genetic tests can distinguish them."[9] The sociologist Alondra Nelson remarked sagely in a 2014 interview about DNA testing commerce, "there's no market," meaning possibilities for profit, "for being told we're all related."[10]

Population geneticists' uses of DNA test results to trace modern populations backwards to previous populations who lived on the same land, in Britain in particular, has been a stark example of interpreting DNA test results to validate other differences among humans. Bryan Sykes's *Seven Daughters of Eve* (2001), which popularized mitochondrial DNA testing based on its geographic signatures, was a key text.[11] Such parsing of "geographic ancestral origins" in test results bears heavy political weight for occurring during an era of mass immigration to Britain and northern Europe. In 2015 alone, one million people, mostly from the global South and especially from the wars in Syria and Afghanistan, fled there. Anti-immigration backlashes have shaped European politics ever since, from Hungary to Germany to France.[12] Like Americans did in the 1890s and 1900s, who labeled themselves Daughters and

Dames and Native Sons of the Golden West, Europeans' representations of their longstanding tenure on their lands set an "us" apart from a "them." But while geography-focused ancestry testing was unavailable to those Americans who funded white-baby monuments, genetic test results have lent a scientific legitimacy and a permanence to Europeans' recent attempts to monopolize the cultures and lands that newcomers were struggling to reach.

Another example of genetic studies serving to legitimize modern-day sorting pertains to Israeli politics. Through DNA testing, some Jews have reached for evidence of genetic overlaps with Jewish populations in ancient Israel and the Roman Empire.[13] For Israeli right-wing politicians and movements, genetic test results legitimized modern conquests of disputed territories, Palestinian populations, and non-Jewish populations within Israel in explicitly hereditarian and scientific terms. In 2018, with the Jewish nation-state basic law, indelible to the same extent as a U.S. constitutional amendment, Benjamin Netanyahu's government chained Israeli national belonging more than ever to inborn, inherited Jewishness and the Hebrew language. Never mind Israel's domestic Arab minority, amounting to 21 percent of the country's population.[14]

In this realm of interpreting genetic test results and other genealogical knowledge to validate racism, nativism, and social sorting, the United States has proven an even worse offender. Even as definitions of whiteness grew broader to encompass all European Americans as white, as the historian Nell Painter and others have shown, racists' and immigration restrictionists' reliance on definitions of Americanness as inherited from generations who lived long ago, has persisted. Moreover, some nonmedical uses of DNA test results represent a fun-house mirror's exaggerations of older exclusivities in genealogists' practices. DNA reckoning aspires to reach further back into the human past—and partakes more directly of inborn, irremovable characteristics of one's bodily substances—than the most stringent Jim Crow-era Racial Integrity Act ever did. No such flexibility as "living as white," which some mixed-race people in history have pursued, is available when others interpret DNA markers to sort them into particular populations.[15]

But recent Americans have followed an even more toxic trend than genetic family reckoning's tendencies to bind identity to the past. Some were unable to make facts obtained from genetic test results and historical documents fit their stringently bigoted theories. So, these Americans simply fabricated allegations that hung in the air, like so many viral droplets. When "birthers" persisted in their mistaken belief in Barack Obama Jr.'s foreign birth after he became America's first nonwhite president in 2009, they denied the results that historical and genealogical research could show when such results allowed nonwhite people into positions of power. Financial angels in their midst, notably the reality-show celebrity and real-estate tycoon Donald J. Trump, lent them a powerful microphone. Birthers pounced on the Constitution's insistence that the president be a "natural born citizen" of the United States when they insisted that the Constitution banned Obama from the presidency because of his supposed birth in his father's homeland of Kenya. But all evidence points to Obama's birth in Hawaii in 1961, two years after Hawaiian statehood. In 2011, the Obama administration felt compelled to post the president's birth certificate online, which documented his birth in a Honolulu maternity hospital.[16] This example suggests that there are worse alternatives to commodified DNA tests, and to genetic-genealogy entertainments that traffic in emotions, and even to the chaining of personhood to the past. Millions of customers and television viewers have gone in pursuit of proof, or watched others uncover proof, instead of turning their backs on proof. These searches for proof, including vicarious ones, signify a salutary, persistent hunger for knowledge among America's nations of descendants.

Acknowledgments

Over sixteen interrupted years, this project and I have accumulated many debts. Repeatedly, the Newberry Library in Chicago has granted Scholar-in-Residence status and a blissfully quiet fourth-floor carrel to me. The Newberry's full runs of print-only genealogy periodicals and hereditary organizations' publications have been treasures. This project and I have also benefited from a New England Regional Fellowship Consortium travel fellowship as well as numerous encouragements from my home university, Northeastern Illinois University (NEIU). NEIU's Office of Academic Affairs graciously bestowed on this project a Summer Faculty Research Stipend, a grant from the Committee on Organized Research, and a yearlong sabbatical.

Numerous librarians and archivists have labored on this project's behalf. The Peabody Museum of Archaeology and Ethnography at Harvard University, Columbia University's Rare Book and Manuscript Library, and Yale University's College Archives have provided me with photocopies and photographs. Librarians at the Peabody Essex Museum (Salem, Mass.) catered to my needs in temporary quarters in an office park in neighboring Danvers when their library was under construction in 2013. Beverly Cook and colleagues at the Chicago Public Libraries' Vivian G. Harsh Research Collection of Afro-American History and Literature; the Massachusetts Historical Society; the New England Historic Genealogical Society, Boston; Special Collections, Main Library, Northwestern University; the Newberry Library's own Special Collections; the New Hampshire Historical Society; Schlesinger Library, Radcliffe Institute for Advanced Study, Harvard University; and the University of Tennessee at Knoxville, Special Collections, also hosted me. Ed Remus, Jesse Franco, and Debbie Siegel at Northeastern Illinois University's Ronald Williams Library also aided the project. Sierra Dixon, Briann Greenfield, Christopher Jones, and Jessica Pigza provided sorely needed long-distance research assistance.

I can now report that I have finally followed two pieces of advice that I first received in the 1990s, during graduate school. Rosalind Rosenberg introduced me to Pauli Murray and *Proud Shoes*, and Richard L. Bushman suggested a business history of genealogy on the internet. Shortly afterward, I heard my husband Chuck Steinwedel, a historian himself, say, "Why don't you write a book on the history of genealogy?" Sven Beckert and Julia Rosenbaum induced me to start writing something while I was doing research. Betsy Blackmar strengthened my resolve decades after any responsibility to me as advisee ended. Additional conversations moved this project forward, with Sharon Adelhelm, Margo Anderson, Erica Ball, Gregg Christie, Kirsten Fermaglich, Ilya Gerasimov, Danny Greene, Briann Greenfield, Katja Hering, Nancy Isenberg, Kellie Carter Jackson, Susan Lee Johnson, Chana Kotzin, Malinda Maynor Lowery, Kahlile Mehr, Sophia Mihic, Marina Mogilner, Michelle Nickerson, Shayne Pepper, Jeff Sklansky, Carolyn Strange, Crispien Van Aelst, François Weil, Karin Wulf, and Russell Zanca. I have presented parts of this project to the Organization of American Historians (twice), the National Council of Public History, the Newberry Library's Seminar on Women and Gender, the Society for

Historians of the Early American Republic, the Mormon History Association, the Women's Studies Program at Brigham Young University, the Phi Alpha Theta History Honors Society at NEIU, and to brown-bags at Loyola University in Chicago, the University of Illinois at Chicago, the Massachusetts Historical Society, and the New Hampshire Historical Society. With my late friends, I have never been able to finish conversations about this project. I still miss Susan Rosa each day. Doria Johnson educated me about descendant communities.

I myself am not Mormon. I grew up no closer to Mormon culture than my childhood friend's Donny and Marie Osmond dolls and the assured voices of the Mormon Tabernacle Choir on the family turntable. Now I am among those scholars who seek the mutual understanding and respect, if not shared belief, that is required for scaling historiographical walls. I experienced ministrations from missionaries, librarians, and archivists at the Church History Library in Salt Lake City, as well from conversation with Jed Woodworth, Kevin Barney, and Megan Stanton. Hosting me in Provo in 2017, Amy L. Harris connected me to a faculty seminar in Mormon and family studies at Brigham Young University that amounted to a dream team.

Amy L. Harris, Susan J. Pearson, Josh Salzmann, and Susan Tucker read and enriched vast swaths of the manuscript. Scott Casper and one who prefers anonymity brought the best out of this project, and out of me, when they served as superb readers for the University of North Carolina Press (UNCP). Theo Anderson also enabled this project's completion. Chuck Grench, Debbie Gershenowitz, Dylan White, and others at UNCP have shown steadfast loyalty to my project throughout my repeated revisions. My pack of running buddies and Zumba classmates in Evanston have helped me stay sane. My mother and stepfather, Mary Rhinelander McCarl and Henry McCarl, furnished multiple opportunities for field research on hereditary organizations. I owe the most towering thanks to my family circle: Chuck, Daniel, and Templeton. I am waiting for my husband to suggest my next project.

This book's dedication requires explanation. A friend asked me to explain a remark in my final, seventh chapter. Just why was I "personally . . . glad to be alone in my house" when I beheld results from my own ancestral DNA testing? I anticipated losing composure if the results suggested something different from what my mother and others' text-driven research had always told me. Besides having been an ardent genealogist for decades, my mother was also a trained and published historian who completed the coursework for two different doctorates. She knew what it is to interrogate and cite evidence. She had an unsentimental personality, bordering on the hard-boiled. If I can't trust dispassionately done, fully documented family history research, whom or what can I trust? In the end, my DNA test results did not suggest anything that differed from her own results.

I have never lived without the ability to name forebears centuries back, nor have I endured the absence of basic facts about parentage. An array of large enterprises and reality shows encourage this ability to know ourselves through our forebears. Implicitly, these cultural productions encourage us to go into crisis from lacking this knowledge. From my scholarly perch, I can pass judgment on all the emotionalism and commercialism that have weighed down genealogists' practices, past and present. But if I suddenly lost the ability to name my own kin, including long-ago kin whom I could never know personally, it would feel like an amputation, even though I know perfectly well that relatedness to people who lived long ago depends as much on an imaginative leap as on documentation or DNA over-laps. I am dedicating this book to my mother because she truly was this book's muse.

Notes

Haley Papers 2280
> Alex Haley Papers (MS.2280), University of Tennessee at Knoxville, Special Collections

Holman Papers
> Winifred Lovering Holman Papers, New England Historic Genealogical Society, Boston

IAG   Institute of American Genealogy

IGI   International Genealogy Index

JAAHGS   *Journal of the Afro-American Historical and Genealogical Society*

JAIFR   *Journal of American Indian Family Research*

Jenks Papers
> William Jenks Papers, Massachusetts Historical Society, Boston

JGS   Jewish Genealogical Society

LDS   Latter-day Saints (Mormons)

MHS   Massachusetts Historical Society, Boston

NAACP   National Association for the Advancement of Colored People

NEHGR   *New England Historical and Genealogical Register*

NEHGS   New England Historic Genealogical Society, Boston

NGS   National Genealogical Society, Washington

NGSQ   *National Genealogical Society Quarterly*

NHB   *Negro History Bulletin*

NHHS   New Hampshire Historical Society

NL   Newberry Library, Chicago

NL Trustees
> Office of the Board of Trustees Records, Newberry Library Archives, Chicago

NLA   Newberry Library Archives

NYGBR   *The New York Genealogical and Biographical Record*

NYGBS   New York Genealogical and Biographical Society

NYPL   New York Public Library

PAJHS   *Publications of the American Jewish Historical Society*

PLR   Patricia Liddell Researchers Archives, Carter G. Woodson Regional Library, Vivian G. Harsh Research Collection of Afro-American History and Literature, Chicago Public Libraries

PLRNJ   *Patricia Liddell Researchers News Journal*

QWHU   *Microfilm Edition of the Papers Relating to the Quincy, Wendell, Holmes, and Upham Families*, 1977, Massachusetts Historical Society, Boston

Romaine Collection
> Anne Romaine Collection, University of Tennessee at Knoxville, Special Collections

Shattuck Papers
> Lemuel Shattuck Papers, Massachusetts Historical Society, Boston

SMD   Society of Mayflower Descendants

TAG   *The American Genealogist*

TJHS   Thomas Jefferson Heritage Society

TJMF   Thomas Jefferson Memorial Foundation

UGHM *The Utah Genealogical and Historical Magazine*
VMHB *Virginia Magazine of History and Biography*
WMQ *William and Mary Quarterly*

Introduction

1. Tocqueville, *Democracy in America*, 884.

2. John Farmer to John Kelly, July 24, 1824, folder 18, box 1, Farmer Papers.

3. Tocqueville, *Democracy in America*, 1,003–1,004; Tucker, *City of Remembering*, 23. Who were these unfortunates who inspired Tocqueville's characterizations? He may have gathered his impressions of Americans' behavior while abroad, from conversations with his peers in France or from personal encounters with travelers. Although Tocqueville met the former U.S. consul David Bailie Warden in France and a "rich New York businessman" surnamed Schermerhorn aboard a ship to New York in 1831, biographer André Jardin points to another, major influence on *Democracy in America*: an American studies "salon" in France that included two former French ambassadors to the United States and Tocqueville's famous cousin, the writer François-Auguste-René, viscount of Chateaubriand, who had recently published his own travelogue of the United States (1828). Jardin, *Tocqueville: A Biography*, 94–95, 99.

4. Matthew Frye Jacobson, *Roots Too*, 46–48.

5. Thanks to Theo Anderson, personal communication, March 20, 2020, for helping me articulate this distinction.

6. These paragraphs owe much to Foucault, *Power/Knowledge*, 93, 98, 104–5, 119–24, 142; Foucault, *The History of Sexuality*, 92–102; Pepper, Poll, Meiners, and Mihic, "Coffee and Conversation on the Work of Michel Foucault."

7. My discussions of laws' reliance on genealogical information-gathering are indebted to Jeffrey Sklansky, personal communication, April 12, 2017.

8. Kimberlé Crenshaw's and others' theories of intersectionality have enabled scholars to articulate intragroup hierarchies as well as those that set groups apart from each other. Cho, Crenshaw, and McCall, "Toward a Field of Intersectionality Studies." Hood, *In Pursuit of Privilege*, 222–27; Strange, "Sisterhood of Blood"; and Hollinger, "National Culture and Communities of Descent," also discuss genealogy activity and social class in U.S. history.

9. See especially Cox, *Dixie's Daughters*; Savage, *Standing Soldiers and Kneeling Slaves*; and Wendt, *The Daughters of the American Revolution*.

10. I owe this formulation to Sobel, *Teach Me Dreams*, 12.

11. Okrent, *The Guarded Gate*; Spiro, *Defending the Master Race*. Painter, *The History of White People*, describes successive enlargements of whiteness's definitions in U.S. history.

12. Haraway, *Modest_Witness@Second_Millennium.FemaleMan_Meets_OncoMouse*, 141–48.

13. Eastman, "Eastman's Online Genealogy Newsletter"; Howells, "Cyndi's List"; Cyndi's List, "About Cyndi"; Groot, "On Genealogy," 115.

14. Lapreel D. Huber, "Historical Report of the Nampa [Idaho] Region Genealogical Mission," (typescript, 1979); "Testimonies and Experiences of the Lehi [Utah] Stake Records Extraction Program" (typescript, n.d. [ca. 1979]); Zelda Merritt, "Experiences and Impressions of Genealogical Missionaries, 1981–1986" (typescript, 1986); copies of all at CHL.

15. FamilySearch.org, "FamilySearch 2019 Year in Review," https://www.familysearch.org/blog/en/familysearch–2019-year-in-review/.

16. My language here is influenced by a business slogan of the *Genealogical Helper*, the popular periodical for the do-it-yourself genealogist, run from Utah in 1947–2009 by multiple generations of a Mormon family: "Dedicated to Helping More People Find More Genealogy," *GH* 29 (January 1975): front cover.

17. Gary Mokotoff, "Jewish Genealogy in the First Decade of the 21st Century," *Avotaynu* 17 (Winter 2001): 3. *Avotaynu*'s name translates to "Our Forefathers," from Hebrew. Mokotoff and Sallyann Amdur Sack, "Statement of the Publishers," *Avotaynu* 1 (January 1985): 2.

18. Also in 2019, FamilySearch.org counted half a million contributors of information (518,563). Typically, these were users of and subscribers to the site. FamilySearch.org, "FamilySearch 2019 Year in Review."

19. Harris, "A Genealogical Turn"; Otterstrom, "Genealogy as Religious Ritual"; Parshall, "Genealogy and Family History." In a recent exception, Julia Creet has set Mormon engagements with the dead and genealogy down among genealogy practices generally: Creet, *The Genealogical Sublime*, 38–70. Scholars of earlier periods in Mormon history have not neglected these topics as much, given genealogy's usefulness to rituals surrounding death and bereavement. Samuel Morris Brown, *In Heaven as It Is on Earth*.

20. Brooks, Steenblik, and Wheelwright, *Mormon Feminism*, timeline on 24–32.

21. Brigham Young, sermon, July 18, 1869, in *Journal of Discourses*, 26 vols. (Liverpool, U.K.: Franklin D. Richards, 1854–86), 13:61, in Arrington and Bitton, *The Mormon Experience*, 228; the Church of Jesus Christ of Latter-day Saints, "Mothers' Employment Outside the Home," https://www.lds.org/manual/eternal-marriage-student-manual/mothers-employment-outside-the-home?lang=eng.

22. Scholarship on feminism and antifeminism in Mormon contexts includes Ulrich, "An Epiphany in a Broom Closet"; Shipps, "Dangerous History"; Brooks, "Mormon Feminism: An Introduction"; McDannell, *Sister Saints*, 65–202; and Petrey, *Tabernacles of Clay*.

23. Weil, *Family Trees*, 4, 140–41.

24. TallBear, *Native American DNA*. See also Round, *Removable Type*; Sturm, *Blood Politics*; and Stremlau, *Sustaining the Cherokee Family*.

25. Pascoe, *What Comes Naturally*, 142–46; Dominguez, *White by Definition*, 36–42; Gross, *What Blood Won't Tell*, 153–55. See chapter 1.

26. See especially Cowan, *Heredity and Hope*, 12–40; Alexandra Minna Stern, *Eugenic Nation*; Müller-Wille and Rheinberger, *A Cultural History of Heredity*; Keller, *The Century of the Gene*; Adam Cohen, *Imbeciles*.

27. Little, "Genealogy as Theatre of Self-Identity," 146–204; Little, "Identifying the Genealogical Self"; Catherine Nash, *Genetic Geographies*, 13, 27, 62–67; Abu El-Haj, *The Genealogical Science*, 136–44, 224–25; Caron, *Se créer des ancêtres*, 223–24, 232; Weil, *Family Trees*, 215–16; Groot, "On Genealogy," 111 (genealogy as "the curation of self"); Hogan, *Roots Quest*, 3, 167–71; Kramer, "Kinship, Affinity, and Connectedness." Steedman, *Strange Dislocations*, 4, 15, 75–76; and Creet, *The Genealogical Sublime*.

28. Weil, "Family Trees."

29. John A. Schutz (University of Southern California), "Those Who Became Tories: Town Loyalty and Revolution in New England," 94–105; Jerrilyn Greene Marston (PhD, Boston University), "The Abdication of George III," 133–49; and Richard W. Van Alstyne

(Callison College, University of the Pacific), review of Bernard Bailyn, *The Ordeal of Thomas Hutchinson* (Cambridge: Harvard University Press, 1974), 172–75. All citations from *NEHGR* 129 (April 1975), the "Bicentennial Issue."

30. See the essays in Robert M. Taylor Jr. and Crandall, *Generations and Change*, especially Hays, "History and Genealogy" (originally published in 1975).

31. Hareven, "The Search for Generational Memory"; Robert M. Taylor Jr., "Summoning the Wandering Tribes." See also Bockstruck, "Four Centuries of Genealogy."

32. At an early date (1986), Robert M. Taylor Jr. and Ralph Crandall's brief history noted genealogy's amorphousness. Robert M. Taylor Jr. and Crandall, "Historians and Genealogists"; Weil, *Family Trees*, 8–41; Wulf, "Of the Old Stock"; Wulf, "Bible, King, and Common Law"; and Wulf, "Ancestry as Social Practice in Eighteenth-Century New England."

33. Rodda, "Trespassers in Time," and Rodda, *Trespassers in Time*, also discuss this matter. Histories that make use of genealogists' findings and evidence include Lois Brown, *Pauline Elizabeth Hopkins*; Emerson W. Baker, *A Storm of Witchcraft*; Ginzberg, *Untidy Origins*, xii, 173n31; Susan Lee Johnson, *Writing Kit Carson* and Susan Lee Johnson, "Writing Kit Carson in the Cold War"; and Young, *Masquerade*. Historians' encounters with genealogists and descendant communities include Bailey, *Weeping Time*, 132–52; Heather Andrea Williams, *Help Me to Find My People*, 196–200; Berry, *We Are Who We Say We Are*; Gordon-Reed, *The Hemingses of Monticello*, 21–22, and Hunter, *Bound in Wedlock*, 1–6.

34. Examples include Hartman, *Lose Your Mother*; Peterson, *Black Gotham*; Johnston, *From Slave Ship to Harvard*; Lawrence P. Jackson, *My Father's Name*; Richard S. White, *Remembering Ahanagran*; Polk, *Polk's Folly*; Lindsay, *Atlantic Bonds*; Light, *Common People*; Dew, *The Making of a Racist*; Lowery, *The Lumbee Indians*; Bynum, *The Free State of Jones*, xiv–xv, 192–93, 200–215.

35. Caron, *Se créer des ancêtres*.

36. Akenson, *Some Family*; Weil, *Family Trees*.

37. Weil, *Family Trees*, 1–3.

38. Banner, *Being a Historian*; Novick, *That Noble Dream*, 512–21; Tosh, *The Pursuit of History*, 278–80. The journal *Public Historian* began publication in 1978.

39. Tucker, *City of Remembering*. "The past is a foreign country. They do things differently there." L. P. Hartley, *The Go-Between* (1953; reprinted NYRB Classics, 1962), in Lowenthal, *The Past Is a Foreign Country: Revisited*, 3.

40. Early American recordkeepers' terminology for relatedness can also confuse the self-taught researcher, working centuries later. The term "natural," for children, was a euphemism for those born out of wedlock, at a time when unmarried motherhood seemed deeply shameful. And the word "sister" in old records could indicate a sister-in-law or stepsister, not just a blood sibling. Donald Lines Jacobus, "Census Records: Divorce: Bastardy," *New Haven Genealogical Magazine* 6 (July 1929): 1,281 (later *TAG*); Jacobus, "Retroactive Dates and Places," *TAG* 43 (January 1967): 31–35; George B. Everton Sr., *The How Book for Genealogists* (1971); Judy Jacobson, *History for Genealogists*.

41. I was part of a working group at the 2016 meeting of the National Council for Public History, titled "Building Capacity to Challenge the Exclusive Past." Beaujot, *"Hear, Here*: The Challenges of Democratizing Historical Narratives," helps illustrate the point. See also Roued-Cunliffe and Copeland, *Participatory Heritage*.

42. Groot, "On Genealogy," 104.

43. Malm et al., "Jerome de Groot on Genealogy," especially Malm, "Genealogy and the Problem of Biological Essentialism."

44. Creet, *The Genealogical Sublime*; Lambert, "Constructing Symbolic Ancestry," and "Descriptive, Narrative, and Experiential Pathways to Symbolic Ancestors"; Kramer, "Kinship, Affinity, and Connectedness"; TallBear, *Native American DNA*; Drake, "Findings from the Fullerton Genealogy Study"; Sarah Franklin and McKinnon, *Relative Values*; Watson, "Ordering the Family"; Zerubavel, *Ancestors and Relatives*; Abu El Haj, *The Genealogical Science*; Hogan, *Roots Quest*; and the work of Catherine Nash and Hannah Mary Little.

45. Weil, *Family Trees*, 8–179.

46. Weil, *Family Trees*, 6–7, 181. Gordon S. Wood, "In Quest of Blood Lines," also stresses continuities. Caron, *Se créer des ancêtres*, and Pass, "Strange Whims of Crest Fiends," have implicitly argued for continuities.

47. Sven Beckert, personal communication, October 20, 2009.

48. Weil, especially "Family Trees."

49. Gillis, *A World of Their Own Making*, 74–75; Weil, "Family Trees"; Weil, *Family Trees*, 3–4, 42–77. Steve Fraser and Gerstle, *Ruling America*; Richard L. Bushman, *The Refinement of America*; Tamarkin, *Anglophilia*; and Prochaska, *The Eagle and the Crown*, describe the class hierarchies that persisted in the United States in the absence of official aristocracy, and stubborn American affection for royals and aristocrats. "Constitution," *NEHGR* 24 (April 1870), 219, specified monthly Wednesday meetings in Boston for the New England Historic Genealogical Society.

50. Carl Smith, communication, October 2, 2013 (Northwestern University).

51. Frederick Jackson Turner, "The Significance of the Frontier in American History."

52. Samuel Morris Brown, *In Heaven as It Is on Earth*, 20.

53. Walkowitz, *City of Dreadful Delight*, 16–17, 21 (on the male flâneur, or wanderer); Schlissel, "Introduction," 13; Bate, *The Women*.

54. Mabelle Post Morley, "Foreword," in Morley, *History of California State Society*, 12. Susan Reynolds Williams, *Alice Morse Earle*, 178–204; Weil, *Family Trees*, 54–57; and Watson, "Ordering the Family," 307, discuss geographical mobility's fostering of genealogy practices, historians' practices (in Earle's case), and nostalgia.

55. Gordon S. Wood, *The Americanization of Benjamin Franklin*, 57; Waldstreicher, *Runaway America*, 27–30; Benjamin Franklin, *The Autobiography of Benjamin Franklin*, 27–31. Laurel Thatcher Ulrich led me to this example. See also Weil, *Family Trees*, 27–28. Wulf, "Of the Old Stock," 305–312. Creet, "Genealogy and Genetics Workshop: Part 8," https://juliacreet.vhx.tv /products/genealogy-and-genetics-workshop, discusses modern genealogy practices in light of past colonization. Matthew Frye Jacobson, *Roots Too*, 48, first described the "roots trip."

56. Jefferson, "Letter to Samuel Kercheval," June 12, 1816, https://founders.archives.gov /documents/Jefferson/03-10-02-0128-0002; Tucker, *City of Remembering*, 22; Weil, *Family Trees*, 26, 92–93.

57. Emerson to John Farmer, February 14, 1829, folder 2, box 3, Farmer Papers; Cole, *Mary Moody Emerson and the Origins of Transcendentalism*, 5, 11, 15–16, 34.

58. Malchelosse, "Quebec."

59. Malchelosse, "Quebec"; Auger, "Québec"; Caron, *Se créer des ancêtres*, 23, 134–70; Joseph A. Marault, "Genealogie de la famille Gill au Canada," *JAIFR* 8 (January 1987): 31–51 (reprinted from his *Histoire des Abenakis*, 1866).

60. Annie Lowrey, "Why Are Americans Staying Put? It's the Economy," *New York Times*, December 10, 2013; Kolko with Cornish, "Fewer Americans Are Moving to Pursue Jobs" (2017). I have in mind enduring relocations, as opposed to the traveling and shorter-term relocations described in Hogan, *Roots Quest*, 71, 184n16.

61. This amount, per share, exceeded the price per share of the previous June—only four months beforehand—by 40 percent. Dezember, "Ancestry.com Sets $1.6 Billion Deal."

62. Oguh, "Blackstone to Acquire Ancestry.com for $4.7 Billion."

63. Sharpe, *Family Matters*, 98–113; Little, "Genealogy as Theatre of Self-Identity," 91–95.

64. Segalen, "The Shift in Kinship Studies in France."

65. Ehrenreich, *The Nazi Ancestral Proof*, 17–24.

66. María Elena Martínez, *Genealogical Fictions*, on colonial periods; Open Library, "Academia Mexicana."

67. Hobsbawm, *Age of Empire*, 345; Anne M. Martínez, "Mexican Revolution."

68. Hierarchies of class and morality among the dead seemed to matter less to Mormon genealogists than they did to non-Mormon practitioners at the time, who often filtered their family reckonings to emphasize successful, pious forebears with values congenial to the descendants' own. Morgan, "Lineage as Capital"; Weil, *Family Trees*, 78–111.

69. Payne, *I've Got the Light of Freedom*, 308.

70. Advertisement, *GH* 37 (July–August 1983): 190; Evelyn M. Rusli, "Ancestry.com Said to Be in Talks for a Buyout," *New York Times*, July 24, 2012.

71. Foster et al., "Jefferson Fathered Slave's Last Child."

72. Over time, since 2017, Ancestry has used varying graphics, such as circling places on maps, to represent test results, and sometimes they have updated results to show different ethnic percentages (more Irishness, in my case) from before. I chose the pie chart representation they sent me right after I tested for illustrating DNA information especially well.

73. Beulah-Rose Gross, "A Jewish Genealogist's Encounter With the IGI," *Avotaynu* 12 (Winter 1996): 9 (reprinted from the Australian Jewish Genealogical Society's *Kosher Koala*); Louie, *Chineseness Across Borders*, 1–94; Hasty, "Rites of Passage, Routes of Redemption"; Saxe and Chazan, *Ten Days of Birthright Israel*, 1–16; Kelner, *Tours That Bind*; Catherine Nash, *Of Irish Descent*; Basu, *Highland Homecomings*.

74. Todd, "More Members Now Outside U.S. than in U.S."

75. At its founding, Ancestry Inc. was based in Provo, Utah—home to Brigham Young University. Ancestry headquarters in 2020 is located in Lehi, Utah, closer to Salt Lake City. Advertisement, *GH* 37 (July–August 1983): 190; Ancestry.com, "Our People"; Scodari, *Alternate Roots*, 22–23; Creet, "Data Mining the Deceased," and *The Genealogical Sublime*, 71–94.

Chapter One

1. Scaff, *Max Weber in America*, 161.

2. Scaff, *Max Weber in America*, 61, 188.

3. Max Weber, "Class, Status, Party," in Max Weber, *From Max Weber*, 188; Dulong, "Genealogical Groups in a Changing Organizational Environment," 14.

4. Casper, "Introduction"; Robert M. Taylor Jr., "Summoning the Wandering Tribes," 23. Hannah Mary Little points to the dropping costs of publication in Britain in "Genealogy as Theatre of Self-Identity," 86.

5. DiMaggio, "Cultural Entrepreneurship in Nineteenth-Century Boston," 42–45; Horowitz, *Culture and the City*.

6. Minutes of Newberry trustees meeting, July 13, 1887, pp. 56–57 of photocopy, folder 8, box 2, NL Trustees, 02/01/30. Ashton, "Curators, Hobbyists, and Historians," delivers a long history of the Newberry Library's commitments to genealogists.

7. William Jenks, note "Transcript, July 11, 1838," January–July 1838 folder, box 14, William Jenks Papers, MHS. Also note the mid-1850s "Gleaner" columns in the *Transcript* of N. I. Bowditch. Winsor, ed., *The Memorial History of Boston*, 2:lvi.

8. Doane, *Searching for Your Ancestors*, 75. Libraries across the country collected the *Transcript* as a result. Following the newspaper's demise in 1941, its genealogy features were anthologized and reprinted. Advertisement, *NEHGR* 129 (July 1975): following 316.

9. New York Public Library, "History of the New York Public Library"; Hering, "We Are All Makers of History," 35 (note 64); Stiles, *A Hand-Book of Practical Suggestions*, 3. Future scholars will benefit from consulting the periodical the *Genealogical Helper* (1947–2009). Its "miscellany" sections contained frequent alerts about new or changing newspaper offerings after 1945.

10. Kimmick, *History of the New Mexico State Organization*, 20–21; Mildred A. Kenney, "Genealogy in a Tax–Supported Library," *Library Journal* 55 (December 15, 1930): 1,011, in Hering, "We Are All Makers of History," 141–42.

11. Hering, "We Are All Makers of History," 142n323.

12. Fredrickson, *The Black Image in the White Mind*, 1 and elsewhere. Shawn Michelle Smith, *American Archives*, 28–30; Strange, "Sisterhood of Blood," 109; Sweeney, "Ancestors, Avotaynu, Roots," 96–97, 106–8, 113–14.

13. Painter, *The History of White People* (multiple "enlargements of whiteness" over time); Matthew Frye Jacobson, *Whiteness of a Different Color*; Reeve, *Religion of a Different Color*; and Fredrickson, *The Black Image in the White Mind*, have all been useful.

14. William Whiting, "An Address Delivered to the Members of the New England Historic-Genealogical Society," *NEHGR* 7 (April 1853), 106; Schutz, *A Noble Pursuit*, 22.

15. Jonathan Brown Bright to Henry Bond, May 20, 1853; Bright to Bond, August 30, 1853; both in folder 8, sub-group 3, box 8, Bond Papers; Weil, *Family Trees*, 74.

16. Painter, *History of White People*, 110–13; Horsman, *Race and Manifest Destiny*. My research on the meaning of "Anglo-Saxon" to indicate contemporaries as well as populations in the ancient and early medieval past, included a search of the *American Antiquarian Society's Historical Periodicals Collection* (through 1877) for "Anglo-Saxon." This effort yielded 667 hits. Americans began applying the term to populations in their own time in the 1840s.

17. McPherson and Hogue, *Ordeal by Fire*, 90–94; Matthew Frye Jacobson, *Whiteness of a Different Color*, 68–72.

18. Six years earlier, the 1850 U.S. census showed Morse as a forty-one-year-old accountant, living in East Boston with his wife Mary Cheever Morse and their seven children. Their oldest son and father's namesake Solomon Bradford Morse Jr. was sixteen years old. "Year: 1850, Census Place: East Boston (Boston Ward 4), Suffolk, MA, Roll M432_335, page 11A, image 26," in Ancestry.com, *1850 U.S. Federal Census*, https://www.ancestry.com/search/collections/8054/?name=Solomon+Bradford_Morse&gender=m&residence=_massachusetts-usa_24.

19. Morse handwrote the secretarial minutes and his own genealogy research in the same notebooks. American Party constitution transcribed by Solomon Bradford Morse Jr. in

Vol. 1, unpaginated, n.d. [1853–56], American Party (Boston, Mass.), Records of the East Boston Chapter, MHS. Vols. 3–4 contain Morse's genealogy notes as well as notes made by his grandson, Horace H. Morse, in 1907. Dean Grodzins led me to this source.

20. Barbara Miller Solomon, *Ancestors and Immigrants*; Benton-Cohen, *Inventing the Immigration Problem*, 15–16.

21. Sharpe, *Family Matters*, 50–62; Little, "Genealogy as Theatre of Self-Identity," 28–32.

22. Wulf, "Bible, King, and Common Law," 491–96; Weil, *Family Trees*, 13–29.

23. Tamarkin, *Anglophilia*, xxv, 69–70; Richard L. Bushman, *The Refinement of America*, 403–6; Tucker, *City of Remembering*, 19–21. Tamarkin, *Anglophilia*, and Prochaska, *The Eagle and the Crown*, discuss the broader point of Americans' fetishization of monarchical tropes.

24. Burke, "Peerages and Genealogies," *North American Review* (July 1863): 37, in Tamarkin, *Anglophilia*, 69; Weil, *Family Trees*, 43.

25. He was an honorary member as of December 1862; he was a corresponding (long-distance) member before that, starting in November 1851. *Rolls of Membership* (1891), 85. Michael Sharpe describes the controversies in Britain that dogged Burke's work even in his lifetime, in *Family Matters*, 68–70.

26. Eliza Susan Quincy to Samuel A. Drake, May 19, 1873, pp. 3–4, reel 61, QWHU.

27. Pass, "The Strange Whims of Crest Fiends"; Thackery, "*Back to Adam*," 17–20. On a similar "lack of heraldic and genealogical regulation" in Early America, see Weil, *Family Trees*, 23–29; Wulf, "Bible, King, and Common Law," 494–96.

28. Frederick Law Olmsted, *Walks and Talks of an American Farmer in England* (1852; reprinted Ann Arbor, University of Michigan Press, 1967), 308–10, in Tamarkin, *Anglophilia*, 70.

29. Slotkin, *Fatal Environment*, 228–32 (on Parker).

30. Emerson, *English Traits*, 41–43, from the chapter titled "Race"; Painter, *History of White People*, 165–89. Details of his travels in Howard Mumford Jones's introduction to Emerson, *English Traits*, x–xiv.

31. Ralph Waldo Emerson, *Journals and Miscellaneous Notebooks of Ralph Waldo Emerson*, vol. 11, 1848–1851 (Cambridge: Harvard University Press, 1975), 376, in Painter, *History of White People*, 188.

32. Werth, *Banquet at Delmonico's*, 11; Conlin, *Evolution and the Victorians*, 154–55; Bederman, *Manliness and Civilization*, 25–31; Fredrickson, *The Black Image in the White Mind*, 254–55; John C. Waller, "Ideas of Heredity," 481–82.

33. Müller-Wille and Rheinberger, *A Cultural History of Heredity*, 79; Müller-Wille and Rheinberger, "Heredity: The Formation of an Epistemic Space," 79.

34. Francis Galton, "Hereditary Talent and Character," *Macmillan's Magazine* (1865): 322; William H. Whitmore, "Hereditary Ability," *NEHGR* 23 (July 1869), 285–89; Weil, *Family Trees*, 116.

35. Derry, *Horses in Society*; Grier, *Pets in America*, 27–35, 207–12; Ritvo, *The Animal Estate*.

36. Charles B. Moore, "Plan of Genealogical Work," *NYGBR* 1 (April 1870): 9. Italics his.

37. Morgan, "Lineage as Capital"; Cotlar, "We Have No Wish *Not* to See."

38. Young, *Masquerade*, 24–25.

39. Weil, *Family Trees*, 115–16, 136.

40. Hering, "We Are All Makers of History," 49.

41. The HSP began admitting women to membership in 1862, and the NYGBS allowed women from its beginnings in 1869, but the NEHGS (1845) in Boston remained all-male

until 1898. Gary B. Nash, *First City*, 225; Jay in "Genealogies in Preparation," *Bulletin of the New York Genealogical and Biographical Society* 1 (December 1869), 5; Schutz, *Noble Pursuit*, vii–viii, 62; Hood, *In Pursuit of Privilege*, 223.

42. Waldstreicher, *In the Midst of Perpetual Fetes*, 69, 88, 90, 101, 117; Weil, *Family Trees*, 44–45.

43. Teachout, "Forging Memory," 19–20, 31–39; "Eligibility," *AMM* 2 (January 1893), 116–118; Wallace Evan Davies, *Patriotism on Parade*, 77. See also Shawn Michelle Smith, *American Archives*, 136–42; Weil, *Family Trees*, 130–32.

44. For example, Strange, "The Battlefields of Personal and Public Memory."

45. *Daily Alta California*, June 26, 1876, in Teachout, "Forging Memory," 33. A later account suggests that men in San Francisco organized the Sires earlier, in October 1875. It is possible that the widow's letter, and the nearness of the 1876 anniversary, invigorated a preexisting Sires group. A Daughters of Revolutionary Sires group also formed in 1876 in San Francisco, alongside the Sires, but it later fell into 'innocuous desuetude.'" "The Origin of Societies Founded on Descent from Revolutionary Patriots," *AMM* 3 (November 1893): 538–40; "Mrs. A. S. Hubbard," *AMM* 1 (October 1892): 326.

46. Conforti, *Imagining New England*, 214–18 (300 pages on 217); Des Jardins, *Women and the Historical Enterprise in America*, 13–52; Susan Reynolds Williams, *Alice Morse Earle*.

47. See this book's Introduction; O'Leary, *To Die For*; Strange, "Sisterhood of Blood"; Wendt, "Nationalist Middle-Class Women" and Wendt, *The Daughters of the American Revolution*. On the rightward turn, see Delegard, *Battling Miss Bolsheviki*; Nielsen, *Un-American Womanhood*; Wendt, "Defenders of Patriotism or Mothers of Fascism?"; and Morgan, *Women and Patriotism in Jim Crow America*, 127–52.

48. Michael O'Brien, *Conjectures of Order*, 370–71, 383–84, 646; Weil, *Family Trees*, 93–94.

49. "Reuben Bartley Memoir" (ca. 1868–69), 17–18, Virginia Historical Society (Richmond), in Varon, *Southern Lady, Yankee Spy*, 140.

50. Mrs. Seddon's full name from House Divided: The Civil War Research Engine at Dickinson College, "Seddon, James Alexander," http://hd.housedivided.dickinson.edu/node/6547.

51. Faust, *This Republic of Suffering*, traces the beginnings of government-funded cemeteries and interments of soldiers.

52. Blight, *Race and Reunion*, 255–99; Janney, *Remembering the Civil War*, 133–59; and Censer, *The Reconstruction of White Southern Womanhood*, 153–206, 275–80, are especially useful. Goleman, *Your Heritage Will Still Remain*, contributes a state-level study of the Lost Cause's development in Mississippi.

53. Janney, *Burying the Dead but Not the Past*, 52, 56–57, 168–78. On later commemorations by southerners, see especially Brundage, *The Southern Past*, 12–54; Cox, *Dixie's Daughters*.

54. Brundage, *The Southern Past*, 105–37 (chapter titled "Archiving White Memory"); Prince, "Jim Crow Memory."

55. Gorn, "Introduction: Educating America"; Novick, *That Noble Dream*, 73.

56. "Proceedings," *VMHB* 2 (January 1895): iii–xiii; "Proceedings," *VMHB* 3 (January 1896): i–xxviii; "Index to Genealogical Periodicals, Chiefly for the Year 1942," *TAG* 19 (April 1943): 233; Doane, *Searching for Your Ancestors*, 72; Weil, *Family Trees*, 150.

57. Brundage, "White Women and the Politics of Historical Memory"; Teachout, "Forging Memory," 108–110; Lamar, *A History of the National Society of the Colonial Dames of Amer-*

ica; Teachout, "Forging Memory," 81–93; Morgan, *Women and Patriotism in Jim Crow America*, 44–45. Tucker, *City of Remembering*, discusses the Daughters of 1812 in New Orleans, 67–68.

58. Elizabeth Hayes Turner, *Women, Culture, and Community*, 169–72; *Fifty Years of Achievement*. After more than a century, the state of Texas took control of the Alamo starting in 2011. The state government and the DRT remain enmeshed in litigation, concerning custody of the Alamo's library. Peet, "Industry News."

59. Whalley was no relative of Franklin's. Franklin mentioned her in his letters home during the trip, but in later accounts of his trip to England, namely his *Autobiography*, he did not refer to her. Her first name has been lost to history. *Papers of Benjamin Franklin*, vol. 8, 137; Benjamin Franklin, *The Autobiography of Benjamin Franklin*, 27–31.

60. John Kelly to John Farmer, August 26, 1826, folder 12, box 2, Farmer Papers.

61. "United Daughters of the Confederacy," *Confederate Veteran* 6 (October 1898): 460.

62. Wallace Evan Davies, *Patriotism on Parade*, 55, 77; O'Leary, *To Die For*, 70–109.

63. See Jane Addams's writings on the "family claim" on adult daughters who stayed single. Addams, "Filial Relations." This was especially true of white women, while educated Black women were likelier to remain in paid employment and to pursue careers after marrying. Shaw, *What a Woman Ought to Be and to Do*.

64. "Memoir of John Farmer, M. A.," *NEHGR* 1 (January 1847): 18.

65. Corinne T. Field and Eliza Byard, personal communication, Spring 1998. An exception that proves the rule appears in Hoffert, "Female Self-Making."

66. Beckert and Rosenbaum, *The American Bourgeoisie*.

67. Winifred Lovering Holman, typescript, Caverley-Adams notes, August 31, 1949, Caverly folder, box 5, Holman Papers.

68. *Constitution and By-Laws of the Daughters of the American Revolution* (1890).

69. Mary Smith Lockwood in "Proceedings of the Second Continental Congress," *AMM* 2 (April 1893): 451; Lizzie Stiles Chandler Sumner (Iowa City) on the fourteen–year–old soldier who was her forebear, in "Work of the Chapters," *DARM* 57 (September 1923), 560.

70. Lamar, *History of the National Society of the Colonial Dames of America*, 41; membership certificate of Kate Singleton Conley, Missouri Society of the Colonial Dames of America, November 26, 1910; Juliet L. Finney to Conley, December 7, 1910, folder 52, box 2, Conley-Miller Family Papers, Western Historical Manuscript Collection, University of Missouri/State Historical Society of Missouri, Columbia; Finney to Conley, November 6, 1911, folder 53, box 2, Conley-Miller Family Papers, Western Historical Manuscript Collection, University of Missouri/State Historical Society of Missouri, Columbia. See also Colonial Dames of America, "CDA Today," https://cda1890.org/aboutcda/; National Society of the Colonial Dames of America, "Membership Inquiries," http://nscda.org/about-us/membership-inquiries/.

71. Membership in the Baronial Order was limited to "men lineally descended in the female or male line" from "an ancestor who rendered actual service in or before the year 1215, toward securing the articles of constitutional liberty, known as the Magna Carta, from John, King of England." Virkus, *The Handbook of American Genealogy* (1932), 373.

72. Kennedy, *Freedom from Fear*, 43–103; Winifred Lovering Holman, typescript, "The Descent of Chauncey Devereux Stillman of New York" (1930), Stillman folder 2, box 29; Cincinnati detail in Holman to Roland Mather Hooker, March 6, 1953, Wilcott folder 1, box 34; both in Holman Papers.

73. An example is Jonathan Pearson, "Contributions to the History of the Ancient Dutch Families of New York," *NYGBR* 2 (January 1871): 22–24; "Societies and Their Proceedings," *NEHGR* 37 (October 1883): 411. Caron, *Se créer des ancêtres*, 63–101, and Weil, *Family Trees*, 135–37, note that 1885 marked the bicentenary of the French government's 1685 revocation of the Edict of Nantes and renunciation of religious toleration, a disastrous turning point in Huguenot history.

74. Davenport, ed., *Hereditary Society Blue Book*, 33; Hering, "We Are All Makers of History," 8, 12, 33, 46. Not until after World War II did Pennsylvania Germans rebrand themselves Pennsylvania Dutch (Deutsch). Hering, "Palatines or Pennsylvania German Pioneers?" 328–29.

75. Morgan, "Home and Country," chart on 557 regarding the DAR.

76. Sweeney, "Ancestors, Avotaynu, Roots," 175.

77. Floyd James Davis, *Who Is Black?* 9–10, 77; Pascoe, *What Comes Naturally*, 142–46. Dominguez, *White by Definition*, 36–42, treats Louisiana.

78. On *Rhinelander v. Rhinelander* (1925), see Earl Lewis and Ardizzone, *Love on Trial*; Smith-Pryor, *Property Rites*; Onwuachi-Willig, "A Beautiful Lie," and Onwuachi-Willig, *According to Our Hearts*. Gross, *What Blood Won't Tell*, discusses "racial identity" and racial-fraud litigation generally.

79. Olive Harwood Lash to Susa Young Gates, November 24, 1925, folder 23, box 69, reel 46, Gates Papers.

80. Lash to Gates, November 24, 1925.

81. "National Board of Management," AMM 4 (April 1894): 404; Statute 44 in *Statutes of the National Society, Daughters of the American Revolution*; Teachout, "Forging Memory," 125–26.

82. David Levering Lewis, *W. E. B. Du Bois*, 13, 374–75, 660n66.

83. McPherson and Hogue, *Ordeal by Fire*, 514–15; Levin, *Searching for Black Confederates*.

84. *Constitution and By-Laws of the National Society of the Daughters of the American Revolution* (1894), 8.

85. "D.A.R. Chapters Will Place Five Memorials Soon," n.d. [1924], otherwise unidentified clipping; "D.A.R. Pays Honor to Harriet Godfrey," May 4, 1924, *Minneapolis Sunday Tribune*, clipping; 1924 folder, box 3, Papers of Jennie Adelaide Holmes Coolidge, Minnesota Historical Society, Minnesota History Center, St. Paul.

86. Clara L. Wood, ed., *History and Register, Idaho State Society*, 74.

87. Brundage, *The Southern Past*, 30, 44–45; Founders' Day, Grand Rapids, 23 June 1909; Founders' Day, Grand Rapids, 23 June 1910; programs, Sophie de Marsac Campau Chapter D.A.R. (Grand Rapids), in scrapbook of chapter activities, vol. 1 (1910–29), p. 44, box 34, Papers of the DAR, Michigan Society, Michigan Historical Collections, Bentley Library, University of Michigan, Ann Arbor. Lowery, *The Lumbee Indians*, 25–27, posits the Roanoke Island colonists' possible adoption by surrounding Indigenous communities.

88. D'Emilio and Freedman, *Intimate Matters*, 57–66.

89. Bederman, *Manliness and Civilization*, 200–206.

90. Lovett, *Conceiving the Future*, 77–130; Painter, *The History of White People*, 245–54; Morgan, "Home and Country," 549–66 (demographic studies based on obituaries of 940 DAR members born before 1900).

91. Brooks to Lemuel Shattuck, August 9, 1838, p. 9, 1833–39 folder, box 1, Shattuck Papers; Weil, *Family Trees*, 47; "Notices of New Publications," *NEHGR* 3 (October 1849): 401–2.

92. Lockwood, *Lineage Book of the Charter Members of the Daughters of the American Revolution*; "National Membership Commission," *DARM* 104 (January 1970): 49; George McCracken, "Reviews," *TAG* 49 (April 1973): 121–22; Weil, *Family Trees*, 132–33.

93. Abigail Harding mentioned in "Work of the Chapters," *DARM* 54 (November 1920), 659; Marling, *George Washington Slept Here*, 226–28, 234; Weil, *Family Trees*, 126–27.

94. Stremlau, *Sustaining the Cherokee Family*, 42–43 (matrilineal kinship reckoning and matrilocal practices, in which newly married couples lived with or near brides' families of origin, among the Cherokee prior to enrollment); Plane, *Colonial Intimacies*, 19–22; Perdue, *Cherokee Women*, 41–59.

95. Wilson, *Agriculture of the Hidatsa Indians*, 9. Wilson included the Hidatsa names of Buffalo Bird Woman's foremothers and relatives.

96. Gillis, *A World of Their Own Making*, 61–80 (Victorians' representations of nuclear families).

97. Sturm, *Blood Politics*, especially 2; Saunt, *Black, White, and Indian*, 156–60; Miles, *Ties That Bind*, 194–203; Garroutte, *Real Indians*, 14–25.

98. Stremlau, *Sustaining the Cherokee Family*, 105–79; Gross, *What Blood Won't Tell*, 153–55, 162–63, 177; Saunt, *Black, White, and Indian*, 152–64; Kent Carter, *The Dawes Commission*.

99. See especially LaVelle, "The General Allotment Act 'Eligibility' Hoax," on the timing of government imposition of race quanta.

100. Kiel, "Bleeding Out," especially 90.

101. Ratteree and Hill, *The Great Vanishing Act*.

102. Cramer, *Cash, Color, and Colonialism*, 119; Stremlau, *Sustaining the Cherokee Family*, 58–59, 142; Sturm, *Blood Politics*, 178–87; Gross, *What Blood Won't Tell*, 140–77; Saunt, *Black, White, and Indian*, 215.

103. Henry Louis Gates, Jr., *Stony the Road*.

104. The literature on this subject is vast. See especially Hale, *Making Whiteness*, 121–98; Kelley, *Right to Ride*.

105. Painter, *Standing at Armageddon*, 227–29; Riser, *Defying Disfranchisement*, 74–111.

106. Foner, *Reconstruction*, 276–91.

107. Galton, *Record of Family Faculties*, 1; Shawn Michelle Smith, *American Archives*, 126.

108. Phillimore, *How to Write the History of a Family*, 6.

109. Weil, *Family Trees*, 112–42; Strange, "Sisterhood of Blood," 109; Sweeney, "Ancestors, Avotaynu, Roots," 24–26, 106–8; Shawn Michelle Smith, *American Archives*, 126–34.

110. Charles Benedict Davenport, *Heredity in Relation to Genetics* (New York: H. Holt, 1911), 241; Rothschild, *The Dream of the Perfect Child*, 36–37; Weil, *Family Trees*, 122. A genealogical tree developed by Davenport and colleagues in 1912 as an example of "cacogenics" (bad descent) appears in Lima, *The Book of Trees*, 124.

111. Rothschild, *The Dream of the Perfect Child*, 45 (statistic); Condit, *The Meanings of the Gene*, 48, and Alexandra Minna Stern, *Eugenic Nation*, 106–7. Cowan, *Heredity and Hope*, 12–40; Rothschild, *The Dream of the Perfect Child*, 29–51; Comfort, *The Science of Human Perfection*, 29–66, especially 38–45; Painter, *The History of White People*, 256–77; Adam Cohen, *Imbeciles*, and Alexandra Minna Stern, *Eugenic Nation*, discuss eugenics generally in the United States.

112. Lovett, *Conceiving the Future*, 137–46.

113. Jordan and Kimball, *Your Family Tree*, v–vi, 13. The most recent biography of Jordan (1953) makes no mention of Kimball. Edward McNall Burns, *David Starr Jordan: Prophet of Freedom*.

114. Alexandra Minna Stern, *Eugenic Nation*, 22–23, 84–85; "Proceedings," *NEHGR* 87 (January 1933): 72 (Harriman's obituary).

115. Jordan and Kimball, *Your Family Tree*, 9.

116. Jordan and Kimball, *Your Family Tree*; v. Zimmer, *She Has Her Mother's Laugh*, 188–89, defends such claims about widespread descent from Charlemagne from a mathematical and scientific standpoint. But the claim is hardly possible to prove using the historical, text-based methods of documentation that genealogists have generally preferred.

117. Jordan and Kimball, *Your Family Tree*, 3–4, 7.

118. Okrent, *The Guarded Gate*, and Margo J. Anderson, *The American Census*, discuss the latter point.

119. Barbara Miller Solomon, *Ancestors and Immigrants*.

120. Takaki, *Strangers from a Different Shore*, 87–112.

121. Painter, *The History of White People*, 132–50, 202–5; Matthew Frye Jacobson, *Whiteness of a Different Color*.

122. Hofstadter, *Age of Reform*, 138–39 (note 8); Wallace Evan Davies, *Patriotism on Parade*, 293–97; O'Leary, *To Die For*, 150–246.

123. Mrs. J. H. Robbins in "What We Are Doing," *AMM* 5 (August 1894): 149.

124. *NEHGR* 89 (October 1934): 402. The General Society of Mayflower Descendants, a national umbrella for preexisting *Mayflower* descendants' groups, subsequently formed in Boston in 1897. The General Society of the Sons of Colonial Wars emerged later than the New York Society of the Sons of Colonial Wars, in May 1893. Mrs. Robert M. Sherman and Mrs. Lester A. Hall, "Notes on the General Society of Mayflower Descendants 1897–1970," *NEHGR* 124 (April 1970): 139; "Book Notices," *NEHGR* 48 (July 1894): 366; Spiro, *Defending the Master Race*, 10–14. On the two separate Colonial Dames groups, see Lamar, *A History of the National Society of the Colonial Dames of America*, 3, 24. Daughters of the Revolution founding in *Proceedings of the Eighteenth Annual Meeting* (1909), 22; Teachout, "Forging Memory," 107–11.

125. New York Genealogical and Biographical Society, *Twenty-Fifth Anniversary*, 10–11; Beckert, *Monied Metropolis*, 270–71.

126. Carr, *Guide to the United States for the Jewish Immigrant*, 63. By 1924, the *Manual for Immigrants* appeared in Italian, Spanish, Polish, German, Hungarian, French, and Russian, as well as in English and Yiddish. *DARPCC* 33 (1924): 204.

127. Matthew Frye Jacobson, *Whiteness of a Different Color*, 83–87; Ngai, *Impossible Subjects*, 3–9, 21–55; Archdeacon, *Becoming American*, 143–201; Higham, *Strangers in the Land*; Okrent, *The Guarded Gate*; Daniels, *Guarding the Golden Door*, 52–58.

128. Margo J. Anderson, *The American Census*, 147–49; Ngai, *Impossible Subjects*, 48–62; Daniels, *Guarding the Golden Door*, 55–58. Anderson's characterization of Barker as a "genealogist" (148) is incomplete. Between 1926 and 1939, Barker published in both scholarly journals (linguistics and history periodicals) and in the popular press, on western European surnames. Though Barker worked on topics of interest to genealogists, I have yet to see evidence of his genealogy activity per se. American Council of Learned Societies, *Surnames in*

the *United States Census of 1790*, 126–360; Barker, "The Ancestry of Family Names" (*Atlantic Monthly*, 1935); Barker, "The Founders of New England" (*American Historical Review*, 1933). Historians' works on Americans' naming practices include Laqueur, *The Work of the Dead*, 365–488, and the work of Kristen Fermaglich.

129. Daniels, *Guarding the Golden Door*, 134–39.

130. I have been unable to ascertain the location within Germany of Virkus's birthplace from Ancestry.com, accessed September 5, 2014.

131. Marquis, *The Book of Chicagoans*, 690.

132. "Chicago Group Ready to Battle for New Alien Act," *Chicago Tribune*, March 24, 1929, 22.

133. Marquis, *The Book of Chicagoans*, 690.

134. Gustaitis, *Chicago Transformed*, 256–74; DeWitt, *Degrees of Allegiance*, 84–110.

135. Virkus, *The Abridged Compendium of American Genealogy: First Families of America* (1925), 1:999.

136. "F. A. Virkus, 75, Dies; Leader of Business Men," *Chicago Daily Tribune*, January 25, 1955.

137. "Genealogical Trust," *Magazine of American Genealogy* 1, no. 2 (September 1929): 7.

138. IAG membership form, February 6, 1930; Susa Young Gates to Frederick Adams Virkus, February 12, 1930; both in folder 13, box 71, reel 48, Gates Papers; IAG postcard addressed to Du Bois, January 8, 1930, in "W. E. B. Du Bois Papers."

139. Virkus, *The Handbook of American Genealogy*, vol. 1 (1932), 17 ("Racial Reference Sources"). Matthew Frye Jacobson, *Whiteness of a Different Color*, discusses the broader point.

140. "Citizenship," *Magazine of American Genealogy* 1, no. 5 (December 1929): 19.

141. Ralph Mitchell, "Group Looks Up Lineage So You May Look Back: Genealogy Institute Gives Help to Historians," *Chicago Daily Tribune*, April 27, 1952.

142. "F. A. Virkus, 75, Dies"; "Frederick A. Virkus Runs for Congress as Foe of New Deal," *Chicago Daily Tribune*, February 9, 1936.

143. Christie, "Forgotten Exodus," and Kazal, *Becoming Old Stock*, discuss assimilation and camouflaging possibilities for white immigrants.

144. I refer to this group as "professional" genealogists, rather than "scholarly" or "scientific" ones, to avoid confusing this category with scholars in academia or with professional scientists. Some genealogy professionals held university posts in other fields, but most did not. Robert Charles Anderson reflects on "scholarly" genealogists in his review of François Weil, *Family Trees: A History of Genealogy in America*, NEHGR 167 (October 2013): 300–301; Weil, *Family Trees*, 159–69. Premises and institutions of professionalism have also been discussed in Tolley-Stokes, "Genealogy"; Macy, "Recognizing Scholarly Genealogy," 10–11; Sheppard, "A Bicentennial Look"; TallBear, *Native American DNA*, 105–41.

145. Jacobus, *Genealogy as Pastime and Profession*, (1st ed., 1930), 11–13.

146. Foucault, "Nietzsche, Genealogy, History," 369–70; Nietzsche, *On the Genealogy of Morals*, section 7, 21. Shklar, "Subversive Genealogies"; Weigel, "Genealogy: On the Iconography and Rhetorics of an Epistemological Topos"; and Creet, *The Genealogical Sublime*, 20–24, discuss both meanings of genealogy, as a method of philosophical analysis as well as a pursuit of knowledge of particular family histories.

147. Riley, *Divorce: An American Tradition*, 16.

148. Jacobus, *Genealogy as Pastime and Profession* (1st ed., 1930), 123–24; Jacobus, "Haphazard Eugenics," 173; Tolley-Stokes, "Genealogy," 522.

149. Rothschild, *The Dream of the Perfect Child*, 47, 237 (note 84); Alexandra Minna Stern, *Eugenic Nation*. In late 2020, immigrant women incarcerated in Immigration and Customs Enforcement facilities in Georgia reported sterilizations (full hysterectomies) against their will: Narea, "The Outcry over ICE and Hysterectomies, Explained."

150. Painter, *History of White People*, 228–44, 327–42; Barkan, *The Retreat of Scientific Racism*.

151. Hulbert, *Raising America*, 117–53.

152. Pascoe, *What Comes Naturally*, 140–50; Whitman, *Hitler's American Model*, 73–131; Okrent, *The Guarded Gate*, 373–90.

153. Hering, "Palatines or Pennsylvania German Pioneers?"

154. Ehrenreich, *The Nazi Ancestral Proof*; Cowan, *Heredity and Hope*, 32–33; Condit, *The Meanings of the Gene*, 27.

155. Cowan, *Heredity and Hope*, 34–35.

156. Alexandra Minna Stern, *Eugenic Nation*, 185. On Mary Williamson Averell Harriman: Sweeney, "Ancestors, Avotaynu, Roots," 106–7; "Proceedings," *NEHGR* 87 (January 1933): 72; "Annual Reports," *NEHGR* 87 (April 1933): 176.

157. Painter, *History of White People*, 343–73.

158. Reeve, *Religion of a Different Color*, 1–13, 43–46; Matthew Frye Jacobson, *Whiteness of a Different Color*, 171–200; Fermaglich, *A Rosenberg by Any Other Name*.

159. Douglas J. Davies, *An Introduction to Mormonism*, 210.

Chapter Two

1. Mauss, *All Abraham's Children*, 17–40, 212–30. Klaus J. Hansen, *Mormonism and the American Experience*, 179–204, and Mueller, *Race and the Making of the Mormon People*, are also useful on Mormonism and race.

2. Arrington and Bitton, *The Mormon Experience*, 60–62; Sharpe, *Family Matters*, 157.

3. Flanders, *Nauvoo*, 207–8; Klaus J. Hansen, *Mormonism and the American Experience*, 1–83.

4. Flake, *The Politics of American Religious Identity*, 27.

5. Mauss, *The Angel and the Beehive*; Flake, *The Politics of American Religious Identity*, and Sarah Barringer Gordon, *The Mormon Question*, 19–83. Arrington and Bitton, *The Mormon Experience*, 180, and Flake, *The Politics of American Religious Identity*, 27–29, 120, describe the Supreme Court's decision in *Reynolds v. United States* (1878).

6. Richard L. Bushman, *Joseph Smith and the Beginnings of Mormonism*, 101.

7. Douglas J. Davies, *An Introduction to Mormonism*, 95, 99–100; Samuel Morris Brown, *In Heaven as It Is on Earth*, 203–47; Tobler, "Saviors on Mount Zion," 187–88; Creet, *The Genealogical Sublime*, 38–39, 44–46; Peters, "Recording Beyond the Grave." Blair Hodges shared the Peters reference.

8. Schantz, *Awaiting the Heavenly Country*, 38–69.

9. Josiah Collins Pumpelly, "Genealogy: Its Aims and Utility," *NYGBR* 25 (January 1894): 24.

10. Douglas J. Davies, *An Introduction to Mormonism*, 79–80, 103–4.

11. Douglas J. Davies, *An Introduction to Mormonism*, 212–13; Richard L. Bushman, assisted by Woodworth, *Joseph Smith: Rough Stone Rolling*, 443–44; Holzapfel and Holzapfel, *Women of Nauvoo*, 71 (children's age of baptism in the nineteenth century). Eight years has remained the minimum age for baptism within the modern church: Church of Jesus Christ of Latter-day Saints, "Age of Accountability," https://www.churchofjesuschrist.org/study/friend/2000/02/the-age-of-accountability-why-am-i-baptized-when-i-am-eight-years-old?lang=eng.

12. Here, Smith paraphrased Malachi 4:5. *Doctrines and Covenants* 2, in Allen, Embry, and Mehr, *Hearts Turned to the Fathers*, 15; Samuel Morris Brown, *In Heaven as It Is on Earth*, 164–69; Parshall, "Genealogy and Family History," 243–46.

13. Joseph Smith Jr., *The History of the Church of Jesus Christ of Latter-day Saints*, 2nd ed. rev. (Salt Lake City: Deseret Books, 1971), 2:380, in Allen, Embry, and Mehr, *Hearts Turned to the Fathers*, 18; Douglas J. Davies, *An Introduction to Mormonism*, 97.

14. Doctrine and Covenants (1986), section 128:18, in Otterstrom, "Genealogy as Religious Ritual," 142; Flanders, *Nauvoo*, 191.

15. Otterstrom, "Genealogy as Religious Ritual," 143; Arrington and Bitton, *The Mormon Experience*, 22; Douglas J. Davies, *An Introduction to Mormonism*, 8 (26,000).

16. Tobler, "Saviors on Mount Zion," 230–32.

17. Black and Black, *Annotated Record of Baptisms for the Dead, 1840-1845*, 1:77.

18. Vilate Murray Kimball to Heber C. Kimball, October 11, 1840, Kimball Papers, LDS Church Archives, in Holzapfel and Holzapfel, *Women of Nauvoo*, 90–91.

19. Charlotte Haven to family, May 2, 1843, in "A Girl's Letters from Nauvoo," *Overland Monthly* 16 (December 1890): 629–30; Holzapfel and Holzapfel, *Women of Nauvoo*, 91; Tobler, "Saviors on Mount Zion," 203–4.

20. Holzapfel and Holzapfel, *Women of Nauvoo*, 90; Tobler, "Saviors on Mount Zion," 195–202, 220–29; Flanders, *Nauvoo*, 198–99; Akenson, *Some Family*, 57; Samuel Morris Brown, *In Heaven as It Is on Earth*, 170–203.

21. Holzapfel and Holzapfel, *Women of Nauvoo*, 91. Refusing to join the westbound exodus after her husband died, Emma went on to help organize the antipolygamy Reorganized Latter-day Saints Church (RLDS). Flanders, *Nauvoo*, 306, 319.

22. Patriarchal blessing given to Anna Ballantyne by William Smith, Nauvoo, 1845, RLDS Church Archives, typescript in Madsen's possession, in Madsen, *In Their Own Words*, 24–25.

23. Allen, Embry, and Mehr, *Hearts Turned to the Fathers*, 33–34.

24. Allen, Embry, and Mehr, *Hearts Turned to the Fathers*, 27, 36–37.

25. Akenson, *Some Family*, 196–97, 199; Allen, Embry, and Mehr, *Hearts Turned to the Fathers*, 42–44, 111–12, 176–85.

26. Douglas J. Davies, *An Introduction to Mormonism*, 211; Stuy, "Wilford Woodruff's Vision." Laurel Thatcher Ulrich traces the beginnings of Woodruff's commitments to the dead in *A House Full of Females*, 44–45. Richard L. Bushman with Woodworth, *Joseph Smith: Rough Stone Rolling*, 422, also describes early Mormons' proxy baptisms of famous, presumably unrelated dead people.

27. Flake, *The Politics of American Religious Identity*, 30–31.

28. Alexander, *Mormonism in Transition*, 14, 300.

29. Douglas J. Davies, *An Introduction to Mormonism*, 102.

30. Allen, Embry, and Mehr, *Hearts Turned to the Fathers*, 42; Samuel Morris Brown, *In Heaven as It Is on Earth*, 202; Megan Ann Stanton, "All in the Family."

31. Thirteen thousand adoptions in Akenson, *Some Family*, 196; Allen, Embry, and Mehr, *Hearts Turned to the Fathers*, 44.

32. Allen, Embry, and Mehr, *Hearts Turned to the Fathers*, 20.

33. Woodruff quotations (1894) from *Deseret Evening News*, April 14, 1894, and *UGHM* 13 (October 1922), 145–52, in Allen, Embry, and Mehr, *Hearts Turned to the Fathers*, 43.

34. Arrington and Bitton, *The Mormon Experience*, 69.

35. Analysis of these 1890s transitions includes Allen, Embry, and Mehr, *Hearts Turned to the Fathers*, 42–44; Akenson, *Some Family*, 63–64, 196; Weil, *Family Trees*, 173–74; Douglas J. Davies, *An Introduction to Mormonism*, 214–15; Parshall, "Genealogy and Family History," 247–248; Samuel Morris Brown, *In Heaven as It Is on Earth*, 203–48.

36. Allen, Embry, and Mehr, *Hearts Turned to the Fathers*, 46.

37. Allen, Embry, and Mehr, *Hearts Turned to the Fathers*, 48.

38. On the GSU's beginnings, see also Otterstrom, "Genealogy as Religious Ritual," 145.

39. Allen, Embry, and Mehr, *Hearts Turned to the Fathers*, 34, 54 (note 6).

40. "Genealogical Matters," *Deseret News Weekly*, April 1, 1885, 174; Allen, Embry, and Mehr, *Hearts Turned to the Fathers*, 23–24.

41. Sarah Barringer Gordon, *The Mormon Question*; Grow, "Contesting the LDS Image."

42. Allen, Embry, and Mehr, *Hearts Turned to the Fathers*, 35.

43. "General Gleanings," *UGHM* 1 (January 1910): 48.

44. "The Genealogical Society of Utah," *UGHM* 1 (January 1910): 40.

45. Susa Young Gates, typescript, "Genesis of Classwork in the G. H. S. U.," n.d. [after 1928], folder 22, box 69, reel 46, Gates Papers; Allen, Embry, and Mehr, *Hearts Turned to the Fathers*, 62, 65.

46. Holzapfel and Holzapfel, *Women of Nauvoo*, 178–80; Madsen, *In Their Own Words*, 18–19.

47. Tait, "The Young Woman's Journal"; Tucker, *City of Remembering*, 17, 25–27, 29.

48. Person, "Susa Young Gates," 206–8; Gates to Laura A. W. Underhill, March 3, 1924, folder 16, box 71, reel 48, Gates Papers.

49. Susa Young Gates, *The Brigham Young Family*.

50. Susa Young Gates, "Lessons in Genealogy," *UGHM* 2 (October 1911): 163. Allen, Embry, and Mehr, *Hearts Turned to the Fathers*, 70; Allen and Embry, "Provoking the Brethren," 130; Weil, *Family Trees*, 175–76.

51. Allen, Embry, and Mehr, *Hearts Turned to the Fathers*, 88 (note 39); Allen and Embry, "Provoking the Brethren," 130.

52. Donald Lines Jacobus, "Notes," *TAG* 11 (July 1934): 51. Gates's published instructions were preceded only by the expository material in Lemuel Shattuck's *Complete System of Family Registration* (1841), Henry Reed Stiles's *Hand-Book of Practical Suggestions* (1899), and Frank Allaben's *Concerning Genealogies* (1904). Stiles and Allaben came the closest to anticipating Gates's advice for beginners, but both authors published privately, presumably in limited runs.

53. Allen, Embry, and Mehr, *Hearts Turned to the Fathers*, 29; Akenson, *Some Family*, 65–66.

54. Susa Young Gates, typescript, "Genesis of Classwork in the G. H. S. U.," n.d. [after 1928], folder 22, box 69, reel 46, Gates Papers; Allen, Embry, and Mehr, *Hearts Turned to the Fathers*, 78, 82–83.

55. William G. Hartley, "From Men to Boys."

56. National Genealogy Hall of Fame, "Archibald Fowler Bennett," pamphlet (1994), folder 2, box 3; business card, n.d. [1950s], "Archibald Bennett, Special Lecturer—Religion," p. 779, folder 4, box 2; Bennett Scrapbooks.

57. National Genealogy Hall of Fame, "Archibald Fowler Bennett," pamphlet, n.d. (1994), folder 2, box 3, Bennett Scrapbooks.

58. Cornwall, "Susa Young Gates: The Thirteenth Apostle," 85–86, Person, "Susa Young Gates," 215–17.

59. Susa Young Gates, typescript, "Genesis of Classwork in the G. H. S. U.," n.d. [after 1928], folder 22, box 69, reel 46, Gates Papers.

60. Gates to Pres. Heber J. Grant and Counsellors, September 1, 1931, folder 20, box 75, reel 51, Gates Papers.

61. Susa Young Gates, typescript, "Biographical Writings," n.d. [1932], folder 18, box 75, reel 51, Gates Papers; Becker, "Everyman His Own Historian." Gates did not annotate or otherwise mark up her copy of Becker's article.

62. Allen, Embry, and Mehr, *Hearts Turned to the Fathers*, 12 (books of remembrance).

63. List of addresses and instructional materials, folder 1, box 1, Genealogical Society of Utah, Biography Class Collection, 1932–37, CHL. Claudia L. Bushman has also explored Mormon women's genealogy practices in this period in Margaret E. P. Gordon, *Pansy's History*, 220–48.

64. J. M. Jensen (Provo, Utah) to Gates, May 12, 1932, folder 19, box 75, reel 51, Gates Papers. Jensen taught at Brigham Young University. Nearly sixty years later, Ulrich, *A Midwife's Tale*, 9, famously affirmed the "dailiness" in women's work and writings as historically meaningful (1991).

65. "Professional Research Service Offered to 'Helper' Subscribers," *GH* 23 (December 1969): 385, 447; Nichols, "Questions and Answers on the Name Tabulation Program" (1971).

66. Des Jardins, *Women and the Historical Enterprise in America*, 1–145.

67. Stuart, "A More Powerful Effect upon the Body"; Bingham, "Curses and Marks." Painter, *History of White People*, 326, describes the Anglo-Israelism, also known as British Israelism, that remains abroad today. Adherents believe in the Anglo-Saxon and northwestern European provenance of Jesus and other biblical figures. Mauss, *All Abraham's Children*, 2–4, 268, 276.

68. Susa Young Gates, *Surname and Racial History*, table of contents.

69. "Susa Young Gates," *UGHM* 24 (July 1933): 97.

70. Flake, *The Politics of American Religious Identity*, 167–68.

71. Bate, *The Women*, 1–2, 16–17.

72. Akenson, *Some Family*, 95.

73. Grow, "Contesting the LDS Image," 128–30.

74. Morgan, *Women and Patriotism in Jim Crow America*, 87–88.

75. Bate, *The Women*, 281–89, 57–59.

76. Allen, Embry, and Mehr, *Hearts Turned to the Fathers*, 96–99, 101.

Chapter Three

1. Pearson, "Infantile Specimens," 343, 358–59.

2. See especially Zelizer, *Pricing the Priceless Child*.

3. M. A. Majors, M. D., "The Negro and Disease," *Voice of the Negro* 3 (February 1906): 130; Gray, "Majors, Monroe Alpheus"; Michele Mitchell, *Righteous Propagation*, 141–72.

4. "Our Baby Pictures," *The Crisis* 8 (October 1914): 298–99. Henry Louis Gates Jr., *Stony the Road*, 196–200, 237–39, describes an antecedent: Du Bois's earlier photographic exhibition of successful African Americans at the Exposition Universelle in Paris in 1900.

5. Tera W. Hunter, "The Long History of Child Snatching," *New York Times*, June 3, 2018; Hunter, *Bound in Wedlock*.

6. Kachun, "The Faith That the Dark Past Has Taught Us," 234.

7. Fermaglich, *A Rosenberg by Any Other Name*, 6–8, 15, 50.

8. Goldstein, *The Price of Whiteness*; Brodkin, *How Jews Became White Folks*.

9. Reflections on this matter include Gaines, *Uplifting the Race*.

10. Rowlandson, *Narrative of the Captivity, Sufferings, and Removes of Mrs. Mary Rowlandson*, 83.

11. Peirce, *Indian History, Biography, and Genealogy*, v–vi (foreword by Mitchell). Mitchell's 1857 petition to the Massachusetts state government suggests at least two decades of controversy on this matter before 1878: "Council Files February 5, 1857, Case of Zerviah Gould Mitchell," Harvard University/Digital Archives of Massachusetts, https://dataverse .harvard.edu/dataset.xhtml?persistentId=doi:10.7910/DVN/WNZNC.

12. Peirce, *Indian History, Biography, and Genealogy*, v–vi, 216, 257–61 (list of subscribers). Lepore, *The Name of War*, 231–35; Mandell, *Tribe, Race, History*, 135–36, 225; and Jean M. O'Brien, *Firsting and Lasting*, 161, 164, also discuss the Mitchell family's endeavors in the nineteenth century.

13. Peirce, *Indian History, Biography, and Genealogy*, illustrations after 216, 218; lineage on 218–19.

14. Peirce, *Indian History, Biography, and Genealogy*, 216.

15. New Perspectives on the West, "Events in the West: 1870–1880"; Richard S. White, "*It's Your Misfortune*," 212–69 (217–20 on bison eradication).

16. Peirce, *Indian History, Biography, and Genealogy*, title page; William R. Cutter, "Proceedings: Ebenezer Weaver Peirce," *NEHGR* 57 (April 1903): lxii–lxiii.

17. Browning, *Americans of Royal Descent* (1st ed., 1883), 121–22. Working through research assistance, I was unable to locate correspondence with Mitchell in Browning's Papers at the New York Public Library.

18. LaPier and Beck, *City Indian*, 106–113.

19. "Excerpts from Mrs. Fowler's 1929 Report," in Mrs. Joseph Lindon Smith, "Extracts from the Reports of My State Chairmen of Indian Welfare" (pamphlet; Denver, 1930), folder 26, box 17, Illinois Federation of Women's Clubs Records, Abraham Lincoln Presidential Library (Springfield, Ill.), in LaPier and Beck, *City Indian*, 107. The club conferred "honorary member" status on non-Indian allies. On Blackstone, also see Wendt, *The Daughters of the American Revolution*, 94–95, 109–110, who describes Blackstone's earlier contact with the DAR when she performed as Tsianina Redfeather, and Troutman, *Indian Blues*, who enabled reconfirmation of Blackstone's identity.

20. Gross, *What Blood Won't Tell*, 9; Miles, *Ties That Bind*; Schwalm, *A Hard Fight for We*, 55–56, 65; Hunter, *Bound in Wedlock*, 27–28; Weil, *Family Trees*, 29–31, 50.

21. Hunter, *Bound in Wedlock*, 26; Sachs, "Freedom by a Judgment," especially 176, 178, 197–201.

22. Bly, "Literacy and Orality"; Byron, "Bible"; Heather Andrea Williams, *Self-Taught*, 8–29.

23. Berlin, *Generations of Captivity*, 179–81.

24. Patricia Cline Cohen, *A Calculating People*, 184–85.

25. Kathleen M. Brown, *Good Wives, Nasty Wenches*, 107–36; Schwartz, *Birthing a Slave*, 9–32; Wulf, "Bible, King, and Common Law," 483–86, 496. Sachs, "Freedom by a Judgment," describes an ironic outcome of enslavement's matrilineal descent that did not reward slaveowners. Freedom suits brought by enslaved people in the Coleman family, who cited an Indian foremother who had been free, resulted in success.

26. Typically, authorities made strenuous efforts to locate fathers and compel couples to marry, or to have the men otherwise financially support the women and their children. Ulrich, *A Midwife's Tale*, 147–60; Hough, *Rural Unwed Mothers*, 30–42.

27. Jacobs, *Incidents in the Life of a Slave Girl*, 88.

28. Godbeer, *Sexual Revolution in Early America*, 7–9, 119–21; Hunter, *Bound in Wedlock*, 13, 104.

29. Death and mortality records were the first to be kept by governments, predating records of marriages and births. Patricia Cline Cohen, *A Calculating People*, 86; Cassedy, *American Medicine and Statistical Thinking*, 17–18.

30. Hunter, *Bound in Wedlock*, 1–85.

31. Frederick Douglass, "My Bondage and My Freedom," in Douglass, *Autobiographies*, 140; Wall, *Worrying the Line*, 10.

32. Gordon-Reed, *Thomas Jefferson and Sally Hemings*, 66, 209; Lucia Stanton, *"Those Who Labor for My Happiness,"* 96–97; Scharff, *The Women Jefferson Loved*, 372–73. Virginia and Ohio shared a border before West Virginia's admittance to statehood in 1864, during the Civil War.

33. "Life Among the Lowly, No. 1," Pike County (Ohio) *Republican*, March 13, 1873, reprinted in Gordon-Reed, *Thomas Jefferson and Sally Hemings*, 245–48; Hemings's dates in Gordon-Reed, *Thomas Jefferson and Sally Hemings*, xxiii. Kerrison, *Jefferson's Daughters*, provides family trees on xiv–xv. Wales's name is sometimes spelled "Wayles."

34. Gordon-Reed, *Thomas Jefferson and Sally Hemings*, 133–35.

35. Gordon-Reed, *The Hemingses of Monticello*, 55–56, 271; Kerrison, *Jefferson's Daughters*, 254–55; Gordon-Reed, *Thomas Jefferson and Sally Hemings*, 15.

36. Gordon-Reed, *The Hemingses of Monticello*, 96, 275, 343–44; Helen F. M. Leary, "Sally Hemings's Children: A Genealogical Analysis of the Evidence," *NGSQ* 89 (September 2001): 196.

37. Gordon-Reed, *Thomas Jefferson and Sally Hemings*, 7–58, 246; Kerrison, *Jefferson's Daughters*, 242–308.

38. Brenda E. Stevenson, *Life in Black and White*, 159–257; Heather Andrea Williams, *Help Me to Find My People*; Gutman, *The Black Family in Slavery and Freedom*; Weil, *Family Trees*, 170 (the end of slavery as a "profoundly genealogical moment").

39. Weil, *Family Trees*, 29–31, 50; Gatewood, *Aristocrats of Color*, 16–29.

40. Novick, *That Noble Dream*, 39, 88; Light, "A Visit to the Dead," 299.

41. George E. Adams et al., typescript, "Report of the Committee on Administration," January 1, 1905, folder 10, box 3, NL Trustees, 02/01/21. They did not divulge the number of genealogy patrons during this year.

42. Steenburg, "Stepping Outside Her Sphere," 57; Shattuck, *A History of Concord* (1835), iv.

43. Shaw, *What a Woman Ought to Be and to Do*, 171; Battles, *The History of Public Library Access*, 23–40; Knott, *Not Free, Not for All*.

44. Cerny, "Black Ancestral Research," 580; James M. Rose and Eichholz, *Black Genesis*, 5. On genealogy indexes, see Bockstruck, "Four Centuries of Genealogy."

45. Biographical information on Day in Harvard University Libraries, "Papers of Caroline Bond Day: A Finding Aid," https://hollisarchives.lib.harvard.edu/repositories/6/resources /4762; Michele Mitchell, *Righteous Propagation*, 213.

46. Broman and Steven Williams, *Anthropology at Harvard*, 297–450. Day's own and her husband's lineages, including mathematical calculations of their "race mixture," appear in Day, *A Study of Some Negro-White Families*, 31, 40.

47. Lee D. Baker, *Anthropology and the Racial Politics of Culture*, 156–220; Gross, *What Blood Won't Tell*, 226–30; Painter, *History of White People*, 228–42, 327–42; Day to Mrs. Jeannette T. Jones, April 30, 1927, folder 6, box 1, Day Papers.

48. Day, *A Study of Some Negro-White Families*, 6.

49. Lynd and Lynd, *Middletown*.

50. Mama Penney (Mrs. Edgar J. Penney) to Day, August 23, 1927, folder 9, box 1, Day Papers.

51. Day, *A Study of Some Negro-White Families*, iii.

52. W. E. B. Du Bois to Day, May 23, 1928; Du Bois to Day, April 25, 1930; folder 3, box 1, Day Papers.

53. Ernest C. Tate to Day, May 7, 1930, folder 11, box 1, Day Papers.

54. Margaret H. Wheeler to Day, April 30, 1928, folder 12, box 1; Harvey/Wheeler "family history," n.d. [1920s], folder 25, box 4; Day Papers.

55. Rampersad, *The Life of Langston Hughes*, 39–40, 108, 116; Langston Hughes, "The Negro Speaks of Rivers," *The Crisis* 22 (June 1921): 71.

56. Rampersad, *The Life of Langston Hughes*, 299; booklet for January 18, 1992, workshop, in folder "Meeting, 2nd Family Reunion Workshop," Box 1, PLR.

57. Hopkins, "William Lloyd Garrison Centennial Speech," *The Guardian* (Boston), December 16, 1905, 1; Lois Brown, *Pauline Elizabeth Hopkins*, 9.

58. Lois Brown, *Pauline Elizabeth Hopkins*, 9–32.

59. "Along the Color Line," *The Crisis* 37 (March 1930), 96; Des Jardins, *Women and the Historical Enterprise in America*, 125. Gatewood, *Aristocrats of Color*, 221, 304, and Weil, *Family Trees*, 139–40, discuss some antecedents, including a 1903 group in Boston with a similar name.

60. Du Bois, *The Souls of Black Folk*, 100.

61. Wells-Barnett, *Crusade for Justice*, 8.

62. Anna Julia Cooper, *A Voice from the South*, 31.

63. Gilmore, *Gender and Jim Crow*, 61–89; Gilmore, "Murder, Memory, and the Flight of the Incubus."

64. I draw this conclusion from tables of contents and book notices in the *NEHGR* and in *TAG*, as well as from the multiple editions of the ASG's Genealogical Research and Methods that were intended for classroom and workshop use after 1960. Exceptions include the NGS's publication of Rabbi Malcolm H. Stern's research before he completed *Americans of Jewish Descent* in 1960: *NGSQ* 46 (June 1958): 63–72. Donald Jacobus, review of David de Sola Pool, *Portraits Edged in Stone: Early Jewish Settlers, 1682-1831* (New York:

Columbia University Press, 1952), in "Recent Books," *TAG* 29 (April 1953): 114–16, was another exception. Pool was a prominent Orthodox rabbi. Ellenson, "Zionism in the Mind of the American Rabbinate," 201–2.

65. Nahum Mitchell's 1840 *History of the Early Settlement of Bridgewater, Massachusetts*, illustrates town histories' melding of history, genealogy, and biography especially well. Mitchell (1769–1853) was a Federalist congressman and judge.

66. "Objects," *PAJHS* 1 (1893): iii; A. Neubauer, "Genealogy of a Family at Augsburg," *JQR* 4 (July 1892): 698; Weil, *Family Trees*, 138.

67. Stern in "Book Reviews," *NGSQ* 66 (June 1978): 145.

68. Monetary figures in August Belmont to Richard J. H. Gottheil, March 16, 1917, box C7, Belmont Family Papers.

69. The mutual friend was a Mr. W. Hoffman. Gottheil to Belmont, February 23, 1917, box C7, Belmont Family Papers.

70. Gottheil, "The Family Almanzi," *Jewish Quarterly Review* 5 (April 1893): 500–505.

71. Gottheil, *The Belmont-Belmonte Family*, 173.

72. Gottheil, *The Belmont-Belmonte Family*, 3–4.

73. Ehrenreich, *The Nazi Ancestral Proof*; Benton-Cohen, *Inventing the Immigration Problem*, 72–103; Painter, *The History of White People*, 278–326; Dinnerstein, *Anti-Semitism in America*, 58.

74. Lederhendler, *American Jewry*, 133–34.

75. Dinnerstein, *Anti-Semitism in America*, 84–93, 158–59; Fermaglich, *A Rosenberg by Any Other Name*, 5–11, 102–18.

76. Dinnerstein, *Anti-Semitism in America*, 128, 78–149 more generally; Fermaglich, *A Rosenberg by Any Other Name*, 69–100.

77. Fermaglich, *A Rosenberg by Any Other Name*, 5–11.

78. Dalzell, *Enterprising Elite*, sheds particular light on Boston's interlocking ruling families, including the Cabots, in the nineteenth century.

79. Kaplan and Bernays, *The Language of Names*, 60–61; "Cabots File Objection to Borrowing of Name," *New York Times*, August 14, 1923, 19; Okrent, *The Guarded Gate*, 347, 428. Some sources spell Kabatchnick as "Kabotchnik."

80. Walter and Marian divorced in the 1920s; Walter remarried in 1929. Malcolm H. Stern, *Americans of Jewish Descent* (1960), 104; "A Conversation with Malcolm H. Stern," *Toledot* 1 (Summer 1977): 10. Starting in the 1880s, old-money Protestant elites in eastern cities published *Social Register* lists, consisting of their own names and those of people like themselves. Implicitly, such lists omitted the newly rich, the middle classes, individuals whose behavior violated agreed-upon class attributes, and, of course, Catholics and Jews and African Americans. In New York in the 1880s, the lists "consisted almost entirely of the names of descendants of seventeenth-and eighteenth-century Dutch and English merchants." Clifton Hood has shown *Social Register* activity persisting into the 1980s. Hood, *In Pursuit of Privilege*, 172, 322–23.

81. Wenger, *History Lessons*, 211; Sallyann Amdur Sack, "Jewish Genealogy: The Past 25 Years," *Avotaynu* 20 (Summer 2004): 6 (on Poland); Alisa Solomon, *Wonder of Wonders*, 319.

82. Novick, *The Holocaust in American Life*, 85–126; Fermaglich, "What's Uncle Sam's Last Name?"; "The Program of the American Jewish Archives," *AJA* 1 (June 1948): 3.

83. Kiron, "Demythologizing 1654"; Alisa Solomon, *Wonder of Wonders*, 59; Kranson, *Ambivalent Embrace*, 14.

84. Selma Stern-Taeubler, "Acquisitions: Genealogy," *AJA* 2 (January 1950): 31–32; Michael Goren, "Reviews of Books," *NEHGR* 133 (October 1979): 313–15.

85. Dinnerstein, *Anti-Semitism in America*, 188; Fisher, "A Place in History," 59.

86. Malcolm H. Stern, *Americans of Jewish Descent*, unpaginated foreword, 104; "A Conversation with Malcolm H. Stern," *Toledot* 1 (Summer 1977): 10; Weil, *Family Trees*, 201.

Chapter Four

1. Nobile and Kenney, "The Search for Roots, a Pre-Haley Movement."

2. Alex Haley to Paul Reynolds, January 30, 1965, folder 10, box 3, Haley Papers 1888; Moore, "Routes," 243. Reynolds was Haley's agent at the time.

3. Marcus Lee Hansen, *The Problem of the Third Generation Immigrant* (1938).

4. Matthew Frye Jacobson, *Roots Too*, especially 2–3.

5. Delmont, *Making "Roots."*

6. Alex Haley, "My Furthest-Back Person—The African," *New York Times Magazine*, July 16, 1972, 12.

7. Russell E. Bidlack, "The Family Periodical," *NGSQ* 66 (December 1978): 267.

8. Carp, *Family Matters*, 40–53.

9. Sheppard, "A Bicentennial Look," 12–13; Connecticut Society of Genealogists, "Save Vital Records," *GH* 25 (March 1971): 166; Kermit B. Karns, "Genealogy and Politics," *GH* 32 (March–April 1978): 8. Peter White, "Privacy: An International Concern," provides chronology on 228–31. Creet, *The Genealogical Sublime*, 161–66, and Creet, "Data Mining the Deceased," discuss genealogy and privacy in modern times. Historians' encounters with such restrictions while doing research include Warshauer and Sturges, "Difficult Hunting," 426–31. Peter White, "Privacy: An International Concern," 238–39, describes the later innovation of Freedom of Information Acts, to work around provisions of privacy legislation.

10. The "72-year rule" regarding disclosure of census records became official in 1978; before that, Congress considered restricting access to the 1900 Census for even longer. Lind, "Public Records: The Census," 72; U.S. Census Bureau, "History: The '72-Year' Rule"; "1900 Census Records Opened Fully to the Public," *GH* 32 (March–April 1978): 5. In 2012, the 1940 U.S. Census was opened to the public.

11. I draw this conclusion from the "sources indexed" lists in Filby with Meyer, *Passenger and Immigration Lists Index* (1981), 1:xiii–xxxv; Filby with Lower, *Passenger and Immigration Lists Index: 1986-1990 Cumulated Supplements*, 1:xiii–lv. While English-language publication of immigration lists from the late nineteenth and early twentieth centuries occurred mostly after 1975, German-language publications on this topic began appearing earlier, in the 1950s and 1960s. P. William Filby, "Passenger and Immigration Lists: An Update," *GH* 37 (July–August 1983): 5, offers a history of these publications.

12. Macy, "Recognizing Scholarly Genealogy," 7–8.

13. Allen, Embry, and Mehr, *Hearts Turned to the Fathers*, 35.

14. Otterstrom, "Genealogy as Religious Ritual," 144; *NGSQ* 34 (September 1946): 96; Shipps, "Surveying the Mormon Image," 98 ("mountain curtain"); Tucker, *City of Remembering*, 17.

15. Creet, *The Genealogical Sublime*, 55.

16. Allen, Embry, and Mehr, *Hearts Turned to the Fathers*, 96–103.

17. Doane, *Searching for Your Ancestors* (1937), 138–39; Donald Lines Jacobus, "Notes," *TAG* 11 (July 1934): 51–52.

18. Bennett, "The Ancestor Quest," September 18, 1938, book of remembrance (p. 224), folder 3, box 1, Bennett Scrapbooks.

19. Bennett, "Utah's Great Research Center for Genealogy and History," n.d. [summer 1961], pp. 981–88, folder 2, box 3, Bennett Scrapbooks; Allen, Embry, and Mehr, *Hearts Turned to the Fathers*, 213–64. On World War II's acceleration of microfilming efforts generally, see Charles Drew, "The War and the Development of Microphotography as Applied to English Records," *TAG* 22 (April 1946): 201–5; Creet, *The Genealogical Sublime*, 53–55. Two decades later, the church had microfilmed half a billion pages of records, or 406,682 hundred-foot rolls. Archibald F. Bennett, "Genealogical Sources in Salt Lake City," *TAG* 42 (April 1966): 89–94.

20. Bennett, "Utah's Great Research Center for Genealogy and History," n.d. [summer 1961], pp. 981–88, folder 2, box 3, Bennett Scrapbooks; Dulong, "Genealogical Groups in a Changing Organizational Environment," 224, 245.

21. Archibald F. Bennett, "Genealogical Sources in Salt Lake City," *TAG* 42 (April 1966): 93; Shoumatoff, *Mountain of Names*, 286–93; Sheppard, "A Bicentennial Look," 9; Allen, Embry, and Mehr, *Hearts Turned to the Fathers*, 236–41; Creet, *The Genealogical Sublime*, 57–58. Unlike later authors, Shoumatoff was able to enter the vault in the 1980s.

22. "Visit to the Library of the Genealogical Society of the Church of the Latter Day Saints," *NGSQ* 42 (December 1954): 160.

23. Noel C. Stevenson to Winifred Lovering Holman, May 30, 1953, Drown folder, box 10, Holman Papers. In 1953, she otherwise held a NEHGS life membership, and membership in the historical societies of Long Island, Maryland, and Virginia. Typescript, "Hubbard Lineage" (1932), title page, William Hubbard folder 1, box 17; typescript, "Richards Lineage" (1954–56), Richards folder 1, box 26; Holman Papers.

24. Karl L. Trever to Bennett, February 10, 1950, book of remembrance, p. 756b, folder 4, box 2, Bennett Scrapbooks. See also Lester J. Cappon to Everett L. Cooley, December 18, 1956, book of remembrance, p. 524, folder 2, box 2, Bennett Scrapbooks.

25. Simultaneously, Walter M. Pratt was also president of the NEHGS. "New England Genealogical Head Praises Utah Society," *Deseret News: The Church Section*, March 27, 1949, 21 (clipping), book of remembrance (p. 443), folder 1, box 2, Bennett Scrapbooks.

26. Gates to Pres. Lewis Anderson, October 19, 1920, folder 21, box 72, reel 48, Gates Papers.

27. Copy of Joseph Fielding Smith to Nicholas G. Smith (Mesa, Ariz.), March 6, 1936, in Genealogical Society Minutes, March 19, 1939, Family History Department, in Allen, Embry, and Mehr, *Hearts Turned to the Fathers*, 111–12; Akenson, *Some Family*, 197; Creet, *The Genealogical Sublime*, 58–59, who links this transition with the beginning of the records' computerization that same year.

28. Akenson, *Some Family*, 199, 201; Mauss, *The Angel and the Beehive*, 88; Nichols, "Questions and Answers on the Name Tabulation Program"; Kif Augustine-Adams, personal communication, March 25, 2017.

29. Akenson, *Some Family*, 69; Archibald F. Bennett, "Genealogical Sources in Salt Lake City," *TAG* 42 (April 1966): 97; Kenneally, *The Invisible History of the Human Race*, 115.

30. Lenstra, "'Democratizing' Genealogy and Family Heritage Practices," contributes a local history of genealogy's expansion in this period, in Urbana, Illinois.

31. James B. Rhoads, "Genealogists and the National Archives: Profile of a Partnership," *NGSQ* 59 (June 1971): 84–85.

32. Phyllis Kendall in "Letters to the Editor," *DARM* 113 (August–September 1979): 791; Carolyn Leopold Michaels and Kathryn Scott, "Daughters Plus," *DARM* 115 (May 1981): 425 (on call numbers).

33. Rymsza-Pawlowska, *History Comes Alive*, 6, 86, credits Jesse Lemisch's *Towards a More Democratic History* (1967) for popularizing the phrase "history from the bottom up." See also Biondi, *Black Revolution on Campus*.

34. Kranson, *Ambivalent Embrace*, 7, who points out that it is historically incorrect to label Jews from German-speaking areas of the 1840s and 1850s "German Jews," since they lived before German unification under Bismarck in 1871. Some American descendants of these central European Jews and earlier-arriving Sephardic populations intermarried, further complicating these numbers and distinctions.

35. Okrent, *The Guarded Gate*, 388–89, 391–93.

36. Fermaglich, *A Rosenberg by Any Other Name*, 63–65.

37. Gibson and Jung, "Historical Census Statistics on Population Totals"; Grieco et al., "The Foreign-Born Population in the United States: 2010."

38. American Council of Learned Societies, *Surnames in the United States Census of 1790*, 126–360; Purvis and Akenson, "The European Ancestry of the United States Population, 1790."

39. Conzen et al., "The Invention of Ethnicity."

40. Matthew Frye Jacobson, *Roots Too*, 222–25; Rapaport, "The Holocaust in American Jewish Life"; Novick, *The Holocaust in American Life*, 133–34, 146–69; Berenbaum, "The Nativization of the Holocaust"; Lipstadt, "America and the Memory of the Holocaust." Hasia R. Diner has challenged this thesis about delayed Holocaust remembering in the U.S. with *We Remember with Reverence and Love*.

41. Fermaglich, *A Rosenberg by Any Other Name*, 101–28.

42. Sack and the Israel Genealogical Society, *A Guide to Jewish Genealogical Research in Israel*, xiii.

43. Kranson, *Ambivalent Embrace*, 36–37; Alisa Solomon, *Wonder of Wonders*, 82–83.

44. Kassow, "Shtetl"; Alisa Solomon, *Wonder of Wonders*, 2, 54–56, 334–36.

45. Alisa Solomon, *Wonder of Wonders*, 90–93. When I was ten years old in 1978, my father and I sang and danced in the chorus in a community theater production of *Fiddler* in suburban Boston. Devising costumes for the same production, my mother found that it was far easier and cheaper to clothe the plain villagers of *Fiddler* than to concoct *The Sound of Music* children's seven sailor suits, or to garb the singing aristocrats of *My Fair Lady*.

46. Kurzweil, *From Generation to Generation*, 22–23.

47. Kurzweil, *From Generation to Generation*, 20; Weil, *Family Trees*, 201–2.

48. The modern English-language Wikipedia page on Dobromil, now located in Ukraine (five kilometers from the Polish border), describes prewar Dobromil's Jewish community as a shtetl from history, a neighborhood within a multi-ethnic town, that Nazis later erased. A Pole from Dobromil became a major in the Polish resistance forces before perishing in

the Soviets' Katyn massacre of Polish officers in 1940. "Dobromyl," page last edited June 18, 2019, https://en.wikipedia.org/wiki/Dobromyl.

49. Dan Rottenberg, "Tracing Jewish Ancestors: A Pioneer Looks Back," *Avotaynu* 5 (Fall 1989): 3.

50. Sweeney, "Ancestors, Avotaynu, Roots," 182n123; Fisher, "A Place in History," 67.

51. The historian Eric Ehrenreich has found an earlier Jewish group than Czellitzer's, in Vienna in 1913, but this group apparently did not last. Neil Rosenstein, "Organized Jewish Genealogy: The Early Years," *Avotaynu* 13 (Spring 1997): 3–5; Ehrenreich, *The Nazi Ancestral Proof*, 19. Translation courtesy of Internet Archive citation at https://archive.org/details /judischefamilien.

52. Fisher, "A Place in History," 55–57 (note 66); Hanns G. Reissner, "Gesellschaft fuer Judische Familienforschung," *Toledot* 1 (Summer 1977): 7–8; Arnon Hershkovitz, "Early Jewish Genealogy Organizations in Berlin and Jerusalem," *Avotaynu* 27 (Summer 2011): 23–26.

53. Arnon Hershkovitz, "Early Jewish Genealogy Organizations in Berlin and Jerusalem," *Avotaynu* 27 (Summer 2011): 25.

54. Sallyann Amdur Sack, "Jewish Genealogy: The Past 25 Years," *Avotaynu* 20 (Summer 2004): 3.

55. "To Our Readers," *Toledot* 1 (Spring 1978): 2; Ehrenreich, *The Nazi Ancestral Proof*. The talk of selfishness came from an unnamed rabbi who presided over the funeral of editor Sally Amdur Sack's uncle. Sack, "As I See It," *Avotaynu* 14 (Spring 1998): 2.

56. Marable, *Malcolm X*, 85, 96.

57. Carter G. Woodson, "Negro Women Eligible to be Daughters of the American Revolution," *NHB* 7 (November 1943): 36–37; Sandage, "A Marble House Divided." Additional examples are Luther P. Jackson, "The Daniel Family of Virginia," *NHB* 10 (December 1947): 51–57; Eunice Shaed Lewis, "Distinguished Americans along the Border: The Cook Family," *NHB* 5 (January 1942): 89–90 (Lewis indicated the border between races); "The Family of Porter William Phillips, Sr.," *NHB* 27 (November 1964): 81–84. See also Brundage, *The Southern Past*, 138–83.

58. Asukile, "Joel Augustus Rogers," 324–25. See also Pinckney, *Out There*, 1–54; Pascoe, *What Comes Naturally*, 186–91; John Ralph Willis, "Talent Showed Brightly from Beneath Their Skin," *New York Times*, February 4, 1973; Rogers, *The Five Negro Presidents*.

59. Jean Stephenson to Alex Haley, August 12, 1965, folder 12, box 3, Haley Papers 1888; Haley, "My Search for Roots" (1965): 7.

60. Peter Kerr, "600 'Cousins' Meet to Celebrate Roots," *New York Times*, June 28, 1982, B11.

61. Haley, "My Search for Roots" (1965): 7 (interviewing Walker).

62. Haley, "My Search for Roots" (1965): 5–6. Beard later published a racially and ethnically inclusive instructional work: Beard with Demong, *How to Find Your Family Roots* (1977).

63. PBS Newshour, "Arresting Dress," summarizes cross-dressing's criminalization in Early America and the United States.

64. Pauli Murray and Eastwood, "Jane Crow and the Law"; Bell-Scott, *The Firebrand and the First Lady*, 322–23. I refer to Murray as "she" because her biographers, including scholars who discuss her as an example of genderqueerness, and Murray herself, also used

the pronoun "she." Brittney C. Cooper, *Beyond Respectability*; Drury, "Love, Ambition, and 'Invisible Footnotes'"; Rosalind Rosenberg, *Jane Crow*; Saxby, *Pauli Murray*.

65. Pauline Fitzgerald Dame to Dear Sisters, March 22, 1954, folder 296, box 11, Murray Papers; Rosalind Rosenberg, *Jane Crow*, 17–20.

66. Pauli Murray, *Song in a Weary Throat*, 30.

67. Stephen Vincent Benét to Pauli Murray, n.d. [after October 23, 1939], folder 1,621, box 93, Murray Papers; Pauli Murray, *Song in a Weary Throat*, 132–33.

68. Washington, "Introduction."

69. The original "400" was the New York socialite Ward McAllister's list of somebodies, circa 1888. Like compilers of the *Social Register*, he omitted the newly rich and middle-class people. Four hundred was the maximum number that most contemporary ballrooms could accommodate. Hood, *In Pursuit of Privilege*, 227–35.

70. Pauli Murray to Mother, Aunt Sallie and Aunt Marie, April 17, 1951, folder 1,360, box 77, Murray Papers.

71. Bell-Scott, *The Firebrand and the First Lady*, 196–201, 205–6, 214; Murray, typed notes, "Fitzgerald Odyssey: Delaware and Pennsylvania," April 29, 1954, p. 4, folder 1,355, box 76, Murray Papers.

72. Pauli Murray, *Proud Shoes*. Treatments of *Proud Shoes* include Azaransky, *The Dream is Freedom*, 39–50; O'Dell, *Sites of Southern Memory*, 104–43; Bell-Scott, *The Firebrand and the First Lady*, 256–57; Rosalind Rosenberg, *Jane Crow*, 203–7; Brittney C. Cooper, *Beyond Respectability*, 87–113; Saxby, *Pauli Murray*, 172–88, 293–94.

73. Pauline F. Dame, "Autobiography of My Life" (1944), typescript, p. 8, folder 275, box 11, Murray Papers.

74. Pauli Murray to Lennox McClennon, March 24, 1951, folder 1360, box 77, Murray Papers; Gilmore, *Defying Dixie*, 247–90; Rosalind Rosenberg, *Jane Crow*, 65–77.

75. Bell-Scott, *The Firebrand and the First Lady*, 255–58.

76. Roi Ottley, "An Unknown Aspect of U.S.," *Chicago Tribune*, November 18, 1956, C18; Henrietta Buckmaster, "Indomitable Family," *New York Times*, October 21, 1956.

77. James M. Rose and Eichholz, *Black Genesis*, 3, and Draznin, *The Family Historian's Handbook*, 8, 11, are exceptions to this pattern. Draznin had previously interviewed Murray on the subject of black genealogy. Yaffa Draznin, audiotape of interview with Murray, February 17, 1977, item 2622at, Murray Papers. Bibliographies from later times, generated from within the Afro-American Genealogical and Historical Society (formed in 1977), include James Dent Walker, "Family History and Genealogy: Avocation or Necessity?" *JAAHGS* 2 (Fall 1981): 103–5; Gloria L. Smith, "Some Family Histories," *JAAHGS* 5 (Spring 1984): 44–45. Smith did not claim to be comprehensive, but her list focused on family genealogies, and neither she nor Walker included *Proud Shoes*.

78. Haley to Paul Reynolds, January 30, 1965, folder 10, box 3; bibliography (omitting *Proud Shoes*), n.d., folder 29, box 29; Haley Papers 1888. Delmont, *Making "Roots,"* emphasizes Haley's prowess when it came to speaking and generating publicity.

79. Pauli Murray, *Song in a Weary Throat*, 300.

80. Norrell, *Alex Haley*, 123–24.

81. Copy of letter and proposal, Pauli Murray to Regina Brough, March 23, 1978, folder 327, box 12, Murray Papers. On January 8, 1977, the sixty-six-year-old Murray was among the first American women of any race to undergo official ordination. The first official woman

priest in the United States preceded her by only a week, on January 1. Episcopal News Service, "First Woman Regularly Ordained to Episcopal Priesthood"; Saxby, *Pauli Murray*, 261–92.

82. Jones and Bullock, "The Two or More Races Population: 2010: Census Briefs."

83. Murray to Alma Fitzgerald Biggers, June 24, 1975, p. 4, folder 331, box 12, Murray Papers.

84. See especially Sharfstein, *The Invisible Line*, 324–26; Dominguez, *White by Definition*, 159–61.

85. D'Emilio and Freedman, *Intimate Matters*, 34–37.

86. Jacobus with Waterman, *The Waterman Family*, 1:1 (Waterman's birthdate on 1:5).

87. Jacobus and Waterman, *The Waterman Family*, 3:672–87. Waterman is listed as coauthor of the third volume.

88. Jacobus and Waterman, *The Waterman Family*, 3:688; George McCracken, "Editor's Note," *TAG* 47 (April 1971): 91.

89. An example is Elizabeth Shown Mills and Gary B. Mills, "Slaves and Masters: The Louisiana Metoyers," *NGSQ* 70 (September 1982): 163–89.

90. Pitre, *In Struggle against Jim Crow*.

91. Mary Ainsworth, "The Registrar General Says—," *DARM* 91 (February 1957): 173–74; Jean Stephenson, "Genealogical Source Material," *DARM* 91 (July 1957): 831.

92. Stephenson to Haley, August 12, 1965, folder 12, box 3, Haley Papers 1888; Alex Haley, "Preserving the Family," *DARM* 118 (August–September 1984): 460–65, 487.

93. James B. Rhoads, "Genealogists and the National Archives: Profile of a Partnership," *NGSQ* 59 (June 1971): 87; Gibson and Jung, "Historical Census Statistics on Population Totals."

94. Thomas H. Roderick, "Negro Genealogy," *TAG* 47 (April 1971): 88–91. Susan Tucker reports that the *NGSQ* published items on free people of color as early as 1970. Tucker, *City of Remembering*, 162.

95. Peggy J. Murrell, "Black Genealogy: Despite Many Problems, More Negroes Search for Their Family Pasts," *Wall Street Journal*, March 9, 1972, clipping, folder 23, box 2, Haley Papers 1888.

96. Milton Rubincam, review of Elizabeth L. Nichols, *Help Is Available* (Logan, Utah: Everton Publishers, 1972), in "Book Reviews," *NGSQ* 60 (December 1972): 313.

97. Shoumatoff, *Mountain of Names*, 258–59.

98. Secondary literature on this transition includes Jacobson, *Roots Too*; Lowenthal, *The Heritage Crusade*, 16–17; Hareven, "The Search for Generational Memory"; and, tangentially, Glenn, "In the Blood?" Light, *Common People*, is especially important on genealogical research on working-class and poor populations.

99. Kenneth Gene Lindsay, *Grandpas, Inlaws, and Outlaws: A Lindsay Family Genealogy* (Evansville, Ind.: Kamma Pub Co., 1976), cited in "New on the Bookshelf," *GH* 31 (March–April 1977): 192.

100. Mary Alice Kellogg, "Climbing Family Trees," *Newsweek*, September 13, 1976, in Sweeney, "Ancestors, Avotaynu, Roots," 144; Hilton, "Bury This One Again," in *Who Do You Think You Are?*, 119–31. Hilton was half-joking with her chapter title.

101. "Forum: Dan Rottenberg's Finding Our Fathers," *Toledot* 1 (Fall 1977): 11–12.

102. Matthew Frye Jacobson, *Roots Too*; Zaretsky, *No Direction Home*, 151; Thomas Lask, "Publishing," *New York Times*, April 30, 1976, 70.

103. Heather Murray, *Not in This Family*, 99–107; Moskowitz, *In Therapy We Trust*, 218–45; Hilton, *Who Do You Think You Are?*, 7–9.

104. See my Introduction; Yokota, *Unbecoming British*, 241–42; Little, "Genealogy as Theatre of Self-Identity," 136–45.

105. "Recent Books," *TAG* 37 (January 1961): 59; "Book Reviews," *NGSQ* 69 (March 1981): 66–67.

106. "To the Sentinel: Alex Haley Writes from London," *Daily Sentinel* (Rome, N.Y.), December 6, 1966, clipping, folder 23, box 2, Haley Papers 1888; Delmont, *Making "Roots,"* 37–52; Norrell, *Alex Haley*, 110–12. Haley continued researching his Irish ancestry after *Roots*: V. Ben Bloxham (London) to Alex Haley, April 17, 1978, folder 17, box 2, Haley Papers 1888.

107. Nobile and Kenney, "The Search for Roots, a Pre-Haley Movement."

108. Dan Rottenberg, "Tracing Jewish Ancestors: A Pioneer Looks Back," *Avotaynu* 5 (Fall 1989): 4–5; Jack Greenwald, "European Cemeteries Visited," *Avotaynu* 2 (May 1986): 20.

109. Pauli Murray, "What is Africa to Me?" (1960), reprinted in *Song in a Weary Throat*, 328–32; Hugh A. Mulligan, "U.S. Blacks Making Painful Hunt for Past," *Chicago Tribune*, April 27, 1975, 4.

110. "Second Trip to Africa," May 1967, pages labeled 3016–17, folder 10, box 46, Haley Papers 1888.

111. Delmont, *Making "Roots,"* 37.

112. Nobile, "Uncovering Roots," 35; Frady, "The Children of Malcolm."

113. Alex Haley to Paul Reynolds, January 30, 1965, folder 10, box 3, Haley Papers 1888.

114. Haley, "My Search for Roots" (1965), 5.

115. Alex Haley, "My Furthest-Back Person—The African," *New York Times Magazine*, July 16, 1972; "Book Reviews," *JAAHGS* 6 (Summer 1985): 86–87; Delmont, *Making "Roots,"* 53–78.

116. "Quest for Identity: Americans Go on a Genealogy Kick," 41.

117. Marty Bell, "Debts, Stubborn Faith Drive Alex Haley to Write 'Roots.'"

118. Haley began attending planning meetings for the televising of *Roots* in April 1975. "Now, on to finishing the book Roots," he wrote in a note to himself. Alex Haley, "Carbons of Synopses for Segments . . . as Projected of Television Series of Roots," May 15, 1975, photocopy, page labeled 5645, folder 9, box 47, Haley Papers 1888. Norrell, *Alex Haley*, 139, and Delmont, *Making "Roots,"* 102–3, agree that Haley submitted his full manuscript to Doubleday following Thanksgiving of 1975.

Chapter Five

1. Moore, "Routes," 6, 10. Other useful work on *Roots* include Delmont, *Making "Roots"*; Norrell, *Alex Haley*, 97–202; Helen Taylor, "The Griot from Tennessee"; Linda Williams, *Playing the Race Card*, 220–52; Landsberg, *Prosthetic Memory*, 100–106; Matthew Frye Jacobson, *Roots Too*, 17, 41–48, 55; Rodgers, *Age of Fracture*, 116–18; Rymsza-Pawlowska, *History Comes Alive*, 30–38.

2. Norrell, *Alex Haley*, 166–67.

3. Joseph Egelhof, "Genealogy: What 'Roots' Has Wrought," *Chicago Tribune*, February 25, 1977, 1; "Archives Offers Genealogy Data," *New York Times*, February 18, 1979, 33.

4. Gelman et al., "Everybody's Search for Roots," 26.

5. Jacobsen, "The World Turned Upside Down."

6. Afro-American Historical and Genealogical Society, "History of AAHGS" (excerpted from Paul E. Sluby Sr.'s "Fifth Anniversary Booklet" of 1982).

7. The documentary *After Stonewall* illustrates the significance of the second meeting, or gathering, for all kinds of organizational histories. Organized commemoration of the Stonewall riots of June 1969 in New York City began with the June 1970 anniversary march there. Featuring some of the earliest sustained groups that were dedicated to gay rights and liberation, the march launched the tradition of the annual June "pride" parade in U.S. cities. Scagliotti, Baus, and Hunt, *After Stonewall*.

8. Jean Sampson Scott to Alex Haley, November 18, 1978, folder 3, box 1, Haley Papers 1888.

9. Chicago Public Library, "Patricia Liddell Researchers Archives."

10. William K. Stevens, "A Detroit Woman's Black Roots Lead to a Welcome in the D. A. R.," *New York Times*, December 28, 1977, 1.

11. My search for "Arthur Kurzweil" in ProQuest's holdings of *New York Jewish Week* yielded seventy-four results, the earliest from May 1, 1977.

12. Sweeney, "Ancestors, Avotaynu, Roots," 182 (note 123); Fisher, "A Place in History," 67, 74 (note 18); Arthur Kurzweil, "Two New 'How To' Books for the Jewish Researcher," *Toledot* 1 (Spring 1978): 5.

13. "Jewish Genealogical Societies Worldwide," *Avotaynu* 8 (Spring 1992): 51–52.

14. Sallyann Amdur Sack, "Jewish Genealogy: The Past 25 Years," *Avotaynu* 20 (Summer 2004): 6.

15. Stanley H. Balducci to Haley, December 16, 1982, folder 11, box 1, Haley Papers 1888.

16. Sinko and Scott N. Peters, "A Survey of Genealogists at the Newberry Library," 102.

17. Gelman et al., "Everybody's Search for Roots," 26.

18. Advertisement, *NEHGR* 149 (July 1995): after 334.

19. "Genealogical Miscellany," *GH* 33 (March–April 1979): 61; "Genealogical Miscellany," *GH* 38 (November–December 1984): 78–79; Polish Genealogical Society of America, "About PGSA," https://pgsa.org/about-pgsa.

20. Draznin, *The Family Historian's Handbook*, 103–13, 130–36; "Book Reviews," *NGSQ* 73 (September 1985): 215–16.

21. Larry S. Watson, "Arrow Tips: American Indian Genealogy and the Oral Tradition," *JAIFR* 2 (March 1981): 4.

22. Joseph Egelhof, "Genealogy: What 'Roots' Has Wrought," *Chicago Tribune*, February 25, 1977, 1.

23. Watson's full name and dates in "Larry Sullivan Watson."

24. Larry S. Watson, "Arrow Tips: Building an Indian Research Collection, Part I," *JAIFR* 11 (January 1990): 2.

25. Lynn C. McMillion, "American Indian Genealogical Research," *JAAHGS* 5 (Summer 1984): 87–89 (bibliography). The five tribes in question are the Cherokee, Chickasaw, Choctaw, Creek, and Seminole. Larry S. Watson, "Genealogical Research: Indian Territory," *JAIFR* 1 (February 1980): 3–5.

26. Carpenter, *How to Research American Indian Blood Lines*; "Talking Leaves," *JAIFR* 9 (July 1988): 55–56.

27. Flyer for the 38th Annual Texas Hispanic Genealogical and Historical Conference, September 2017, posted at the Newberry Library (Chicago). At its inception in 1977, the Austin group called itself the Sociedad Genealógica de Austin. Tejano Genealogical Society of Austin, "About TGSA," https://www.tgsaustin.org/about.

28. The term "Hispanic" is truer than "Latino" or Latinx to the period under study in this chapter (post-1945 history up to the 1990s). But starting in the late 1960s, Chicano activists who fostered pride in Indian and mestizo ancestry strongly criticized the term "Hispanic" as Spanish-centric and therefore white supremacist. Oboler, "Hispanics? That's What They Call Us," and George Hartley, "I Am Joaquín."

29. Margaret B. Harvey, "California in the Revolution," *AMM* 21 (October 1902): 283.

30. Chávez, *Origins of New Mexico Families* (1954), xvii; Milton Rubincam, "Genealogy for All People," *NGSQ* 66 (December 1978), 247. Anglos in New Mexico, including Ralph Emerson Twitchell, who had moved there from Iowa, had been publishing historical and genealogical content since the early 1910s in their magazine *Old Santa Fe.* However, Chávez condemned Twitchell's work as often "misleading." *Origins of New Mexico Families* (1954), 338.

31. Susan Lee Johnson, "Writing Kit Carson in the Cold War"; Pablo Mitchell, *Coyote Nation,* 101–21.

32. Chávez, *Origins of New Mexico Families* (1954), xiv; Chávez, *Origins of New Mexico Families* (1992), xviii.

33. Ryskamp, *Tracing Your Hispanic Heritage* (1984). The same preoccupation with antecedents in Spain is evident in an earlier work by a genealogist employed by the LDS Church. He addressed all Spanish-speaking Latin Americans, beyond Latinx people in the U.S. Platt, *Genealogical Historical Guide to Latin America* (1978).

34. Roland C. Barksdale-Hall, review of Nora Louis Hicks, *Slave Girl Reba and Her Descendants in America* (Jericho, N.Y.: Exposition Press, 1974), in "Book Reviews," *JAAHGS* 9 (Winter 1988): 180–81.

35. Elizabeth Clark-Lewis, "Oral History: Its Utilization in the Genealogical Research Process," *NGSQ* 67 (March 1979): 27–31.

36. "Officers and Board Members," *JAAHGS* 3 (Spring 1982): front matter; Clark-Lewis, *Living In, Living Out.*

37. His 2016 obituary lists his graduate institutions and degrees. "Larry Sullivan Watson." Garroutte, *Real Indians,* 118–20, also argues for the value of formal genealogy activity, stressing the gathering of documents, in modern Indian life.

38. "Arrow Tips: Finding Obscure Government Documents Pertaining to Indian Records," *JAIFR* 1 (January 1981): 4.

39. Carpenter, *How to Research American Indian Blood Lines.*

40. Hareven, "The Search for Generational Memory," 139.

41. John Brooks, "The Epic of the Black Man as Told, at Last, by a Black Man," *Chicago Tribune,* September 26, 1976, F1 (reprinted from *The New Yorker*); George McCracken, "Recent Books and Reprints," *TAG* 53 (April 1977): 122–23.

42. Mel Watkins, "A Talk with Alex Haley," *New York Times,* September 26, 1976.

43. Willie Lee Rose, "An American Family."

44. Ottaway, "Tangled Roots."

45. Toby Waller was renamed Toby Reynolds in the televised version of *Roots.*

46. Gary B. Mills and Elizabeth Shown Mills, "'Roots' and the New 'Faction,'" 9.

47. Wright, "Uprooting Kunta Kinte"; Delmont, *Making "Roots,"* 51. Other discussions of challenges to *Roots* include Nobile, "Uncovering Roots"; Weil, *Family Trees*, 196–97; Norrell, *Alex Haley*, 175–77, 183–98; Delmont, *Making "Roots,"* 181–98.

48. Wolfgang Saxon, "Harold Courlander, 82, Author and Expert on World Folklore," *New York Times*, March 19, 1996, D22. Discussions of Margaret Walker include Parry, "The Politics of Plagiarism"; Delmont, *Making "Roots,"* 74, 190.

49. Haley, "Blacks, Oral History, and Genealogy" (1973), 20.

50. Nancy L. Arnez, "From His Story to Our Story: A Review of 'Roots,'" *Journal of Negro Education* 46 (Summer 1977): 367–72, in Sweeney, "Ancestors, Avotaynu, Roots," 160.

51. AAHGS founders spoke to him as an old friend in 1978: "Many of your friends, Paul Sluby, Debra Newman, Milton Rubincam and I . . . are on the executive board" of the AAHGS. Jean Sampson Scott to Haley, November 18, 1978, folder 3, box 1, Haley Papers 1888.

52. Gary B. Nash, Crabtree, and Dunn, *History on Trial*.

53. John J. O'Connor, "TV: The Return of 'Palmerstown,'" *New York Times*, March 17, 1981.

54. "Book Reviews," *JAAHGS* 6 (Summer 1985): 86–87; Saundra Oliver Brown, "James Dent Walker," *PLRNJ* 1 (Fall–Winter 1993): 32–33, copy in box 5, PLR.

55. Haley titled an acclaimed 1971 lecture "A Saga of Black History"; the book *Roots* had as its subtitle *The Saga of an American Family*. Item 3,272, folder 2, box 45, Haley Papers 1888. Named for a deceased member, Patricia Liddell Researchers (PLR) was and is the records of the AAHGS chapter in Chicago. This collection includes a vast, ongoing collection of funeral programs. These are useful source materials for genealogists because of the birthdates, death dates, and other demographic information they contain. Chicago Public Library, "Patricia Liddell Researchers Archives."

56. Weil, *Family Trees*, 6–7, 181; Hogan, *Roots Quest*, 22.

57. Matthew Frye Jacobson, *Roots Too*; Formisano, *Boston Against Busing*; Corbould, "Roots, the Legacy of Slavery, and Civil Rights Backlash."

58. The April 1970 issue of the NEHGS's *Register* was its "Pilgrim Anniversary" issue, devoted to 1620s content. *NEHGR* 124 (April 1970).

59. Hijiya, "Roots," 550; "Book Ends," *New York Times*, July 11, 1976; advertisement for *Adams Chronicles*, *DARM* 110 (January 1976): 161. *Roots*' publisher, Doubleday, did not advertise *Roots* in this same publication, the *Daughters of the American Revolution Magazine*, in 1976–77.

60. Jeannette Osborn Baylies, "Report of the President General," *DARM* 114 (August–September 1980): 922–23; "National Board of Management," *DARM* 118 (December 1984): 738.

61. Jeannette Osborn Baylies, "From the Office of the President General," *DARM* 111 (October 1977): 807. Wendt, *The Daughters of the American Revolution*, 162–204, also discusses the DAR after 1945.

62. Karen E. Sutton was a nurse in Maryland. "African American Revolutionary War Patriot Qualifies Descendant for Membership," *PLRNJ* 1 (Fall–Winter 1993): 39–40, copy in box 5, PLR; Morgan, *Women and Patriotism in Jim Crow America*, 236 (note 32); Wendt, *The Daughters of the American Revolution*, 194–98. I have not seen evidence of Latina Daughters,

but Simon Wendt has documented Native American Daughters in the 1920s in *The Daughters of the American Revolution*, 94–95, 109.

63. Sharfstein, *The Invisible Line*, and Gaines, *Uplifting the Race*, make this point especially powerfully.

64. Streets, *Slave Genealogy*.

65. "Brief Biography of Adlean Harris," folder "Speakers' Biographical Materials," box 6, PLR.

66. William K. Stevens, "A Detroit Woman's Black Roots Lead to a Welcome in the D. A. R." *New York Times*, December 28, 1977, 1; Bardaglio, "Shameful Matches," 123.

67. Haley, "My Search for Roots," 6.

68. Bonnie G. Smith, *The Gender of History*; Fitzpatrick, *History's Memory*; Des Jardins, *Women and the Historical Enterprise in America*; Susan Lee Johnson, "Writing Kit Carson in the Cold War," 294–96.

69. J. Carlyle Parker, "Discrimination Against Genealogists," *Wilson Library Bulletin* 47 (November 1972): 254; Sweeney, "Ancestors, Avotaynu, Roots," 134.

70. Hijiya, "Roots," 549, 552; Lasch, *Culture of Narcissism*; Kranson, *Ambivalent Embrace*.

71. Howe, "Tevye on Broadway"; Alisa Solomon, *Wonder of Wonders*, 119, 229.

72. "To Our Readers," *Toledot* 1 (Fall 1977): 2.

73. Howe, "The Limits of Ethnicity," 18.

74. "To Our Readers," *Toledot* 1 (Fall 1977): 3.

75. Strong, "To Forget Their Tongue, Their Name, and Their Whole Relation."

76. Cramer, *Cash, Color, and Colonialism*, 7–8.

77. Information from library catalog webpage for the Brotherton Indian Collection, NEHGS, at http://library.nehgs.org/record=b1057565~So.

78. Larry S. Watson, "Arrow Tips: Further Thoughts on Discovering Your American Indian Ancestors," *JAIFR* 7 (October 1986): 5; Watson, "Arrow Tips: What Cherokee Records Should You Search?" *JAIFR* 9 (October 1988): 6–8. Generally, allotment rolls were drawn up for tribes west of the Appalachians, as tribes closer to the Atlantic had dealt with colonial governments rather than with the post-1789 U.S. government.

79. TallBear, *Native American DNA*, 47; Gover, *Tribal Constitutionalism*, 108–56.

80. George Morrison Bell Sr., *Genealogy of "Old and New Cherokee Families,"* 63.

81. See especially Sturm, *Blood Politics*, 168–200.

82. Gilmore, *Gender and Jim Crow*, xvi, xxii, 313. See also Blouin and William G. Rosenberg, *Archives, Documentation, and Institutions of Social Memory*; Steedman, *Dust*, 6 (drawing on Jacques Derrida's *Archive Fever*).

83. Noel C. Stevenson, *Genealogical Evidence* (1979).

84. Arthur Adams, "Introduction," 1. This statement did not appear in the revised edition of the volume from 1980. Shah, *Stranger Intimacy*, 6–8, discusses the broader point about transience.

85. Elizabeth Shown Mills, "Spanish Records: Locating Anglo and Latin Ancestry in the Colonial Southeast," *NGSQ* 73 (December 1985): 243–61; Auger, "Québec"; Malchelosse, "Quebec"; Kathryn Burns, "Notaries, Truth, and Consequences."

86. Gilbert Harry Doane, "The Editor's Notes," *NEHGR* 119 (July 1965): 230.

87. Of those patrons who reported an interest in attending genealogy classes or workshops, 60.4 percent were interested in classes on particular kinds of documents, and 53.6

percent of the sample evinced interest in geographical areas, contrasted with only 26 percent who reported an interest in programs on particular groups. Sinko and Scott N. Peters, "A Survey of Genealogists at the Newberry Library," 103.

88. "Statement of Ownership, Management, and Circulation," *GH* 31 (November–December 1977): 666; *NEHGR* 130 (April 1976): inside front cover. Both were dwarfed by the partial example of the DAR's magazine, which featured history and Americana much more than genealogy per se. The members, numbering over two hundred thousand by 1976, were asked to subscribe. "President General's Message," *DARM* 110 (May 1976): 507.

89. Phyllis Pastore Preece, "Guide to Genealogical Research in Italy," *GH* 27 (January 1973): 1, 4–7; Larry O. Jensen, "Genealogical Research in Poland," *GH* 28 (January 1974): 1.

90. An exception is Marjory Allen Perez (Wayne County, N.Y.), "Descendants of Aaron and Betsey Brister/Bristol," *JAAHGS* 7 (Summer 1986): 60–62.

91. An exception among white-run journals is the *National Genealogical Society Quarterly*, which published myriad source studies between the 1960s and 1980s. William H. Dumont, "Burke County, Georgia," *NGSQ* 54 (March 1966): 3; Kenneth Scott, "Runaways, Excerpts from the Pennsylvania Gazette, 1775-1783," *NGSQ* 64 (December 1976): 243–60.

92. Agnes Kane Callum, then president of the Baltimore chapter of the AAHGS, had "traced her family tree back to 1798." Circular in folder titled "2nd workshop & lecture, 2/13/1991," box 1, PLR.

93. "James Dent Walker," *PLRNJ* 1 (Fall–Winter 1993): 32–35, copy in box 5, PLR.

94. Alex Haley to Paul Reynolds, June 16, 1967, photocopy (3148), folder 1, box 45, Haley Papers 1888; Haley, *Roots*, 715–16; Marty Bell, "Debts, Stubborn Faith Drive Alex Haley to Write 'Roots.'"

95. Alice Suggs, "Interracial Marriage: Barrier or Challenge to a Family Search," *JAAHGS* 7 (Summer 1986): 82–87.

96. Gwendolyn Hackley Austin, "The African Lady," *JAAHGS* 8 (Summer 1987): 69.

97. See especially Linda Williams, *Playing the Race Card*, on this point.

98. An American's feat of tracing ancestors back to Africa seemed unattainable to many in 1977, but it has moved closer to possibility since then. Multiple historians in modern times have managed to trace the American posterity of Africans. Johnston, *From Slave Ship to Harvard*; Lawrence P. Jackson, *My Father's Name*; Lindsay, *Atlantic Crossings* (on African descendants of American slaves).

99. On *Roots'* reverberations overseas, see Sharpe, *Family Matters*, 178–79; Stollery, "The Same, But a Step Removed"; Norvella P. Carter, Chalken, and Zungu, "Re-Rooting Roots"; and Yang, "One Man's Quest."

100. Helen Taylor, "The Griot from Tennessee," 48; Moore, "Routes," 6; U.S. Department of Commerce, Bureau of the Census, *Statistical Abstract of the United States, 1977*, xiii.

101. Matthew Frye Jacobson, *Roots Too*, 44; Zaretsky, *No Direction Home*, 155–57; Little, "Genealogy as Theatre of Self-Identity," 185–92.

102. Haley, "What Roots Means to Me" (May 1977), 159.

103. Bidlack, "Genealogy Today," 7.

104. Rymsza-Pawlowska, *History Comes Alive*, 31.

105. Alex Haley to Paul Reynolds, October 15, 1964, photocopy (2712–2714); campaign materials for George Haley (1964), photocopy (2718); folder 14, box 44, Alex Haley Papers 1888; Campbell, "George Haley."

106. Marable, *Malcolm X*, 220; Alex Haley to Paul Reynolds, September 3, 1963, photocopy (2506), folder 13, box 44, Alex Haley Papers 1888.

107. Alex Haley to Charles W. Ferguson, August 16, 1964, photocopy (2671), folder 14, box 44, Haley Papers 1888; Marable, *Malcolm X*, 9, 259, 331.

108. Horwitz, *Confederates in the Attic*; Webb, *Massive Resistance*; McRae, *Mothers of Massive Resistance*.

109. Peter Applebome, "Enduring Symbols of the Confederacy Divide the South Anew," *New York Times*, January 27, 1993, A16.

110 Janney, *Remembering the Civil War*, 303–4.

111. Helen Taylor, "The Griot from Tennessee," 44.

112. Dulong, "Genealogical Groups in a Changing Organizational Environment," 316.

113. Hudson, "The Effect of 'Roots' and the Bicentennial on Genealogical Interest"; Zaretsky, *No Direction Home*, 155–57; Tammy S. Gordon, *The Spirit of 1976*.

114. Berenbaum, "The Nativization of the Holocaust," 448; Novick, *The Holocaust in American Life*, 209–20.

115. Seltzer, "Introduction: The Ironies of American Jewish History"; Gilman, "There Ain't No There There"; Krah, "Further Forward Through the Past."

116. David Einsiedler, "My Mistress: Genealogy"; "A Branch of the Family Menorah"; *Avotaynu* 3 (Fall 1987): 30–31. The journal sometimes spelled his surname "Einseidler."

117. YIVO Institute for Jewish Research, "YIVO Archives & Library Collections."

118. Zachary Baker and Dina Abramowicz, interviews in Arthur Kurzweil, "Former YIVO Head Librarian Lauds Genealogy," *Avotaynu* 12 (Summer 1996): 65.

119. Daniel J. Cohen, "The Gathering of Jewish Records to Israel"; "Abstracts of Papers Given," *JAAHGS* 5 (Summer 1984): 85 (Lynn C. McMillion bibliography on "Native American Genealogical Research").

120. "World Conference on Records," *TAG* 46 (January 1970): 29. The church continued after 1980 to hold big conferences on genealogy, including annual RootsTech conferences (2014 onward) that attracted 25,000 participants in 2017 alone. Creet, *The Genealogical Sublime*, 68.

121. Douglas J. Davies, *An Introduction to Mormonism*, 212; Mauss, *All Abraham's Children*, 231–41; Reeve, *Religion of a Different Color*, 259–61; Britsch, "The Church in Asia," 77; Britsch, "The Church in Oceana," 1,024–25; and Chadwick and Garrow, "Native Americans," 985.

122. Mauss, *All Abraham's Children*, 218–20, 276; Arrington and Bitton, *The Mormon Experience*, 322–24; Claudia L. Bushman, *Contemporary Mormonism*, 91–109.

123. Haley, "Family: A Humanizing Force"; Haws, *The Mormon Image in the American Mind*, 67.

124. Glenda T. Owen of Bountiful, Utah, in Zelda Merritt, "Experiences and Impressions of Genealogical Missionaries, 1981–1986" (typescript, 1986), copy at CHL.

125. Ozick, "Who Owns Anne Frank?"

126. Allen, Embry, and Mehr, *Hearts Turned to the Fathers*, 318–19.

127. Gary Mokotoff, "Mormons Baptize Holocaust Victims," *Avotaynu* 10 (Spring 1994): 11.

128. Petrovsky-Shtern, *Jews in the Russian Army*, 1–27, 90–104; Litvak, *Conscription and the Search for Modern Russian Jewry*, 140–99. Chuck Steinwedel shared these references.

129. Sallyann Amdur Sack, "As I See It," *Avotaynu* 7 (Summer 1991): 2. She published or coauthored multiple advice books for Americans about researching family history in Israel:

Sack, *A Guide to Jewish Genealogical Research in Israel* (1987); Sack and the Israel Genealogical Society, *A Guide to Jewish Genealogical Research in Israel* (1995).

130. Sallyann Amdur Sack, "Seminar Will Return to Jerusalem in May 1994," *Avotaynu* 9 (Summer 1993): 14.

131. Advertisement, *Avotaynu* 10 (Spring 1994): 36; Mokotoff, "Mormons Baptize Holocaust Victims," *Avotaynu* 10 (Spring 1994): 11.

132. Beulah-Rose Gross, "A Jewish Genealogist's Encounter with the IGI," *Avotaynu* 12 (Winter 1996): 9–10.

133. Advertisement, *Avotaynu* 18 (Spring 2002): 20; Sack and Mokotoff, *Avotaynu Guide to Jewish Genealogy*, 61–67.

134. Mark Oppenheimer, "A Twist on Posthumous Baptisms Leaves Jews Miffed at Mormon Rite," *New York Times*, March 3, 2012; Church of Jesus Christ of Latter-day Saints, the First Presidency, "Names Submitted for Temple Ordinances," https://www.churchofjesuschrist.org/church/news/names-submitted-for-temple-ordinances?lang=eng; Weaver, "Church Asks Members to Understand Policies," https://www.churchofjesuschrist.org/church/news/church-asks-members-to-understand-policies?lang=eng. Claudia L. Bushman and Ardis E. Parshall, writing separately, suggest that the church began discouraging the baptism of nonrelatives slightly earlier, in the 2000s: Claudia L. Bushman, *Contemporary Mormonism*, 86–87; Parshall, "Genealogy and Family History," 250.

Chapter Six

1. Haley, "What Roots Means to Me" (May 1977), 159.
2. Moskowitz, *In Therapy We Trust.*
3. Hilton, *Who Do You Think You Are?* (1976), 8–9.
4. Wolfe, "The 'Me' Decade and the Third Great Awakening."
5. Cross, *An All-Consuming Century*, 170–91. A contemporary jeremiad on the subject was Lasch, *Culture of Narcissism*. I thank Josh Salzmann and Theo Anderson for inspiring these paragraphs.
6. Friedan, *The Feminine Mystique*, 258–80 (the chapter titled "The Forfeited Self").
7. Terry Greene, "The Anguish of Alex Haley's Widow," *Phoenix New Times* 23 (November 11–17, 1992): 21, folder 20, box 1, Romaine Collection (George counted ten "mortgaged properties").
8. Fred Brown, "Costly Success," *Knoxville* (Tenn.) *News-Sentinel*, March 1, 1992; Terry Greene, "The Anguish of Alex Haley's Widow"; both clippings in folder 20, box 1, Romaine Collection; "Alex Haley Literary Work is Auctioned for $100,000," *New York Times*, October 2, 1992, A12.
9. Jennifer Schuessler, "Malcolm X Writings Are Sold, Including Rumored Lost Portions," *New York Times*, July 27, 2018, A1.
10. The show aired on Sundays at 1 p.m. on KDYL, starting on January 24, 1954. "Pres. Eisenhower on Genealogy TV Show," *Deseret News: Church News*, January 30, 1954, 6, scrapbook p. 789; Martha Roach, typescript, "What's Your Name? Selections from the Television Program on Ancestral Research," n.d. [1980s or 1990s], pp. 791–95; folder 4, box 2, Bennett Scrapbooks.

11. This phrase is inspired by Mokotoff and Sack with Sharon, *Where Once We Walked*.

12. H. G. Somerby (London) to Henry Bond, November 28, 1851; Somerby to Bond, February 19, 1852; Somerby to Bond, January 26, 1855; all in folder 50, sub-group 3, box 10; Abbott Lawrence to Bond, February 23, 1855, folder 36, sub-group 3, box 9; Bond Papers; Weil, *Family Trees*, 75–76. Somerby's full name and occupation in G. Andrews Moriarty, "Pre-American Ancestries: The Lawrence Family," *TAG* 10 (October 1933): 79.

13. Morgan, *Women and Patriotism in Jim Crow America*, 11; Jane Farwell Smith, "President General's Message," *DARM* 110 (May 1976): 507.

14. Doane, *Searching for Your Ancestors*, 158.

15. Stiles, *A Hand-Book of Practical Suggestions*, 3.

16. A punctilious insurance agent named George Ernest Bowman (1860–1941) launched the GSMD in Boston in 1897, three years after New Yorkers developed a local Mayflower descendants' society in 1894. At a time when others infused the pursuit of Mayflower descent with passion, Bowman and colleagues adhered to unsentimental emphasis on primary documents. In its early decades, the SMD devoted its periodical to reprinting original records. Bowman, "The Brewster Book," *Mayflower Descendant* 1 (January 1899): 1–8; "The Mayflower Descendant in 1900," *Mayflower Descendant* 1 (October 1899): 256; Donald Jacobus, "Book Reviews," *New Haven Genealogical Magazine* 8 (April 1932): 2,064–67; "Memoirs," *NEHGR* 96 (January 1942): 78–79; Mrs. Robert M. Sherman and Mrs. Lester A. Hall, "Notes on the General Society of Mayflower Descendants 1897–1970," *NEHGR* 124 (April 1970): 139–42. Consider the title of the DAR's 1958 manual for applicants: *Is That Lineage Right?* Historical accuracy became a positive good by then.

17. Advertisement, *AMM* 1 (August 1892): following 191.

18. Edward A. Claypool, printed circular, n.d., inserted in front of December 17, 1906 entry, Harriet Taylor diary (1900–1907), box 1, Harriet Taylor Papers, NLA 11/15/01.

19. M. S. H., "Mrs. Henry Lewis Pope," *AMM* 2 (April 1893): 401–3; Sarah Lloyd Moore Ewing Pope, "Ancestry of Mrs. S. L. M. E. Pope," *AMM* 2 (April 1893): 404–5; "Mrs. Mary McKinlay Nash," *AMM* 2 (April 1893): 461–70.

20. A partial exception from earlier times, that used radiating circles instead of lines, comes from Lemuel Shattuck's circular radial chart (1841) that placed the descendant in the center. Shattuck, *A Complete System of Family Registration*, unpaginated (family chart, first form). Entrepreneurs in addition to Browning also preferred ascendant genealogies. Virkus, *The Abridged Compendium of American Genealogy: First Families of America*, vol. 2, 1926, 9, called the living descendant "the subject." Allaben claimed inaccurately in 1904 to have invented them in *Concerning Genealogies*, 46, 50, but see Stiles, *Hand-Book of Practical Suggestions* (1899), 35. In later times, ascendant lineages changed in meaning. Professionals came to prize them for promoting accuracy: "The only way to trace a line is to begin with the present generation and go back year by year." Jean Stephenson, "Genealogical Source Material," *DARM* 91 (December 1957): 1,337; James M. Rose and Eichholz, *Black Genesis*, 3.

21. Allaben, *Concerning Genealogies*, 13 (on clients); Washburn and Allaben, *How to Trace and Record Your Own Ancestry*, 24; Pass, "Strange Whims of Crest Fiends," 14–21; biographical information on Washburn from Washburn, *Washburn Family Foundations*, 75–76.

22. Washburn and Allaben, *How to Trace and Record Your Own Ancestry*, 56–59.

23. "Let's Do It Now!" *Magazine of American Genealogy* 1, no. 10 (May 1930): 37.

24. Virkus, *The Handbook of American Genealogy*, vol. 1 (1932), 351 (list of "heraldic artists"), 353–71.

25. *Encyclopaedia Britannica*, "John Harvard."

26. Hassam to Waters, May 12, 1884, folder 4, box 3, Waters Papers.

27. Hassam to Waters, April 18, 1885, folder 4, box 3, Waters Papers.

28. Hassam to Waters, August 13, 1885; Hassam to Waters, November 6, 1885; folder 4, box 3, Waters Papers.

29. Waters to Hassam, December 1885, folder 13, box 1, Hassam Papers.

30. Samuel A. Eliot to Waters, July 6, 1885, folder 4, box 2, Waters Papers.

31. John Farmer (1789–1838) of Concord, New Hampshire, authored the first-ever American genealogy publication about more than one family, in 1829. He was frequently bedridden due to digestive ailments and the tuberculosis that eventually took his life and, as a result, he conducted much of his research by mail. Friends went to historical societies and town archives and borrowed library books on his behalf. Nearly five hundred letters survive. The finding aid to his papers at the New Hampshire Historical Society is available at https://www.nhhistory.org/finding_aids/finding_aids/Farmer_John_Papers.pdf; Farmer, *A Genealogical Register of the First Settlers of New-England*; Papers of Cyrus Parker Bradley, NHHS; Weil, "John Farmer and the Making of American Genealogy"; Morgan, "Lineage and Capital."

32. "Genealogical Trust," *Magazine of American Genealogy* 1, no. 2 (September 1929): 7.

33. Allaben and Washburn, *How to Trace and Record Your Own Ancestry*, 58.

34. Jacobus, *Genealogy as Pastime and Profession* (2nd ed., 1968), 5.

35. Doane, *Searching for Your Ancestors*, 201–4.

36. Gelber, *Hobbies*, 42.

37. Doane, *Searching for Your Ancestors*, 75.

38. "Annual Reports," *NEHGR* 88 (April 1934): 166. Not until 1964 did the NEHGS move to its current location in Boston's Back Bay. On the 1930s, see also Corinne Miller Simons, "Genealogical Interest in Cincinnati," *TAG* 11 (October 1934): 65–69.

39. Hering, "We Are All Makers of History,'" 10, 295; Tucker, *City of Remembering*, 47, 109–11, 118–20; Margo Burns and Rosenthal, "Examination of the Records of the Salem Witch Trials."

40. McCoy, "The Struggle to Establish a National Archives in the United States"; "A Message to the President General," *DARM* 57 (February 1923): 70.

41. Tolley-Stokes, "Genealogy," 521; Weil, *Family Trees*, 167–69; Macy, "Recognizing Scholarly Genealogy," 10–11.

42. Sheppard, "A Bicentennial Look," 7–8; Weil, *Family Trees*, 204; Macy, "Recognizing Scholarly Genealogy," 10; Pass, "The Strange Whims of Crest Fiends." Doane, *Searching for Your Ancestors*, vii, described a similar fly-by-night operation in the 1930s (not by name) that worked through unsolicited mailings.

43. Sheppard, "A Bicentennial Look," 8.

44. Advertisement for sixth annual Institute in *NEHGR* 109 (April 1955): xix; Tolley-Stokes, "Genealogy," 521; Weil, *Family Trees*, 187–88. The institute resulted from cooperation between the National Archives and the ASG. Falley, *Irish and Scots-Irish Ancestral Research*, 1 (first volume of a two-volume work):v, ix.

45. Milton Rubincam, "A Program for Certifying Genealogists, Lineage Specialists, and Record Searchers," *NGSQ* 61 (March 1973): 11–15; Archibald F. Bennett, "Genealogical Sources in Salt Lake City," *TAG* 42 (April 1966): 94.

46. "Utah Genealogists Organize," *GH* 25 (March 1971): 41; Walter Lee Sheppard Jr., "Professional Ethics in Genealogical Research," *NGSQ* 67 (March 1979): 4–6.

47. Noel C. Stevenson, *Search and Research*; Noel C. Stevenson, *Genealogical Evidence*.

48. Adult-education courses dated from 1953. "Pres. Smith Speaks to Genealogy Graduates," n.d. [March 1957], otherwise unidentified clipping, book of remembrance (p. 528), folder 2, box 2, Bennett Scrapbooks. This article refers to church president Joseph Fielding Smith.

49. Novick, *That Noble Dream*, 52–54, 372–76; Townsend, *History's Babel*.

50. "At the Editor's Desk," *TAG* 12 (April 1936): 263; "More Subscribers Needed," *TAG* 34 (January 1958): 2 (typing); Jacobus to Winifred Lovering Holman, December 21, 1959, Dunsmoor folder 2, box 10, Holman Papers (no car); "Ida Wilmot Lines Jacobus," *TAG* 28 (July 1952): 193–96; John Insley Coddington, "Donald Lines Jacobus," *NEHGR* 125 (January 1971): 4.

51. Stiles, *A Hand-Book of Practical Suggestions*, 11–12.

52. Browning's own pedigree, which he traced through his mother, appears in Browning, *Americans of Royal Descent* (1883), 12–17.

53. William H. Whitmore, "Crossing the Water," *NEHGR* 14 (July 1860), 193–94.

54. "The Editor's Notes," *NEHGR* 119 (January 1965): 70.

55. "Towards an Index Expurgatorius," *TAG* 52 (July 1976): 182. Other examples of professionals' debunking previous findings include G. Andrews Moriarty, "Pre-American Ancestries: The Lawrence Family," *TAG* 10 (October 1933): 78–83 (on Somerby); Donald Lines Jacobus, "Royal Ancestry," *TAG* 9 (October 1932): 95 (on Browning); "Book Reviews," *New Haven Genealogical Magazine* 8 (April 1932): 2064–67 (on Virkus); Coddington, "Royal and Noble Genealogy," 299–303.

56. Shirley Langdon Wilcox, "The National Genealogical Society: A Look at Its First One Hundred Years," *NGSQ* 91 (December 2003): 255; Waters listed in National Genealogical Society, "National Genealogy Hall of Fame Members," https://www.ngsgenealogy .org/hall-of-fame-members.

57. Eugene A. Stratton, "The Validity of Genealogical Evidence," *NGSQ* 72 (December 1984): 276, 286n25. More recent heraldry commerce is addressed in Helen Hinchliff, "A Right to Bear Arms? An Examination of Commercial Offerings for 'Henderson of St. Laurence, Scotland," *NGSQ* 87 (March 1999): 6–15; Pass, "Strange Whims of Crest Fiends."

58. Sinko and Scott N. Peters, "A Survey of Genealogists at the Newberry Library," 102. Similar arguments for the predominance of freelance hobbyists among genealogists appear in Drake, "Findings from the Fullerton Genealogy Study" (2001), and Stratton, "The Validity of Genealogical Evidence," 273, 286 (note 25).

59. Walter M. Everton, *The Everton Knowles Book*.

60. George B. Everton Jr., "Helper Celebrates Twentieth Anniversary of Its Founding," *GH* 21 (March 1967): 1; "Mr. and Mrs. Everton Observe 50th Wedding Anniversary," *GH* 28 (November 1974): 585, 646.

61. "Evertons Microfilming in the British Isles," *GH* 21 (March 1967): 36; *NEHGR* 124 (April 1970): inside back cover; Weil, *Family Trees*, 184.

62. "New Edition," *GH* 19 (June 1965): 37; "Evertons Microfilming in the British Isles," *GH* 21 (March 1967): 36.

63. Jeanne Christensen, "Genealogy is Fast-Growing Business," *GH* 19 (December 1965): 297, 329; George B. Everton Jr., "Helper Celebrates Twentieth Anniversary of Its Founding," *GH* 21 (March 1967): 1; masthead, *GH* 31 (January–February 1977): 3; "Family Tree Climbing on the Move," *GH* 38 (July–August 1984): 186; "Publisher Dies," *GH* 53 (March–April 1999): 3. Alma Lee appeared as A. Lee Everton on the *Genealogical Helper*'s masthead into the 2000s. I no longer saw his name by 2005.

64. "'Helper' Rate Increases," *GH* 19 (September 1965): 73.

65. Advertising insert, *GH* 31 (May–June 1977): after 245; advertising insert, *GH* 31 (July–August 1977): after 418.

66. Hays, "History and Genealogy," 29.

67. *GH* 1 (October 1947): 1; *GH* 29 (January 1975): front cover.

68. J. Adolph Bishop, "An Introduction to Heraldry," *NGSQ* 54 (March 1966): 55–56 (at this time, Bishop served as the NGS's "herald"); Walter Lee Sheppard Jr., "A Bicentennial Look," 14–15. Peter Wilson Coldham's feature titled "Genealogical Gleanings in England" (named in tribute to Henry FitzGilbert Waters's nineteenth-century feature on the same subject) appeared regularly in the *NGSQ* in the late 1970s.

69. Stuart L. Cohen, review of Neil Rosenstein and Charles B. Bernstein, *From King David to Baron David: The Genealogical Connections between Baron Guy de Rothschild and Baroness Alix de Rothschild*, in *Avotaynu* 6 (Summer 1990): 23–24. This item was not representative of the journal's content.

70. "1981 Directory," *GH* 35 (July–August 1981): 17; Frederick J. Haskin, "Coats of Arms and How to Obtain Them," *UGHM* 7 (July 1916): 150–53; Susa Young Gates, "Language of Heraldry," *UGHM* 12 (January 1921): 38–41.

71. P. William Filby, "The Compiler," *GH* 41 (July–August 1987): 5.

72. Pass, "The Strange Whims of Crest Fiends," 20–23.

73. Susa Young Gates, *Surname and Racial History*, table of contents, discussed both categories of descent (biblical and aristocratic).

74. List of headings for genealogy lessons [1930–31], book of remembrance (p. 33), folder 1, box 1, Bennett Scrapbooks.

75. Typescript, "Promises in Patriarchal Blessings," n.d. [after 1927], book of remembrance (p. 957), folder 2, box 3, Bennett Scrapbooks; Madsen, *In Their Own Words*, 181; Allen, Embry, and Mehr, *Hearts Turned to the Fathers*, 53 (note 2).

76. See chapter 2.

77. Delmont, *Making "Roots,"* 69.

78. Farnham, "Who's Your Daddy?" (2012); Rodriguez, "How Genealogy Became Almost as Popular as Porn" (2014). Both journalists caution that statistics on genealogy's popularity are unreliable. Sweeney, "Ancestors, Avotaynu, Roots," 130, addresses the 1970s.

79. Rosenzweig and Thelen, *The Presence of the Past*, 12, 19, 219.

80. Andereck and Pence, *Computer Genealogy*; Eakle and Cerny, *The Source* (1984). Regarding Ancestry Inc., as publisher in the 1980s and 1990s, my search in library catalogs yielded more than eighty results among print books (some are multiple editions of the same work).

81. Groot, "Genealogy and Family History," 75; Creet, *The Genealogical Sublime*, 75.

82. Esther A. Anderson, "On Getting Involved with Computers: Some Guidelines for Genealogists," *NGSQ* 70 (September 1982): 203; Nichols, *Genealogy in the Computer Age*, 27–28.

83. Benton-Cohen, *Inventing the Immigration Problem*, 85.

84. Susan E. King, "The Future of JewishGen," *Avotaynu* 19 (Spring 2003): 3.

85. Hogan, *Roots Quest*, 37–38; Amy L. Harris, personal communication, July 1, 2017; Tanner, "About Microfilm and FamilySearch," http://rejoiceandbeexceedingglad.blogspot.com/2017/04/about-microfilm-and-familysearch.html; Creet, *The Genealogical Sublime*, 69.

86. Hogan, *Roots Quest*, 128.

87. Buzzy Jackson, *Shaking the Family Tree*, 181–82; Church of Jesus Christ of Latter-day Saints, "Tithing," https://www.lds.org/topics/tithing?lang=eng.

88. Groot, "Genealogy and Family History"; Abu El-Haj, *The Genealogical Science*, 144–59 (on the Jewish genealogist and entrepreneur Bennett Greenspan); Otterstrom, "Genealogy as Religious Ritual," 145; Ancestry.com advertisement, *NEHGR* 153 (January 1999): 128; Kenneally, *The Invisible History of the Human Race*, 207; Scodari, *Alternate Roots*, 23; Creet, *The Genealogical Sublime*, 71, 86–91.

89. See my Introduction. Julia Creet offers a history of Ancestry.com and its interrelated enterprises in *The Genealogical Sublime*, 71–94.

90. Amy Zipkin, "A Personal Sort of Time Travel: Ancestry Tourism," *New York Times*, July 29, 2016; Ancestry.com, "Subscribe," https://www.ancestry.com/cs/offers/subscribe?sub=1. Kenneally, *The Invisible History of the Human Race*, 127–30, notes an exception for public libraries, for which there was an abbreviated, gratis version of Ancestry.com.

91. Ancestry.com, "Company Facts," https://www.ancestry.com/corporate/about-ancestry/company-facts; Oguh, "Blackstone to Acquire Ancestry.com for $4.7 Billion."

92. Chakraborty and Bosman, "Measuring the Digital Divide in the United States" (pertaining to personal computers); Comito, *Tech for All*.

93. The NEHGS was in sound financial health, with an endowment of $16.5 million. The amount expended on the site's content that year was $450,000. "2003 Annual Report," *NEHGR* 158 (April 2004): 167, 172.

94. Groot, "On Genealogy," 114. On the commercialization of historical recordkeeping, see also Drakes, "Who Owns Your Archive?"

95. She found even more pronounced instances of monetized handling of information in the recent history of genealogy-driven DNA testing. Creet, "Data Mining the Deceased," and *The Genealogical Sublime*, 92–93, 131–32. Jerome de Groot has recently published a more benign portrayal of Ancestry.com, as advancing popular engagement with the past such as through its co-sponsorship of the Disney film *Coco* (2017): Groot, "Ancestry.com and the Evolving Nature of Historical Information Companies."

Citing stricter consumer-privacy legislation in the European Union and California, Ancestry has itself revised its terms and conditions and provided a formal "privacy statement" dated September 23, 2020 (with links to presumably more stringent privacy statements for customers in California and the European Union). The company admitted "[using] some Personal Information to market products and offers from us or our business partners. This includes advertising personalized to you based on your interests" but the company "does not share your Genetic Information with third-party marketers, insurance companies, or employers, and we will not use your Genetic Information for marketing or personalized advertising without getting your explicit consent." Ancestry.com, "Your Privacy," https://www.ancestry.com/cs/legal/privacystatement#personal-info-use.

96. Hering, "Review of Ancestry.com."

97. Watson, "Ordering the Family," 307; Hogan, *Roots Quest*, 134.

98. Quayle, "Address to the Commonwealth Club of California (Family Values)," May 22, 1992.

99. Klatch, *Women of the New Right*, 119–73; De Hart and Donald G. Mathews, *Sex, Gender, and the Politics of ERA*; Spruill, *Divided We Stand*; Rivers, *Radical Relations*, 173–206.

100. Social scientists have long disproven the falsehood that half of modern marriages end in divorce. The 35 percent figure results from longitudinal tracing of marriages that began in the same timeframe. Claire Cain Miller, "The Divorce Surge is Over, But the Myth Lives On," *New York Times*, December 2, 2014.

101. Stephanie Coontz, "Divorce, No-Fault Style," *New York Times*, June 17, 2010; Castells, *The Power of Identity*, 134–242.

102. In 2018, the American birth rate stood at 1,728 births per one thousand women. Liam Stack, "U. S. Birthrate Drops 4th Year in a Row, Possibly Echoing the Great Recession," *New York Times*, May 17, 2019, 17.

103. "Illegitimacy Noted," *New York Times*, April 30, 1962, 45; Ventura and Bachrach, "Nonmarital Childbearing in the United States, 1940-99," 1–2; Natalie Angier, "The Changing American Family," *New York Times*, November 25, 2013.

104. Rivers, *Radical Relations*, 53–79; Weston, *Families We Choose*, 195–213.

105. Batza, "Against Doctors' Orders"; Rivers, *Radical Relations*; Weston, *Families We Choose*, 165–93; Halloran, "How Vermont's 'Civil' War Fueled the Gay-Marriage Movement."

106. Chauncey, *Why Marriage?*, 87–136.

107. Sarah Franklin and McKinnon, *Relative Values*; Strathern, "Refusing Information"; Strathern, *Reproducing the Future*; Carsten, *After Kinship*.

108. Madilyn Coen Crane (Richardson, Tex.), "Numbering Your Genealogy—Special Cases: Surname Changes, Step Relationships, and Adoptions," *NGSQ* 83 (June 1995): 86–95.

109. Richard L. Bushman with Woodworth, Joseph Smith: *Rough Stone Rolling*, 443–44; Daynes, *More Wives Than One*, 4.

110. Utah has consistently been among the five states with the highest marriage rates since 1980. The state's fertility rate has long exceeded the national birth rate and the population replacement rate. U.S. Centers for Disease Control and Prevention, National Center for Health Statistics, "Marriage Rates by State, 1990, 1995, 1999–2018"; T. J. Mathews and Brady E. Hamilton, "Total Birth Rate by State and Race and Hispanic Origin: United States, 2017."

111. Petrey, *Tabernacles of Clay*, interprets the church's conservatism on matters of gender identity, sexual orientation, and marriage, as stemming from an underlying knowledge of these three matters' malleability.

112. Brooks, *The Book of Mormon Girl*, 161–80; Haws, *The Mormon Image in the American Mind*, 240–42; Peggy Fletcher Stack and Gehrke, "In Major Move, Mormon Leaders Call for Statewide LGBT Protections" (January 27, 2015); MormonNewsroom.org, "Church Leaders Counsel Members after Supreme Court Same-Sex Decision" (July 1, 2015), https://

www.lds.org/church/news/church-leaders-counsel-members-after-supreme-court-same
-sex-marriage-decision?lang=eng; Petrey, *Tabernacles of Clay.*

113. Cross, *An All-Consuming Century,* 170–91. More recent boycotts and threats to boy-
cott that express political and partisan divides have since challenged Cross's optimism. Julie
Cresswell and Tiffany Hsu, "Companies Cut Ties to the N.R.A., But Find There is No Neu-
tral Ground," *New York Times,* February 23, 2017.

114. Akenson, *Some Family,* 105, 118.

115. Robert Sink, comment in Organization of American Historians panel "Family History, Genealogy, and Historical Practice: New Directions in Teaching and Scholarship,"
New Orleans, April 7, 2017; Sink, *NYPL Librarians.*

116. Bishop, "In the Grand Scheme of Things," 399, 405–7.

117. Kenneally, *The Invisible History of the Human Race,* 116–17; "Family Tree," at Family-
Search.org, https://familysearch.org/treeview=tree&section=pedigree&person=L58F-
MQW; Akenson, *Some Family,* 7. I created a FamilySearch.org account, at no charge, to
access this webpage.

118. Amy L. Harris, review of Donald Harman Akenson, *Some Family: The Mormons and
How Humanity Keeps Track of Itself* (Montreal and Kingston, Can.: McGill-Queen's University Press, 2007), in *Journal of Interdisciplinary History* 39 (Winter 2009): 450.

119. Noel C. Stevenson, "Declarations of Pedigree and Family History and the Hearsay
Rule," *TAG* 21 (July 1944): 41–47; Donald Lines Jacobus, "On the Nature of Genealogical
Evidence," *NEHGR* 92 (July 1938): 213–20; Jacobus, "To Trace Your Ancestry," *TAG* 40
(October 1964): 240–45. Hogan, *Roots Quest,* 32, describes the BCG's more recent Genea-
logical Proof Standard (2015).

120. Burroughs, *Black Roots,* 351–74.

121. J. Kugelmass, "The Rites of the Tribe: American Jewish Tourism in Poland," in I.
Karp et al., *Museums and Communities: The Politics of Public Culture* (Washington: Smithsonian Institution Press, 1992), 415, in Stein, "Trauma and Origins," 302; Wendy Roth interview in Kenneally, *The Invisible History of the Human Race,* 25–26.

122. Scodari, *Alternate Roots,* 15. M. J. Rymsza-Pawlowska describes transformations before *Roots* in which 1970s television began favoring nostalgic and historical content, in contrast to the futuristic fare of the 1960s. An example is the *Little House on the Prairie* series,
launched in 1974. Rymsza-Pawlowska, *History Comes Alive,* 12–38.

123. Note the title of Wulf, "Not Your Grandmother's Genealogy." Demographic studies
of genealogy practitioners have found that they were not necessarily elderly. Pamela J.
Drake's 2001 sample showed only 20 percent who were older than sixty-five. Drake, "Findings from the Fullerton Genealogy Study."

124. Vincent Waller, "Pest of the West." My own children led me to this material.

125. Scholarship on modern roots travel includes Louie, *Chineseness Across Borders;* Timothy, "Genealogical Mobility"; Bruner, "Tourism in Ghana"; Hasty, "Rites of Passage,
Routes of Redemption," 56–58; Catherine Nash, "Genealogical Identities" and *Of Irish Descent;* Hogan, *Roots Quest,* 139–66.

126. J. Kugelmass, "The Rites of the Tribe: American Jewish Tourism in Poland," in I.
Karp et al., *Museums and Communities: The Politics of Public Culture* (Washington: Smithso-
nian Institution Press, 1992), 403, in Stein, "Trauma and Origins," 302; Fisher, "A Place in
History," 133–38.

127. Amy Hilliard's LinkedIn page lists her graduation date as 1978: https://www.linkedin.com/in/amy-hilliard-b2134/; statistic on the Class of 1978 (indicating completed degrees) from Cullen Schmitt, Harvard Business School, personal communication, June 28, 2016.

128. Anne Romaine, transcript of interview with Amy Hillard-Jones, n.d. [1993 or 1994], folder 22, box 2, Romaine Collection.

129. Romaine, transcript of interview with Hillard-Jones. See also Romaine, interview with Earl Jones, September 19, 1994; folder 22, box 2, Romaine Collection.

130. Description and visuals of "Tarzan: Lord of the Jungle" (1976–78) on Internet Movie Database: https://www.imdb.com/title/tt0149533/. The original character of Tarzan from 1912 was the orphaned son of a British lord and lady. Bederman, *Manliness and Civilization*, 217–40.

131. Ebron, "Tourists as Pilgrims." Alex Haley's kin on the 1994 trip included his son William (Bill), a businessman, who had first devised the McDonald's contest; his daughter Lydia Anne (Ann); his first wife, Nan (Branch) Haley; and his ninety-year-old cousin, Beatrice Neeley. Romaine, list of interviews, n.d. [1994], folder 23, box 2, Romaine Collection.

132. Ebron, "Tourists as Pilgrims," 925.

133. Hartman, *Lose Your Mother*, 57, 162–63 (statistic on 162); Hogan, *Roots Quest*, 156–66.

Chapter Seven

1. Mukherjee, *The Gene*, offers a useful overview of the history of genetics as a science.

2. Nikolas Rose, *The Politics of Life Itself*; TallBear, *Native American DNA*, 41–44; Abu El-Haj, *The Genealogical Science*, 229–41; Milanich, *Paternity*, 246–67.

3. Greely, "Genetic Genealogy"; Groot, "Genealogy and Family History," 80–83: Jennifer A. Hamilton, "The Case of the Genetic Ancestor"; Nelson, *The Social Life of DNA*; Hogan, *Roots Quest*, 83–100, 186 note 14; Weil, *Family Trees*, 209–10; Catherine Nash, *Genetic Geographies*, 141, 186 (note 6); Creet, *The Genealogical Sublime*, 119–43. Buzzy Jackson, *Shaking the Family Tree*, 123–40, delivers a vivid account of revelations from a woman's own DNA results.

4. Canonical studies of nonbiological relatedness include Carol B. Stack, *All Our Kin*, and Weston, *Families We Choose*, 106. Susan Pearson shared the Stack reference. Here I am also indebted to Benedict Anderson, *Imagined Communities*, for my language on imagined bonds. Sweet, "Defying Social Death," and Carsten, *After Kinship*, are among those who have repudiated the term "fictive" kin.

5. Zachary M. Baker, "Eastern European 'Jewish Geography': Some Problems and Suggestions," *Toledot* 2 (Winter 1978–79): 9.

6. Weil, *Family Trees*, 211–12; Abu El-Haj, *The Genealogical Science*, 28, 234–41; Catherine Nash, *Genetic Geographies*, 56–57.

7. Kenneally, *The Invisible History of the Human Race*, 19–21; Pinker, "Strangled by Roots"; Catherine Nash, *Genetic Geographies*, especially 31–68; Dawkins, with Wong, *Ancestor's Tale*; Strathern, "Nostalgia and the New Genetics."

8. Duster, *Backdoor to Eugenics*; Duster, "Welcome, Freshmen. DNA Swabs, Please"; Weil, *Family Trees*, 215; Hogan, *Roots Quest*, 83–100 ("The New Blood Quantum"). A dissenting view, in response to Duster, is Comfort, *The Science of Human Perfection*, 238–39, 244–46.

9. Genesis 5, 11:10–27; First Chronicles 1–8; Delaney, "Cutting the Ties That Bind"; Goody, *The Development of the Family and Marriage in Europe*; Karlsen, *Devil in the Shape of a Woman*, 77–116; Hogan, *Roots Quest*, 12.

10. D'Emilio and Freedman, *Intimate Matters*, 344–60; Zaretsky, *No Direction Home*; Weston, *Families We Choose*, 110–11.

11. Katya Maslakowski (Loyola University of Chicago), personal communication, spring 2014; Hammack et al., "Queer Intimacies."

12. Leonardo, "The Female World of Cards and Holidays," 442–43; Richards, "Knitting the Transatlantic Bond." Stein, "Trauma and Origins," and Hogan, *Roots Quest*, 11, have both applied di Leonardo's thesis to modern genealogy practices because of organized genealogy's preponderance of women.

13. Drake, "Findings from the Fullerton Genealogy Study"; Hogan, *Roots Quest*, 9, 11.

14. See especially Bonnie G. Smith, *The Gender of History*, and Des Jardins, *Women and the Historical Enterprise*.

15. Women's percentages dropped in the 1950s and 1960s. ASG fellows numbered, cumulatively, ninety-nine by 1973. Eighteen of these, or nearly 18 percent, were women, and of those eighteen, ten had been elected before 1953. Women's percentages have grown since 1973, though they have not reached parity. At least fifteen (30 percent) of the fifty ASG fellows of 2018 appeared to be women, judging from their names. Holman to Roland Mather Hooker, November 11, 1952, Wilcott folder 2, box 34, Holman Papers; Walter Lee Sheppard Jr., "The American Society of Genealogists," *NGSQ* 61 (June 1973): 104–6; American Society of Genealogists, "Current Fellows," https://fasg.org/fellows/current-fellows/. Female professionals' opuses have included Ferris, *Dawes-Gates Ancestral Lines*, and Falley, *Irish and Scots-Irish Ancestral Research*.

16. George McCracken, review of *Mayflower Families through Five Generations: Descendants of the Pilgrims*, ed. Lucy Mary Kellogg (Plymouth, Mass.: General Society of Mayflower Descendants, 1975), in *TAG* 52 (April 1976): 121; "Reviews," *TAG* 51 (January 1975): 60 (description of Detroit Society for Genealogical Research's festschrift publication in Kellogg's memory). Lee van Antwerp, "The Mayflower, Her Passengers and Their Descendants," *NEHGR* 124 (April 1970): 110–13, delivers an overview of the Five Generation Project.

17. Elizabeth Shown Mills and Gary B. Mills, "The Genealogist's Assessment of Alex Haley's Roots," *NGSQ* 73 (March 1984): 38.

18. Haley, "Blacks, Oral History, and Genealogy."

19. Haley, "A Search for Roots: A Black American's Story," *Reader's Digest* (May 1974), 74; Sweeney, "Ancestors, Avotaynu, Roots," 156.

20. Names of forebears in Haley, "My Furthest-Back Person—The African," *New York Times Magazine*, July 16, 1972; Haley, *Roots*, 725.

21. Sallyann Amdur Sack, "Jewish Genealogy: The Past 25 Years," *Avotaynu* 20 (Summer 2004): 5.

22. Ulrich, "Creating Lineages," 5–7; Ulrich, *Art of Homespun*, 111, 133, 135; Maureen A. Taylor, "Tall Oaks from Little Acorns Grow"; Nylander, "Preserving a Legacy"; Tucker, *City of Remembering*, 139–57; Little, "Genealogy as Theatre of Self-Identity," 104–15.

23. Shawn Michelle Smith, *American Archives*, 140–41; Bate, *The Women*.

24. Helene Enid Schwartz in "Bookshelf," *Toledot* 1 (Summer 1977): 7.

25. Moynihan, *The Negro Family*. The literature analyzing it includes Gutman, *The Black Family in Slavery and Freedom*; Deborah Gray White, *Too Heavy a Load*; and Geary, *Beyond Civil Rights*.

26. Robert Martin, interview of Murray, August 15 and 17, 1968, pp. 7–8, for the Civil Rights Documentation Project (Washington, D.C.), photocopied typescript, folder 8, box 1, Murray Papers.

27. Milton Rubincam, review of Mrs. J. M. Wood Jr., *Those Reeves Girls*, 2 vols. (Lubbock, Tex.: privately published, 1973), in "Book Reviews," *NSGQ* 64 (December 1976): 315; Mrs. J. M. Wood Jr., *Those Reeves Girls*, 2:158.

28. Ulrich, "Creating Lineages," 5–6; Maureen A. Taylor, "Tall Oaks from Little Acorns Grow," 76. Edward Jarvis, M.D., "The Supposed Decay of Families," *NEHGR* 38 (October 1884): 387, reflected that the early death or absence of males in any generation meant that a family name, and with that the family, was "extinguished."

29. Sunners, "Elizabeth Sunners: Uncovering a Secret Feminist History," http://www.youtube.com/watch?v=HmddommMhHQ. Netiva Caftori shared this reference.

30. Lorde, *Zami: A New Spelling of My Name*, 104; Wall, *Worrying the Line*, 21, 42–48; Weston, *Families We Choose*, 205–6.

31. Wall, *Worrying the Line*, 21.

32. Women in the professions, in government employment, and in the military endured particularly severe consequences. Canaday, *The Straight State*, 174–213; David K. Johnson, *The Lavender Scare*, 147–49, 155–57; Faderman, *Odd Girls and Twilight Lovers*, 139–58.

33. D'Emilio, *Sexual Politics, Sexual Communities*.

34. Weston, *Families We Choose*, 126–27; Howard, *Men Like That*, 282–83; Livingston, *Paris is Burning*.

35. Haraway, *Modest_Witness@Second_Millennium.FemaleMan_Meets_OncoMouse*, 265; Sarah Franklin, "Biologization Revisited," 316.

36. Sarah Franklin with Haraway, "Staying with the Manifesto."

37. Martin, *A Narrative of a Revolutionary Soldier*, 6.

38. Carp, *Family Matters*, 102–37.

39. Scholars of adoption have described the recent and ongoing treasuring of biological relatedness, although they have not invoked laypeople's investment in genetics per se. Modell, *Kinship with Strangers*, 4–5, 135–39, 225–38; Melosh, *Strangers and Kin*, 272, 287–91; Carp, *Family Matters*, 211, 228–29.

40. H. J. Sants, "Genealogical Bewilderment in Children with Substitute Parents," *Child Adoption* 47 (1965): 32–42, and Arthur D. Sorosky, Annette Baran, and Reuben Pannor, *The Adoption Triangle: Sealed or Opened Records—How They Affect Adoptees, Birth Parents, and Adoptive Parents* (1978; reprinted Garden City, N.Y.: Doubleday/Anchor, 1984), both cited in Melosh, *Strangers and Kin*, 312n2. See also Melosh, *Strangers and Kin*, 241–43; Modell, *Kinship with Strangers*, 137, 253n19. Little, "Genealogy as Theatre of Self-Identity," 146–47, and Deborah Cohen, *Family Secrets*, 124–55, 251–52, describe adult adoptees' protests in Britain.

41. Susan Carroll, "Genealogy for Adult Adopted Persons: Not an Insoluble Problem," *GH* 32 (November–December 1978): 8; Carp, *Family Matters*, 140–47; Pearson, "Age Ought to Be a Fact."

42. Meredith B. Colket Jr., "Some Trends in Genealogy," *NGSQ* 68 (March 1980): 4.

43. Cynthia A. Ortega, "Adoption Records: Buried Roots," *New York Times*, February 25, 1977, 16; Modell, *Kinship with Strangers*, 135–39.

44. Thomas H. Roderick, "Negro Genealogy," TAG 47 (April 1971): 88; Catherine Nash, *Genetic Geographies*, 179–81, on later periods.

45. "DAR Developments," *DARM* 118 (November 1984): 615.

46. Examples include Mrs. J. M. Wood Jr., *Those Reeves Girls*; Rath, *The Rath Trail*; and Rhinelander, *On Coming to America*. I am proud to call Rhinelander my aunt.

47. "National Board of Management," *DARM* 112 (December 1978): 973. White's position title was Registrar General.

48. Milton Rubincam, "Book Reviews," *NGSQ* 68 (March 1980): 64.

49. Milton Rubincam, review of Virginia H. Rollins, *Basic Course in Genealogy: Instruction to Help Beginners in Genealogical Research*, rev. ed., 1975), in "Book Reviews," *NGSQ* 68 (March 1980): 65.

50. Louise M. Everton, review of Katrina Maxtone-Graham, *An Adopted Woman: Her Search, Her Discoveries. A True Story* (New York: Kampomann and Co., 1983), in "New on the Bookshelf," *GH* 37 (July–August 1983): 151.

51. Keller, *The Century of the Gene*, 72; Gabriel, "A Biologist's Perspective on DNA and Race."

52. Carey, *The Epigenetics Revolution*; Zimmer, *She Has Her Mother's Laugh*, 370–403; Kenneally, *The Invisible History of the Human Race*, 216–18.

53. Keller, *The Century of the Gene*, 67–68; Müller-Wille and Rheinberger, *A Cultural History of Heredity*, xi, 217–18; Condit, *The Meanings of the Gene*.

54. Patricia J. Williams, *The Alchemy of Race and Rights*, 217.

55. Judy Siegel-Itzkovich, "Using a Rare Mutation to Find a Relative," *Avotaynu* 10 (Summer 1994): 37 (on thalassemia research); Cowan, *Heredity and Hope*.

56. Foster et al., "Jefferson Fathered Slave's Last Child," 27; Creet, *The Genealogical Sublime*, 119–21. I browsed the following journals before and after the Foster article's publication: the *New England Historical and Genealogical Register* (NEHGR), the *National Genealogical Society Quarterly* (NGSQ), and the *Genealogical Helper* (GH). I found considerable advocacy of medical studies of genetics within families, including recent generations, as with the *NGSQ*'s special issue on the subject in June 1994. But with the exception of a small study done by geneticist/genealogist Thomas H. Roderick of Bar Harbor, Maine, I found no interest in DNA testing directed at nonmedical purposes, focused on remote ancestry, before the early 2000s. Thomas H. Roderick, "Umbilical Lines and the mtDNA Project," *NGSQ* 82 (June 1994): 144–45. I also found no examples of genetic genealogy commerce, including in advertisements, in these publications before 2000. I found plenty of examples of both phenomena after 2000.

57. Horn, Jan Ellen Lewis, and Onuf, *The Revolution of 1800*.

58. Gordon-Reed, *Thomas Jefferson and Sally Hemings*, 59–62.

59. Gordon-Reed, *Thomas Jefferson and Sally Hemings*, 98–102; Nieman, "Coincidence or Causal Connection?" (2000).

60. Gordon-Reed, *Thomas Jefferson and Sally Hemings*, 25–46; Kerrison, *Jefferson's Daughters*, 242–308.

61. Gordon-Reed, *Hemingses of Monticello*, 655–57; Lucia Stanton, *"Those Who Labor for My Happiness,"* 69–70.

62. See Bailey, *The Weeping Time*, and Heather Andrea Williams, *Help Me to Find My People*.

63. Foster et al., "Jefferson Fathered Slave's Last Child," 27; Kenneally, *The Invisible History of the Human Race*, 228–33; Shepard, Honenberger, and Megill, "A Case Study in Historical Epistemology." Mark Schmeller shared the latter citation.

64. Regarding the last point, consider the title of Passley, Robertson, and Waldstreicher, *Beyond the Founders*.

65. Cogliano, *Thomas Jefferson*, 119, 178–79.

66. Randall Mikkelson, "Jefferson Kin, Black and White, Meet at White House," *Boston Globe*, April 13, 2001, 7; Cogliano, *Thomas Jefferson*, 170.

67. Cogliano, *Thomas Jefferson*, 180–81.

68. Michael Kilian, "Jefferson's Heirs Reject Hemings' Kin," *Chicago Tribune*, May 6, 2002; Cogliano, *Thomas Jefferson*, 196 (note 42).

69. See Duncan, *Where Death and Glory Meet*, 115, 120, on Confederates' insistence on interring white Union officer Robert Gould Shaw in South Carolina with the African American soldiers he commanded in 1863. Confederates intended a deep insult to Shaw and his family in Boston in burying him with Black people.

70. Weil, *Family Trees*, 208–9; Frank D. Cogliano, review of Andrew Holowchak, *Framing a Legend: Exposing the Distorted History of Thomas Jefferson and Sally Hemings*, in *Journal of American History* 101 (September 2014): 564–66.

71. Cogliano, *Thomas Jefferson*, 195 (note 33); Greely, "Genetic Genealogy"; Sommer, "DNA and Cultures of Remembrance"; Abu El-Haj, *The Genealogical Science*, 141–79; Sharpe, *Family Matters*, 248–53; Creet, *The Genealogical Sublime*, 121–30.

72. Abu El-Haj, *The Genealogical Science*, 144–59 (on the Jewish genealogist and entrepreneur Bennett Greenspan); Otterstrom, "Genealogy as Religious Ritual," 145; Ancestry.com advertisement, *NEHGR* 153 (January 1999): 128; Kenneally, *The Invisible History of the Human Race*, 207.

73. Alondra Nelson contributes a history of African Ancestry and of Kittles in her *Social Life of DNA* and other essays; founding date in Nelson, *The Social Life of DNA*, 11.

74. TallBear, *Native American DNA*, 68–69.

75. Kenneally, *The Invisible History of the Human Race*, 162.

76. Nelson, *The Social Life of DNA*, 74.

77. Hogan, *Roots Quest*, 186, note 14.

78. Roth, Yaylaci, Jaffe, and Richardson, "Do Genetic Ancestry Tests Increase Racial Essentialism?" 1–2.

79. TallBear, *Native American DNA*, 41–44.

80. Kenneally, *The Invisible History of the Human Race*, 210.

81. Kenneally, *The Invisible History of the Human Race*, 3; Abu El-Haj, *The Genealogical Science*, 227–28; Caron, *Se créer des ancêtres*, 202. Translation is mine.

82. Stallard and de Groot explore this point in depth in interviews of genealogists in "Things Are Coming Out That Are Questionable."

83. Len Yodaiken, "21st-Century DNA Confirms 18th-Century Relationship," *Avotaynu* 18 (Spring 2002): 19–22; Abu El-Haj, *The Genealogical Science*, 159–69.

84. Abu El-Haj, *The Genealogical Science*, 146–47.

85. Hogan, *Roots Quest*, 88–91. On ethnic labels in flux over time, a classic historical work is Eugen Weber, *Peasants into Frenchmen*. Creet's 2018 interdisciplinary panel at the Archives

of Ontario, of scientists and social scientists, is also helpful on this point: Creet, "Genealogy and Genetics Workshop: Part 8," https://juliacreet.vhx.tv/products/genealogy-and-genetics-workshop.

86. Milanich, *Paternity*, 258–60.

87. Nelson, *The Social Life of DNA*, 88–93; summary of *Motherland* from British Broadcasting Company, Press Office, "Press Release: Long-Lost Roots of Black Britons" (2003), http://www.bbc.co.uk/pressoffice/pressreleases/stories/2003/02_february/05/motherland.shtml.

88. Little, "Genealogy as Theatre of Self-Identity," 156–57, 160, 171–85; Little, "Identifying the Genealogical Self," 245–50; Deborah Cohen, *Family Secrets*, 257–65; Hogan, *Roots Quest*, 101–20. Jerome de Groot lists the sixteen other countries (besides the United States and Britain) that, as of 2015, broadcast adaptations of *Who Do You Think You Are?* in Groot, "On Genealogy," 112; Groot, "History on Television," 194–202.

89. Hogan, *Roots Quest*, 36–37; Creet, *The Genealogical Sublime*, 84–85 (NBC-era growth); Ancestry.com, "See Celebrities Discover Family Stories as Entertaining as They Are," https://www.ancestry.com/cs/who-do-you-think-you-are.

90. Nededog, "Bryan Cranston and More to Appear on New Season"; Scodari, *Alternate Roots*, 41. The sociologist Anne-Marie Kramer analyzed the original British version of *Who Do You Think You Are?* in "Mediatizing Memory."

91. Lowery, *The Lumbee Indians*, 6. Circe Sturm has described similar criteria for Cherokee belonging as Cherokees defined it in the 1990s: Sturm, *Blood Politics*, 108–41.

92. While on the show, Erdrich spurned the "reveal" also because, she said, she did not want to add to "confusion" among her relatives. Poetry Foundation, "Louise Erdrich," https://www.poetryfoundation.org/poems-and-poets/poets/detail/louise-erdrich; Erdrich in MacArthur, "Genetic Ancestry Testing," https://www.wired.com/2010/03/genetic-ancestry-testing-people-who-dont-want-to-know.

93. Nelson, *The Social Life of DNA*, 16.

94. Maggie Astor, "Why Many Native Americans Are Angry with Elizabeth Warren," *New York Times*, October 17, 2018; Miranda et al., "Rapid Response History: Native American Identities, Racial Slurs, and Elizabeth Warren"; TallBear, "Elizabeth Warren's Claim to Cherokee Ancestry is a Form of Violence"; Creet, *The Genealogical Sublime*, 157–58.

95. Woodtor, *Finding a Place Called Home*; Woodtor to "Coy," n.d. [1991], folder 5, box 1, Afro-American Family History Outreach Project (1987-1988), NL; H. Gregory Meyer, "Delores 'Dee' Parmer Woodtor," *Chicago Tribune*, August 14, 2002. Her colleague may have been Coy D. Robbins, who published *Black Indiana Pioneers* with the Indiana AAHGS in 1990. Result of Google searches for "coy" and "Black genealogy." It is unclear whether Woodtor sent the letter to Coy.

Epilogue

1. Fermaglich, *A Rosenberg by Any Other Name*, 159–71 (166–70 on wiping away inconsistencies after 9/11).

2. Tatelman, "The REAL ID Act of 2005"; Eyre, *The Real ID Act*; Krajewska, *Documenting Americans*, 157–244.

3. Catherine Nash, *Genetic Geographies*, especially 12–13, 171–83, makes a similar point.

4. Hogan, *Roots Quest*, 99–100, 134–35.

5. Roth, Yaylaci, Jaffe, and Richardson, "Do Genetic Ancestry Tests Increase Racial Essentialism?" 3.

6. U.S. National Institutes of Health, National Human Genome Research Institute, "Why Mouse Matters" (2010), https://www.genome.gov/10001345/importance-of-mouse-genome.

7. Creet, *The Genealogical Sublime*, 1–25; Creet, "Genealogy and Genetics Workshop: Part 8," https://juliacreet.vhx.tv/products/genealogy-and-genetics-workshop. Creet describes Icelandic records that originated before the year 1000 as well as Confucian traditions in China. But millennium-length pedigrees, especially in textual form, are uncommon in the Americas except possibly among some Indigenous populations.

8. An ever-increasing literature from nonhistorians supports this point. See in particular Catherine Nash, *Genetic Geographies*; Nelson, *The Social Life of DNA*; Roth, Yaylaci, Jaffe, and Richardson, "Do Genetic Ancestry Tests Increase Racial Essentialism?"; Roth and Ivemark, "Genetic Options"; Creet, "Data Mining the Deceased"; Creet, *The Genealogical Sublime*; and Creet, "Genealogy and Genetics Workshop: Part 8."

9. Roth, Yaylaci, Jaffe, and Richardson, "Do Genetic Ancestry Tests Increase Racial Essentialism?" 2.

10. Alondra Nelson interviewed (2014) in Creet, *The Genealogical Sublime*, 151; Creet, "Data Mining the Deceased."

11. Kenneally, *The Invisible History of the Human Race*, 159–78; Catherine Nash, *Genetic Geographies*, 101–69; Creet, *The Genealogical Sublime*, 125.

12. British Broadcasting Company, "Migrant Crisis: One Million Enter Europe in 2015"; K. Biswas, "How the Far Right Became Europe's New Normal," *New York Times*, February 4, 2020.

13. Creet, *The Genealogical Sublime*, 119–23; Abu El-Haj, *The Genealogical Science*.

14. David M. Halbfinger and Isabel Kershner, "Israel Enshrines Rights for Jews," *New York Times*, July 20, 2018.

15. Sharfstein, *The Invisible Line*, and Saunt, *Black, White, and Indian*, are especially insightful works on Americans' living as white.

16. Sheryl Gay Stolberg, "In Defining Obama, Misperceptions Stick," *New York Times*, August 19, 2010; "President Obama's Long-Form Birth Certificate," https://www.slideshare.net/whitehouse/birth-certificatelongform; Obama, "Remarks by the President," https://www.whitehouse.gov/the-press-office/2011/04/27/remarks-president.

Bibliography

Archival Materials

Illinois
  Chicago
    Newberry Library Archives, Special Collections, Newberry Library
      Afro-American Family History Outreach Project (1987–88), Local and Family
        History Section Records, 11/04/60
        Office of the Board of Trustees Records
          Minutes and Agendas, 02/01/30
          Trustee Reports and Documents, 02/01/21
            Personal Papers: Eliphalet Wickes Blatchford Papers, 02/15/01
          Harriet Taylor Papers, 11/15/01
      Vivian G. Harsh Research Collection of Afro-American History and Literature,
        Chicago Public Library
    Patricia Liddell Researchers Archives
Massachusetts
  Amherst
    University of Massachusetts-Amherst
      "W. E. B. Du Bois Papers." Last accessed March 8, 2021. http://credo.library
        .umass.edu/view/full/mums312-b054-i263
  Boston
    Massachusetts Historical Society
      American Party, Records of the East Boston Chapter, 1853–56
      William Jenks Papers
      Microfilm Edition of the Papers Relating to the Quincy, Wendell, Holmes,
        and Upham Families. Boston: Massachusetts Historical Society, 1977.
    Lemuel Shattuck Papers
    New England Historic Genealogical Society
      Henry Bond Papers
      Winifred Lovering Holman Papers
  Cambridge
    Peabody Museum of Archaeology and Ethnography, Harvard University
      Caroline Bond Day Papers
    Arthur and Elizabeth Schlesinger Library on the History of Women in America,
      Radcliffe Institute for Advanced Study, Harvard University
    Pauli Murray Papers
    "Antislavery Massachusetts Petitions Dataverse." Harvard University and Digital
      Archives of Massachusetts

"Council; Council Files February 5, 1857, Case of Zerviah Gould Mitchell, GC3/
　　Series 378, Petition of Zerviah Gould Mitchell." Published 2015. https://
　　dataverse.harvard.edu/dataset.xhtml?persistentId=doi:10.7910/DVN
　　/WNZNC.
Salem
　Peabody Essex Museum, Phillips Library
　　John Tyler Hassam Papers
　　Henry FitzGilbert Waters Papers
Michigan
　Ann Arbor
　　Michigan Historical Collections, Bentley Library, University of Michigan
　　　Papers of the Daughters of the American Revolution, Michigan Society
Minnesota
　St. Paul
　　Minnesota Historical Society, Minnesota History Center
　　　Papers of Jennie Adelaide Holmes Coolidge
Missouri
　Columbia
　　Western Historical Manuscript Collection, University of Missouri/State Historical
　　　Society of Missouri
　　　Helm-Davidson Family Papers
New Hampshire
　Concord
　　New Hampshire Historical Society, Tuck Library
　　　John Farmer Papers
　　　Cyrus Parker Bradley Papers
New York
　New York City
　　Columbia University Rare Book and Manuscript Library
　　　Belmont Family Papers
Tennessee
　Knoxville
　　University of Tennessee at Knoxville, Special Collections
　　　Alex Haley Papers, 1870–1991 (MS.1888)
　　　Alex Haley Papers (MS.2280)
　　　Anne Romaine Collection
Utah
　Provo
　　Ancestry.com, "1850 United States Federal Census." Last accessed March 7, 2021.
　　　https://www.ancestry.com/search/collections/8054/
　Salt Lake City
　　Church History Library, Church of Jesus Christ of Latter-day Saints
　　　Archibald F. Bennett scrapbooks ("From His Book of Remembrance"), 1928–65
　　　Susa Young Gates Papers

Genealogical Society of Utah. Biography Class Collection, 1932–37
"The GIANT System." Typed script for slideshow, n.d. (ca. 1969)
Lapreel D. Huber. "Historical Report of the Nampa [Idaho] Region Genealogical
Mission." Typescript, 1979
Zelda Merritt, comp. "Experiences and Impressions of Genealogical Missionaries,
1981–1986." Typescript, 1986
"Testimonies and Experiences of the Lehi [Utah] Stake Records Extraction
Program." Typescript, n.d. (ca. 1979)
Family History Library and FamilySearch.org, Church of Jesus Christ of Latter-
day Saints. "Family History Books" collection. Last accessed March 7,
2021. http://books.familysearch.org/

Periodicals, Newspapers, and Databases

*American Antiquarian Society Historical
Periodicals Collection*
American Genealogist
American Jewish Archives
*American Jewish Historical Society
Publications*
American Monthly Magazine
*Avotaynu: The International Review of
Jewish Genealogy*
Colored American Magazine
The Crisis: Record of the Darker Races
*Daughters of the American Revolution
Magazine*
Daughters of the American Revolution,
Proceedings of the Continental Congress
Eugenical News
Genealogical Computer Pioneer
Genealogical Computing
*Genealogical Helper/Everton's Genealogical
Helper*
Jewish Quarterly Review
*Journal of the Afro-American Historical and
Genealogical Society*
Journal of American Genealogy
Journal of American Indian Family Research
Journal of Negro History

Library Journal
Library Trends
Magazine of American Genealogy
Massachusetts Historical Society
Collections
Mayflower Descendant
Mayflower Quarterly
National Genealogical Society Quarterly
Negro History Bulletin
*New England Historical and Genealogical
Register*
New Haven Genealogical Magazine
*New York Genealogical and Biographical
Record*
New York Jewish Week (1973–85)
(Manhattan Edition), ProQuest LLC
ProQuest Historical Newspapers: *Chicago
Tribune*, ProQuest LLC
ProQuest Historical Newspapers:
New York Times, ProQuest LLC
Toledot
Utah Genealogical and Historical Magazine
Virginia Magazine of History and Biography
Voice of the Negro
William and Mary Quarterly
The Woman's Era

Publications

Abu El-Haj, Nadia. *The Genealogical Science: The Search for Jewish Origins and the Politics of Epistemology*. Chicago and London: University of Chicago Press, 2012.

Adams, Arthur. "Introduction." In *Genealogical Research: Methods and Sources, by the American Society of Genealogists*, edited by Milton Rubincam, 1–2. Washington, D.C.: The American Society of Genealogists, 1960.

Adams, Henry. *The Education of Henry Adams*, with an introduction by James Truslow Adams. New York: The Modern Library, 1931. First published 1918.

Addams, Jane. "Filial Relations." In *Democracy and Social Ethics*, 71–102. New York: The Macmillan Company, 1907.

Afro-American Historical and Genealogical Society. "History of AAHGS," 1982. Last accessed March 7, 2021. https://www.aahgs.org/index.cfm?fuseaction=Page.ViewPage &pageId=597.

Akenson, Donald Harman. *Some Family: The Mormons and How Humanity Keeps Track of Itself*. Montreal and Kingston, Can.: McGill-Queen's University Press, 2007.

Alexander, Thomas G. *Mormonism in Transition: A History of the Latter-day Saints, 1890–1930*. Urbana and Chicago: University of Illinois Press, 1986.

Allaben, Frank. *Concerning Genealogies: Being Suggestions of Value for All Interested in Family History*. New York: Grafton Press, 1904.

Allaben, Frank, and Mabel Washburn. *How to Trace and Record Your Own Ancestry*. New York: National Historical Company, 1932.

Allen, James B., and Jessie L. Embry. "'Provoking the Brethren to Good Works': Susa Young Gates, the Relief Society, and Genealogy." *Brigham Young University Studies* 31 (Spring 1991): 115–38.

Allen, James B., Jessie L. Embry, and Kahlile B. Mehr. *Hearts Turned to the Fathers: A History of the Genealogical Society of Utah, 1894–1994*. Provo, Utah: BYU Studies, Brigham Young University, 1995.

American Council of Learned Societies. Report of Committee on Linguistics and National Stocks in the Population of the United States. *Surnames in the United States Census of 1790: An Analysis of National Origins of the Population*. Baltimore: Genealogical Publishing Co., 1971. First published in 1932.

American Society of Genealogists. "Current Fellows." 2019. https://fasg.org/fellows /current-fellows/.

Andereck, Paul Arthur, and Richard A. Pence. *Computer Genealogy: A Guide to Research through High Technology*. Salt Lake City: Ancestry Incorporated, 1985.

Anderson, Benedict. *Imagined Communities: Reflections on the Origin and Spread of Nationalism*. Rev. ed. London: Verso, 1991.

Anderson, Margo J. *The American Census: A Social History*. New Haven and London: Yale University Press, 1988.

Angela C. "Pioneer Day Tips for Mormon Muggles and Mudbloods." Blog post, published June 1, 2015. *By Common Consent*, https://bycommonconsent.com/2015/06/01 /pioneer-day-tips-for-mormon-muggles-mudbloods/.

Archdeacon, Thomas J. *Becoming American: An Ethnic History*. New York: The Free Press, 1983.

Arrington, Leonard J., and Davis Bitton. *The Mormon Experience: A History of the Latter-day Saints.* New York: Alfred A. Knopf, 1979.

Ashton, Rick J. "Curators, Hobbyists, and Historians: Ninety Years of Genealogy at the Newberry Library." *Library Quarterly* 47 (April 1977): 149–62.

Asukile, Thabiti. "Joel Augustus Rogers: Black International Journalism, Archival Research, and Black Print Culture." *Journal of African American History* 95 (Summer/Fall 2010): 322–47.

Auger, Roland J. "Québec." In *Genealogical Research: Methods and Sources, by the American Society of Genealogists.* Vol. 1, 338–51. Rev. ed. Washington, D.C.: The American Society of Genealogists, 1980.

Axelrod, Alan. *The Colonial Revival in America.* New York: W. W. Norton for the Henry Francis du Pont Winterthur Museum, 1985.

Azaransky, Sarah. *The Dream is Freedom: Pauli Murray and American Democratic Faith.* New York: Oxford University Press, 2011.

Baden-Lasar, Eli, and Susan Dominus. "A Family Portrait: Brothers, Sisters, Strangers." *New York Times Magazine*, June 26, 2019. Interactive version at https://www.nytimes .com/interactive/2019/06/26/magazine/sperm-donor-siblings.html.

Bailey, Anne C. *The Weeping Time: Memory and the Largest Slave Auction in American History.* Cambridge: Cambridge University Press, 2017.

Baker, Emerson W. *A Storm of Witchcraft: The Salem Trials and the American Experience.* New York: Oxford University Press, 2015.

Baker, Lee D. *Anthropology and the Racial Politics of Culture.* Durham, N.C.: Duke University Press, 2010.

Baldwin, James. "How One Black Man Came to Be an American." *New York Times Book Review*, September 26, 1976.

Ball, Erica, and Kellie Carter Jackson, eds. *Reconsidering* Roots: *Race, Politics, and Memory.* Athens: University of Georgia Press, 2017.

Banner, James M., Jr. *Being a Historian: An Introduction to the Professional World of History.* Cambridge: Cambridge University Press, 2012.

Bardaglio, Peter W. "'Shameful Matches': The Regulation of Interracial Sex and Marriage in the South before 1900." In *Sex, Love, Race: Crossing Boundaries in North American History*, edited by Martha Hodes, 112–40. New York: New York University Press, 1999.

Barkan, Elazar. *The Retreat of Scientific Racism: Changing Concepts of Race in Britain and the United States between the World Wars.* Cambridge: Cambridge University Press, 1992.

Barker, Howard F. "The Ancestry of Family Names." *The Atlantic Monthly* (August 1935): 182–86.

———. "The Founders of New England." *American Historical Review* 38 (July 1933): 702–13.

Barnhill, Georgia Brady. "'Keep Sacred the Memory of Your Ancestors': Family Registers and Memorial Prints." In *The Art of Family: Genealogical Artifacts in New England*, edited by D. Brenton Simons and Peter Benes, 60–74. Boston: New England Historic Genealogical Society, 2002.

Basu, Paul. *Highland Homecomings: Genealogy and Heritage Tourism in the Scottish Diaspora.* New York: Routledge, 2007.

Bate, Kerry William. *The Women: A Family Story.* Salt Lake City: University of Utah Press, 2016.

Battles, David M. *The History of Public Library Access for African Americans in the South, or, Leaving Behind the Plow.* Lanham, Md.: Scarecrow Press, 2009.

Beaujot, Ariel. "*Hear, Here*: The Challenges of Democratizing Historical Narratives." Case statement, February 3, 2016, National Council of Public History. http://ncph.org/phc /ncph-working-groups/building-capacity3016-working-group/ariel-beaujot-case-statement/.

Beard, Timothy Field, with Denise Demong. *How to Find Your Family Roots.* New York: McGraw-Hill, 1977.

Becker, Carl L. "Everyman His Own Historian." *American Historical Review* 37 (January 1932): 221–36.

Beckert, Sven. *The Monied Metropolis: New York City and the Consolidation of the American Bourgeoisie, 1850–1896.* Cambridge and New York: Cambridge University Press, 2001.

Beckert, Sven, and Julia Rosenbaum, eds. *The American Bourgeoisie: Distinction and Identity in Nineteenth-Century America.* New York: Palgrave Macmillan, 2010.

Bederman, Gail. *Manliness and Civilization: A Cultural History of Gender and Race in the United States, 1880–1917.* Chicago: University of Chicago Press, 1995.

Bell, George Morrison, Sr. *Genealogy of "Old and New Cherokee Families."* Bartlesville, Okla.: Leonard Printing Company, 1972.

Bell, Marty. "Debts, Stubborn Faith Drive Alex Haley to Write 'Roots.'" *Chicago Tribune*, February 27, 1977, 12.

Bell-Scott, Patricia. *The Firebrand and the First Lady: Portrait of a Friendship: Pauli Murray, Eleanor Roosevelt, and the Struggle for Social Justice.* New York: Alfred A. Knopf, 2016.

Benton-Cohen, Katherine. *Inventing the Immigration Problem: The Dillingham Commission and Its Legacy.* Cambridge, Mass., and London: Harvard University Press, 2018.

Berenbaum, Michael. "The Nativization of the Holocaust." *Judaism* 35 (Fall 1986): 447–57.

Berlin, Ira. *Generations of Captivity: A History of African-American Slaves.* Cambridge, Mass.: Harvard University Press, 2003.

Berry, Mary Frances. *We Are Who We Say We Are: A Black Family's Search for Home across the Atlantic World.* New York: Oxford University Press, 2015.

Bidlack, Russell E. "Genealogy Today." *Library Trends* 32 (Summer 1983): 7–23.

Billingsley, Frank. *Swabbed and Found: An Adopted Man's DNA Journey to Discover His Family Tree.* Houston: Bright Sky Press, 2017.

Bingham, Ryan Stuart. "Curses and Marks: Racial Dispensations and Dispensations of Race in Joseph Smith's Bible Revision and the Book of Abraham." *Journal of Mormon History* 41 (July 2015): 22–57.

Biondi, Martha. *The Black Revolution on Campus.* Berkeley and Los Angeles: University of California Press, 2012.

Bishop, Ronald. "In the Grand Scheme of Things: An Exploration of the Meaning of Genealogical Research." *Journal of Popular Culture* 41 (June 2008): 393–412.

Biswas, K. "How the Far Right Became Europe's New Normal." *New York Times*, February 4, 2020.

Black, Susan Easton, and Harvey Bischoff Black, comps. *Annotated Record of Baptisms for the Dead, 1840–1845: Nauvoo, Hancock County, Illinois.* 7 vols. Provo, Utah: Center for Family History and Genealogy, Brigham Young University, 2002.

Blight, David W. *Frederick Douglass: Prophet of Freedom.* New York: Simon and Schuster, 2018.

———. *Race and Reunion: The Civil War in American Memory*. Cambridge, Mass.: Harvard University Press, 2001.

Blouin, Francis X., Jr., and William G. Rosenberg, eds. *Archives, Documentation, and Institutions of Social Memory: Essays from the Sawyer Seminar*. Ann Arbor: University of Michigan Press, 2006.

Bly, Antonio T. "Literacy and Orality." In *World of a Slave: Encyclopedia of the Material Life of Slaves in the United States*, edited by Martha B. Katz-Hyman and Kym S. Rice, 14. Santa Barbara, Calif.: Greenwood Press, 2011.

Bockstruck, Lloyd DeWitt. "Four Centuries of Genealogy: A Historical Overview." *RQ* 23, no. 2 (Winter 1983): 162–70.

Bottero, Wendy. "Practising Family History: 'Identity' as a Category of Social Practice." *British Journal of Sociology* 66, no. 3 (September 2015): 534–56.

———. "Who Do You Think They Were? How Family Historians Make Sense of Social Position and Inequality in the Past." *British Journal of Sociology* 63, no. 1 (March 2012): 54–74.

Bouquet, Mary. "Family Trees and Their Affinities: The Visual Imperative of the Genealogical Diagram." *Journal of the Royal Anthropological Institute* 2, no. 1 (March 1996): 43–66.

Bourdieu, Pierre. *Distinction: A Social Critique of the Judgement of Taste*. Translated by Richard Nice. Cambridge, Mass.: Harvard University Press, 1984.

Bowditch, Harold. "Heraldry." In *Genealogical Research: Methods and Sources, by the American Society of Genealogists*, edited by Milton Rubincam, 411–27. Washington, D.C.: The American Society of Genealogists, 1960.

Bowditch, Harold, with Sir Anthony Wagner. "Heraldry." In *Genealogical Research: Methods and Sources, by the American Society of Genealogists*. Vol. 1, 531–47. Rev. ed. Washington, D.C.: The American Society of Genealogists, 1980.

Boyd, Nan Alamilla. *Wide-Open Town: A History of Queer San Francisco to 1965*. Berkeley and Los Angeles: University of California Press, 2003.

British Broadcasting Company. "Migrant Crisis: One Million Enter Europe in 2015." Published December 22, 2015. https://www.bbc.com/news/world-europe-35158769.

British Broadcasting Company, Press Office. "Press Release: Long-Lost Roots of Black Britons." Published February 5, 2003. http://www.bbc.co.uk/pressoffice/pressreleases /stories/2003/02_february/05/motherland.shtml.

Britsch, R. Lanier. "The Church in Asia." In *Encyclopedia of Mormonism: The History, Scripture, Doctrine, and Procedure of The Church of Jesus Christ of Latter-day Saints*, edited by Daniel H. Ludlow, 75–81. New York: Macmillan Publishing Company, 1992.

———. "The Church in Oceana." In *Encyclopedia of Mormonism: The History, Scripture, Doctrine, and Procedure of The Church of Jesus Christ of Latter-day Saints*, edited by Daniel H. Ludlow, 1022–26. New York: Macmillan Publishing Company, 1992.

Brodkin, Karen. *How Jews Became White Folks and What That Says About Race in America*. New Brunswick, N.J.: Rutgers University Press, 1998.

Brogan, Hugh. *Alexis de Tocqueville: A Life*. New Haven, Conn.: Yale University Press, 2006.

Broman, David L., and Steven Williams. *Anthropology at Harvard: A Biographical History, 1790–1940*. Cambridge, Mass.: Peabody Museum Press of Harvard University, 2013.

Brooks, Joanna. *The Book of Mormon Girl: A Memoir of an American Faith.* New York: Free Press, 2012.

————. "Feminism, Theology, and the Personal in American Studies." *Legacy: A Journal of American Women Writers* 32, no. 2 (2015): 173–76.

————. "Mormon Feminism: An Introduction." In *Mormon Feminism: Essential Writings,* edited by Brooks, Rachel Hunt Steenblik, and Hannah Wheelwright, 1–23. New York: Oxford University Press, 2016.

Brooks, Joanna, Rachel Hunt Steenblik, and Hannah Wheelwright, eds. *Mormon Feminism: Essential Writings.* New York: Oxford University Press, 2016.

Brown, Kathleen M. *Good Wives, Nasty Wenches, and Anxious Patriarchs: Gender, Race, and Power in Colonial Virginia.* Chapel Hill: University of North Carolina Press, 1996.

Brown, Lois. *Pauline Elizabeth Hopkins: Black Daughter of the Revolution.* Chapel Hill: University of North Carolina Press, 2008.

Brown, Samuel Morris. *In Heaven as It Is on Earth: Joseph Smith and the Early Mormon Conquest of Death.* New York: Oxford University Press, 2012.

Browning, Charles Henry. *Americans of Royal Descent.* Philadelphia: Porter & Coates, 1883.

————. *Americans of Royal Descent: Collections of Genealogies of American Families Whose Lineage is Traced to the Legitimate Issue of Kings.* 2nd ed. Philadelphia: Porter & Coates, 1891.

————. *Americans of Royal Descent: Collections of Genealogies Showing the Lineal Descent from Kings of Some American Families.* 7th ed. Baltimore: Genealogical Publishing Co., 1998. First published 1911.

Bruinius, Harry. *Better for All the World: The Secret History of Forced Sterilization and America's Quest for Racial Purity.* New York: Alfred A. Knopf, 2006.

Brundage, W. Fitzhugh. *The Southern Past: A Clash of Race and Memory.* Cambridge, Mass., and London: Harvard University Press, 2005.

————. "White Women and the Politics of Historical Memory in the New South, 1880–1920." In *Jumpin' Jim Crow: Southern Politics from Civil War to Civil Rights,* edited by Jane Dailey, Glenda Elizabeth Gilmore, and Bryant Simon, 115–39. Princeton, N.J.: Princeton University Press, 2000.

Bruner, Edward M. "Tourism in Ghana: The Representation of Slavery and the Return of the Black Diaspora." *American Anthropologist* 98 (June 1996): 290–305.

Burns, Edward McNall. *David Starr Jordan: Prophet of Freedom.* Stanford, Calif.: Stanford University Press, 1953.

Burns, Kathryn. "Notaries, Truth, and Consequences." *American Historical Review* 110 (April 2005): 350–79.

Burns, Margo, and Bernard Rosenthal. "Examination of the Records of the Salem Witch Trials." *William and Mary Quarterly* 65 (July 2008): 401–22.

Burroughs, Tony. *Black Roots: A Beginner's Guide to Tracing the African American Family Tree.* New York: Simon and Schuster, 2001.

Burton, H. David. "Baptism for the Dead." In *The Encyclopedia of Mormonism: The History, Scripture, Doctrine, and Procedure of the Church of Jesus Christ of Latter-day Saints.* Vol. 1, edited by Daniel H. Ludlow, 95–96. New York: Macmillan Publishing Company, 1992.

Bushman, Claudia L. *Contemporary Mormonism: Latter-Day Saints in Modern America.* Lanham, Md., and Plymouth, U.K.: Rowman & Littlefield, 2006.

Bushman, Richard L. *Believing History: Latter-day Saint Essays*. Edited by Reid L. Neilson and Jed Woodworth. New York: Columbia University Press, 2004.

———. *Joseph Smith and the Beginnings of Mormonism*. Urbana and Chicago: University of Illinois Press, 1984.

———. *The Refinement of America: Persons, Houses, Cities*. New York: Alfred A. Knopf, 1992.

Bushman, Richard L., with the assistance of Jed Woodworth. *Joseph Smith: Rough Stone Rolling: A Cultural Biography of Mormonism's Founder*. New York: Alfred A. Knopf, 2005.

Bynum, Victoria E. *The Free State of Jones: Mississippi's Longest Civil War*. Rev. ed. Chapel Hill: University of North Carolina Press, 2016.

Byron, Tammy K. "Bible." In *World of a Slave: Encyclopedia of the Material Life of Slaves in the United States*, edited by Martha B. Katz-Hyman and Kym S. Rice, 67. Santa Barbara, Calif.: Greenwood Press, 2011.

Campbell, Matt. "George Haley, One of the First African-Americans to Be Elected to the Kansas Senate, Dies at 89." *Kansas City Star*, May 14, 2015. https://www.kansascity.com/news/local/article21053835.html.

Canaday, Margot. *The Straight State: Sexuality and Citizenship in Twentieth-Century America*. Princeton and Oxford: Princeton University Press, 2009.

Carey, Nessa. *The Epigenetics Revolution: How Modern Biology Is Rewriting Our Understanding of Genetics, Disease, and Inheritance*. New York: Columbia University Press, 2012.

Caron, Caroline-Isabelle. *Se créer des ancêtres: Un parcours généalogique Nord-Américain, XIXe-XXe siècles (To Create Ancestors: A North American Family Journey, 19th–20th Centuries)*. Sillery, Québec: Septentrion, 2006.

Carp, E. Wayne. *Family Matters: Secrecy and Disclosure in the History of Adoption*. Cambridge, Mass.: Harvard University Press, 1998.

Carpenter, Cecelia Svinth. *How to Research American Indian Blood Lines*. South Prairie, Wash: Meico Associates, 1984.

Carr, John Foster. *Guide to the United States for the Jewish Immigrant: A Nearly Literal Translation of the Second Yiddish Edition*. n.p.: Connecticut Daughters of the American Revolution, 1912.

Carsten, Janet. *After Kinship*. Cambridge: Cambridge University Press, 2004.

Carter, Kent. *The Dawes Commission and the Allotment of the Five Civilized Tribes, 1893–1914*. Orem, Utah: Ancestry.com, 1999.

Carter, Norvella P., Warren Chalklen, and Bhekuyise Zungu. "Re-Rooting *Roots*: The South African Perspective." In *Reconsidering Roots: Race, Politics, and Memory*, edited by Erica L. Ball and Kellie Carter Jackson, 165–81. Athens: University of Georgia Press, 2017.

Casper, Scott E. "Introduction." In *A History of the Book in America. Vol. 3. The Industrial Book, 1840–1880*, edited by Casper, Jeffrey D. Groves, Stephen W. Nissenbaum, and Michael Winship, 1–39. Chapel Hill: University of North Carolina Press, 2007.

Cassedy, James H. *American Medicine and Statistical Thinking, 1800–1860*. Cambridge, Mass., and London: Harvard University Press, 1984.

———. *Medicine and American Growth, 1800–1860*. Madison: University of Wisconsin Press, 1986.

"Cast and Details: Who Do You Think You Are." *TV Guide*. July 23, 2014. http://www
.tvguide.com/tvshows/who-do-you-think-you-are/296860/.

Castells, Manuel. *The Power of Identity*. Malden, Mass., and Oxford, U.K.: Blackwell
Publishing, 1997.

———. *The Rise of the Network Society*. 2nd ed. Malden, Mass., and Oxford, U.K.:
Blackwell Publishing, 2000.

Censer, Jane Turner. *The Reconstruction of White Southern Womanhood, 1865–1895*.
Baton Rouge: Louisiana State University Press, 2003.

Cerny, Johni. "Black Ancestral Research." In *The Source: A Guidebook of American Genealogy*,
edited by Arlene Eakle and Cerny, 579–95. Salt Lake City: Ancestry Publishing
Company, 1984.

Chadwick, Bruce A., and Thomas Garrow. "Native Americans." In *Encyclopedia of
Mormonism: The History, Scripture, Doctrine, and Procedure of The Church of Jesus Christ
of Latter-day Saints*, edited by Daniel H. Ludlow, 981–85. New York: Macmillan
Publishing Company, 1992.

Chakraborty, Jayajit, and M. Martin Bosman. "Measuring the Digital Divide in the United
States: Race, Income, and Personal Computer Ownership." *The Professional Geographer*
57 (August 2005): 395–410.

Chauncey, George. *Why Marriage? The History Shaping Today's Debate over Gay Equality*.
New York: Basic Books, 2004.

Chávez, Fray Angélico. *Origins of New Mexico Families in the Spanish Colonial Period. In
Two Parts: The Seventeenth (1598-1693) and the Eighteenth (1693–1821) Centuries*. Santa
Fe: The Historical Society of New Mexico, 1954.

———. *Origins of New Mexico Families: A Genealogy of the Spanish Colonial Period*. Rev. ed.
Santa Fe: Museum of New Mexico Press, 1992.

Chicago Public Library. "Patricia Liddell Researchers Archives." Last accessed March 7,
2021. https://www.chipublib.org/fa-patricia-liddell-researchers-archive/.

Cho, Sumi, Kimberlé Williams Crenshaw, and Leslie McCall. "Toward a Field of
Intersectionality Studies: Theory, Applications, and Praxis." *Signs* 38 (Summer 2013):
785–810.

Chomsky, Martin J., John Erman, David Greene, and Gilbert Moses, dirs. *Roots: Thirtieth
Anniversary Edition*. Burbank, Calif.: Warner Home Video, 2007. 6 discs. DVD, 573 min.

The Church of Jesus Christ of Latter-day Saints. "Age of Accountability: Why Am I
Baptized When I'm Eight Years Old?" Published February 2000. https://www
.churchofjesuschrist.org/study/friend/2000/02/the-age-of-accountability-why-am-i
-baptized-when-i-am-eight-years-old?lang=eng.

———. "Mothers' Employment outside the Home." In *Eternal Marriage Student Manual*
(2003), 237–40. https://www.lds.org/manual/eternal-marriage-student-manual
/mothers-employment-outside-the-home?lang=eng.

———. "Tithing." Last accessed March 7, 2021. https://www.lds.org/topics/tithing?lang=eng.

The Church of Jesus Christ of Latter-day Saints, The First Presidency. "Names Submitted
for Temple Ordinances." March 1, 2012. https://www.churchofjesuschrist.org/church
/news/names-submitted-for-temple-ordinances?lang=eng.

Clark-Lewis, Elizabeth. *Living In, Living Out: African American Domestics in Washington,
D.C., 1910–1940*. Washington, D.C.: Smithsonian Institution Press, 1994.

Cleves, Rachel Hope. *Charity and Sylvia: A Same-Sex Marriage in Early America.* New York: Oxford University Press, 2014.

Coddington, John Insley. "Royal and Noble Genealogy." In *Genealogical Research: Methods and Sources, by the American Society of Genealogists,* edited by Milton Rubincam, 299–319. Washington, D.C.: The American Society of Genealogists, 1960.

Cogliano, Francis D. *Thomas Jefferson: Reputation and Legacy.* Charlottesville: University of Virginia Press, 2006.

Cohen, Adam. *Imbeciles: The Supreme Court, American Eugenics, and the Sterilization of Carrie Buck.* New York: Penguin Books, 2016.

Cohen, Daniel J. "The Gathering of Jewish Records to Israel." *World Conference on Records and Genealogical Seminar, August 5–8, 1969.* Vol. A, typescript, 70–84. FamilySearch Digital Library, Church of Jesus Christ of Latter-day Saints. https://www.familysearch.org.

Cohen, Deborah. *Family Secrets: Shame and Privacy in Modern Britain.* New York and Oxford: Oxford University Press, 2013.

Cohen, Patricia Cline. *A Calculating People: The Spread of Numeracy in Early America.* Chicago and London: University of Chicago Press, 1982.

Cole, Phyllis. *Mary Moody Emerson and the Origins of Transcendentalism: A Family History.* New York and Oxford: Oxford University Press, 1998.

Colonial Dames of America. "CDA Today." https://cda1890.org/aboutcda/.

Comaroff, John L., and Jean Comaroff. *Ethnicity, Inc.* Chicago and London: University of Chicago Press, 2009.

Comfort, Nathaniel. *The Science of Human Perfection: How Genes Became the Heart of American Medicine.* New Haven and London: Yale University Press, 2012.

Comito, Lauren, ed. *Tech for All: Moving Beyond the Digital Divide.* Lanham, Md.: Rowman and Littlefield, 2019.

Condit, Celeste Michelle. *The Meanings of the Gene: Public Debates about Human Heredity.* Madison: University of Wisconsin Press, 1999.

Conforti, Joseph A. *Imagining New England: Explorations of Regional Identity from the Pilgrims to the Mid-Twentieth Century.* Chapel Hill: University of North Carolina Press, 2001.

Conlin, Jonathan. *Evolution and the Victorians: Science, Culture and Politics in Darwin's Britain.* London and New York: Bloomsbury, 2014.

Constitution and By-Laws of the Daughters of the American Revolution. Washington, D.C.: Press of Gedney & Roberts, 1890.

Constitution and By-Laws of the National Society of the Daughters of the American Revolution. Washington, D.C.: Press of W. F. Roberts, 1894.

Conzen, Kathleen Neils, David A. Gerber, Ewa Morawska, George E. Pozzetta, and Rudolph J. Vecoli. "The Invention of Ethnicity: A Perspective from the U. S. A." *Journal of American Ethnic History* 12 (Fall 1992): 3–41.

Coontz, Stephanie. *The Way We Never Were: American Families and the Nostalgia Trap.* New York: Basic Books, 1992.

Cooper, Anna Julia. *A Voice from the South,* with an introduction by Mary Helen Washington. New York: Oxford University Press, 1988.

Cooper, Brittney C. *Beyond Respectability: The Intellectual Thought of Race Women.* Urbana and Chicago: University of Illinois Press, 2017.

Corbould, Clare. "*Roots*, the Legacy of Slavery, and Civil Rights Backlash in 1970s America." In *Reconsidering Roots: Race, Politics, and Memory*, edited by Erica L. Ball and Kellie Carter Jackson, 25–46. Athens: University of Georgia Press, 2017.

Cordell, Sigrid Anderson. "'The Case Was Very Black Against' Her: Pauline Hopkins and the Politics of Racial Ambiguity at the *Colored American Magazine*." *American Periodicals* 16, no. 1 (March 2006): 52–73.

Cornwall, Rebecca Foster. "Susa Young Gates: The Thirteenth Apostle." In *Sister Saints*, edited by Vicky Burgess-Olson, 61–93. Provo, Utah: Brigham Young University Press, 1978.

Cott, Nancy F. *Public Vows: A History of Marriage and the Nation*. Cambridge, Mass.: Harvard University Press, 2000.

Cowan, Ruth Schwartz. *Heredity and Hope: The Case for Genetic Screening*. Cambridge, Mass., and London: Harvard University Press, 2008.

Cox, Karen L. *Dixie's Daughters: The United Daughters of the Confederacy and the Preservation of Southern Culture*. Gainesville: University Press of Florida, 2003.

Cramer, Renée Ann. *Cash, Color, and Colonialism: The Politics of Tribal Acknowledgment*. Norman: University of Oklahoma Press, 2005.

Creet, Julia. "The Archive as Temporary Abode." In *Memory and Migration: Multidisciplinary Approaches to Memory Studies*, edited by Creet and Andreas Kitzmann, 280–98. Toronto and Buffalo: University of Toronto Press, 2011.

———. *The Genealogical Sublime*. Amherst and Boston: University of Massachusetts Press, 2019.

———. "Genealogy and Genetics Workshop: Part 8." Filmed at the Archives of Ontario. Posted September 2018. https://juliacreet.vhx.tv/products/genealogy-and-genetics -workshop.

———. "Introduction: The Migration of Memory and Memories of Migration." In *Memory and Migration: Multidisciplinary Approaches to Memory Studies*, edited by Creet and Andreas Kitzmann, 3–26. Toronto and Buffalo: University of Toronto Press, 2011.

———, dir. "Data Mining the Deceased: Ancestry and the Business of Family." 56 minutes. Toronto, Can.: Past Productions, 2017. https://juliacreet.vhx.tv/.

Cross, Gary. *An All-Consuming Century: Why Commercialism Won in Modern America*. New York: Columbia University Press, 2000.

Cyndi's List. "About Cyndi." Last accessed March 7, 2021. http://www.cyndislist.com /aboutus/.

Dakhlia, Jocelyne. "Collective Memory and the Story of History: Lineage and Nation in a North African Oasis." *History and Theory* 32 (December 1993): 57–79.

Dalzell, Robert F., Jr. *Enterprising Elite: The Boston Associates and the World They Made*. Cambridge, Mass., and London: Harvard University Press, 1987.

Daniels, Roger. *Guarding the Golden Door: American Immigration Policy and Immigrants since 1882*. New York: Hill and Wang, 2004.

———. "United States Policy toward Asian Immigrants: Contemporary Developments in Historical Perspective." *International Journal* 48 (Spring 1993): 310–34.

Darwin, Charles. *The Variation of Animals and Plants under Domestication*. Vol. 2, with a foreword by Harriet Ritvo. Baltimore: Johns Hopkins University Press, 1998. First published 1868.

Davenport, Robert R., ed. *Hereditary Society Blue Book*. Baltimore: Genealogical Publishing Co.; Beverly Hills, Calif.: Eastwood Publishing Co., 1994.

Davies, Douglas J. *An Introduction to Mormonism*. Cambridge: Cambridge University Press, 2003.

Davies, Wallace Evan. *Patriotism on Parade: The Story of Veterans' Organizations and Hereditary Organizations in America, 1783–1900*. Cambridge, Mass.: Harvard University Press, 1955.

Davis, Floyd James. *Who Is Black? One Nation's Definition*. University Park, Pa.: Pennsylvania State University Press, 1991.

Dawkins, Richard, with Yan Wong. *The Ancestor's Tale: A Pilgrimage to the Dawn of Life*. London: Weidenfeld & Nicholson, 2004.

Day, Caroline Bond. *A Study of Some Negro-White Families in the United States*. Westport, Conn.: Negro Universities Press, 1970. First published 1932.

Daynes, Kathryn M. *More Wives than One: Transformation of the Mormon Marriage System, 1840–1910*. Urbana and Chicago: University of Illinois Press, 2001.

De Hart, Jane Sherron, and Donald G. Mathews. *Sex, Gender, and the Politics of ERA: A State and the Nation*. New York: Oxford University Press, 1990.

Delaney, Carol. "Cutting the Ties That Bind: The Sacrifice of Abraham and Patriarchal Kinship." In *Relative Values: Reconfiguring Kinship Studies*, edited by Sarah Franklin and Susan McKinnon, 445–67. Durham, N.C., and London: Duke University Press, 2001.

Delegard, Kirsten Marie. *Battling Miss Bolsheviki: The Origins of Female Conservatism in the United States*. Philadelphia: University of Pennsylvania Press, 2012.

Delmont, Matthew F. *Making* Roots: *A Nation Captivated*. Berkeley and Los Angeles: University of California Press, 2016.

DeLucia, Christine M. *Memory Lands: King Philip's War and the Place of Violence in the Northeast*. New Haven and London: Yale University Press, 2018.

D'Emilio, John. *Sexual Politics, Sexual Communities: The Making of a Homosexual Minority in the United States, 1940–1970*. Chicago and London: University of Chicago Press, 1983.

D'Emilio, John, and Estelle B. Freedman. *Intimate Matters: A History of Sexuality in America*. 2nd ed. Chicago: University of Chicago Press, 1997.

De Platt, Lyman. *Genealogical Historical Guide to Latin America*. Detroit: Gale Research Company, 1978.

Derry, Margaret E. *Horses in Society: A Story of Animal Breeding and Marketing, 1800–1920*. Toronto and London: University of Toronto Press, 2006.

Des Jardins, Julie. *Women and the Historical Enterprise in America: Gender, Race, and the Politics of Memory, 1880–1945*. Chapel Hill: University of North Carolina Press, 2003.

Dew, Charles B. *The Making of a Racist: A Southerner Reflects on Family History, Slavery, and the Slave Trade*. Charlottesville and London: University of Virginia Press, 2016.

DeWitt, Petra. *Degrees of Allegiance: Harassment and Loyalty in Missouri's German-American Community during World War I*. Athens: Ohio University Press, 2012.

Dezember, Ryan. "Ancestry.com Sets $1.6 Billion Deal." *Wall Street Journal*, October 22, 2012. http://www.wsj.com/articles/SB10001424052970203406404578071390645955994.

DiMaggio, Paul. "Cultural Entrepreneurship in Nineteenth-Century Boston: The Creation of an Organizational Base for High Culture in America." *Media, Culture and Society* 3 (January 1982): 33–50.

Diner, Hasia R. *We Remember with Reverence and Love: American Jews and the Myth of Silence about the Holocaust, 1945–1962*. New York: New York University Press, 2009.

Dinnerstein, Leonard. *Anti-Semitism in America*. Oxford and New York: Oxford University Press, 1994.

Doane, Gilbert Harry. *Searching for Your Ancestors: The Why and How of Genealogy*. New York and London: Whittlesey House/McGraw Hill Book Company, 1937.

Dominguez, Virginia R. *White by Definition: Social Classification in Creole Louisiana*. New Brunswick, N.J.: Rutgers University Press, 1986.

Dorman, John Frederick. "Virginia." In *Genealogical Research: Methods and Sources*, by the American Society of Genealogists. Vol. 1, 281–93. Rev. ed. Washington, D.C.: The American Society of Genealogists, 1980.

Douglass, Frederick. *Autobiographies*. Edited by Henry Louis Gates Jr. New York: Library of America, 1994.

Drakes, Gail. "Who Owns Your Archive? Historians and the Challenge of Intellectual Property Law." In *Doing Recent History: On Privacy, Copyright, Video Games, Institutional Review Boards, Activist Scholarship, and History That Talks Back*, edited by Claire Bond Potter and Renee C. Romano, 83–111. Athens and London: University of Georgia Press, 2012.

Draznin, Yaffa. *The Family Historian's Handbook*. New York: Jove Publications, 1978.

Drury, Doreen M. "Love, Ambition, and 'Invisible Footnotes' in the Life and Writing of Pauli Murray." *Souls* 11, no. 3 (2009): 295–309.

Du Bois, W. E. B. *The Souls of Black Folk*. Edited with an introduction by David W. Blight and Robert Gooding-Williams. Boston: Bedford Books, 1997.

Duncan, Russell. *Where Death and Glory Meet: Colonel Robert Gould Shaw and the Massachusetts 54th Massachusetts Infantry*. Athens: University of Georgia Press, 1999.

Duster, Troy. *Backdoor to Eugenics*. New York: Routledge, 1990.

———. "Welcome, Freshmen. DNA Swabs, Please." *Chronicle of Higher Education*, May 28, 2010. https://www.chronicle.com/article/welcome-freshmen-dna-swabs-please/M.

Eagleton, Terry. *Ideology: An Introduction*. London and New York: Verso, 1991.

Eakle, Arlene, and Johni Cerny, eds. *The Source: A Guidebook of American Genealogy*. Salt Lake City: Ancestry Publishing Company, 1984.

Eastman, Dick. "Eastman's Online Genealogy Newsletter." https://eogn.com/.

Ebron, Paulla. "Tourists as Pilgrims: Commercial Fashioning of Transatlantic Politics." *American Ethnologist* 26 (November 1999): 910–32.

Ehrenreich, Eric. *The Nazi Ancestral Proof: Genealogy, Racial Science, and the Final Solution*. Bloomington: Indiana University Press, 2007.

Ellenson, David. "Zionism in the Mind of the American Rabbinate during the 1940s." In *The Americanization of the Jews*, edited by Robert M. Seltzer and Norman J. Cohen, 193–212. New York: New York University Press, 1995.

Emerson, Ralph Waldo. *English Traits*. Edited with an introduction by Howard Mumford Jones. Cambridge, Mass.: Harvard University Press, 1966. First published 1856.

Encyclopaedia Britannica. "John Harvard," June 9, 2006. https://www.britannica.com /biography/John-Harvard.

Enke, Anne. *Finding the Movement: Sexuality, Contested Space, and Feminist Activism*. Durham, N.C.: Duke University Press, 2007.

Episcopal News Service. "First Woman Regularly Ordained to Episcopal Priesthood." The Archives of the Episcopal Church. January 6, 1977. Last accessed March 7, 2021. http://www.episcopalarchives.org/cgi-bin/ENS/ENSpress_release.pl?pr_number=77002.

Everton, George B., Sr. *The How Book for Genealogists.* 7th ed. Logan, Utah: Everton Publishers, 1971.

Everton, Walter M. *The Everton Knowles Book: The Life Story of Walter Marion Everton with Some Account of Their Ancestors and Their Descendants.* Typescript, November 1942.

Eyre, William. *The Real ID Act: Privacy and Government Surveillance.* El Paso, Tex.: LFB Scholarly Publishing, 2011.

Faderman, Lillian. *Odd Girls and Twilight Lovers: A History of Lesbian Life in Twentieth-Century America.* New York: Penguin Books, 1992. First published 1991.

Falley, Margaret Dickson. *Irish and Scots-Irish Ancestral Research: A Guide to the Genealogical Records, Methods and Sources in Ireland.* 2 vols. Strasburg, Va.: Shenandoah Publishing House, 1961–62.

Farley, John. *Gametes and Spores: Ideas about Sexual Reproduction, 1750–1914.* Baltimore and London: Johns Hopkins University Press, 1982.

Farmer, John. *A Genealogical Register of the First Settlers of New-England.* Lancaster, Mass.: Carter, Andrews, & Co., 1829.

Farnham, Alex. "Who's Your Daddy? Genealogy Becomes a $1.6B Hobby." *ABC News,* October 24, 2012. http://abcnews.go.com/Business/genealogy-hot-hobby-worth-16b-mormons/story?id=17544242.

Faust, Drew Gilpin. *This Republic of Suffering: Death and the American Civil War.* New York: Alfred A. Knopf, 2008.

Fermaglich, Kirsten. *A Rosenberg by Any Other Name: A History of Jewish Name Changing in America.* New York: New York University Press, 2018.

———. "'What's Uncle Sam's Last Name?': Jews and Name Changing in New York City during the World War II Era." *Journal of American History* 102 (December 2015): 719–45.

Ferris, Mary Walton, comp. *Dawes-Gates Ancestral Lines.* 2nd ed. 2 vols. Milwaukee, Wis.: privately published, 1943.

Fifty Years of Achievement: History of the Daughters of the Republic of Texas, Together with the Charter, By-Laws, Constitution and List of Members. Dallas: Banks Upshaw and Company. 1942.

Filby, P. William, ed., with Mary K. Meyer. *Passenger and Immigration Lists Index.* 1st ed. 3 vols. Detroit: Gale Research Company, 1981.

Filby, P. William, ed., with Dorothy M. Lower. *Passenger and Immigration Lists Index: 1986–1990 Cumulated Supplements.* 3 vols. Detroit: Gale Research, 1990.

Firth, Lucy, and Eric Blyth. "Assisted Reproductive Technology in the U.S.A.: Is More Regulation Needed?" *Reproductive Medicine Online* 29 (October 2014): 516–23. https://www.rbmojournal.com/article/S1472–6483(14)00368-X/fulltext.

Fitzpatrick, Ellen. *History's Memory: Writing America's Past, 1880–1980.* Cambridge, Mass., and London: Harvard University Press, 2002.

Flake, Kathleen. *The Politics of American Religious Identity: The Seating of Senator Reed Smoot, Mormon Apostle.* Chapel Hill: University of North Carolina Press, 2004.

Flanders, Robert Bruce. *Nauvoo: Kingdom on the Mississippi.* Urbana: University of Illinois Press, 1965.

Foner, Eric. *Reconstruction, 1863–1877: America's Unfinished Revolution.* New York: Harper and Row, 1988.

Formisano, Ronald P. *Boston Against Busing: Race, Class, and Ethnicity in the 1960s and 1970s.* Chapel Hill: University of North Carolina Press, 2004.

Foster, Eugene A., M. A. Jobling, P. G. Taylor, P. Donnelly, P. DeKnijf, Rene Mieremet, T. Zerjal, and C. Tyler-Smith. "Jefferson Fathered Slave's Last Child." *Nature* 396, no. 6706 (November 5, 1998): 27–28.

Foucault, Michel. *The History of Sexuality: An Introduction,* Vol. 1. Translated by Robert Hurley. New York: Vintage Books, 1990. First published 1978.

———. "Nietzsche, Genealogy, History." In *Essential Works of Foucault, 1954–1984,* Vol. 2. Edited by James D. Faubion, translated by Robert Hurley and others, 369–91. New York: The New Press, 1998.

———. *Power/Knowledge: Selected Interviews and Other Writings, 1972–1977.* Edited by Colin Gordon; translated by Gordon, Leo Marshall, John Mepham, and Kate Soper. New York: Pantheon, 1980.

Frady, Marshall. "The Children of Malcolm." *The New Yorker* (October 12, 1992): 65–81.

Franklin, Benjamin. *The Autobiography of Benjamin Franklin, with Related Documents,* edited with an introduction by Louis P. Masur. 2nd ed. Boston and New York: Bedford/St. Martin's, 2003.

Franklin, Sarah. "Biologization Revisited: Kinship Theory in the Context of the New Biologies." In *Relative Values: Reconfiguring Kinship Studies,* edited by Franklin and Susan McKinnon, 302–25. Durham, N.C., and London: Duke University Press, 2001.

Franklin, Sarah, with Donna Haraway. "Staying with the Manifesto: An Interview with Donna Haraway." *Theory, Culture, and Society* 34 (July 2017): 49–63.

Franklin, Sarah, and Susan McKinnon, eds. *Relative Values: Reconfiguring Kinship Studies.* Durham, N.C., and London: Duke University Press, 2001.

Fraser, Steve, and Gary Gerstle, eds. *Ruling America: A History of Wealth and Power in a Democracy.* Cambridge, Mass., and London: Harvard University Press, 2005.

Fredrickson, George M. *The Black Image in the White Mind: The Debate on Afro-American Character and Destiny, 1817–1914.* New York: Harper & Row, 1971.

Friedan, Betty. *The Feminine Mystique.* Edited by Kirsten Fermaglich and Lisa M. Fine. New York: W. W. Norton, 2013. First published 1963.

Fulton, Crystal. "The Genealogist's Information World: Creating Information in the Pursuit of a Hobby." *Journal of Multidisciplinary Research* 8 (Spring 2016): 85–100.

Gabel, Lauren K. "'By this you see we are but dust': The Gravestone Art and Epitaphs of Our Ancestors." In *The Art of Family: Genealogical Artifacts in New England,* edited by D. Brenton Simons and Peter Benes, 150–75. Boston: New England Historic Genealogical Society, 2002.

Gabriel, Abram. "A Biologist's Perspective on DNA and Race." In *Genetics and the Unsettled Past: The Collision of DNA, Race, and History,* edited by Keith Wailoo, Alondra Nelson, and Catherine Lee, 43–66. New Brunswick, N.J.: Rutgers University Press, 2012.

Gaines, Kevin K. *African Americans in Ghana: Black Expatriates and the Civil Rights Era.* Chapel Hill: University of North Carolina Press, 2006.

———. *Uplifting the Race: Black Leadership, Politics, and Culture in the Twentieth Century.* Chapel Hill: University of North Carolina Press, 1996.

Galton, Francis. *Record of Family Faculties; consisting of Tabular Forms and Directions for Entering Data, with an Explanatory Preface*. London: Macmillan, 1884.

Galvin, John T. *The Gentleman Mr. Shattuck: A Biography of Henry Lee Shattuck, 1879–1971*. Boston: Tontine Press, 1996.

Gardner, Marvin K. "General Authorities." In *Encyclopedia of Mormonism: The History, Scripture, Doctrine, and Procedure of The Church of Jesus Christ of Latter-day Saints*, edited by Daniel H. Ludlow, 538–40. New York: Macmillan Publishing Company, 1992.

Garroutte, Eva Marie. *Real Indians: Identity and the Survival of Native America*. Berkeley and Los Angeles: University of California Press, 2003.

Gates, Henry Louis, Jr. *Finding Oprah's Roots, Finding Your Own*. New York: Crown Publishing, 2007.

———. *Stony the Road: Reconstruction, White Supremacy, and the Rise of Jim Crow*. New York: Penguin Books, 2019.

Gates, Susa Young. "Family Life Among the Mormons." *North American Review* 150, no. 400 (March 1890): 339–50.

———, comp. *The Brigham Young Family*. Salt Lake City: Young Family Association, n.d. (ca. 1897).

———, ed. and comp. *Surname and Racial History: A Compilation and Arrangement of Historical Data for Use of the Students and Members of the Relief Society of the Church of Jesus Christ of Latter-day Saints*. Salt Lake City: n.p., 1918.

Gates, Susa Young, and Leah D. Widtsoe. *Women of the 'Mormon' Church*. Independence, Mo.: Press of Zion's Printing and Publishing Company, 1928.

Gatewood, Willard B. *Aristocrats of Color: The Black Elite, 1880–1920*. Indianapolis: Indiana University Press, 1990.

Geary, Daniel. *Beyond Civil Rights: The Moynihan Report and Its Legacy*. Philadelphia: University of Pennsylvania Press, 2015.

Gelber, Steven M. *Hobbies: Leisure and the Culture of Work in America*. New York: Columbia University Press, 1999.

Gelman, David, Betsy Carter, Peter S. Greenberg, Martin Kasindorf, and Pamela Ellis Simons. "Everybody's Search for Roots: Better than Bingo?" *Newsweek*, July 4, 1977, 26.

Gibson, Campbell J., and Kay Jung. "Historical Census Statistics on Population Totals by Race, 1790 to 1990, and by Hispanic Origin, 1970 to 1990, for the United States, Regions, Divisions, and States." Working Paper No. 56, September 2002. https://www.census .gov/content/dam/Census/library/working-papers/2002/demo/POP-twps0056.pdf.

Gillis, John R. *A World of Their Own Making: Myth, Ritual, and the Quest for Family Values*. New York: Basic Books, 1996.

Gilman, Sander L. "There Ain't No There There: Reimagining Eastern European Jewish Culture in the 21st Century." *Shofar* 25 (Fall 2006): 1–4.

Gilmore, Glenda Elizabeth. *Defying Dixie: The Radical Roots of Civil Rights, 1919–1950*. New York: W. W. Norton & Company, 2008.

———, *Gender and Jim Crow: Women and Politics of White Supremacy in North Carolina, 1896–1920*. Chapel Hill: University of North Carolina Press, 1996.

———, "Murder, Memory, and the Flight of the Incubus." In *Democracy Betrayed: The Wilmington Race Riot of 1898 and Its Legacy*, edited by David S. Cecelski and Timothy B. Tyson, 73–94. Chapel Hill: University of North Carolina Press, 1998.

Ginzberg, Lori D. *Untidy Origins: A Story of Woman's Rights in Antebellum New York.* Chapel Hill: University of North Carolina Press, 2005.

Glenn, Susan A. "In the Blood? Consent, Descent, and the Ironies of Jewish Identity." *Jewish Social Studies* 8 (Winter/Spring 2002): 139–52.

Godbeer, Richard. *Sexual Revolution in Early America.* Baltimore: Johns Hopkins University Press, 2002.

Goetz, Rebecca Anne. *The Baptism of Early Virginia: How Christianity Created Race.* Baltimore: Johns Hopkins University Press, 2012.

Goldstein, Eric L. *The Price of Whiteness: Jews, Race, and Identity.* Princeton, N.J.: Princeton University Press, 2008.

Goleman, Michael J. *Your Heritage Will Still Remain: Racial Identity and Mississippi's Lost Cause.* Jackson: University Press of Mississippi, 2017.

Goody, Jack. *The Development of the Family and Marriage in Europe.* Cambridge: Cambridge University Press, 1983.

Gordon, Margaret E. P. *Pansy's History: The Autobiography of Margaret E. P. Gordon, 1866–1966.* Edited and annotated by Claudia L. Bushman. Logan, Utah: Utah State University Press, 2011.

Gordon, Sarah Barringer. *The Mormon Question: Polygamy and Constitutional Conflict in Nineteenth-Century America.* Chapel Hill: University of North Carolina Press, 2002.

Gordon, Tammy S. *The Spirit of 1976: Commerce, Community, and the Politics of Commemoration.* Amherst and Boston: University of Massachusetts Press, 2013.

Gordon-Reed, Annette. *The Hemingses of Monticello: An American Family.* New York: W. W. Norton, 2008.

———. *Thomas Jefferson and Sally Hemings: An American Controversy.* Charlottesville and London: University Press of Virginia, 1997.

Goren, Arthur A. *The Politics and Public Culture of American Jews.* Bloomington and Indianapolis: Indiana University Press, 1999.

Gorn, Elliott J. "Introduction: Educating America." In *The McGuffey Readers: Selections from the 1879 Edition*, edited by Elliott Gorn, 1–36. Boston: Bedford/St. Martin's, 1998.

Gottheil, Richard James Horatio. *The Belmont-Belmonte Family: A Record of Four Hundred Years.* New York: privately published, 1917.

Gover, Kirsty. *Tribal Constitutionalism: States, Tribes, and the Governance of Membership.* New York: Oxford University Press, 2010.

Gray, John S., III. "Majors, Monroe Alpheus." Texas State Historical Association, 2010. https://tshaonline.org/handbook/online/articles/fmacq.

Greely, Henry T. *The End of Sex and the Future of Human Reproduction.* Cambridge, Mass., and London: Harvard University Press, 2016.

———. "Genetic Genealogy: Genetics Meets the Marketplace." In *Revisiting Race in a Genomic Age*, edited by Barbara A. Koenig, Sandra Soo-Jin Lee, and Sarah Richardson, 215–35. Piscataway, N.J.: Rutgers University Press, 2008.

Greene, Daniel. *The Jewish Origins of Cultural Pluralism: The Menorah Association and American Diversity.* Bloomington and Indianapolis: Indiana University Press, 2011.

Grieco, Elizabeth M., Yesenia D. Acosta, Patricia de la Cruz, Christine Gambino, Thomas Gryn, Luke J. Larsen, Edward N. Trevelyan, and Nathan P. Walters. "The Foreign-Born

Population in the United States: 2010." U. S. Census Bureau, Library. May 2012. https:// www.census.gov/library/publications/2012/acs/acs-19.html.

Grier, Katherine C. *Pets in America: A History*. Chapel Hill: University of North Carolina Press, 2006.

Groot, Jerome de. "Ancestry.com and the Evolving Nature of Historical Information Companies." *Public Historian* 42 (February 2020): 8–28.

———. "Genealogy and Family History." In *Consuming History: Historians and Heritage in Contemporary Popular Culture*, 71–86. 2nd ed. London and New York: Routledge, 2016.

———. "The Genealogy Boom: Inheritance, Family History, and the Popular Historical Imagination." In *The Impact of History? Histories at the Beginning of the 21st Century*, edited by Bernard Taithe and Pedro Ramos Pinto, 21–34. New York: Routledge, 2015.

———. "On Genealogy." *The Public Historian* 37 (August 2015): 102–27.

———. "History on Television: Reality, Professional Reality, Celebrity and Object History." In *Consuming History: Historians and Heritage in Contemporary Popular Culture*, 183–214. 2nd ed. London and New York: Routledge, 2016.

Gross, Ariela. *What Blood Won't Tell: A History of Race on Trial in America*. Cambridge, Mass.: Harvard University Press, 2008.

Grow, Matthew J. "Contesting the LDS Image: The *North American Review* and the Mormons, 1881–1907." *Journal of Mormon History* 32 (Summer 2006): 111–38.

Guelke, Jeanne Kay, and Dallen J. Timothy. "Locating Personal Pasts: An Introduction." In *Geography and Genealogy: Locating Personal Pasts*, edited by Timothy and Guelke, 1–22. Aldershot, U.K., and Burlington, Vt.: Ashgate Publishing, Ltd., 2008.

Gustaitis, Joseph. *Chicago Transformed: World War I and the Windy City*. Carbondale: Southern Illinois University Press, 2016.

Gutman, Herbert G. *The Black Family in Slavery and Freedom, 1750–1925*. New York: Vintage Books, 1976.

Hackstaff, Karla B. "Who Are We? Genealogists Negotiating Ethno-Racial Identities." *Qualitative Sociology* 32 (June 2009): 173–94.

Hale, Grace Elizabeth. *Making Whiteness: The Culture of Segregation in the South, 1890–1940*. New York: Pantheon Books, 1998.

Haley, Alex. "Blacks, Oral History, and Genealogy." *Oral History Review* 1 (1973): 1–25.

———. "Family: A Humanizing Force." *World Conference on Records: Preserving Our Heritage, August 12-15, 1980*. Vol. 1, 8–18. FamilySearch Digital Library, Church of Jesus Christ of Latter-day Saints. https://www.familysearch.org.

———. "Hope Springs Eternal." *Atlantic Monthly* 195 (January 1955): 89–90.

———. "My Search for Roots." *Tuesday Magazine* 1 (October 1965): 4–7.

———. "My Search for Roots: A Black American's Story." *Reader's Digest* (May 1974): 73–78.

———. *Roots: The Saga of an American Family*. New York: Dell Publishing, 1977. First published 1976.

———. "What *Roots* Means to Me" (May 1977). In *Reader's Digest, Alex Haley: The Man Who Traced America's Roots*, 159–62. New York: Reader's Digest Association, 2007.

Halloran, Liz. "How Vermont's 'Civil' War Fueled the Gay-Marriage Movement." *All Things Considered*, National Public Radio, March 23, 2013. http://www.npr.org/2013 /03/27/174651233/how-vermonts-civil-war-fueled-the-gay-marriage-movement.

Hamilton, Jennifer A. "The Case of the Genetic Ancestor." In *Genetics and the Unsettled Past: The Collision of DNA, Race, and History*, edited by Keith Wailoo, Alondra Nelson, and Catherine Lee, 266–78. New Brunswick, N.J.: Rutgers University Press, 2012.

Hammack, Philip L., David M. Frost, and Sam D. Hughes. "Queer Intimacies: A New Paradigm for the Study of Relationship Diversity." *Journal of Sex Research* 56 (May/June 2019): 556–92.

Hansen, Klaus J. *Mormonism and the American Experience*. Chicago and London: University of Chicago Press, 1981.

Hansen, Marcus Lee. *The Problem of the Third Generation Immigrant*. Rock Island, Ill.: Augustana College Library, 1987. First published 1938.

Haraway, Donna. *Modest_Witness@Second_Millennium.FemaleMan_Meets_OncoMouse: Feminism and Technoscience*. New York: Routledge, 1997.

Hareven, Tamara K. "The Search for Generational Memory: Tribal Rites in Industrial Society." *Daedalus* 107 (Fall 1978): 137–49.

Harper, Steven C. "'Dictated by Christ': Joseph Smith and the Politics of Revelation." *Journal of the Early Republic* 26 (Summer 2006), 275–304.

Harris, Amy L. "A Genealogical Turn: Possibilities for Mormon Studies and Genealogical Scholarship." *Mormon Studies Review* 5 (2018): 73–88.

Hartley, George. "*I Am Joaquín*: Rodolfo 'Corky' Gonzales and the Retroactive Construction of Chicanismo." In *The Latino/a Condition: A Critical Reader*, edited by Richard Delgado and Jean Stefancic, 241–48. 2nd ed. New York: New York University Press, 2011.

Hartley, William G. "From Men to Boys: LDS Aaronic Priesthood Offices, 1829–1996." *Journal of Mormon History* 22, no. 1 (1996): 80–136.

Hartman, Saidiya. *Lose Your Mother: A Journey Along the Atlantic Slave Route*. New York: Farrar, Straus, and Giroux, 2007.

Hasty, Jennifer. "Rites of Passage, Routes of Redemption: Emancipation Tourism and the Wealth of Culture." *Africa Today* 49, no. 3 (Autumn 2002): 47–76.

Hawkins, Mike. *Social Darwinism in European and American Thought, 1860–1945: Nature as Model and Nature as Threat*. Cambridge: Cambridge University Press, 1997.

Haws, J. B. *The Mormon Image in the American Mind: Fifty Years of Public Perception*. New York: Oxford University Press, 2013.

Hays, Samuel P. "History and Genealogy: Patterns of Change and Prospects for Cooperation." In *Generations and Change: Genealogical Perspectives in Social History*, edited by Robert M. Taylor, Jr., and Ralph J. Crandall, 29–52. Mercer, Ga.: Mercer University Press, 1986.

Heaton, Tim B., and Sandra Calkins. "Family Size and Contraceptive Use among Mormons: 1965–75." *Review of Religious Research* 25 (December 1983): 102–13.

Hering, Katharina. "Palatines or Pennsylvania German Pioneers? The Development of Transatlantic Pennsylvania German Family and Migration History, 1890s–1966." *Pennsylvania Magazine of History and Biography* 140 (October 2016): 305–34.

Herman, Ellen. *Kinship by Design: A History of Adoption in the Modern United States*. Chicago: University of Chicago Press, 2008.

Hershkovitz, Arnon. "Editorial: Genealogy and Family History through Multiple Academic Lenses: An Introduction to the Special Issue." *Journal of Multidisciplinary Research* 8 (Spring 2016): 5–10.

Hertzel, David. *Ancestors: Who We Are and Where We Come From.* Lanham, Md.: Rowman & Littlefield, 2017.

Hiden, Martha W. "Virginia." In *Genealogical Research: Methods and Sources, by the American Society of Genealogists,* edited by Milton Rubincam, 212–20. Washington, D.C.: The American Society of Genealogists, 1960.

Higham, John. *Strangers in the Land: Patterns of American Nativism, 1890–1925.* 2nd ed. New York: Atheneum, 1963.

Hijiya, James A. "Roots: Family and Ethnicity in the 1970s." *American Quarterly* 30 (Autumn 1978): 548–56.

Hillstrom, Kevin. *Defining Moments: The Internet Revolution.* Detroit: Omnigraphics, 2005.

Hilton, Suzanne. *Who Do You Think You Are? Digging for Your Family Roots.* Philadelphia: Westminster Press, 1976.

Hobsbawm, Eric J. *The Age of Empire, 1875–1914.* New York: Vintage Books, 1989. First published 1987.

———. "Mass-Producing Traditions: Europe, 1870–1914." In *The Invention of Tradition,* edited by Hobsbawm and Terence Ranger, 263–307. Cambridge: Cambridge University Press, 1983.

Hoffert, Sylvia D. "Female Self-Making in Mid-Nineteenth-Century America." *Journal of Women's History* 20 (Fall 2008): 34–59.

Hofstadter, Richard. *The Age of Reform: From Bryan to F.D.R.* New York: Vintage Books, 1955.

Hogan, Jackie. *Roots Quest: Inside America's Genealogy Boom.* Lanham, Md.: Rowman and Littlefield, 2019.

Hollinger, David A. "National Culture and Communities of Descent." *Reviews in American History* 26 (March 1998): 312–28.

Holt, Thomas C. "Du Bois, W. E. B." In *African American National Biography,* edited by Henry Louis Gates Jr. and Evelyn Brooks Higginbotham. New York: Oxford University Press, 2008. https://hutchinscenter.fas.harvard.edu/web-dubois.

Holzapfel, Richard Neitzel and Jeni Broberg Holzapfel. *Women of Nauvoo.* Salt Lake City: Bookcraft, 1992.

Hood, Clifton. *In Pursuit of Privilege: A History of New York City's Upper Classes and the Making of a Metropolis.* New York: Columbia University Press, 2017.

Horn, James, Jan Ellen Lewis, and Peter S. Onuf, eds. *The Revolution of 1800: Democracy, Race, and the New Republic.* Charlottesville: University of Virginia Press, 2002.

Horowitz, Helen Lefkowitz. *Culture and the City: Cultural Philanthropy in Chicago from the 1880s to 1917.* Chicago and London: University of Chicago Press, 1989. First published 1976.

———. *Rereading Sex: Battles over Sexual Knowledge and Suppression in Nineteenth-Century America.* New York: Alfred A. Knopf, 2002.

Horsman, Reginald. *Race and Manifest Destiny: The Origins of American Racial Anglo-Saxonism.* Cambridge, Mass.: Harvard University Press, 1981.

Horwitz, Tony. *Confederates in the Attic: Dispatches from the Unfinished Civil War.* New York: Vintage Books, 1998.

Hough, Mazie. *Rural Unwed Mothers: An American Experience, 1870–1950.* Brookfield, Vt., and London: Pickering & Chatto, 2010.

House Divided: The Civil War Research Engine at Dickinson College. "Seddon, James Alexander." Carlisle, Pa.: Dickinson College, 2007–16. Last accessed March 7, 2021. http://hd.housedivided.dickinson.edu/node/6547.

Howard, John. *Men Like That: A Southern Queer History*. Chicago and London: University of Chicago Press, 1999.

Howe, Irving. "The Limits of Ethnicity." *The New Republic* (June 25, 1977): 17–19.

———. "Tevye on Broadway." *Commentary* 38 (November 1964): 73–75.

———. *World of Our Fathers*. New York: Harcourt Brace Jovanovich, 1976.

Howells, Cyndi. "Cyndi's List." *Utne Reader* (May–June 1999): 78.

Hudson, Michelle. "The Effect of 'Roots' and the Bicentennial on Genealogical Interest among Patrons of the Mississippi Department of Archives and History." *Journal of Mississippi History* 53, no. 4 (1991): 321–36.

Hulbert, Ann. *Raising America: Experts, Parents, and a Century of Advice about Children*. New York: Knopf, 2003.

Hunter, Tera W. *Bound in Wedlock: Slave and Free Black Marriage in the Nineteenth Century*. Cambridge, Mass., and London: Harvard University Press, 2017.

Ingold, Tim. *Lines: A Brief History*. London and New York: Routledge, 2007.

Is That Lineage Right? A Training Manual for the Examiner of Lineage Papers, With Helpful Hints for the Beginner in Genealogy Research. Washington, D.C.: National Society Daughters of the American Revolution, 1958.

Isenberg, Nancy. *White Trash: The 400-Year Untold History of Class in America*. New York: Viking, 2016.

Jackson, Buzzy. *Shaking the Family Tree: Blue Bloods, Black Sheep, and Other Obsessions of an Accidental Genealogist*. New York: Touchstone, 2010.

Jackson, Lawrence P. *My Father's Name: A Black Virginia Family after the Civil War*. Chicago and London: University of Chicago Press, 2012.

Jacobs, A. J. "Are You My Cousin?" *New York Times*, January 31, 2014.

———. *It's All Relative: Adventures Up and Down the World's Family Tree*. New York: Simon and Schuster, 2017.

Jacobs, Harriet A. *Incidents in the Life of a Slave Girl, Written by Herself*. New York: Penguin Books, 2000. First published 1861.

Jacobsen, Phebe R. "The World Turned Upside Down: Reference Priorities and the State Archives." *American Archivist* 44 (Fall 1981): 341–45.

Jacobson, Judy. *History for Genealogists: Using Chronological Time Lines to Find and Understand Your Ancestors*. Rev. ed. Baltimore: Genealogical Publishing Company for Clearfield Publishing, 2016.

Jacobson, Matthew Frye. *Roots Too: White Ethnic Revival in Post–Civil Rights America*. Cambridge, Mass.: Harvard University Press, 2006.

———. *Whiteness of a Different Color: European Immigrants and the Alchemy of Race*. Cambridge, Mass., and London: Harvard University Press, 1998.

Jacobus, Donald Lines. *Genealogy as Pastime and Profession*. New Haven, Conn.: The Tuttle, Morehouse & Taylor Company, 1930.

———. *Genealogy as Pastime and Profession*. 2nd ed., revised. Baltimore: Genealogical Publishing Company, 1968.

———. "Haphazard Eugenics." *The North American Review* 228, no. 840 (February 1928): 168–74.

———, comp., with the assistance of Edgar Francis Waterman. *The Waterman Family.* 3 vols. New Haven, Conn.: The Tuttle, Morehouse, & Taylor Company, 1939–54.

Janney, Caroline E. *Burying the Dead but Not the Past: Ladies' Memorial Associations and the Lost Cause.* Chapel Hill: University of North Carolina Press, 2008.

———. *Remembering the Civil War: Reunion and the Limits of Reconciliation.* Chapel Hill: University of North Carolina Press, 2013.

Jardin, André. *Tocqueville: A Biography.* New York: Farrar Straus Giroux, 1988.

Jefferson, Thomas. "Letter to Samuel Kercheval," June 12, 1816. Published by the U.S. National Archives and Records Administration, Founders Online. Last accessed March 7, 2021. https://founders.archives.gov/documents/Jefferson/03-10-02-0128-0002.

Jelks, Joyce E., and Janice White Sikes. "Approaches to Black Family History." *Library Trends* 32 (Summer 1983): 139–51.

Johnson, David K. *The Lavender Scare: The Cold War Persecution of Gays and Lesbians in the Federal Government.* Chicago: University of Chicago Press, 2004.

Johnson, Susan Lee. *Writing Kit Carson: Fallen Heroes in a Changing West.* Chapel Hill: University of North Carolina Press, 2020.

———. "Writing Kit Carson in the Cold War: 'The Family,' 'The West,' and Their Chroniclers." In *On the Borders of Love and Power: Families and Kinship in the Intercultural American Southwest,* edited by David Wallace Adams and Crista DeLuzio, 278–318. Berkeley and Los Angeles: University of California Press, 2012.

Johnston, James H. *From Slave Ship to Harvard: Yarrow Mamout and the History of an African American Family.* New York: Fordham University Press, 2012.

Jones, Nicholas A., and Jungmiwha Bullock. "The Two or More Races Population: 2010: 2010 Census Briefs." U.S. Census Bureau. September 2012. https://www.census.gov/prod/cen2010/briefs/c2010br-13.pdf.

Jordan, David Starr, and Sarah Louise Kimball. *Your Family Tree: Being a Glance at Scientific Aspects of Genealogy, with a Variety of Illustrative Examples from the Lineage of Families Prominent in America and Great Britain.* New York and London: D. Appleton and Company, 1929.

Kaplan, Justin, and Anne Bernays. *The Language of Names.* New York: Simon and Schuster, 1997.

Karlsen, Carol F. *Devil in the Shape of a Woman: Witchcraft in Colonial New England.* New York: W. W. Norton, 1987.

Kassow, Samuel. "Shtetl." YIVO Institute for Jewish Research, *The YIVO Encyclopedia of Jews in Eastern Europe.* 2010. http://www.yivoencyclopedia.org/article.aspx/Shtetl#author.

Kazal, Russell A. *Becoming Old Stock: The Paradox of German-American Identity.* Princeton and Oxford: Princeton University Press, 2004.

Keller, Evelyn Fox. *The Century of the Gene.* Cambridge, Mass., and London: Harvard University Press, 2000.

Kelley, Blair L. M. *Right to Ride: Streetcar Boycotts and African American Citizenship in the Era of Plessy v. Ferguson.* Chapel Hill: University of North Carolina Press, 2010.

Kelner, Shaul. *Tours That Bind: Diaspora, Pilgrimage, and Israeli Birthright Tourism.* New York: New York University Press, 2010.

Kenneally, Christine. *The Invisible History of the Human Race: How DNA and History Shape Our Identities and Our Futures.* New York: Viking, 2014.

Kennedy, David M. *Freedom from Fear: The American People in Depression and War, 1929–1945.* New York: Oxford University Press, 1999.

Kerber, Linda K. *"No Constitutional Right to Be Ladies": Women and the Obligations of Citizenship.* New York: Hill and Wang, 1998.

Kerrison, Catherine. *Jefferson's Daughters: Three Sisters, White and Black, in a Young America.* New York: Ballantine Books, 2018.

Kessel, Barbara. *Suddenly Jewish: Jews Raised as Gentiles Discover Their Jewish Roots.* Hanover and London: Brandeis University Press/University Press of New England, 2000.

Kiel, Doug. "'Bleeding Out': Histories and Legacies of 'Indian Blood.'" In *The Great Vanishing Act: Blood Quantum and the Future of Native Nations,* edited by Kathleen Ratteree and Norbert Hill, 80–97. Golden, Colo.: Fulcrum Publishing, 2017.

Kimmick, Elizabeth, comp. and ed. *History of the New Mexico State Organization of the National Society, Daughters of the American Revolution.* n.p., 1957.

Kiron, Arthur. "Mythologizing 1654." *Jewish Quarterly Review* 94 (Autumn 2004): 583–94.

Klapisch-Zuber, Christiane. "The Genesis of the Family Tree." *I Tatti Studies: Essays in the Renaissance* 4 (1991): 105–30.

Klatch, Rebecca E. *Women of the New Right.* Philadelphia: Temple University Press, 1987.

Klepp, Susan E. *Revolutionary Conceptions: Women, Fertility, and Family Limitation in America, 1760–1820.* Chapel Hill: University of North Carolina Press, 2009.

Kline, Wendy. *Building a Better Race: Gender, Sexuality, and Eugenics from the Turn of the Century to the Baby Boom.* Berkeley and London: University of California Press, 2001.

Knott, Cheryl. *Not Free, Not for All: Public Libraries in the Age of Jim Crow.* Amherst and Boston: University of Massachusetts Press, 2015.

Kolko, Jed, with Audie Cornish. "Fewer Americans Are Moving to Pursue Jobs Across the Nation." Transcript of interview. *All Things Considered.* National Public Radio, August 4, 2017. https://www.npr.org/2017/08/04/541675186/fewer-americans-are-moving-to -pursue-better-jobs-across-the-nation?smid=nytcore-ios-share.

Korn, Bertram W. *Jewish Roots in America.* New York: The American Jewish Tercentenary, 1954.

Krah, Markus. "Further Forward Through the Past: Postwar American Jews Reconfigure the East European Tradition in Cultural Terms." *Shofar* 35 (Summer 2017): 111–55.

Krajewska, Magdalena. *Documenting Americans: A Political History of National ID Card Proposals in the United States.* Cambridge: Cambridge University Press, 2017.

Kramer, Anne-Marie. "Kinship, Affinity, and Connectedness: Exploring the Role in Genealogy in Personal Lives." *Sociology* 45, no. 3 (June 2011): 379–95.

———. "Mediatizing Memory: History, Affect, and Identity in *Who Do You Think You Are?*" *European Journal of Cultural Studies* 14, no. 4 (2011): 428–45.

Kranson, Rachel. *Ambivalent Embrace: Jewish Upward Mobility in Postwar America.* Chapel Hill: University of North Carolina Press, 2017.

Kurzweil, Arthur. *From Generation to Generation: How to Trace Your Jewish Genealogy and Personal History.* New York: William Morrow and Company, 1980.

Lamar, Mrs. Joseph Rucker (Clarinda Huntington Lamar). *A History of the National Society of the Colonial Dames of America, from 1891 to 1933.* Atlanta: The Walter W. Brown Publishing Company, 1934.

Lambert, Ronald D. "Constructing Symbolic Ancestry: Befriending Time, Confronting Death." *Omega: Journal of Death and Dying* 46, no. 4 (January 2002–3): 303–21.

———. "Descriptive, Narrative, and Experiential Pathways to Symbolic Ancestors." *Mortality* 11 (November 2006): 317–35.

Lander, Eric S., and Joseph J. Ellis. "Founding Father." *Nature* 396, no. 6706 (November 5, 1998): 13–14.

Landsberg, Alison. *Prosthetic Memory: The Transformation of American Remembrance in the Age of Mass Culture.* New York: Columbia University Press, 2004.

LaPier, Rosalyn R. and David R. M. Beck. *City Indian: Native American Activism in Chicago, 1893–1934.* Lincoln and London: University of Nebraska Press, 2015.

Laqueur, Thomas W. *The Work of the Dead: A Cultural History of Mortal Remains.* Princeton, N.J.: Princeton University Press, 2015.

"Larry Sullivan Watson." *The Lawton (Okla.) Constitution,* November 4, 2016. https:// www.swoknews.com/almanac/larry-sullivan-watson/article_e4b7f5c4-0259-54f0-8f80 -83534ad65668.html.

Lasch, Christopher. *The Culture of Narcissism: American Life in an Age of Diminishing Expectations.* New York: W. W. Norton and Company, 1978.

Laugesen, Amanda. *The Making of Public Historical Culture in the American West, 1880– 1910: The Role of Historical Societies.* Lewiston, N.Y., and Lampeter, U.K.: The Edwin Mellen Press, 2006.

LaVelle, John. "The General Allotment Act 'Eligibility' Hoax: Distortions of Law, Policy, and History in Derogation of Indian Tribes." *Wicazo Sa Review* 14 (Spring 1999): 251–302.

Lederhendler, Eli. *American Jewry: A New History.* Cambridge: Cambridge University Press, 2017.

Lenstra, Noah. "'Democratizing' Genealogy and Family Heritage Practices: The View from Urbana, Illinois." In *Encounters with Popular Pasts: Cultural Heritage and Popular Culture,* edited by Mike Robinson and Helaine Silverman, 203–18. Cham, Switzerland, and New York: Springer International, 2015.

di Leonardo, Micaela. "The Female World of Cards and Holidays: Women, Families, and the Work of Kinship." *Signs* 12 (Spring 1987): 440–53.

Lepore, Jill. *The Name of War: King Philip's War and the Origins of American Identity.* New York: Vintage Books, 1999. First published 1998.

Lerner, Gerda. "The Lady and the Mill Girl: Changes in the Status of Women in the Age of Jackson." In Lerner, *The Majority Finds Its Past: Placing Women in History,* 15–30. New York: Oxford University Press, 1979.

Levin, Kevin M. *Searching for Black Confederates: The Civil War's Most Persistent Myth.* Chapel Hill: University of North Carolina Press, 2019.

Lewis, David Levering. *W. E. B. Du Bois: Biography of a Race, 1868–1919.* New York: Henry Holt and Co., 1993.

Lewis, Earl, and Heidi Ardizzone. *Love on Trial: An American Scandal in Black and White.* New York: W. W. Norton, 2001.

Light, Alison. *Common People: In Pursuit of My Ancestors*. Chicago: University of Chicago Press, 2015.

———. "A Visit to the Dead: Genealogy and the Historian." In *History after Hobsbawm: Writing the Past for the Twenty-First Century*, edited by John H. Arnold, Matthew Hilton, and Jan Rüger, 292–305. Oxford, U.K.: Oxford University Press, 2018.

Lima, Manuel. *The Book of Trees: Visualizing Branches of Knowledge*. New York: Princeton Architectural Press, 2014.

Lind, William. "Public Records: The Census." In *Genealogical Research: Methods and Sources, by the American Society of Genealogists*. Vol. 1, 71–73. Rev. ed. Washington, D.C.: The American Society of Genealogists, 1980.

Lindgren, James M. *Preserving Historic New England: Preservation, Progressivism, and the Remaking of Memory*. New York and Oxford: Oxford University Press, 1995.

Lindsay, Lisa A. *Atlantic Bonds: A Nineteenth-Century Odyssey from America to Africa*. Chapel Hill: University of North Carolina Press, 2017.

Lineage Book, National Society of the Daughters of the American Revolution, Vol. 2, 1892. Harrisburg, Pa.: Harrisburg Publishing Co., n.d. [ca. 1892].

Lipstadt, Deborah. "America and the Memory of the Holocaust, 1950–1965." *Modern Judaism* 16 (October 1996): 195–214.

Little, Hannah. "Identifying the Genealogical Self." *Archival Science* 11, nos. 3–4 (November 2011): 241–52.

Litvak, Olga. *Conscription and the Search for Modern Russian Jewry*. Bloomington and Indianapolis: Indiana University Press, 2006.

Livingston, Jennie, dir. *Paris is Burning*. Burbank, Calif.: Miramax Home Entertainment, 2005. DVD, 78 minutes. Originally released 1990.

Lockwood, Mary S. *Lineage Book of the Charter Members of the Daughters of the American Revolution*. Rev. ed. Harrisburg, Pa.: Harrisburg Publishing Co., 1895.

Lorde, Audre. *Zami: A New Spelling of My Name: A Biomythography*. Berkeley, Calif.: Ten Speed Press, 1982.

Louie, Andrea. *Chineseness across Borders: Renegotiating Chinese Identities in China and in the United States*. Durham, N.C., and London: Duke University Press, 2004.

Lovett, Laura L. *Conceiving the Future: Pronatalism, Reproduction, and the Family in the United States, 1890–1938*. Chapel Hill: University of North Carolina Press, 2007.

Lowenthal, David. *The Heritage Crusade and the Spoils of History*. Cambridge: Cambridge University Press, 1998. First published 1996.

———. *The Past is a Foreign Country: Revisited*. Cambridge: Cambridge University Press, 2015.

Lowery, Malinda Maynor. *The Lumbee Indians: An American Struggle*. Chapel Hill: University of North Carolina Press, 2018.

Lynd, Robert, and Helen Merrell Lynd. *Middletown: A Study in Modern American Culture*. New York: Harcourt Brace & Company, 1957. First published 1929.

MacArthur, Daniel. "Genetic Ancestry Testing: People Who Don't Want to Know." *Wired* (March 8, 2010), later edited by MacArthur. https://www.wired.com/2010/03/genetic-ancestry-testing-people-who-dont-want-to-know/.

Macy, Harry, Jr. "Recognizing Scholarly Genealogy and Its Importance to Scholars and Historians." *New England Historic Genealogical Register* 150 (January 1996): 7–28.

Madsen, Carol Cornwall, ed. *In Their Own Words: Women and the Story of Nauvoo.* Salt Lake City: Deseret Book Company, 1994.

Malchelosse, Gérard. "Quebec." In *Genealogical Research: Methods and Sources, by the American Society of Genealogists,* edited by Milton Rubincam, 265–76. Washington, D.C.: The American Society of Genealogists, 1960.

Malm, Carolina Johnsson. "Genealogy and the Problem of Biological Essentialism." Blog post, published September 10, 2015. *History@Work.* http://ncph.org/history-at-work /genealogy-and-biological-essentialism/.

Malm, Carolina Johnsson, Regina Poertner, Paul Knevel, and Sara Trevisan. "Jerome de Groot on Genealogy." Blog posts, published August 7–21, 2015. *History@Work.* http:// ncph.org/history-at-work/tag/jerome-de-groot-on-genealogy/.

Mandell, Daniel R. *Tribe, Race, History: Native Americans in Southern New England, 1780–1880.* Baltimore: The Johns Hopkins University Press, 2008.

Marable, Manning. *Malcolm X: A Life of Reinvention.* New York: Viking, 2011.

Marks, Jonathan. "'We're Going to Tell These People Who They Really Are': Science and Relatedness." In *Relative Values: Reconfiguring Kinship Studies,* edited by Sarah Franklin and Susan McKinnon, 355–83. Durham, N.C., and London: Duke University Press, 2001.

Marling, Karal Ann. *George Washington Slept Here: Colonial Revivals and American Culture, 1876–1896.* Cambridge, Mass., and London: Harvard University Press, 1988.

Marquis, Albert Nelson, ed. *The Book of Chicagoans: A Biographical Dictionary of Leading Living Men of the City of Chicago.* Chicago: A. N. Marquis and Company, 1911.

Martin, Joseph Plumb. *A Narrative of a Revolutionary Soldier: Some of the Adventures, Dangers, and Sufferings of Joseph Plumb Martin.* Introduction by Thomas Fleming. Afterword by William Chad Stanley. New York: Signet Classics, 2001.

Martínez, Anne M. "Mexican Revolution." In *The Oxford Encyclopedia of Latinos and Latinas in the United States,* edited by Suzanne Oboler and Deena M. González. New York: Oxford University Press, 2005. https://www-oxfordreference-com.

Martínez, María Elena. *Genealogical Fictions: Limpieza de Sangre, Religion, and Gender in Colonial Mexico.* Stanford, Calif.: Stanford University Press, 2008.

Mathews, T. J., and Brady E. Hamilton. "Total Birth Rate by State and Race and Hispanic Origin: United States, 2017." *National Vital Statistics Reports* 68 (January 10, 2019): 1–10. U.S. Centers for Disease Control and Prevention. https://www.cdc.gov/nchs/data /nvsr/nvsr68/nvsr68_01-508.pdf.

Mauss, Armand L. *All Abraham's Children: Changing Mormon Conceptions of Race and Lineage.* Urbana and Chicago: University of Illinois Press, 2003.

———. *The Angel and the Beehive: The Mormon Struggle with Assimilation.* Urbana and Chicago: University of Illinois Press, 1994.

Maxwell, William. *Ancestors.* New York: Alfred A. Knopf, 1971.

May, Elaine Tyler. *Homeward Bound: American Families in the Cold War Era.* New York: Basic Books, 1988.

McClung, Quantrille D., comp. *Carson-Bent-Boggs Genealogy: Line of William Carson, Ancestor of "Kit" Carson, Famous Scout and Pioneer of the Rocky Mountain Area, with the Western Branches of the Bent and Boggs Families with whom "Kit" was Associated.* Denver: Denver Public Library, 1962.

McConnell, Stuart. "Reading the Flag: A Reconsideration of the Patriotic Cults of the 1890s." In *Bonds of Affection: Americans Define Their Patriotism*, edited by John Bodnar, 102–19. Princeton, N.J.: Princeton University Press, 1996.

McConville, Brendan. *The King's Three Faces: The Rise and Fall of Royal America, 1688–1776*. Chapel Hill: University of North Carolina Press, 2006.

McCoy, Donald R. "The Struggle to Establish a National Archives in the United States." In *Guardian of Heritage: Essays on the History of the National Archives*, edited by Timothy Walch. Washington, D.C.: National Archives and Records Administration, 1985. https://www.archives.gov/about/history/sources/mccoy.pdf.

McDannell, Colleen. *Sister Saints: Mormon Women since the End of Polygamy*. New York: Oxford University Press, 2019.

McDannell, Colleen, and Bernhard Lang. "Modern Heaven . . . and a Theology." In *Mormons and Mormonism: An Introduction to an American World Religion*, edited by Eric A. Eliason, 137–46. Urbana and Chicago: University of Illinois Press, 2001.

McMullen, Haynes. *American Libraries before 1876*. Westport, Conn., and London: Greenwood Press, 2000.

McPheeters, Annie L. *Library Service in Black and White: Some Personal Recollections, 1921–1980*. Metuchen, N.J., and London: The Scarecrow Press, 1988.

McPherson, James M., and James K. Hogue. *Ordeal by Fire: The Civil War and Reconstruction*. 4th ed. New York: McGraw-Hill Higher Education, 2010.

McRae, Elizabeth Gillespie. *Mothers of Massive Resistance: White Women and the Politics of White Supremacy*. New York: Oxford University Press, 2018.

Melosh, Barbara. *Strangers and Kin: The American Way of Adoption*. Cambridge, Mass.: Harvard University Press, 2002.

Meyer, Melissa L. "American Indian Blood Quantum Requirements: Blood is Thicker than Family." In *Over the Edge: Remapping the American West*, edited by Valerie J. Matsumoto and Blake Allmendinger, 231–52. Berkeley and Los Angeles: University of California Press, 1999.

Milanich, Nara B. *Paternity: The Elusive Quest for the Father*. Cambridge, Mass., and London: Harvard University Press, 2019.

Miles, Tiya. *Ties That Bind: The Story of an Afro-Cherokee Family in Slavery and Freedom*. Berkeley and Los Angeles: University of California Press, 2005.

Mills, Gary B., and Elizabeth Shown Mills. "The Genealogist's Assessment of Alex Haley's *Roots*." *National Genealogical Society Quarterly* 73 (March 1984): 35–49.

———. "'Roots' and the New 'Faction': A Legitimate Tool for Clio?" *Virginia Magazine of History and Biography* 89 (January 1981): 3–26.

Mims, Bob. "For Black Mormons, Black DNA Testing a Revelation of Roots—and of Faith." *Salt Lake Tribune*, March 28, 2017. http://www.sltrib.com/lifestyle/faith /5010095-155/for-black-mormons-dna-testing-a.

Miranda, Deborah, Jean M. O'Brien-Kehoe, Julie L. Reed, Doug Kiel, Malinda Maynor Lowery, and Alyssa Mt. Pleasant. "Rapid Response History: Native American Identities, Racial Slurs, and Elizabeth Warren." American Historical Association panel, January 5, 2019, Chicago. https://aha.confex.com/aha/2019/webprogram/Session18835.html.

Mitchell, Michele. *Righteous Propagation: African Americans and the Politics of Racial Destiny after Reconstruction*. Chapel Hill: University of North Carolina Press, 2004.

Mitchell, Nahum. *History of the Early Settlement of Bridgewater in Plymouth County, Massachusetts, Including an Extensive Family Register.* Boston: Kidder & Wright, 1840.

Mitchell, Pablo. *Coyote Nation: Sexuality, Race, and Conquest in Modernizing New Mexico, 1880–1920.* Chicago: University of Chicago Press, 2005.

Modell, Judith S. *Kinship with Strangers: Adoption and Interpretations of Kinship in American Culture.* Berkeley and Los Angeles: University of California Press, 1994.

Mokotoff, Gary, and Sallyann Amdur Sack, with Alexander Sharon. *Where Once We Walked: A Guide to the Jewish Communities Destroyed in the Holocaust.* Rev. ed. New Haven, Conn.: Avotaynu, 2002.

Molho, Anthony, Roberto Barducci, Gabriella Batista, and Francesco Donnini. "Genealogy and Marriage Alliance: Memories of Power in Late Medieval Florence." In *Portraits of Medieval and Renaissance Living: Essays in Memory of David Herlihy,* edited by Samuel K. Cohn Jr. and Steven A. Epstein, 39–70. Ann Arbor: University of Michigan Press, 1996.

Moore, David Chioni. "Revisiting a Silenced Giant: Alex Haley's *Roots*—A Bibliographic Essay, and a Research Report on the Haley Archives at the University of Tennessee, Knoxville." *Resources for American Literary Study* 22 (Summer 1996): 195–249.

———. "Routes: Alex Haley's *Roots* and the Rhetoric of Genealogy." *Transition* 64 (1994): 4–21.

Morgan, Francesca. "Lineage as Capital: Genealogy in Antebellum New England." *New England Quarterly* 83, no. 1 (June 2010): 250–82.

———. "'My Furthest-Back Person': *Roots* and the History of Black Genealogy." In *Reconsidering Roots: Race, Politics, and Memory,* edited by Erica L. Ball and Kellie Carter Jackson, 63–79. Athens: University of Georgia Press, 2017.

———. "A Noble Pursuit? Bourgeois America's Uses of Lineage." In *The American Bourgeoisie: Distinction and Identity in the Nineteenth Century,* edited by Sven Beckert and Julia Rosenbaum, 135–52. New York: Palgrave Macmillan, 2010.

———. *Women and Patriotism in Jim Crow America.* Chapel Hill: University of North Carolina Press, 2005.

Morley, Mrs. Walter S. (Mabelle Post Morley), comp. *History of California State Society, Daughters of the American Revolution, 1891–1938.* Berkeley, Calif.: Lederer, Street and Zeus Co., 1938.

MormonNewsroom.org. "Church Leaders Counsel Members after Supreme Court Same-Sex Decision." Church of Jesus Christ of Latter-day Saints, July 1, 2015. https://www.lds.org/church/news/church-leaders-counsel-members-after-supreme-court-same-sex-marriage-decision?lang=eng.

Moskowitz, Eva S. *In Therapy We Trust: America's Obsession with Self-Fulfillment.* Baltimore and London: Johns Hopkins University Press, 2001.

Moynihan, Daniel Patrick. *The Negro Family: The Case for National Action.* Washington, D.C.: U.S. Department of Labor, 1965.

Mueller, Max Perry. *Race and the Making of the Mormon People.* Chapel Hill: University of North Carolina Press, 2017.

Mukherjee, Siddhartha. *The Gene: An Intimate History.* London: The Bodley Head, 2016.

Müller-Wille, Staffan, and Hans-Jörg Rheinberger. *A Cultural History of Heredity.* Chicago: University of Chicago Press, 2012.

Müller-Wille, Staffan, and Hans-Jörg Rheinberger. "Heredity: The Formation of an Epistemic Space." In *Heredity Produced: At the Crossroads of Biology, Politics, and Culture, 1500–1870*, edited by Müller-Wille and Rheinberger, 3–34. Cambridge, Mass., and London: Massachusetts Institute of Technology Press, 2007.

Murray, Heather. *Not in This Family: Gays and the Meaning of Kinship in Postwar North America*. Philadelphia: University of Pennsylvania Press, 2010.

Murray, Pauli. *Proud Shoes: The Story of an American Family*. New York: Harper & Row, 1987. First published 1956.

———. *Song in a Weary Throat: An American Pilgrimage*. New York: Harper & Row, 1987.

Murray, Pauli, and Mary O. Eastwood. "Jane Crow and the Law: Sex Discrimination and Title VII." *George Washington Law Review* 34, no. 2 (1965): 232–56.

Nagel, Joane. *American Indian Ethnic Renewal: Red Power and the Resurgence of Identity and Culture*. New York: Oxford University Press, 1996.

Narea, Nicole. "The Outcry Over ICE and Hysterectomies, Explained." *Vox*, September 15, 2020; updated September 18, 2020. https://www.vox.com/policy-and-politics/2020/9/15/21437805/whistleblower-hysterectomies-nurse-irwin-ice.

Nash, Catherine. *Genetic Geographies: The Trouble with Ancestry*. Minneapolis: University of Minnesota Press, 2015.

———. "Genealogical Identities." *Environment and Planning D: Space and Society* 20 (2002): 27–52.

———. *Of Irish Descent: Origin Stories, Genealogy, and the Politics of Belonging*. Syracuse, N.Y.: Syracuse University Press, 2008.

Nash, Gary B. *First City: Philadelphia and the Forging of Historical Memory*. Philadelphia: University of Pennsylvania Press, 2002.

Nash, Gary B., Charlotte Crabtree, and Ross E. Dunn. *History on Trial: Culture Wars and the Teaching of the Past*. New York: Vintage Books, 2000. First published 1997.

Naughton, John. *A Brief History of the Future: From Radio Days to Internet Years in a Lifetime*. Woodstock, N.Y.: The Overlook Press, 2000.

Nededog, Jethro. "Bryan Cranston and More to Appear on New Season." *Business Insider*, June 25, 2015. http://www.businessinsider.com/tlc-who-do-you-think-you-are-summer-lineup-celebrity-guests-2015-6.

Nelson, Alondra. "The Factness of Diaspora: The Social Sources of Genetic Genealogy." In *Revisiting Race in a Genomic Age*, edited by Barbara Koenig, Sandra Soo-Jin Lee, and Sarah S. Richardson, 253–67. New Brunswick, N.J., and London: Rutgers University Press, 2008.

———. *The Social Life of DNA: Race, Reparations, and Reconciliation after the Genome*. Boston: Beacon Press, 2016.

———. "The Social Life of DNA: Racial Reconciliation and Institutional Morality After the Genome: A Response." *British Journal of Sociology* 69 (September 2018): 575–79.

New Perspectives on the West. "Events in the West: 1870–1880." Washington, D.C.: The West Film Project and WETA, 2001. https://www.pbs.org/weta/thewest/events/1870_1880.htm.

New York Genealogical and Biographical Society. *Twenty-Fifth Anniversary of the New York Genealogical and Biographical Society, February 27th, 1894*. New York: Printed for the Society by T. A. Wright, 1895.

New York Public Library. "Charles Henry Browning Papers." Last accessed March 7, 2021. http://archives.nypl.org/mss/419.

———. "History of the New York Public Library." Last accessed March 7, 2021. https://www.nypl.org/help/about-nypl/history.

Ngai, Mae M. *Impossible Subjects: Illegal Aliens and the Making of Modern America.* Princeton, N.J.: Princeton University Press, 2004.

Nichols, Elizabeth L. *Genealogy in the Computer Age: Understanding FamilySearch. Part I. Genealogical Resource Files.* Salt Lake City: Family History Educators, 1991.

———. "Questions and Answers on the Name Tabulation Program." *Ensign* 1 (November 1971): unpaginated. Last accessed March 7, 2021. https://www.lds.org/ensign/1971/11?lang=eng.

Nielsen, Kim E. *Un-American Womanhood: Antiradicalism, Antifeminism, and the First Red Scare.* Columbus: The Ohio State University Press, 2001.

Nieman, Fraser D. "Coincidence or Causal Connection? The Relationship between Thomas Jefferson's Visits to Monticello and Sally Hemings's Conceptions." *William and Mary Quarterly* 57 (January 2000): 198–211.

Nietzsche, Friedrich. *On the Genealogy of Morals.* Translated and edited by Walter Kaufmann. New York: Vintage Books, 1967.

Nixon, George J. "Genealogical and Historical Sources in the Spanish and Mexican Southwest." In *The Source: A Guidebook of American Genealogy,* edited by Arlene Eakle and Johni Cerny, 558–77. Salt Lake City: Ancestry Publishing Company, 1984.

———. "Records Relating to Native American Research: The Five Civilized Tribes." In *The Source: A Guidebook of American Genealogy,* edited by Arlene Eakle and Johni Cerny, 534–57. Salt Lake City: Ancestry Publishing Company, 1984.

Nobile, Philip. "Uncovering *Roots,*" *Village Voice,* February 23, 1993, 31–38.

Nobile, Philip, and Maureen Kenney. "The Search for Roots, a Pre-Haley Movement." *New York Times,* February 27, 1977.

Norrell, Robert J. *Alex Haley and the Books That Changed a Nation.* New York: St. Martin's Press, 2015.

Novick, Peter. *The Holocaust in American Life.* Boston: Mariner Books, 2000. First published 1999.

———. *That Noble Dream: The "Objectivity Question" and the American Historical Profession.* Cambridge: Cambridge University Press, 1988.

Nylander, Jane Cayford. "Preserving a Legacy." In *The Art of Family: Genealogical Artifacts in New England,* edited by D. Brenton Simons and Peter Benes, 201–21. Boston: New England Historic Genealogical Society, 2002.

Obama, Barack, Jr. "Remarks by the President," April 27, 2011. https://www.whitehouse.gov/the-press-office/2011/04/27/remarks-president.

Oboler, Suzanne. "Hispanics? That's What They Call Us." In *The Latino/a Condition: A Critical Reader,* edited by Richard Delgado and Jean Stefancic, 8–10. 2nd ed. New York: New York University Press, 2011.

O'Brien, Jean M. *Firsting and Lasting: Writing Indians Out of Existence in New England.* Minneapolis and London: University of Minnesota Press, 2010.

O'Brien, Michael. *Conjectures of Order: Intellectual Life in the American South, 1810–1860.* 2 vols. Chapel Hill: University of North Carolina Press, 2004.

O'Dell, Darlene. *Sites of Southern Memory: The Autobiographies of Katharine Du Pre Lumpkin, Lillian Smith, and Pauli Murray.* Charlottesville and London: University Press of Virginia, 2001.

Oguh, Chibuike. "Blackstone to Acquire Ancestry.com for $4.7 Billion." *Reuters*, August 5, 2020. https://www.reuters.com/article/us-ancestry-m-a-blackstone-group/blackstone -to-acquire-ancestry-com-for-4-7-billion-idUSKCN2512ES.

O'Hare, Sheila. "Genealogy and History." *Common-Place: The Interactive Journal of Early American Life* 2 (April 2002). http://commonplace.online/.

Okrent, Daniel. *The Guarded Gate: Bigotry, Eugenics, and the Law That Kept Two Generations of Jews, Italians, and Other European Immigrants Out of America.* New York: Scribner, 2019.

O'Leary, Cecilia Elizabeth. *To Die For: The Paradox of American Patriotism.* Princeton, N.J.: Princeton University Press, 1999.

Onwuachi-Willig, Angela. *According to Our Hearts:* Rhinelander v. Rhinelander *and the Law of the Multiracial Family.* New Haven, Conn.: Yale University Press, 2013.

———. "A Beautiful Lie: Exploring *Rhinelander v. Rhinelander* as a Formative Lesson on Race, Identity, Marriage, and Family." *California Law Review* 95 (December 2007): 2,393–2,458.

Open Library. "Academia Mexicana de Genealogía y Heráldica." Created January 12, 2009. https://openlibrary.org/authors/OL6551204A/Academia_Mexicana_de_Genealog %C3%ADa_y_Her%C3%A1ldica.

Ottaway, Mark. "Tangled Roots: Doubts Raised Over the Story of the Big TV Slave Saga." *The Times* (London), April 10, 1977, 1, 17, 21.

Otterstrom, Samuel M. "Genealogy as Religious Ritual: The Doctrine and Practice of Family History in the Church of Jesus Christ of Latter-day Saints." In *Geography and Genealogy: Locating Personal Pasts,* edited by Dallen J. Timothy and Jeanne Kay Guelke, 137–53. Aldershot, U.K., and Burlington, Vt.: Ashgate Publishing, Ltd., 2008.

Ozick, Cynthia. "Who Owns Anne Frank?" *The New Yorker* 73, no. 30 (October 6, 1997): 76.

Painter, Nell Irvin. *The History of White People.* New York: W. W. Norton and Company, 2010.

———. *Standing at Armageddon: The United States, 1877–1919.* New York: W. W. Norton, 1987.

Papers of Benjamin Franklin. Vol. 8, April 1, 1758 through December 31, 1759. Edited by Leonard W. Labaree. New Haven and London: Yale University Press, 1965.

Parshall, Ardis E. "Genealogy and Family History." In *Mormonism: A Historical Encyclopedia,* edited by W. Paul Reeve and Parshall, 243–250. Santa Barbara, Calif., and Oxford: ABC Clio, 2010.

Parry, Tyler D. "The Politics of Plagiarism: *Roots,* Margaret Walker, and Alex Haley." In *Reconsidering Roots: Race, Politics, and Memory,* edited by Erica L. Ball and Kellie Carter Jackson, 47–62. Athens: University of Georgia Press, 2017.

Pascoe, Peggy. *What Comes Naturally: Miscegenation Law and the Making of Race in America.* New York: Oxford University Press, 2009.

Pass, Forrest D. "Strange Whims of Crest Fiends: Marketing Heraldry in the United States, 1880–1980." *Journal of American Studies* 49 (July 2015): 1–25.

Pasley, Jeffrey L., Andrew W. Robertson, and David Waldstreicher, eds. *Beyond the Founders: New Approaches to the Political History of the Early American Republic*. Chapel Hill: University of North Carolina Press, 2004.

Paul, Diane B. *Controlling Human Heredity, 1865 to the Present*. Amherst, N.Y.: Humanities Books, 1998.

Payne, Charles M. *I've Got the Light of Freedom: The Organizing Tradition and the Mississippi Freedom Struggle*. 2nd ed. Berkeley and Los Angeles: University of California Press, 2007.

PBS Newshour. "Arresting Dress: A Timeline of Anti-Cross-Dressing Laws in the United States," May 31, 2015. https://www.pbs.org/newshour/nation/arresting-dress-timeline -anti-cross-dressing-laws-u-s/.

Pearson, Susan J. "'Age Ought to Be a Fact': The Campaign Against Child Labor and the Rise of the Birth Certificate." *Journal of American History* 101 (March 2015): 1,144–65.

———. "'Infantile Specimens': Showing Babies in Nineteenth-Century America." *Journal of Social History* 42 (Winter 2008): 341–70.

Peet, Lisa. "Industry News: Daughters of the Republic of Texas Retain Control of Library Collection—for Now." *Library Journal* (October 27, 2015). http://lj.libraryjournal.com /2015/10/litigation/daughters-of-the-republic-of-texas-retain-control-of-alamo-library -collection-for-now/#.

Peirce, Ebenezer Weaver. *Indian History, Biography, and Genealogy, Pertaining to the Good Sachem Massasoit of the Wampanoag Tribe, and His Descendants*. North Abington, Mass.: Zerviah Gould Mitchell, 1878.

Perdue, Theda. *Cherokee Women: Gender and Culture Change, 1700–1835*. Lincoln, Neb., and London: University of Nebraska Press, 1998.

Perego, Ugo A., Natalie M. Myres, and Scott R. Woodward. "Reconstructing the Y-Chromosome of Joseph Smith: Genealogical Applications." *Journal of Mormon History* 31 (Fall 2005): 42–60.

Person, Carolyn W. D. "Susa Young Gates." In *Mormon Sisters: Women in Early Utah*, edited by Claudia L. Bushman, 199–223. Logan: Utah State University Press, 1997. First published 1976.

Peters, John Durham. "Recording Beyond the Grave: Joseph Smith's Celestial Bookkeeping." *Critical Inquiry* 42 (Summer 2016): 842–69.

Peterson, Carla L. *Black Gotham: A Family History of African Americans in Nineteenth Century New York City*. New Haven and London: Yale University Press, 2011.

Petrey, Taylor G. *Tabernacles of Clay: Sexuality and Gender in Modern Mormonism*. Chapel Hill: University of North Carolina Press, 2020.

Petrovsky-Shtern, Yohanan. *Jews in the Russian Army, 1827–1917: Drafted into Modernity*. Cambridge: Cambridge University Press, 2009.

Phillimore, W. P. W. *How to Write the History of a Family: A Guide for the Genealogist*. Boston: Cupples and Hurd, 1887.

Pinckney, Darryl. *Out There: Mavericks of Black Literature*. New York: BasicCivitas Books, 2002.

Pinker, Steven. "Strangled by Roots: The Genealogy Craze in America." *The New Republic*, August 5, 2007. https://newrepublic.com/article/77729/strangled-roots.

Pitre, Merline. *In Struggle Against Jim Crow: Lulu B. White and the NAACP, 1900–1957*. College Station: Texas A & M University Press, 1999.

Plane, Ann Marie. *Colonial Intimacies: Indian Marriage in Early New England.* Ithaca, N.Y., and London: Cornell University Press, 2000.

Polk, William R. *Polk's Folly: An American Family History.* New York: Anchor Books, 2000.

"President Obama's Long-Form Birth Certificate." Published April 27, 2011. https://www .slideshare.net/whitehouse/birth-certificatelongform.

Prince, K. Stephen. "Jim Crow Memory: Southern White Supremacists and the Regional Politics of Remembrance." In *Remembering Reconstruction: Struggles Over the Meaning of America's Most Turbulent Era,* edited by Carole Emberton and Bruce E. Baker, 17–34. Baton Rouge: Louisiana State University Press, 2017.

Prochaska, Frank. *The Eagle and the Crown: Americans and the British Monarchy.* New Haven and London: Yale University Press, 2008.

Purcell, Sarah J. *Sealed with Blood: War, Sacrifice, and Memory in Revolutionary America.* Philadelphia: University of Pennsylvania Press, 2002.

Purvis, Thomas L., and Donald H. Akenson. "The European Ancestry of the United States Population, 1790: A Symposium." *William and Mary Quarterly* 41 (January 1984): 85–101.

Quayle, Dan. "Address to the Commonwealth Club of California (Family Values)." Transcript, May 22, 1992. Reprinted Scottsdale, Ariz.: The Dan Quayle, 2004. http:// www.vicepresidentdanquayle.com/speeches_StandingFirm_CCC_3.html.

"Quest for Identity: Americans Go on a Genealogy Kick." *U.S. News and World Report,* July 29, 1974, 41.

Rampersad, Arnold. *The Life of Langston Hughes, Vol. 1, 1902–1941: I, Too, Sing America.* 2nd ed. New York: Oxford University Press, 2002.

Rapaport, Lynn. "The Holocaust in American Jewish Life." In *The Cambridge Companion to American Judaism,* edited by Dana Evan Kaplan, 187–208. Cambridge: Cambridge University Press, 2005.

Rath, Ida Ellen. *The Rath Trail: Non-Fiction Biography of Charles Rath.* Wichita, Kans.: McCormick-Armstrong Co., 1961.

Ratteree, Kathleen, and Norbert Hill, eds. *The Great Vanishing Act: Blood Quantum and the Future of Native Nations.* Golden, Colo.: Fulcrum Publishing, 2017.

Rattley, Sandra. "The Impact of Roots." *Africa Report* 22 (May–June 1977): 12–16.

Reed, Ann. *Pilgrimage Tourism of Diaspora Africans to Ghana.* New York: Routledge, 2015.

Reeve, W. Paul. *Religion of a Different Color: Race and the Mormon Struggle for Whiteness.* New York and Oxford: Oxford University Press, 2015.

Report of the Trustees of the Newberry Library for the Year 1899. Chicago: Hollister Brothers, 1900.

Report of the Trustees of the Newberry Library for the Year 1901. Chicago, 1902.

Report of the Trustees of the Newberry Library for the Year 1902. Chicago, 1903.

Report of the Trustees of the Newberry Library for the Year 1905. Chicago, 1906.

Rhinelander, Jeanne C. *On Coming to America: A Discussion of the German Roots of the Rhinelander Family and 18th Century Life in Philadelphia, Tulpehocken, New Rochelle, Colonial New-York, and New York in the Gilded Age.* Gloucester, Mass.: privately published, 2015.

Richards, Penny L. "Knitting the Transatlantic Bond: One Woman's Letters to America, 1860–1910." In *Geography and Genealogy: Locating Personal Pasts,* edited by Dallen J.

Timothy and Jeanne Kay Guelke, 83–98. Aldershot, U.K., and Burlington, Vt.: Ashgate Publishing, Ltd., 2008.

Riley, Glenda. *Divorce: An American Tradition*. Lincoln: University of Nebraska Press, 1997. First published 1991.

Riser, R. Volney. *Defying Disfranchisement: Black Voting Rights Activism in the Jim Crow South, 1890–1908*. Baton Rouge: Louisiana State University Press, 2010.

Ritvo, Harriet. *The Animal Estate: The English and Other Creatures in the Victorian Age*. Cambridge, Mass.: Harvard University Press, 1987.

———. *The Platypus and the Mermaid and Other Figments of the Classifying Imagination*. Cambridge, Mass.: Harvard University Press, 1997.

Rivers, Daniel Winunwe. *Radical Relations: Lesbian Mothers, Gay Fathers, and Their Children in the United States since World War II*. Chapel Hill: University of North Carolina Press, 2013.

Rodda, Anne Patterson. *Trespassers in Time: Genealogists and Microhistorians*. N.p.: Published by the author, 2012.

Rodgers, Daniel T. *Age of Fracture*. Cambridge, Mass., and London: Harvard University Press, 2011.

Rodriguez, Gregory. "How Genealogy Became Almost as Popular as Porn." *Time*, May 30, 2014. http://time.com/133811/how-genealogy-became-almost-as-popular-as-porn/.

Rogers, Joel Augustus. *The Five Negro Presidents: According to What White People Said They Were*. New York: Helga M. Rogers, 1965.

Rolls of Membership of the New-England Historic Genealogical Society, 1844–1890. Boston: Printed for the Society/Cambridge, Mass.: John Wilson and Son, 1891.

Rose, James M., and Alice Eichholz. *Black Genesis*. Detroit: Gale Research Company, 1978.

Rose, Nikolas. *The Politics of Life Itself: Biomedicine, Power, and Subjectivity in the Twenty-First Century*. Princeton, N.J.: Princeton University Press, 2006.

Rose, Willie Lee. "An American Family: A Review of *Roots*, by Alex Haley." *New York Review of Books* 23 (November 11, 1976): 3–6.

Rosenberg, Rosalind. *Jane Crow: The Life of Pauli Murray*. New York: Oxford University Press, 2017.

———. "Pauli Murray and the Killing of Jane Crow." In *Forgotten Heroes: Inspiring American Portraits from Our Leading Historians*, edited by Susan Ware, 279–88. New York: The Free Press, 1998.

Rosenzweig, Roy, and David Thelen. *The Presence of the Past: Popular Uses of History in American Life*. New York: Columbia University Press, 1998.

Roth, Wendy D., and Biorn Ivemark. "Genetic Options: The Impact of Genetic Ancestry Testing on Consumers' Racial and Ethnic Identities." *American Journal of Sociology* 124 (July 2018): 150–84.

Roth, Wendy D., Sule Yaylaci, Kaitlyn Jaffe, and Lindsey Richardson. "Do Genetic Ancestry Tests Increase Racial Essentialism? Findings from a Randomized Controlled Trial." *PLoS ONE* 15 (January 29, 2020): 1–17.

Rothschild, Joan. *The Dream of the Perfect Child*. Bloomington and Indianapolis: Indiana University Press, 2005.

Rottenberg, Dan. *Finding Our Fathers: A Guidebook to Jewish Genealogy*. New York: Random House, 1977.

Roued-Cunliffe, Henriette, and Andrea Copeland, eds. *Participatory Heritage*. London: Facet Publishing, 2017.

Round, Philip H. *Removable Type: Histories of the Book in Indian Country, 1663–1880*. Chapel Hill: University of North Carolina Press, 2010.

Rowlandson, Mary. *Narrative of the Captivity, Sufferings, and Removes of Mrs. Mary Rowlandson*. Boston: Massachusetts Sabbath School Society, 1856. GoogleBooks edition. First printed 1791.

Rubincam, Milton. "Adventures in Genealogy." In *Genealogical Research: Methods and Sources, by the American Society of Genealogists*, 5–13. Washington, D.C.: The American Society of Genealogists, 1960.

———. "Adventures in Genealogy." In *Genealogical Research: Methods and Sources, by the American Society of Genealogists*. Vol. 1, 5–12. Rev. ed. Washington, D.C.: The American Society of Genealogists, 1980.

———. "Secondary Materials." In *Genealogical Research: Methods and Sources, by the American Society of Genealogists*, 91–95. Washington, D.C.: The American Society of Genealogists, 1960.

———, ed. *Genealogical Research: Methods and Sources, by the American Society of Genealogists*. Washington, D.C.: The American Society of Genealogists, 1960.

———, ed. *Genealogical Research: Methods and Sources, by the American Society of Genealogists*. Vol. 1. Rev. ed. Washington, D.C.: The American Society of Genealogists, 1980.

Rymsza-Pawlowska, M. J. *History Comes Alive: Public History and Popular Culture in the 1970s*. Chapel Hill: University of North Carolina Press, 2017.

Ryskamp, George R. *Tracing Your Hispanic Heritage*. Riverside, Calif.: Hispanic Family History Research, 1984.

Sachs, Honor. "'Freedom by a Judgment': The Legal History of an Afro-Indian Family." *Law and History Review* 30 (February 2012): 173–203.

Sack, Sallyann Amdur. *A Guide to Jewish Genealogical Research in Israel*. Baltimore: Genealogical Publishing Company, 1987.

Sack, Sallyann Amdur, and Gary Mokotoff, eds. Avotaynu *Guide to Jewish Genealogy*. Bergenfield, N.J.: Avotaynu, 2004.

Sack, Sallyann Amdur, and the Israel Genealogical Society. *A Guide to Jewish Genealogical Research in Israel*. Teaneck, N.J.: Avotaynu, 1995.

Sagers, Diane. "FamilySearch 2016 Year in Review." In *FamilySearch Blog*, January 4, 2017. https://familysearch.org/blog/en/familysearch-2016-year-review/.

Samuel, Lawrence R. *Shrink: A Cultural History of Psychoanalysis in America*. Lincoln: University of Nebraska Press, 2013.

Saunt, Claudio. *Black, White, and Indian: Race and the Unmaking of an American Family*. New York: Oxford University Press, 2005.

Savage, Kirk. *Standing Soldiers, Kneeling Slaves: Race, War, and Monument in Nineteenth-Century America*. Princeton, N.J.: Princeton University Press, 1997.

Saxby, Troy R. *Pauli Murray: A Personal and Political Life*. Chapel Hill: University of North Carolina Press, 2020.

Saxe, Leonard, and Barry Chazan. *Ten Days in Birthright Israel: A Journey in Young Adult Identity*. Waltham, Mass.: Brandeis University Press, 2008.

Scaff, Lawrence A. *Max Weber in America*. Princeton: Princeton University Press, 2011.

Scagliotti, John, Janet Baus, and Dan Hunt, dirs. *After Stonewall*. New York: First Run Features, 1999. DVD, 88 minutes.

Scarupa, Harriet Jackson. "Margaret Walker Alexander." *American Visions* 1 (March/April 1986): 48–52.

Schantz, Mark S. *Awaiting the Heavenly Country: The Civil War and America's Culture of Death*. Ithaca and London: Cornell University Press, 2008.

Scharff, Virginia. *The Women Jefferson Loved*. New York: HarperCollins, 2010.

Schlissel, Lillian. "Introduction." In *Women's Diaries of the Westward Journey*, edited by Schlissel, 9–145. Expanded ed. New York: Schocken Books, 1992.

Schutz, John A. *A Noble Pursuit: The Sesquicentennial History of the New England Historic Genealogical Society, 1845–1995*. Boston: The New England Historic Genealogical Society, 1995.

Schwalm, Leslie A. *A Hard Fight for We: Women's Transition from Slavery to Freedom in South Carolina*. Urbana and Chicago: University of Illinois Press, 1997.

Schwartz, Marie Jenkins. *Birthing a Slave: Motherhood and Medicine in the Antebellum South*. Cambridge, Mass.: Harvard University Press, 2006.

Scodari, Christine. *Alternate Roots: Ethnicity, Race, and Identity in Genealogy Media*. Jackson: University of Mississippi Press, 2018.

———. "Recuperating Ethnic Identity through Critical Genealogy." *Journal of Multidisciplinary Research* 8 (Spring 2016): 47–62.

———. "Roots, Representation, and Resistance? Family History Media and Culture through a Critical Lens." *Journal of American Culture* 24, no. 3 (September 2013): 206–20.

Seelye, John. *Memory's Nation: The Place of Plymouth Rock*. Chapel Hill: University of North Carolina Press, 1998.

Segalen, Martine. "The Shift in Kinship Studies in France: The Case of Grandparenting." In *Relative Values: Reconfiguring Kinship Studies*, edited by Sarah Franklin and Susan McKinnon, 246–73. Durham, N.C., and London: Duke University Press, 2001.

Seltzer, Robert M. "Introduction: The Ironies of American Jewish History." In *The Americanization of the Jews*, edited by Seltzer and Norman J. Cohen, 1–16. New York: New York University Press, 1995.

Shah, Nayan. *Stranger Intimacy: Contesting Race, Sexuality, and the Law in the North American West*. Berkeley and Los Angeles: University of California Press, 2011.

Sharfstein, Daniel J. *The Invisible Line: Three American Families and the Secret Journey from Black to White*. New York: The Penguin Press, 2011.

Sharpe, Michael. *Family Matters: A History of Genealogy*. South Yorkshire, U.K.: Pen & Sword Books, 2011.

Shattuck, Lemuel. *A Complete System of Family Registration*. Boston: William D. Ticknor, 1841.

———. *A History of Concord; Middlesex County, Massachusetts, from its Earliest Settlement to 1832, and of the Adjoining Towns, Bedford, Acton, Lincoln, and Carlisle*. Boston: Russell, Odiorne, and Company/Concord, Mass.: John Stacy, 1835.

———. *Memorials of the Descendants of William Shattuck, the Progenitor of the Families in America That Have Borne His Name*. Boston: Dutton and Wentworth, 1855.

Shaw, Stephanie J. *What a Woman Ought to Be and to Do: Black Professional Women Workers During the Jim Crow Era*. Chicago: University of Chicago Press, 1996.

Shepard, Steven, Philip Honenberger, and Alan Megill. "A Case Study in Historical Epistemology: What Did the Neighbors Know about Thomas Jefferson and Sally Hemings?" In Megill, *Historical Knowledge, Historical Error: A Contemporary Guide to Practice*, 125–50. Chicago and London: University of Chicago Press, 2007.

Sheppard, Walter Lee, Jr. "A Bicentennial Look at Genealogy Methods, Performance, Education, and Thinking." *National Genealogical Society Quarterly* 65 (March 1977): 3–15.

Shipps, Jan. "Dangerous History: Laurel Thatcher Ulrich and Her Mormon Sisters." In *Sojourner in the Promised Land: Forty Years Among the Mormons*, 193–203. Urbana and Chicago: University of Illinois Press, 2000.

———. "Surveying the Mormon Image since 1960." In *Sojourner in the Promised Land: Forty Years Among the Mormons*, 98–123. Urbana and Chicago: University of Illinois Press, 2000.

Shklar, Judith. "Subversive Genealogies." *Daedalus* 101 (Winter 1972): 129–54.

Shoumatoff, Alex. *The Mountain of Names: A History of the Human Family*. New York: Kodansha International, 1995. First printed 1985.

Simons, D. Brenton, and Peter Benes, eds. *The Art of Family: Genealogical Artifacts in New England*. Boston: New England Historic Genealogical Society, 2002.

Sink, Robert. *NYPL Librarians*. Blog posts (2011–15). Last accessed March 7, 2021. http://nypl-librarians.blogspot.com.

Sinko, Peggy Tuck, and Scott N. Peters. "A Survey of Genealogists at the Newberry Library." *Library Trends* 32 (Summer 1983): 97–109.

Slotkin, Richard. *The Fatal Environment: The Myth of the Frontier in the Age of Industrialization, 1800–1890*. New York: HarperPerennial, 1994. First printed 1985.

Smedley, Audrey, and Brian D. Smedley. *Race in North America: Origin and Evolution of a Worldview*. 4th ed. Boulder, Colo.: Westview Press, 2012.

Smith, Bonnie G. *The Gender of History: Men, Women, and Historical Practice*. Cambridge, Mass.: Harvard University Press, 1998.

Smith, Jessie Carney. *Ethnic Genealogy: A Research Guide*. Westport, Conn.: Greenwood Press, 1983.

Smith, Shawn Michelle. *American Archives: Gender, Race, and Class in Visual Culture*. Princeton, N.J.: Princeton University Press, 1999.

Smith-Pryor, Elizabeth M. *Property Rites: The Rhinelander Trial, Passing, and the Protection of Whiteness*. Chapel Hill: University of North Carolina Press, 2009.

Sobel, Mechal. *Teach Me Dreams: The Search for Self in the Revolutionary Era*. Princeton, N.J.: Princeton University Press, 2000.

Solomon, Alisa. *Wonder of Wonders: A Cultural History of* Fiddler on the Roof. New York: Picador, 2013.

Solomon, Barbara Miller. *Ancestors and Immigrants: A Changing New England Tradition*. Boston: Northeastern University Press, 1989. First printed 1956.

———. *In the Company of Educated Women: A History of Women and Higher Education in America*. New Haven, Conn.: Yale University Press, 1985.

Sommer, Marianne. "DNA and Cultures of Remembrance: Anthropological Genetics, Biohistories, and Biosocialities." *BioSocieties* 5, no. 3 (2010): 366–90.

Spiro, Jonathan Peter. *Defending the Master Race: Conservation, Eugenics, and the Legacy of Madison Grant*. Burlington: University of Vermont Press; Hanover, N.H., and London: University Press of New England, 2009.

Spruhan, Paul. "A Legal History of Blood Quantum in Federal Law to 1935." *South Dakota Law Review* 51, no. 1 (2006): 1–50.

Spruill, Marjorie Julian. *Divided We Stand: The Battle over Women's Rights and Family Values that Polarized American Politics*. New York: Bloomsbury, 2017.

Stack, Carol B. *All Our Kin: Strategies for Survival in a Black Community*. New York: Harper and Row, 1974.

Stack, Peggy Fletcher, and Robert Gehrke. "In Major Move, Mormon Leaders Call for Statewide LGBT Protections." *Salt Lake Tribune*, January 27, 2015. http://www.sltrib .com/home/2106982-155/in-major-move-mormon-apostles-call.

Stallard, Matthew, and Jerome de Groot. "'Things Are Coming Out That Are Questionable, We Never Knew About': DNA and the New Family History." *Journal of Family History* 45, no. 3 (July 2020): 274–94.

Stanton, Lucia. *"Those Who Labor for My Happiness": Slavery at Thomas Jefferson's Monticello*. Charlottesville and London: University of Virginia Press, 2012.

Statutes of the National Society, Daughters of the American Revolution. Washington, D.C.: National Society, Daughters of the American Revolution, n.d. [ca. 1897].

Steedman, Carolyn. *Dust: The Archive and Cultural History*. 2001; New Brunswick, N.J.: Rutgers University Press, 2002.

———. *Strange Dislocations: Childhood and the Idea of Human Interiority, 1780–1830*. Cambridge, Mass.: Harvard University Press, 1995.

Steenburg, Nancy. "Stepping Outside Her Sphere: The Intellectual Adventures of Frances Mainwaring Caulkins." *Connecticut History* 51 (Spring 2012): 40–64.

Stein, Arlene. "Trauma and Origins: Post-Holocaust Genealogists and the Work of Memory." *Qualitative Sociology* 32 (September 2009): 293–309.

Stern, Alexandra Minna. *Eugenic Nation: Faults and Frontiers of Better Breeding in Modern America*. Berkeley and London: University of California Press, 2005.

Stern, Malcolm H. *Americans of Jewish Descent: A Compendium of Genealogy*. Cincinnati: Hebrew Union College Press, 1960.

Stevenson, Brenda E. *Life in Black and White: Family and Community in the Slave South*. New York: Oxford University Press, 1997.

Stevenson, Noel C. *Genealogical Evidence: A Guide to the Standard of Proof Relating to Pedigrees, Ancestry, Heirship and Family History*. Laguna Hills, Calif.: Aegean Park Press, 1979.

———. "Genealogical Evidence: A Practical System for Accepting or Rejecting Research Results." In *Genealogical Research: Methods and Sources, by the American Society of Genealogists*. Vol. 1, 38–49. Rev. ed. Washington, D.C.: The American Society of Genealogists, 1980.

———. *Search and Research, the Researcher's Handbook: A Guide to Official Records and Library Sources for Investigators, Historians, Genealogists, Lawyers, and Librarians*. Rev. ed. Salt Lake City: Deseret Book Company, 1959.

Stiles, Henry R. *A Hand-Book of Practical Suggestions, for Use of Students in Genealogy*. Albany, N.Y.: Joel Munsell's Sons, 1899.

Stollery, Martin. "The Same, but a Step Removed: Aspects of the British Reception of *Roots*." In *Reconsidering Roots: Race, Politics, and Memory*, edited by Erica L. Ball and Kellie Carter Jackson, 147–64. Athens: University of Georgia Press, 2017.

Strange, Carolyn. "The Battlefields of Personal and Public Memory: Commemorating the Battle of Saratoga (1777) in the Late Nineteenth Century." *Journal of the Gilded Age and Progressive Era* 14 (April 2015): 194–221.

———. "Sisterhood of Blood: The Will to Descend and the Formation of the Daughters of the American Revolution." *Journal of Women's History* 26 (Fall 2014): 105–28.

Strathern, Marilyn. *Kinship, Law and the Unexpected: Relatives Are Always a Surprise.* Cambridge: Cambridge University Press, 2005.

———. "Nostalgia and the New Genetics." In *Rhetorics of Self-Making*, edited by Debbora Battaglia, 97–120. Berkeley and Los Angeles: University of California Press, 1995.

———. "Refusing Information." In *Property, Substance and Effect: Anthropological Essays on Persons and Things*, 64–86. London and New Brunswick, N.J.: Athlone Press, 1999.

———. *Reproducing the Future: Essays on Anthropology, Kinship, and the New Reproductive Technologies.* New York: Routledge, 1992.

Stratton, Eugene A. "The Validity of Genealogical Evidence." *National Genealogical Society Quarterly* 72 (December 1984): 273–87.

Streets, David H. *Slave Genealogy: A Research Guide with Case Studies.* Bowie, Md.: Heritage Books, 1986.

Stremlau, Rose. *Sustaining the Cherokee Family: Kinship and the Allotment of an Indigenous Nation.* Chapel Hill: University of North Carolina Press, 2011.

Strong, Pauline Turner. "To Forget Their Tongue, Their Name, and Their Whole Relation: Captivity, Extra-Tribal Adoption, and the Indian Child Welfare Act." In *Relative Values: Reconfiguring Kinship Studies*, edited by Sarah Franklin and Susan McKinnon, 468–93. Durham, N.C., and London: Duke University Press, 2001.

Stryker-Rodda, Kenn, ed. *Genealogical Research: Methods and Sources.* Vol. 2. Rev. ed. Washington, D.C.: American Society of Genealogists, 1983.

———. *Genealogical Research.* Vol. 2. Washington, D.C.: American Society of Genealogists, 1971.

Stuart, Joseph R. "'A More Powerful Effect upon the Body': Early Mormonism's Theory of Racial Redemption and American Religious Theories of Race." *Church History* 87 (September 2018): 768–96.

Sturm, Circe. *Blood Politics: Race, Culture, and Identity in the Cherokee Nation of Oklahoma.* Berkeley and Los Angeles: University of California Press, 2002.

Stuy, Brian H. "Wilford Woodruff's Vision of the Signers of the Declaration of Independence." *Journal of Mormon History* 26 (Spring 2000): 64–90.

Sunners, Amy. "Elizabeth Sunners: Uncovering a Secret Feminist History." YouTube video, May 23, 2010. http://www.youtube.com/watch?v=HmddommMhHQ.

Sweet, James H. "Defying Social Death: The Multiple Configurations of African Slave Family in the Atlantic World." *William and Mary Quarterly* 70 (April 2013): 251–72.

Tait, Lisa Olsen. "Between Two Economies: The Business Development of the *Young Woman's Journal*." *Journal of Mormon History* 38, no. 4 (Fall 2012): 1–54.

———. "Susa Young Gates and the Vision of the Redemption of the Dead: D&C 138." *Revelations in Context*, August 14, 2015. "Church History," Church of Jesus Christ of

Latter-day Saints. https://history.lds.org/article/susa-young-gates-vision-of
-redemption?lang=eng.

————. "'Thank God That I Have Been Counted Worthy': Susa Amelia Young Dunford
Gates." In *Women of Faith in the Latter Days. Vol. 3, 1846–1870*, edited by Richard E.
Turley Jr. and Brittany A. Chapman, 57–68. Salt Lake City: Deseret Books, 2014.

————. "The *Young Woman's Journal*: Gender and Generations in a Mormon Women's
Magazine." *American Periodicals* 22 (Spring 2012): 51–71.

Takaki, Ronald. *Strangers from a Different Shore: A History of Asian Americans*. New York:
Penguin Books, 1989.

TallBear, Kim. "Elizabeth Warren's Claim to Cherokee Ancestry is a Form of Violence."
High Country News (Paonia, Colo.), January 17, 2019. https://www.hcn.org/issues
/51.2/tribal-affairs-elizabeth-warrens-claim-to-cherokee-ancestry-is-a-form-of-
violence.

————. "Making Love and Relations Beyond Settler Sex and Family." In *Making Kin Not
Population*, edited by Adele E. Clarke and Donna Haraway, 145–66. Chicago: Prickly
Pear Press, 2018.

————. *Native American DNA: Tribal Belonging and the False Promise of Genetic Science*.
Minneapolis: University of Minnesota Press, 2013.

Tamarkin, Elisa. *Anglophilia: Deference, Devotion, and Antebellum America*. Chicago:
University of Chicago Press, 2008.

Tanner, James. "About Microfilm and FamilySearch." *Rejoice and Be Exceedingly Glad:
Genealogy from the Perspective of a Member of the Church of Jesus Christ of Latter-day
Saints* (blog), April 13, 2017. http://rejoiceandbeexceedingglad.blogspot.com/2017
/04/about-microfilm-and-familysearch.html.

Taylor, Helen. "'The Griot from Tennessee': The Saga of Alex Haley's *Roots*." *Critical
Quarterly* 37 (Summer 1995): 46–62.

Taylor, Maureen A. "Tall Oaks from Little Acorns Grow: The Family Tree Lithograph in
America." In *The Art of Family: Genealogical Artifacts in New England*, edited by D.
Brenton Simons and Peter Benes, 75–89. Boston: New England Historic Genealogical
Society, 2002.

Taylor, Robert M., Jr. "Summoning the Wandering Tribes: Genealogy and Family
Reunions in American History." *Journal of Social History* 16 (Winter 1982): 21–37.

Taylor, Robert M., Jr., and Ralph J. Crandall. "Historians and Genealogists: An Emerging
Community of Interest." In *Generations and Change: Genealogical Perspectives in Social
History*, edited by Robert M. Taylor Jr. and Ralph J. Crandall, 1–28. Mercer, Ga.: Mercer
University Press, 1986.

————, eds. *Generations and Change: Genealogical Perspectives in Social History*. Mercer, Ga.:
Mercer University Press, 1986.

Teachout, Woden. *Capture the Flag: A Political History of American Patriotism*. New York:
Basic Books, 2009.

Tejano Genealogical Society of Austin. "About TGSA." Last updated 2020; last accessed
March 7, 2021. https://www.tgsaustin.org/about.

Tenenbaum, Shelly, and Lynn Davidman. "It's in My Genes: Biological Discourse and
Essentialist Views of Identity among Contemporary American Jews." *Sociological
Quarterly* 48 (Summer 2007): 435–50.

Thackery, David T. *"Back to Adam": A Survey of Genealogy in the Western World, as Illustrated in the Collections of the Newberry Library, Chicago, Illinois. An Exhibition Catalogue.* Chicago: Newberry Library, 1992.

———. *Finding Your African American Ancestors: A Beginner's Guide.* Provo, Utah: Ancestry Publishing, a Division of Generations Network, 2000.

Thompson, Charis. "Strategic Naturalizing: Kinship in an Infertility Clinic." In *Relative Values: Reconfiguring Kinship Studies,* edited by Sarah Franklin and Susan McKinnon, 175–202. Durham, N.C., and London: Duke University Press, 2001.

Thornton, Russell. *American Indian Holocaust and Survival: A Population History since 1492.* Norman and London: University of Oklahoma Press, 1987.

Timothy, Dallen J. "Genealogical Mobility: Tourism and the Search for a Personal Past." In *Geography and Genealogy: Locating Personal Pasts,* edited by Timothy and Jeanne Kay Guelke, 115–36. Aldershot, U.K., and Burlington, Vt.: Ashgate Publishing, Ltd., 2008.

Timothy, Dallen J., and Jeanne Kay Guelke, eds. *Geography and Genealogy: Locating Personal Pasts.* Aldershot, U.K., and Burlington, Vt.: Ashgate Publishing, Ltd., 2008.

Tobler, Ryan G. "'Saviors on Mount Zion': Mormon Sacramentalism, Mortality, and the Baptism for the Dead." *Journal of Mormon History* 39, no. 4 (Fall 2013): 182–238.

Tocqueville, Alexis de. *Democracy in America.* 2 vols. Edited by Eduardo Nolla; translated by James T. Schleifer. Indianapolis: Liberty Fund, 2012.

Todd, Jay M. "More Members Now Outside U.S. than in U.S." *Ensign* (March 1996). https://www.lds.org/ensign/1996/03/news-of-the-church/more-members-now -outside-us-than-in-us?lang=eng.

Tolley-Stokes, Rebecca. "Genealogy." In *Dictionary of American History.* Vol. 3, 3rd ed., edited by Stanley Kutler, 3:521–23. 10 vols. New York: Charles Scribner's Sons, 2003.

Tosh, John. *The Pursuit of History: Aims, Methods, and New Directions in the Study of History.* 6th ed. New York and London: Routledge, 2015.

Townsend, Robert B. *History's Babel: Scholarship, Professionalization, and the Historical Enterprise in the United States, 1880–1940.* Chicago and London: University of Chicago Press, 2013.

Troutman, John William. *Indian Blues: American Indians and the Politics of Music, 1879-1934.* Norman: University of Oklahoma Press, 2012.

Tucker, Susan. *City of Remembering: A History of Genealogy in New Orleans.* Jackson: University of Mississippi Press, 2016.

Turley, Richard E., Jr. "The Latter-day Saint Doctrine of Baptism for the Dead." Brigham Young University, *Family History Fireside,* published November 9, 2001. https:// brightspotcdn.byu.edu/b4/68/ec96ff354cbdbb861d43b6598055/2001-11-09.pdf.

Turner, Elizabeth Hayes. *Women, Culture, and Community: Religion and Reform in Galveston, 1880–1920.* New York: Oxford University Press, 1997.

Turner, Frederick Jackson. "The Significance of the Frontier in American History." In Turner, *The Frontier in American History,* 1–38. Tucson and London: University of Arizona Press, 1994. First printed 1920.

Tyrrell, Ian. *Historians in Public: The Practice of American History, 1890–1970.* Chicago and London: University of Chicago Press, 2005.

Ulrich, Laurel Thatcher. *The Age of Homespun: Objects and Stories in the Creation of an American Myth.* New York: Alfred A. Knopf, 2001.

———. "Creating Lineages." In *The Art of Family: Genealogical Artifacts in New England,* edited by D. Brenton Simons and Peter Benes, 5–11. Boston: New England Historic Genealogical Society, 2002.

———. "An Epiphany in a Broom Closet." *Weber Studies* 10 (Fall 1993). https://weberstudies.weber.edu/archive/archive%20A%20%20Vol.%201-10.3/Vol.%2010.3/10.3Ulrich.htm.

———. *A House Full of Females: Plural Marriage and Women's Rights in Early Mormonism, 1835–1870.* New York: Alfred A Knopf, 2017.

———. *A Midwife's Tale: The Life of Martha Ballard, Based on Her Diary, 1785–1812.* New York: Vintage, 1991. First printed 1990.

U.S. Census Bureau, Department of Commerce. "History: The '72-Year' Rule." Last updated December 17, 2019. https://www.census.gov/history/www/genealogy/decennial_census_records/the_72_year_rule_1.html.

———. *Statistical Abstract of the United States, 1977: 98th Annual Edition.* Washington, D.C.: Government Printing Office, 1977. https://www.census.gov/library/publications/1977/compendia/statab/98ed.html.

U.S. Centers for Disease Control and Prevention. National Center for Health Statistics. "Marriage Rates by State, 1990, 1995, 1999–2018." Last accessed March 7, 2021. https://www.cdc.gov/nchs/data/dvs/state-marriage-rates-90-95-99-18.pdf.

U.S. Department of State, Office of the Historian. "The Immigration Act of 1924 (the Johnson-Reed Act)." Last updated April 8, 2018. https://history.state.gov/milestones/1921-1936/immigration-act.

U.S. Library of Congress. "The Loc.gov Wise Guide: A (Family) Tree Grows in the Library." Published July 2008. https://www.loc.gov/wiseguide/jul08/tree.html.

U.S. National Institutes of Health. National Human Genome Research Institute. "Why Mouse Matters." Published July 23, 2010. https://www.genome.gov/10001345/importance-of-mouse-genome.

Varon, Elizabeth R. *Southern Lady, Yankee Spy: The True Story of Elizabeth Van Lew, a Union Agent in the Heart of the Confederacy.* New York: Oxford University Press, 2003.

Veblen, Thorstein. *The Theory of the Leisure Class.* New York: Penguin Books, 1979. First printed 1899.

Ventura, Stephanie J., and Christine A. Bachrach. "Nonmarital Childbearing in the United States, 1940–99." Revised ed. *National Vital Statistics Reports* 48, no. 16 (October 18, 2000): 1–39. https://www.cdc.gov/nchs/data/nvsr/nvsr48/nvs48_16.pdf.

Vetterli, R. Richard. "Elder, Melchizedek Priesthood." In *Encyclopedia of Mormonism: The History, Scripture, Doctrine, and Procedure of The Church of Jesus Christ of Latter-day Saints,* edited by Daniel H. Ludlow, 447–48. New York: Macmillan Publishing Company, 1992.

Virkus, Frederick Adams, ed. *The Abridged Compendium of American Genealogy: First Families of America.* Vol. 2, 1926. Chicago: F. A. Virkus, 1926.

———, ed. *The Abridged Compendium of American Genealogy: First Families of America.* Vol. 2, 1928. Chicago: F. A. Virkus, 1928.

———, ed. *The Handbook of American Genealogy.* 4 vols. Chicago: Institute of American Genealogy, 1932–43.

Virkus, Frederick Adams, ed., under direction of Albert Nelson Marquis. *The Abridged Compendium of American Genealogy: First Families of America: A Genealogical*

Encyclopedia of the United States. 7 vols. Chicago: A. N. Marquis & Company, 1925–43. Latter volumes published Chicago: F. A. Virkus.

Waldstreicher, David. *In the Midst of Perpetual Fetes: The Making of American Nationalism, 1776–1820.* Chapel Hill: University of North Carolina Press, 1997.

———. *Runaway America: Benjamin Franklin, Slavery, and the American Revolution.* New York: Hill and Wang, 2004.

Walkowitz, Judith R. *City of Dreadful Delight: Narratives of Sexual Danger in Late-Victorian London.* Chicago: University of Chicago Press, 1992.

Wall, Cheryl A. *Worrying the Line: Black Women Writers, Lineage, and Literary Tradition.* Chapel Hill: University of North Carolina Press, 2005.

Waller, John C. *Heredity: A Very Short Introduction.* New York: Oxford University Press, 2017.

———. "Ideas of Heredity, Reproduction, and Eugenics in Britain, 1800–1875." *Studies in History and Philosophy of Biology and Biomedical Science* 32, no. 3 (2001): 457–89.

———. "Poor Old Ancestors: The Popularity of Medical Hereditarianism, 1770–1870." Preprint 247, *A Cultural History of Heredity II: 18th and 19th Centuries,* 131–44. Berlin, Germany: Max Planck Institute for the History of Science, 2003.

Waller, Vincent, dir. "Pest of the West." In *Pest of the West: SpongeBob SquarePants.* New York: Nickelodeon, 2008. DVD, 74 minutes. Originally aired April 11, 2008.

Ware, Susan. "Dialogue: Pauli Murray's Notable Connections." *Journal of Women's History* 14 (Summer 2002): 54–87.

Warshauer, Matthew, and Michael Sturges. "Difficult Hunting: Accessing Connecticut Patient Records to Learn about Post-Traumatic Stress Disorder during the Civil War." *Civil War History* 59 (December 2013): 419–52.

Washburn, Mabel Thacher Rosemary. *Washburn Family Foundations in Normandy, England and America.* Greenfield, Ind.: William Mitchell Printing Company, 1953.

Washington, Mary Helen. "Introduction." In Anna Julia Cooper, *A Voice from the South,* xxvii–liv. New York: Oxford University Press, 1988.

Watson, Julia. "Ordering the Family: Genealogy as Autobiographical Pedigree." In *Getting a Life: Everyday Uses of Autobiography,* edited by Sidonie Smith and Watson, 297–323. Minneapolis: University of Minnesota Press, 1996.

Weaver, Sarah Jane. "Church Asks Members to Understand Policies," March 1, 2012. https://www.churchofjesuschrist.org/church/news/church-asks-members-to -understand-policies?lang=eng.

Webb, Clive, ed. *Massive Resistance: Southern Opposition to the Second Reconstruction.* New York: Oxford University Press, 2005.

Weber, Eugen. *Peasants into Frenchmen: The Modernization of Rural France, 1870–1914.* Stanford, Calif.: Stanford University Press, 1976.

Weber, Max. *From Max Weber: Essays in Sociology.* Translated, edited, and with an introduction by H. H. Gerth and C. Wright Mills. New York: Oxford University Press, 1971. First printed 1946.

Weed, James A. "Vital Statistics in the United States: Preparing for the Next Century." *Population Index* 61 (Winter 1995): 527–39.

Weigel, Sigrid. "Genealogy: On the Iconography and Rhetorics of an Epistemological Topos." Published January 2006. https://www.researchgate.net/publication

/280836714_Genealogy_On_the_iconography_and_rhetorics_of_an_epistemological
_topos.

Weil, François. *Family Trees: A History of Genealogy in America.* Cambridge and London: Harvard University Press, 2013.

———. "John Farmer and the Making of American Genealogy." *New England Quarterly* 80 (September 2007): 408–34.

Weinberg, Sydney Stahl. *The World of Our Mothers: The Lives of Jewish Immigrant Women.* Chapel Hill: University of North Carolina Press, 1988.

Wells-Barnett, Ida B. *Crusade for Justice: The Autobiography of Ida B. Wells.* Edited by Alfreda M. Duster. Chicago and London: University of Chicago Press, 1970.

Wendt, Simon. *The Daughters of the American Revolution and Patriotic Memory in the Twentieth Century.* Gainesville: University Press of Florida, 2020.

———. "Defenders of Patriotism or Mothers of Fascism? The Daughters of the American Revolution, Antiradicalism, and Un-Americanism in the Interwar Period." *Journal of American Studies* 47 (November 2013): 943–69.

———. "Nationalist Middle-Class Women, Memory, and Conservative Family Values, 1890–1945." In *Inventing the Modern American Family: Family Values and Social Change in the 20th Century United States,* edited by Isabel Heinemann, 31–58. Frankfurt, Germany: Campus Verlag, 2012.

Wenger, Beth S. *History Lessons: The Creation of American Jewish Heritage.* Princeton, N.J.: Princeton University Press, 2010.

Werth, Barry. *Banquet at Delmonico's: Great Minds, the Gilded Age, and the Triumph of Evolution in America.* New York: Random House, 2009.

Weston, Kath. *Families We Choose: Lesbians, Gays, Kinship.* New York: Columbia University Press, 1991.

White, Deborah Gray. *Too Heavy a Load: Black Women in Defense of Themselves, 1894–1994.* New York: W. W. Norton and Company, 1999.

White, Peter. "Privacy: An International Concern." *International Library Review* 12 (March 1980): 223–42.

White, Richard S. *"It's Your Misfortune and None of My Own": A New History of the American West.* Norman and London: University of Oklahoma Press, 1991.

———. *Remembering Ahanagran: A History of Stories.* New York: Hill and Wang, 1998.

Whitman, James Q. *Hitler's American Model: The United States and the Making of Nazi Race Law.* Princeton, N.J.: Princeton University Press, 2017.

Wiencek, Henry. *Master of the Mountain: Thomas Jefferson and His Slaves.* New York: Macmillan, 2012.

Williams, Heather Andrea. *Help Me to Find My People: The African American Search for Family Lost in Slavery.* Chapel Hill: University of North Carolina Press, 2012.

———. *Self-Taught: African American Education in Slavery and Freedom.* Chapel Hill: University of North Carolina Press, 2005.

Williams, Linda. *Playing the Race Card: Melodramas of Black and White from Uncle Tom to O. J. Simpson.* Princeton, N.J.: Princeton University Press, 2001.

Williams, Patricia J. *The Alchemy of Race and Rights: Diary of a Law Professor.* Cambridge, Mass., and London: Harvard University Press, 1991.

Williams, Susan Reynolds. *Alice Morse Earle and the Domestic History of Early America.* Amherst and Boston: University of Massachusetts Press, 2013.

Wilson, Gilbert Livingstone. *Agriculture of the Hidatsa Indians: An Indian Interpretation.* Lincoln, Neb.: J & L Reprint Company, 1977. First printed 1917. http://digital.library.upenn.edu/women/buffalo/garden/garden.html#I.

Winsor, Justin, ed. *The Memorial History of Boston, Including Suffolk County, Massachusetts, 1630-1880, in Four Volumes. Vol. 2, The Provincial Period.* Boston: James R. Osgood and Company, 1881.

Wolfe, Tom. "The 'Me' Decade and the Third Great Awakening." *New York* (August 23, 1976): 1–13. http://nymag.com/news/features/45938/.

Wood, Clara L., ed. *History and Register, Idaho State Society, Daughters of the American Revolution.* Caldwell, Idaho: Caxton Printers, 1936.

Wood, Gordon S. *The Americanization of Benjamin Franklin.* New York: The Penguin Press, 2004.

———. "In Quest of Blood Lines." *New York Review of Books,* May 23, 2013. https://www.nybooks.com/articles/2013/05/23/quest-blood-lines/.

———. *The Radicalism of the American Revolution.* New York: Alfred A. Knopf, 1992.

Wood, Mrs. J. M., Jr. (Christine Knox Wood). *Those Reeves Girls.* 2 vols. Lubbock, Tex.: privately published, 1973.

Woodruff, Wilford. *Wilford Woodruff's Journal: 1833–1898: Typescript.* Edited by Scott G. Kenney. 9 vols. Midvale, Utah: Signature Books, 1983.

Woodtor, Dee Parmer. *Finding a Place Called Home: A Guide to African-American Genealogy and Historical Identity.* New York: Random House, 1999.

Wright, Donald R. "Uprooting Kunta Kinte: On the Perils of Relying on Encyclopedic Informants." *History in Africa* 8 (1981): 205–17.

———. "The Effect of Alex Haley's 'Roots' on How Gambians Remember the Atlantic Slave Trade." *History in Africa* 38 (2011): 295–318.

Wulf, Karin A. "Bible, King, and Common Law: Genealogical Literacies and Family History Practices in British America." *Early American Studies* 10 (Fall 2012): 467–502.

———. "Not Your Grandmother's Genealogy." *William and Mary Quarterly* 59 (October 2002): 1,000–1,003.

———. "'Of the Old Stock': Quakerism and Transatlantic Genealogies in Colonial British America." In *The Creation of the British Atlantic World,* edited by Elizabeth Mancke and Carole Shammas, 304–20. Baltimore and London: Johns Hopkins University Press, 2005.

Yang, Domenic Meng-Hsuan. "One Man's Quest: Chiang Su-chang, *Roots,* and the Mainland Homebound Movement in Taiwan." In *Reconsidering Roots: Race, Politics, and Memory,* edited by Erica L. Ball and Kellie Carter Jackson, 182–202. Athens: University of Georgia Press, 2017.

YIVO Institute for Jewish Research, New York. "YIVO Archives & Library Collections." Last accessed March 7, 2021. https://yivo.org/archives-library.

Yokota, Kariann Akemi. *Unbecoming British: How Revolutionary America Became a Postcolonial Nation.* New York: Oxford University Press, 2011.

Young, Alfred S. *Masquerade: The Life and Times of Deborah Sampson, Continental Soldier.* New York: Alfred A. Knopf, 2004.

Younkin, C. George. "Searching for American Indian Genealogy." *Stirpes: Texas State Genealogical Society* 17 (December 1977): 167–82.

Zaretsky, Natasha. *No Direction Home: The American Family and Fear of National Decline, 1968–1980.* Chapel Hill: University of North Carolina Press, 2007.

Zelizer, Viviana A. *Pricing the Priceless Child: The Changing Social Value of Children.* Princeton, N.J.: Princeton University Press, 1985.

Zerubavel, Eviatar. *Ancestors and Relatives: Genealogy, Identity, and Community.* New York: Oxford University Press, 2012.

Zimmer, Carl. *She Has Her Mother's Laugh: The Powers, Perversions, and Potential of Heredity.* New York: Dutton, 2018.

Unpublished Works

Batza, Catherine. "Against Doctors' Orders: Lesbian Motherhood and the Battle for Medical Authority in the 1970s." Paper presented at the Seminar on Women and Gender, Newberry Library, Chicago, January 16, 2009.

Christie, Gregg. "A Forgotten Exodus: The Importance of Nineteenth-Century Canadian Immigration to the American Midwest." Unpublished seminar paper, Northeastern Illinois University, April 2, 2012.

Cotlar, Seth. "'We Have No Wish *Not* to See': Nostalgic Local Historians and the Unlikely Origins of a Modern Historical Sensibility." Presented to the English Atlantic Writing Group, Loyola University, Chicago, February 3, 2016.

Creet, Julia. "Arborescent Archives: or, the Aesthetic Roots of the Family Tree." Online working paper, 2014. https://www.academia.edu/503106/Arborescent_Archives_or_the_Aesthetic_Roots_of_the_Family_Tree.

Drake, Pamela J. "Findings from the Fullerton Genealogy Study." Master's thesis, California State University at Fullerton, 2001. http://psych.fullerton.edu/genealogy/#RESULT.

Dulong, John P. "Genealogical Groups in a Changing Organizational Environment: From Lineage to Heritage." PhD diss., Wayne State University, 1986.

Fermaglich, Kirsten. "Married Names, Middle Names, and Maiden Names: Gender and Name-Changing in the New York City Civil Court in the Twentieth Century." Paper presented at the Seminar on Women and Gender, Newberry Library, Chicago, February 19, 2016.

Fisher, Rachel Eskin. "A Place in History: Genealogy, Jewish Identity, and Modernity." PhD diss., University of California at Santa Barbara, 1999.

Hering, Katharina. "'We Are All Makers of History': People and Publics in the Practice of Pennsylvania-German Family History, 1891–1966." PhD diss., George Mason University, 2009.

———. "Review of Ancestry.com" (May 2018). Accepted for publication in *Beyond Citation*, in progress.

Kachun, Mitch. "The Faith That the Dark Past Has Taught Us: African-American Commemorations in the North and West and the Construction of a Usable Past, 1808–1915." PhD diss., Cornell University, 1997.

Little, Hannah Mary. "Genealogy as Theatre of Self-Identity: A Study of Genealogy as a Cultural Practice within Britain since c. 1850." PhD diss., University of Glasgow, 2009.

Lynott, Patricia A. "Susa Young Gates, 1856–1933: Educator, Suffragist, Mormon."
  PhD diss., Loyola University Chicago, 1996.

Morgan, Francesca Constance. "'Home and Country': Women, Nation, and the
  Daughters of the American Revolution, 1890–1939." PhD diss., Columbia University,
  1998.

Pearson, Susan J. "Documentary Proof: Evidence of Age and the Campaign Against Child
  Labor." Paper presented at the Seminar on Labor and Working-Class History,
  Newberry Library, Chicago, January 14, 2012.

Pepper, Shayne D., Ryan Poll, Erica Meiners, and Sophia Mihic. "Coffee and Conversation
  on the Work of Michel Foucault." Faculty roundtable discussion at Northeastern
  Illinois University, September 26, 2019.

Rodda, Anne Patterson. "Trespassers in Time: Genealogists and Microhistorians."
  PhD diss., Drew University, 2010.

Stanton, Megan Ann. "All in the Family: Ecclesiastical Authority and Family Theology in
  the Church of Jesus Christ of Latter-day Saints." PhD diss., University of Wisconsin at
  Madison, 2018.

Sweeney, Michael S. "Ancestors, Avotaynu, Roots: An Inquiry into American Genealogical
  Discourse." PhD diss., University of Kansas, 2010.

Tatelman, Todd B. "The REAL ID Act of 2005: Legal, Regulatory, and Implementation
  Issues." Washington, D.C.: Congressional Research Service, April 1, 2008.

Teachout, Woden Sorrow. "Forging Memory: Hereditary Societies, Patriotism, and the
  American Past, 1876–1898." PhD diss., Harvard University, 2003.

Weil, François. "Family Trees: A History of Genealogy in America." Presentation at the
  Department of History, Northwestern University, Evanston, Ill., October 2, 2013.

Wulf, Karin. "Ancestry as Social Practice in Eighteenth-Century New England: The
  Origins of Early Republic Genealogical Vogue." Presented at the Boston Area Early
  America Seminar, Massachusetts Historical Society, Boston, March 2012.

———. "Representing the Family to the State; Or, Lineage in a New Nation." Presented at
  the annual meeting of the Organization of American Historians, Washington, April
  2006.

Index